YOU MUST BE DREAMING

BARBARA NOËL

with KATHRYN WATTERSON

POSEIDON PRESS

New York   London   Toronto   Sydney   Tokyo   Singapore

POSEIDON PRESS

Simon & Schuster Building
Rockefeller Center
1230 Avenue of the Americas
New York, New York 10020

POSEIDON PRESS is a registered trademark
of Simon & Schuster Inc.

POSEIDON PRESS colophon is a trademark
of Simon & Schuster Inc.

Designed by Karolina Harris
Manufactured in the United States of America

10 9 8 7 6 5 4 3 2 1

Library of Congress Cataloging in Publication Data
Noël, Barbara.
    You must be dreaming / Barbara Noël, with Kathryn
Watterson.
        p.   cm.
    Includes bibliographical references.
    1. Noël, Barbara.   2. Sexually abused patients—United
States—Biography.   3. Masserman, Jules Hymen, 1905–
        4. Psychiatrists—Professional ethics—United
States—Case studies.   I. Watterson, Kathryn, date.
II. Title.
RC455.2.A28N64   1992
362.88'3'092—dc20
[B]   92-16265
                                                    CIP

ISBN: 0-671-74153-5

For my mother and father and the people they might have become were it not for their struggles with their own heritage.
—*Barbara Noël*

A Note to Readers

Unless otherwise indicated, the names in this book are true and have not been changed. Recent interviews with lawyers, doctors, and others of Dr. Jules H. Masserman's former patients who have brought charges against him have illuminated this story. In addition, Barbara Noël's vivid recollections about her Amytal sessions and the content of some of her therapy sessions are confirmed in large part by Jules Masserman's own recorded testimony about his administration of Amytal and his perceptions of Barbara Noël, during his discovery and evidence depositions in the Circuit Court of Cook County, Illinois. Dr. Masserman's insurers have made four out-of-court settlements against him. He has also signed a consent order with the state of Illinois agreeing to give up his license to prescribe drugs or practice any form of psychotherapy or medicine. Additionally, he has received notice of his suspension from the American Psychiatric Association and the Illinois Psychiatric Society for violating the principles of medical ethics. Nevertheless, Dr. Masserman has denied all allegations that he is guilty of misconduct. During an interview before this book was published, Dr. Masserman again categorically denied all the allegations against him and told Kathryn Watterson that during his forty years of medical practice, "I have never done anything unethical to any patient." That interview, documenting Dr. Masserman's further commentary and defense, is included as an Afterword on page 307. For further reference and additional information on each chapter, please see documentary research Notes and Sources at the back of this book.

"I swear by Apollo the physician and by Aesculapius to keep the following oath: I will prescribe for the good of my patients and never do harm to anyone. In every house where I come I will enter only for the good of my patients, keeping myself far from all intentional ill-doing and all seduction, and especially from the pleasures of love with women or men, be they free or slaves."

—from the physician's Hippocratic Oath

"Twenty-three-hundred years ago Hippocrates, a famous Greek still revered as the father of medicine, observed that the ladies of his day had long since developed a striking capacity to get their way by staging histrionic tantrums or, when necessary, dramatic faints. Hippocrates, as the progenitor of a long line of physicians and gentlemen, professed to overlook the fact that many of his charming patients cast such 'spells' in obvious attempts to evade some unpleasant situation, elicit sympathy and service, and so exert control over those about them."

—Jules Masserman, in "The
Convenience of a Nervous Breakdown,"
A Psychiatric Odyssey (pp. 271–72)

CONTENTS

CONTENTS

PROLOGUE *My Early Training*

This is a story about knowing and not knowing, telling and not telling, living and not living.

It's a story that will feel familiar to people who have been sexually abused by their parents or other adults when they were children—as I was.

It's a story that will feel familiar to people who have been sexually abused by their therapists or someone else who has power over them—as I also was.

In particular, this is the story of an experience that started the day I woke up in a drugged state and discovered I was being raped by my psychiatrist, Dr. Jules H. Masserman. I know now that what Dr. Masserman did to me is not all that extraordinary. Studies suggest that at least one out of every ten male psychotherapists—including psychiatrists, psychologists, social workers, and marriage counselors—has had sexual contact with at least one patient. In a survey of psychiatrists conducted by Dr. Nanette Gartrell and her colleagues at Harvard Medical School, 7.1 percent of male psychiatrists and 3 percent of female psychiatrists *admitted* to having broken the ethical rule against sexual contact with a patient during or after treatment.

What compounds the treachery of Dr. Masserman's actions is that he was a man so visibly at the top of his profession—a teacher and model for other therapists, both nationally and internationally. Dr. Masserman, a psychoanalyst and a neurologist as well as a psychiatrist, served as trustee, secretary, vice-president, and president of the American Psychiatric Association. Known by his colleagues as an articulate, somewhat eccentric, critic of psychoanalytic orthodoxy, he was co-chairman of the Department of Neurology and Psychiatry at Northwestern University Medical School from 1964 to 1969 and remained with the department as a professor until 1974, when he became professor emeritus.

Dr. Masserman's theory of "biodynamics" and his research in experimental neurosis are still widely studied by students of psychology. He has held high elective office in many organizations and is a past president of the American Academy of Psychoanalysis, the American Society for Group Therapy, the Illinois Psychiatric Society, the Chicago Psychoanalytic Society, the American Association for Social Psychiatry, and the International Association for Social Psychiatry. He is honorary president for life of the World Association for Social Psychiatry.

Dr. Harold M. Visotsky, professor and former chairman of the Department of Psychiatry and Behavioral Sciences at Northwestern University Medical School, described Jules Masserman in 1979 as "psychiatry's ambassador to the world—having visited, lectured, or chaired conferences in almost every Western European country and in South America, Africa, and the Near and Far East . . ." Dr. Visotsky said Dr. Masserman is "a scholar who grasps the principles of mathematics and physics as readily as those of musical composition. [He's] an iconoclast who respects tradition . . . a gentleman and a gentle man."

On another occasion, Dr. Visotsky said that Dr. Masserman "is a teacher of teachers, internationally recognized and respected. The reputation enjoyed by Chicago as a psychiatric research and training center is due in large measure to his presence."

In 1987, Dr. John Carlton, then president of the World Association of Social Psychiatry, called him "the most prominent psychiatrist in the world."

What I know now, but didn't know the day I "woke up" in Dr. Jules Masserman's office, is this: When I was a little girl, both of my parents sexually molested me. I was a good little girl for them by pretending what they did to me never happened—and thus I learned to be a perfect victim. In the same way, I was a good little girl for Dr. Masserman until that September day in 1984 when some inner strength allowed me to see what he was doing to me.

I'm writing this story now because I've been sleepwalking all my life—and I refuse to do that anymore. I'm writing it because I don't want what happened to me to happen to other women or men. I'm also writing this because I'm angry. I was doubly betrayed, because of what Dr. Masserman did to me and because of what my parents did—using me for their needs and never giving me what I needed.

I was a patient of Dr. Masserman's for eighteen years, six months, and two weeks. My ex-husband and I have been able to locate a large number of our calendars and checkbooks from those years. Those records alone—which are partial—document 1,256 of my sessions with Jules Masserman during that time. In fact, if the records were complete, they would show that I had 2,000 or more sessions with him and paid him approximately $100,000 of my own money, without the benefit of health insurance reimbursements.

As a result of my "therapy" with him, I became addicted to Amytal, a potentially dangerous barbiturate Dr. Masserman administered to me by intravenous injection on at least two hundred occasions, ostensibly to lower my defenses and overcome my resistances to getting at "the truth." In addition to serving as an unconscious body for Dr. Masserman's sexual gratification when I was knocked out by the Amytal, I also became addicted to alcohol while under his medical care.

For a long time after the curtain of pretense and naïveté that had protected me was lifted, I remembered clues and events that made me sure Dr. Masserman had raped me more than once over the years. Perhaps he had done it dozens of times—if not more.

In the normal course of therapy, Dr. Masserman also behaved in other inappropriate and questionable ways. When he traveled to far-away places for psychiatric conferences or speeches, he brought me back records, coins, trinkets, or other gifts. From time to time, he gave me copies of articles, poems, and music he had written. After my husband Richard and I were divorced, Dr. Masserman repeatedly invited me to go sailing on his yacht and flying in his airplane. I felt uncomfortable about his invitations and accepted only one of them, but I was flattered. In the summer of 1982, he persuaded me to go to France with him and several of his other patients. He was president-elect of the World Congress for Social Psychiatry, and in Paris, I acted as his hostess and translator during an evening event he hosted. At the time, basking in the glow of Dr. Masserman's aura along with his other patients and admirers, I felt I had joined a magic circle. It didn't occur to me that his solicitations would have been considered clearly unethical by his colleagues. I had no idea that he himself, as president of the American Psychiatric Association, had condemned such behavior.

After the fact, of course, the unethical nature of his conduct seemed obvious, and I felt ashamed of my obliviousness, mortified at how I had managed to explain away these obvious indicators of impropriety and abuse. It seemed any "normal" person would have suspected something extremely odd was going on; any "normal" person would have gotten out of the situation. Why didn't I? After all, it wasn't as if I'd been an isolated human being, locked away from reality. I read newspapers every day, I read books. I was a grown woman with a successful career as a professional singer. I ran my own business. I sang with many bands, performed on camera, and did voice-overs in commercials; I sang jingles, wrote lyrics, composed music, taught voice students, kept appointments, paid taxes, noticed other people and their lives. I thought: How could I have not known? How could I have been so stupid?

You, too, must wonder: How could anyone be so moronic as to have stayed in therapy all that time? How could anyone take a barbiturate like Amytal for nearly seventeen years and not realize she's addicted? How could any woman have intercourse, even when she's unconscious, and not know it afterward? The answers to these questions boil down to this: I doubted my own reality and suppressed the truth, just as I had been trained to do in my early life. The clues weren't recognizable; I tried to make the truth not the truth.

I still don't know if Dr. Masserman ejaculated inside me. If he did, I assume he used a condom, but I will probably never know. I didn't feel anything; I was numb in more ways than one. As his prey, I didn't feel and I didn't think. My mind could never accept the unbearable truth that my parents exploited me sexually. In the same way, I couldn't believe that my therapist, my "healthy" father figure, was abusing me. I knew, though, how to deny and pretend, even to myself. And after Dr. Masserman started giving me the Amytal and I became addicted to it, seeing him became a habit I couldn't break, primarily because he also became my pusher: he gave me my drugs.

Eventually, I learned that many victims of incest have no conscious memory of their childhood sexual abuse. Like others, I had lived in a nightmare and denied or "dissociated" the horrible reality I lived with.

Dissociation allowed me to separate myself: *it wasn't really happening to me.* I blocked out the nightmare in order to appear normal—even when I knew things were not normal. Like any child, I wanted to be like other kids at school and church—participating in all the ordinary activities. To do that I had to hide the truth and pretend everything was fine. I used magical thinking to make up outlandish stories about my wonderful family and repressed my memories through a creative adaptation that made me forget and helped me survive. Therapists call that process "traumatic amnesia" or "psychogenic amnesia." Hundreds of thousands of men and women like me deny or don't remember their abuse until they're adults and start having sexual problems, phobias, flashbacks, or other symptoms that lead them to get help.

Because I had no conscious memory of my parents' behavior, I wasn't aware that with Dr. Masserman, I was recreating a highly charged, interior motif from my childhood. On some internal, unconscious level, shame and mortification obliterated any healthy sense of myself and my rights. This is why I was so pliable, naive, and blind when it came to Dr. Masserman's behavior. I was a willing victim, participating in and responding to a familiar, abusive pattern in the only way I knew.

I sometimes now imagine that when I first went into therapy with Dr. Masserman, in 1966, I wanted to uncover and come to terms with what had happened to me when I was a child. If I could have found a therapist aware of the symptoms of childhood sexual abuse, who could have helped me explore and deal with the incest then, when I was in my twenties, I believe I could more easily have resolved it and put it to rest. But in those days, very little had been written on the subject, and most therapists weren't alert to it. Besides that, the psychiatrist I was seeing had no real interest in helping me; he was helping only himself. So I never dealt with my childhood traumas until much, much later.

Dr. Ann Jernberg, the psychologist who finally helped me understand the role I played as a victim, says that today Dr. Masserman or almost any experienced therapist would probably have surmised after a few sessions that I had been a sexually abused child. I wonder if Dr. Masserman did not suspect it even then. It would not have been a difficult guess: for the past thirty-five years, surveys consistently have shown that one out of every three to five women in the United States has been sexually molested by an adult male before she reaches her late teens. Most of these girls were molested by someone they knew or were related to. (Between 4 and 12 percent of all women report a sexual experience with a relative, and one out of every one hundred women reports a sexual experience with her father or stepfather. Some research indicates that the incidence of incest is much higher.)*

It was clear that like many children who have been emotionally neglected, I had very low self-esteem, felt isolated, and was eager for acceptance and approval. But my detachment from my feelings, my shame and mortification about my body, my fear of the dark, my sleep disturbances, and the occasional terrifying flashbacks I experienced were all typical of children who have been sexually abused. Additional symptoms—dissociation, with headaches, the loss of my voice, startle reactions, facial tension, vocal distress, and the feeling that I was being gagged or choked—are classic suggestors of childhood abuse. Yet Dr. Masserman never addressed any of these issues. If he became aware in the 1970s or '80s of any possibility of early sexual abuse, he allowed me to continue to repress it; he never helped me bring it forth. But then that would not have been in his interest. Sex offenders regularly pick out victims like me; we are out-of-touch prey who won't challenge them, won't stand up for ourselves or cope aggressively with what is happening. I was a sitting duck.

What I didn't know—and what Dr. Masserman failed to imagine— was that I would ever be strong enough to wake up and have the courage to tell the truth. But the struggle between truth and repression finally comes down to a choice between life and death. My past, so full of illusion and people wearing two faces, working from two scripts, has prodded me into going through the pain of discovery to get at the truth about myself. As it turns out, I'm not a victim; I'm a survivor. I always was a survivor; all I had to do was wake up to that fact.

*For further reference, see Notes, page 288.

1 *Under the Influence*

FRIDAY, SEPTEMBER 21, 1984 From somewhere in the foggy depths of my mind, I heard someone groaning. He was on top of me; his weight was pinning me down. I suddenly realized that he was raping me, thrusting back and forth inside me like a grunting animal burrowing for food.

Slow, as if counting out time on my fingers, I realized I wasn't dreaming; I *knew* I was awake.

I was terrified, overwhelmed by a horrible, cold fear. I could hardly breathe. But almost instantly, my panic was followed by a calm that made me as alert as a stalked deer—ears raised, body immobilized—sensing the close threat of death.

I was lying on a hard surface, my head flat and my eyes closed, like a person in a casket. I didn't dare move a muscle, so I did the only thing I could do. In rhythm with my breathing, in slowly, out slowly, I inhaled the air and regarded it intensely and analytically before quietly exhaling. The smell was familiar, but I couldn't place it. At least I hadn't been knocked in the head and dragged to some strange, dark alley; this was a place I knew, even though I didn't yet know where it was.

I felt the man shifting his weight on me. I became aware of his hot breath on my shoulder. If I looked straight up, he wouldn't know I was awake, and I could see where I was. I could hardly breathe, I was so scared. Please, God, don't let my eyes make any sound as they open; don't let the lashes stick together. My eyes opened slowly, and then I was looking up at familiar long, oblong panels in a ceiling. I let my breath out very slowly. I was in Dr. Jules Masserman's examination room. Dr. Masserman was my psychoanalyst, and for years I had been coming into this room so he could give me Amytal, a "truth serum" that put me to sleep and was supposed to help me open up my subconscious. What I was smelling was rubbing alcohol and the familiar musty odor of the room.

At that moment, I felt frantic, practically hysterical. I thought: Whoever this is, he's got to get off me. I can't stand this anymore. I can't stand it! I couldn't bear his weight or the pressure of his body on mine. I was terrified that if he didn't get off me immediately, I would start screaming. I closed my eyes again, and keeping my body limp, I moved ever so slightly. I made a small, stirring noise and voiced a guttural "ummm," as if I were about to wake up. The man stopped groaning, stopped moving. He lay very still.

Then I felt his weight carefully but quickly lifting off me. Within a couple of seconds, I heard water running in the sink. I could visualize the hot plate by the sink, next to the refrigerator and the storage cabinet, but I had to see the man who had just been on top of me. Very slowly, miming a sleeping person, I rolled my head to the side. The water was still running. I opened my eyes only enough to look out through a narrow wedge of my eyelashes.

A man was standing with his back to me, and when I saw his bald head and the shape of his body, I felt a shudder of shock and nausea. It was Dr. Masserman, my trusted and renowned psychoanalyst. He was totally naked. The water was running, and his arms were moving up and down at the sink as he washed his genitals. His bottom was white. The suntan lines from his sailing trips were distinct. In contrast with his dark legs and tan back, his white bottom gleamed.

I looked for another few seconds, and then I closed my eyes as a rush of hot, thick, ugly feeling, like putrid black oil, churned through my body. I slowly rolled my head back. I felt like bellowing out the hideousness of this betrayal, howling like a hurt wolf. But I had to play dead. I prayed that the anger beginning to seethe within me wouldn't seep through my skin.

I heard him turn off the water and walk back across the room toward me. I wondered if I was going to die now. An irrational unjustifiable thought jumped into my mind, unbidden: Oh, my God, now he's going to kill me just like he killed Billie. Billie had been Dr. Masserman's secretary for years, but three months before, she had died suddenly, unexpectedly, in her sleep. She was a vital single woman, only sixty-three years old, who had raised two boys, now fourteen and eighteen years old. The last time I had seen her, I'd run into the office to pay a bill, and Billie had been sitting at her desk. I'd said, "Billie, what are you doing here? Aren't you going on vacation?" Billie, looking very upset, had said, "Well, I will if I live that long." One week later, Billie Laird was dead.

Now crazy thoughts still raced through my mind: If he knows I know what he just did to me, will he kill me? Was that his plan? Was that what came next? Maybe, just maybe, if I didn't stir, he would think I was still asleep and didn't know what he'd done. I heard a jingling sound and the rustle of material. He was getting dressed. Coins in his pockets clinked and fabric swished as he pulled on his pants and zipped them up. Within moments, I felt him standing over me. I hoped I was breathing normally and that the hairs had not risen on my arms. I felt him pull up my underpants. He drew blankets over me and tucked them around my shoulders and under my chin. I heard footsteps moving away, and then I heard the door open and shut.

I lay perfectly motionless for a while. But the horror began to overtake me, and I started shaking with repulsion and rage. How dare he? How *dare* he? I knew he had all kinds of implements over there by his hot plate. I thought that if I could get up fast enough and get a knife, I would kill him. I imagined trying to stick a knife into his chest. And then I knew that if I tried, he would kill me first. He could kill me easily and write it off to some medical reason. He'd given me flu shots every fall. When I was sick, he often gave me antibiotics. He could just give me a lethal injection of something and say I'd had a heart attack or died of "cardiac arrest." Or he could say he'd killed me in self-defense. The only thing I could do to stay alive was play it out. *I had to pretend I'd been asleep the whole time. I was supposed to be asleep; I should go back to sleep.*

I started to cry. My tears were hot as they ran down my face into my ears and down into the pillow. I had to stop crying, I had to control myself. But my skin was crawling, and a hideous, sickening stench clung to my shoulders. It was the scent of his body—of old flesh and sweat and after-shave lotion. I felt totally nauseated, but I fought my urge to vomit.

What was worse was the sudden sensation of having smelled this horrible body odor before. I thought: Dr. Masserman has been giving me Amytal for years. Has he done this before when I didn't wake up? I thought: Maybe I'm hallucinating. Maybe this isn't happening at all, and I'm lost somewhere in the middle of a gruesome dream.

I looked through my tear-fogged vision at the geometric designs in the large rug hanging on the wall next to the daybed. Was it real? I lifted my arm to touch it; my fingers felt the texture of its bumpy threads, and I knew the rug was genuine, not woven into an illusion. My fingers were real. The air around my arm was real.

I have heard about people waking up unable to move. But this wasn't paralysis. It wasn't a dream. And it wasn't fantasy or hallucination. My psychiatrist had raped me.

But I wanted desperately for it not to be true.

Usually, I woke up in stages from the Amytal. At the first, I often heard the doctor talking with a patient in his office, which adjoined the examination room where I had been sleeping. After I listened to the conversation for a few minutes and tried to visualize the speakers, I would fall back asleep until stage two, when the doctor flicked the overhead lights on and off and spoke to me. Then he would leave on the light and suggest I rest awhile before getting dressed. Sometimes I would doze off again before I finally got up and dressed.

Now I tried to get a grip on myself. I had to pretend that it hadn't happened, that I was back in stage one: This meant I *must* go back to sleep. Slowly, I took deep breaths and started feeling the effects of the drug again. One breath at a time, I submerged my mind and reentered that deep, black, drugged sleep where I could leave my pain and rage behind and float in a cloudless, painless universe.

The overhead light blinked on and off, on and off. Dr. Masserman, his shirt sleeves rolled up to his elbows and his tie askew, stood in the doorway, flipping the switch. Sometimes when he woke me, he would come in and sit on the ottoman beside me and say, "Are you ready to wake up now?" Today he stayed in the doorway, which made me feel safer.

"Ah, little lady, you're awake, I see," he said with his kind, familiar smile. "How do you feel?"

"Just fine, thank you," I said, attempting to speak normally. I tried to smile, tried to will myself to act naturally, but my lips started to tremble and I was terrified he would notice.

"Well, be certain to rest a bit until you're sure that you can maneuver," he said. "And come in and see me before you go."

For an instant after he closed the door, I wondered again if I might have been dreaming. But before the question was fully formed in my mind, his repellent body odor wafted up from my shoulders. I knew it had been no dream.

2 Back to the Beginning

I still shake hands with my patients, help old ladies off with their
coats and pat gentlemen on the shoulders. Why? Because immediately
beneath his formal adult clothing, every patient who comes to a
trusted physician is a hurt, hurting and frightened child anxiously
seeking a devoted parent. Accordingly, he wants to be immediately
and warmly welcomed, soothingly spoken to and gently touched.

JULES MASSERMAN, March 1960

CHICAGO: MARCH 7, 1966 My heartbeat sounded like ca-
lypso drums as I pressed the button in the Willoughby Tower elevator
that would carry me up to the fourteenth floor and my first appointment
with Dr. Jules Masserman, one of the most famous psychoanalysts in
the world.

I didn't want to be here. The problems I'd been having with my
husband, Richard, my feelings of being trapped, my headaches, the
way I fell apart in anticipation of professional performances—all skit-
tered out of my mind. I could only think: This is a bad idea. I want
to go home.

I'd spent the morning rummaging through my closet. As a singer, I
knew costumes and wasn't normally at a loss about the right attire for
a recording session, a performance with a band, or a dinner party. But
I couldn't decide what to wear to my first meeting with Dr. Masserman.
Finally, I settled on a soft, teal-blue wool jumper and a silvery silk
blouse patterned with intertwined leaves of blue and taupe. Thinking

of the half-frozen slush clogging the streets, I pulled on tan boots, and for the fifth time in two hours, I brushed my hair. I looked out the large window in our Lake Shore Drive apartment and watched a few thin rays of white-gold sunshine slanting through the gray Monday morning.

In a cab, speeding over the Chicago River into the Loop, I panicked. The cabbie was raving on about some new health care program called Medicare, but I couldn't concentrate on his words. I kept thinking: What will Dr. Masserman ask me? Will this great doctor think I'm a fraud? A piece of fluff? I may look good, but he won't be fooled by a glamorous appearance; he'll see right through me. After all, he's a brilliant psychoanalyst. Grow up, I commanded myself as the cab pulled up at Willoughby Tower, on South Michigan Avenue, near the Art Institute and Orchestra Hall. Sit up straight! You're lucky to be seeing this man!

Our family internist, Dr. Ivan Keever, had initially recommended Dr. Charles Adams, a psychiatrist who said he was too busy to take any new patients. Dr. Adams, however, had given me the names of several doctors, including Dr. Masserman. Of those doctors, Dr. Keever thought Dr. Masserman would be the best. "He was a prodigy on the violin, Barbara," Dr. Keever said. "That's right up your alley." He also told me Dr. Masserman was about sixty years old, was professor and cochairman of the Department of Psychiatry and Neurology at Northwestern University, and had a dazzling career. I was desperate and relieved. An eminent professional who loved music sounded perfect.

I had gone to the library to look him up. A recent issue of *Who's Who in America* said that Jules Hymen Masserman,* physician and psychiatrist, was director of education and training psychiatrist at Illinois State Psychiatric Institute and was past president of many prestigious groups, including the Illinois Psychiatric Society, the American Society for Group Therapy, the Illinois Society for Group Therapy, and the American Society for Biological Psychiatry. He had also been a founding member and president of the Amercian Academy of Psychoanalysis. It was quite impressive.

When I mentioned Dr. Masserman's name to friends, they had all heard of him. I didn't know it then, but part of the unspoken aura around Jules Masserman came from his being an analytic descendant

---

*In later sources, Jules Masserman's middle name is often given as Homan.

of Sigmund Freud. The lineage came to Dr. Masserman from his brief analysis and subsequent friendship with Franz Alexander, a Hungarian neuropsychiatrist who had had a personal relationship with Freud and had been analyzed and trained by Hanns Sachs, a member of Freud's inner circle. Dr. Alexander was with Sachs in Vienna as well as in Berlin, where their illustrious company included Karl Abraham, Max Eitingon, Karen Horney, Sándor Radó, Siegfried Bernfeld, and Otto Fenichel.

Freud thought Franz Alexander was one of the most brilliant and promising of the "new" generation. In the early 1920s, Freud sent his son Oliver into analysis with Alexander in Berlin, and for many years during and after that time, Freud and Alexander corresponded.

As one of the first psychoanalysts to emigrate to the United States, Alexander became an influential voice in American psychoanalysis. He started the Chicago Institute for Psychoanalysis and was its director for twenty-five years. He also garnered great credibility for a new field when he was appointed professor of psychoanalysis at the University of Chicago—the first such appointment in the country. His research on psychosomatic disorders during the 1930s and '40s was so significant that a large number of illnesses became classed as psychosomatic and doctors began to recognize that even when diseases had an organic basis, psychosomatic factors could play a role.

I would later learn that it was a great source of pride to Jules Masserman that his analytic lineage could be traced to Freud through Franz Alexander. He was also proud that his early research in animal behavior had been supervised by Horsley Gantt, who had trained with Pavlov, and that the renowned psychiatrist Adolf Meyer had supervised his work at the Johns Hopkins University Medical School. It seems that Jules Masserman's own rise to power in the established psychoanalytic community had more than a little to do with his following in the footsteps of his distinguished therapeutic "ancestry."

I stood outside the office door of Suite 1404, trying to remind myself why I had come. Self-discovery? Happiness? Self-fulfillment? That's what I wanted, but it all seemed illusory at the time. I forced myself to mouth the names Freud, Jung, Fromm, Maslow, whom I'd read about in college. At the moment, I couldn't remember a single thing about any one of them. Before I'd come, I had thought: This will help me understand myself and my southern childhood. It will help me establish priorities. I'll be able to resolve what Dr. Keever calls my "case of nerves" about performing.

I pushed open the door with extra force and found myself standing in Dr. Masserman's surprisingly small reception room. A thin, wiry woman with a cap of permed blond hair looked up from an old manual typewriter and smiled at me.

She greeted me and said she was Billie Laird, Dr. Masserman's secretary. I nodded, unable to find my voice. She handed me a form to fill out and a pencil, and then she lit an unfiltered cigarette. I watched her inhale. I liked her rough, gritty smile and hunched-over posture.

I filled out the card and had a fantasy of sitting in a chair with my hands folded in my lap, as Dr. Masserman said, "That's just a case of whosiewatsis. You are now cured and you can go home feeling like a million dollars." Then I imagined myself saying, "I feel inferior," and his replying, "You feel inferior because you *are* inferior." What *would* he say to me? What would he want to know?

As I was giving the card back to Billie Laird, two tall, elegant, fur-coated women burst into the reception room and told Billie they needed just a moment of the doctor's time. Almost simultaneously, the door to the left of the receptionist's desk opened, and a man padded out— pale, nearly bald, and short, barely taller than the receptionist. His shirt sleeves were rolled up to his elbows, and he wore leather bedroom slippers, well past their prime. He looked up at the women descending on him and smiled in surprise. The women, who appeared to be sisters, seemed to talk at once, in strong British accents, saying they simply *had* to say goodbye before going on to San Francisco; it had been absolutely *divine* to see him, and they couldn't *bear* to leave without seeing him again first. They interrupted each other continuously, with great enthusiasm and confidence.

Dr. Masserman laughed softly and spoke in a subdued, yet melodious voice that had a weathered, slightly rough quality to it. He reminded them that he would see them both in London in just a few months and asked them to give their father his greetings in the meantime. The kindness and power in his voice was compelling; I was mesmerized by it.

The doctor shook hands with the women, and they left in a flurry of goodbyes. When the door closed behind them, Billie Laird rather loudly introduced me.

He turned toward me with a small, concerned smile. "Oh, yes," he said. "Won't you come in?" In what would become a familiar ritual, he held the door open for me, then took my coat.

I sat down in an old leather armchair on one side of his desk and watched as he carefully hung my white wool coat on the coat tree behind the door. As he padded slowly toward his desk, he pulled on a green jacket that looked as old and worn as his office furniture. He then made a small, slow turn before sitting down in the soft-looking leather chair behind his desk. "Courtly" was the word that came to my mind. He was courtly and kind. He was looking at me rather solemnly, and I couldn't remember anything I had planned to say.

Fortunately for me, the phone rang, and he picked it up, listened, then started talking.

While he spoke on the phone, I looked around his office. It looked like something straight out of a 1940s Hollywood version of a psychiatrist's office—small, messy, and cluttered with Oriental rugs and books and papers and small mementos from all over the world. A low bookcase along the length of the right wall was filled with books; many of them had "Masserman" on the spine. A dark-brown leather couch, just like the ones in the movies, was against the opposite wall, and at its foot was an Oriental-looking three-paneled lacquered screen that had birds flying and ships sailing across a brown background. Looking at that screen, I felt an amazing calm. I thought: I am safe here. I will be made whole here.

I looked at some ivory and wood figurines and a framed letter from Albert Einstein. Another framed letter was signed by Adlai Stevenson, and yet another was a recent letter from President Lyndon B. Johnson, thanking Dr. Masserman for his contributions to mental health on behalf of the U.S. State Department. The letters were next to a picture of Jules H. Masserman standing beside former President Dwight D. Eisenhower. Dr. Masserman was much shorter than Ike, and while he looked solid, he didn't appear as robust as the ex-President. His chest was small and his shoulders were quite narrow. I thought that with his large nose, little chin, and triangular face, the doctor was rather homely. Almost ugly.

In the picture with Ike, Dr. Masserman had black hair, and only the very peak of his head was bald. I furtively looked over at Dr. Masserman, still on the phone. Now the entire top of his head was bald and shiny, and the thick fringe of hair above his ears was gray. It occurred to me that even if his mouth was too wide and his nose bulbous and gnarled, his face was interesting. It was a face that seemed to possess exceptional strength and intelligence. I turned in my chair and stared out the large windows that overlooked the icy-blue waters of Lake Michigan. I didn't dare look at the doctor anymore. He might sense my gaze and ask me about it, and I would die if I had to tell him what I thought about his looks. I wasn't very good at lying.

He hung up, sighed, and placed his elbows on the desk. Then, in a gesture that would become as familiar to me as the way he walked or spoke, Dr. Masserman placed his fingertips together and formed a steeple that touched the bottom of his nose and made an arch in front of his thin gray mustache and narrow lips.

He studied me a long moment and then smiled. His kind gray eyes radiated such generosity and thoughtfulness that tears immediately welled up in my eyes. I looked down at the tiny bows edging the sleeves of my silk blouse. My hands were shaking. I spread my fingers on my arms, trying to still them.

"Well, now, young lady, what seems to have brought you here?"

My chest felt as if it were going to burst. I wanted to say something, but I couldn't open my mouth.

"Are you having some problems with your husband, Miz Nole?" he asked, rhyming Nole with Mole.

"It's pronounced No-elle," I managed to say in a whisper. "Not Nole. No-elle."

"All right, Miz No-*elle*," he said, smiling. "You were referred by Dr. Keever."

"Yes."

"What seems to be the problem?" He paused.

When I didn't say anything, he said I could start anywhere I liked, and if I wanted, I could tell him about my husband first.

"Well, my husband is a singer—one of the best in the commercial business," I said, speaking in a voice so tiny it embarrassed me. "He's done television and radio in Chicago for a long time. When we met in California, he was a regular on the Tennessee Ernie Ford show on ABC, and I was a vocalist on the Dick Stewart show. We've been married seven months."

My mind flew over some of the major issues: Richard and I had started seeing each other when we were both married to other people, and within months, both our marriages had broken up. While I was getting my divorce, I moved back to New York, where a spectacular agent had lined me up with great work.

But Richard pressured me to leave it all and come to Chicago to marry him—and I was a southern girl who wanted to do the proper thing. When I told my agent I was leaving, he was livid, and now I thought he'd been right: I shouldn't have left New York. Now that we were married, Richard was angry at me almost every time I got a job. Instead of getting mad back, I walked around the house trying to act like a good girl so he wouldn't stay angry, which made me feel absurd.

But I didn't say any of those things. I kept my hands together in my lap and felt the tears spilling down my cheeks. At last I managed to say, "Richard thinks I came here to talk about our problems, but that's not really why I'm here."

"I see. There is another reason you're here?"

"Yes."

"Well, think for a bit. How would you best describe that other problem?"

I leaned forward in my seat: I was blowing my work, and that worried me more than anything else. It was the worst thing that had ever happened to me, and it seemed to be the center of things, including the problems in my marriage. "I'm a singer," I said, "but sometimes . . . I can't control what comes out of my mouth. There are times when I get up in front of a microphone and I feel exhausted before I start to sing or, even worse, nothing comes out."

"Times when you can't talk?" he asked gently.

"Sing *or* talk," I replied. "Sometimes when I sing, I have particularly successful sessions, and I'm wonderful. But there's always a chance I'll lose my voice and nothing will come out."

I watched the doctor's placid expression and gray eyes, looking for his reaction, but I couldn't tell what he was thinking. I didn't understand how desperate I was for approval. I started experiencing the panic I had each time I went into a recording booth and felt the walls closing in on me, terrified I would fall apart in front of the other singers, the musicians, producers, and recording engineers. It didn't matter if I was singing, "New, mean Mr. Clean; he hates dirt!" or "You'll love that Roman Meal bread." I was even petrified when I went to sing studio backup with a four-part group for rhythm-and-blues singers Junior Walker, Major Lance, Betty Everett or Donny Hathaway.

What was most tormenting was the unpredictability of my voice. Sometimes I'd go into the studio and feel great and sing without a glitch, and then, another time, I'd have terrible pains in my face—sometimes even my ears would hurt—and I'd go through incredible torture to finish a session. I never knew what to expect in terms of quality of sound or pain levels, but more and more, especially when Richard was around, I felt hysterical. I thought I must be crazy. I couldn't figure out any other logical reason for the unexplained head-aches and facial pain, nor was there a reason for the voice loss and lack of consistency.

"Losing my voice makes me feel crazy," I said.

"Perhaps there is something you don't want to say," he said.

A chill went down my back, but no thought came to mind. Dr. Masserman leaned back in his chair.

"Now, Miz Nole, you must know, don't you, that you have complete control over everything you do," he said. "We human beings are always responsible for our own actions. You know that? Perhaps you'd feel better if you could tell me why you sometimes don't want something to come out of your mouth. What might it be that you're afraid of saying?"

I was silent, trying to think. Then I knew. I said, "They'll find out."

"What will they find out?"

"I'm a fake, or I'm no good." My strong, matter-of-fact voice surprised me. I sounded almost defiant.

"And why do you think you're no good?"

"I don't know," I said, crossing my arms tightly in front of my body, trying to think. "I think I'm good—a lot of people have told me I am. My New York agent said I could really go to the upper limits if I worked at it. But I'm afraid they're wrong—maybe I've been faking it. Maybe I have no talent at all."

Dr. Masserman removed his glasses and wiped each lens with a white handkerchief he had pulled from his pocket. Then he looked up and smiled at me again. "Do you suppose it might be all right with you if I spoke to your husband one day?" he said. "Alone, I mean? I'd never betray a confidence of yours, but perhaps if I could get a better idea as to how your husband is feeling these days, it would help. Then we both—you and I—could better understand what might be causing you to feel the way you do."

Even though he spoke so softly I had to lean forward to hear him,

Dr. Masserman's voice was making a surprising impact on me. He spoke carefully, distinctly, and his words were well chosen and filled with enormous concern and compassion. Now he was pressing his fingertips together again as if in prayer, and I almost felt as though I were in a holy place, a place for healing.

"That's fine," I said, relieved and yet agitated about the idea of Richard talking with him alone. "It might help."

Dr. Masserman smiled at me. "And you and I will get together a few more times, shall we? That way, we can come to a decision as to what direction we will finally take."

During our second session, I was much more comfortable. Dr. Masserman took notes and often smiled at me as if he were an old, wise, and comforting friend. I was still nervous, but I managed to tell him that Richard's fits of temper about my work made me feel desperate. I told him how I used to be so thrilled that Richard, unlike my father, thought I was a gifted singer. "At least with my father, I knew where I stood," I said. Dr. Masserman wrote something down and then looked at me.

"You knew where you stood with your father?" he asked.

"Yes."

"I see."

I looked at the doctor. I didn't know what he meant when he said "I see," so I just went on trying to explain myself in a way that would make sense. "My father's poor opinion of me never wavered. He always put me down. He taught music at my college, and in my senior year, when I got voted Most Popular in my class, he told me, 'They always choose a compromise.' When I got elected May Queen, his sarcastic response was, 'Oh, no! What is this going to cost us?' And when I was already a professional and sang at my best friend's wedding, he came up afterward and said, 'I've had freshmen students who sounded better than that!' I think that's why Richard's praise of my work was so important to me. When we were first seeing each other, he used to tell me how much he admired my work—and it felt wonderful. I thought he understood that music was my life.

"But now he's treating this part of my life—which is so *big* to me— as trivial. Last week, he said, 'I will not have you out at a club or auditioning for a bunch of ad executives who'll make passes at you. Can't you understand that? You're my wife now.' Whenever I go for a job, he gets *so* grim and rigid. And even though we worked together before, now he just wants me to stay home, take care of his children when they visit, entertain his friends, and make his special meals. He goes off to work, and I'm supposed to stay home."

"Miz Nole, do you think you might be jealous of your husband's relationship with his children?"

I thought for a minute. "Yes, I suppose so."

"Now, why would that be?"

"Well, his kids hate me," I said. "When they come to visit, they stonewall me. Richard is so guilty about having left them that he dotes on them, even to the point of letting them sit in the front and relegating me to the back seat when he drives—as if I were a child. I try to win them over by cooking their favorite meals and making special desserts, but nothing works. And Richard's allegiance is totally with them. Once I insisted on getting to sit in the front, like a grown woman, and Richard still hasn't forgiven me for it."

"Now, now. Do you really think it's as bad as all that?" Dr. Masserman said, leaning back in his chair with a little sigh. "Is it so hard for you to play second fiddle every now and then?"

Between my second and third sessions, Richard met with Dr. Masserman. I didn't ask Richard anything about his visit, because I didn't want him asking *me* any questions about what I said. I had read a lot on psychiatry and respected the privacy and sanctity involved. I also knew Dr. Masserman was on my side and was simply trying to understand me from Richard's perspective.

By my fourth session, I told Dr. Masserman a big thing about my mother. I told him how in 1965, when I was getting my divorce from my first husband, Robin Stark,* my mother said she was worried about me. I was back down South on a visit, and Mother and I were standing in her kitchen, putting away groceries. A record of Prokofiev's Violin Concerto in D was playing in the background. "Mother had a kind of nervous expression on her face," I said, "and she dropped a box of raisins. She picked them up, and then she straightened her back and looked at me with her mouth all pursed and tight, like she was holding something in. Suddenly, in a rush of words, she said, 'Barbara, I just want to tell you something. . . . I want you to know . . . your father

*This is not his real name.

and I made some big mistakes with you when you were little, and you might want to see a psychiatrist sometime to talk about it.'

"I had a head of lettuce and a package of carrots in my hands, and I just froze. We stood there looking at each other, and I felt cold and scared. I knew she was saying something significant. I had never heard her say it might help anybody to see a psychiatrist. I didn't know what she meant, or what kind of mistakes she or my father had made, but I didn't ask. Somehow I couldn't; I couldn't even formulate a question. I only knew she wasn't criticizing me; she was giving me a personal message. She was trying to be a good mother."

I paused, and Dr. Masserman stopped his note taking.

I waited, but he didn't say anything.

Then I continued. "I feel good about her having said that to me. It made me feel she *cares*. I think I'll tell her sometime soon that I'm in therapy with you. I know she'll be glad I'm taking care of myself," I said. "I also feel good about seeing you—and I'm enjoying talking. It makes me feel more optimistic."

Dr. Masserman leaned back in his chair, folded his hands behind his head, and said: "My dear young lady, I believe these problems you've brought to me, even though they trouble you deeply now, can be resolved. They are not too deep, and I don't think it will take too long to get everything straight.

"You are a relatively well-adjusted young person. It won't take more than a year, perhaps two years, for a different woman, a calmer woman, to sit here in front of me. She'll be a woman with a healthier way of looking at life, a woman in a happy marriage."

I saw a vision of myself happy, content, enjoying my career and my husband. Richard and I were onstage, singing "Everything's Coming Up Roses" together, holding the high notes. It made me feel great, imagining myself like that. I felt so grateful I thought I would explode. In a torrent of words, I thanked him again and again and asked him if he really thought so.

"Of course," he said, laughing at my outburst.

He spoke with such candor and wisdom. I knew I was in good hands.

3 *In Good Hands*

SEPTEMBER 1966 I sat in Dr. Masserman's waiting room like an old pro, thumbing through a magazine that had graphic pictures from the Chicago dormitory where eight student nurses had been murdered in July by a crazy man named Richard Speck. The murders were so disgusting and grisly that the pictures made me sick. I changed magazines, looking up every now and then at Billie Laird, who cracked jokes and lit one cigarette after another at her cluttered desk. The magazines seemed full of problems—student protests at Columbia University and the University of Wisconsin, voting rights demonstrations in Mississippi and Washington, D.C., the war in Vietnam, old pictures of Lenny Bruce, who had died in August. Miniskirts were the only fun news—and I didn't even like them, though I had just bought a chic black-and-white suit that was *almost* a mini.

Between telephone calls and sips of Coke, Billie typed letters or journal articles for the doctor on her old manual and did a lot of paperwork; nevertheless, she always took time to joke around. Billie knew how to laugh. She had once been an army nurse and had retained that down-to-earth quality I associated with her former profession. It was her relaxed manner that made the place friendly and took away my fears of not being "normal." She made appointments and collected payments for the doctor and knew exactly what everyone needed to be comfortable. Sometimes, when glamorous, wealthy patients strolled out after a session with the doctor, Billie raised her eyebrows and

shared a smile with me. She confirmed my observation of some of the
doctor's patients as Social Register favorites. They were the people at
all the showings of new fashion collections; they flew to the Metropolitan Opera in New York for special performances, to Hollywood
and San Francisco. In Chicago, they were at all the fancy museum
benefits; they danced for cancer and either gave or attended all the
right parties.

I liked to think that even though I wasn't famous, the doctor noticed
me because of the progress I'd made over the six months I'd been
seeing him. I was much more open than I had been at the beginning.
During our sessions now, I lay on the couch and free-associated. He
told me when I started it that this was "an important part of the dynamic
psychotherapeutic process" I would be going through. He said I should
always report everything that occurred to me, no matter how trivial it
seemed. It needn't be coherent or focused; I should simply let myself
float and say whatever came into my head. Free-flowing thought eventually would bring me to those areas of conflict most basic to my
difficulties. Then it was *his* job to help me understand the issues and
work through them.

I loved free-associating and looked forward to it. Each session, I felt
I was making progress. I enjoyed seeing Dr. Masserman open the door
from his office. His rolled-up shirt sleeves, his worn pants and slippers,
his lack of pretension, only emphasized his greatness to me. I thought
Dr. Masserman looked exactly as a psychiatrist should—quaint, slightly
ugly, small, and very wise—above any interest in fashion or any pho-
niness. The character actors who played psychiatrists in old Hollywood
movies were usually weather-beaten, had beards or goatees and foreign
accents—all of which invested them with an appearance of wisdom.
Dr. Masserman didn't have a foreign accent, but he pronounced some
words oddly, he looked somewhat alien, and he was *perfectly* wise. I
knew he taught and trained other psychiatrists, and that pushed him
even higher up on the ladder of my admiration.

Dr. Masserman also happened to look a lot like Gandhi, and I started
thinking of him as Gandhi's twin. Besides his small size, Dr. Masserman
had that same energy and spark in his eyes. Like Gandhi, he was a
peacemaker, a spokesman for his times. I loved seeing Dr. Masserman's
name in the paper: he was quoted on world peace or China or the
cold war or women's roles—whatever topic he was asked about.
Clearly, he was a man of breadth and wisdom, a distinguished intel-

lectual others looked to for larger understanding, not only of themselves, but of our society.

I was seeing him three times a week now, and his kind smile, his
soft, soothing voice, kept me spellbound. Today, as he opened the
door to the waiting room, he looked at me, as usual, for maybe five
seconds with no emotion or expression whatsoever, as if trying to get
his bearings. Then he said, "Ah, Miz Nole, won't you come in?" I felt
my normal moment of irritation, which I quickly suppressed. After all
these months, I had become used to his calling me "Miz Nole" instead
of Mrs. Noël, but it still bothered me. On some level, it made me feel
worthless that the man didn't know my name. I figured he didn't mean
any harm by it, but over the years, even though I corrected his pro-
nunciation a number of times, his faulty articulation of my name became even more fixed unless he was in the presence of my husband.
Many, many years later, I heard that President Lyndon Johnson purposely mispronounced people's names when he wanted to put them
down or keep them in their place, and it made me rethink Dr. Masserman's seeming inability to say my name properly. I began to wonder
whether he didn't do this on purpose, perhaps as an experiment in
depersonalizing the patient.

At that time, however, I didn't question any of Dr. Masserman's
motives. I only felt tremendous gratitude toward him for being so
gracious and listening to me. When I walked into his cluttered office,
he would take my coat and hang it up as I walked across the worn-
out brown carpet that covered the floor. Sometimes when I'd head for
the chair next to his desk, he'd tell me to go to the couch. Or if I went
straight to the couch, he'd tell me to sit in the chair first. As soon as
I got settled, he'd say, "Now, Miz Nole, what seems to be bothering
you today?"

Lying on his couch, before I began to talk, I looked up at that
wonderful three-paneled lacquered screen with its flying birds and ships
sailing across a brown background. I loved looking at it, and I loved
the freedom of being able to free-associate and not worry about making
sense, just letting myself go and knowing that ultimately it would lead
us to the important issues. Whenever I hit a topic that made me squirm,
looking at the screen let me relax, gave me a feeling of calm. I couldn't
see Dr. Masserman, who sat behind me at his desk, but I could hear
his pen scratching. I felt comforted by his presence even when he said
nothing; the silence didn't bother me because I knew from what I'd

read about analysis that more often than not, the psychoanalyst doesn't say anything at all. He lets you talk it out with yourself and intervenes only when he can help you steer in the right direction.

At the beginning, I spoke a lot about my childhood and my glamorous, charming parents. They were gifted professional musicians, and their personal life was steeped in etiquette and graciousness. I told Dr. Masserman how my parents got married onstage, between the matinee and evening performances of a light opera they were performing. My brother, Warren, and I were both born in Indiana, but we moved to Virginia when we were little because my parents got jobs as music professors at a small college there.*

"When I was a teenager," I told Dr. Masserman at one afternoon session, "my mother used to give little parties for me and my friends, so I would know exactly how the silver was placed, how the napkins were folded. My friends were always saying, 'If I could pick any family to belong to, it would be yours.' The walls in our house were lined with books, and chamber music and concertos and symphonies were playing all the time. My parents gave recitals, spoke in soft southern accents and did all the southern things, plus some."

I told Dr. Masserman of my current worries about my mother. She was not only crippled with arthritis but was in a wheelchair because she had fallen and broken her hip. She was only in her late fifties, but she had a hard time even turning her head. In addition, her body had rejected two pacemakers, and in spite of my father's taking her to Florida to recover, she was failing fast. I went to visit her several times, and when I was with her she talked compulsively.

"Even though she keeps saying, 'I'm not one of those mothers who whines that her children don't pay enough attention to her,' my father says the only time Mother is really happy is when I'm home," I said. "But being there confuses me. I forget who I am. I don't know why. I can't stand to listen to her. I *hate* seeing her all twisted up. I also hate seeing her so dependent on Dad. Everywhere she wants to go, he has to push her in her wheelchair. He has to help her from her chair to her bed, and from her chair to the toilet."

I told Dr. Masserman about a strange incident on my last trip home. I had just seen the movie *Who's Afraid of Virginia Woolf?* with Richard

*The name of Barbara Noël's brother and the states mentioned here have been changed for the purpose of protecting the family's privacy.

Burton and Elizabeth Taylor, and whenever my parents bickered over something, it made me think of the movie. "And then one day," I told him, "Daddy was really angry about something—I don't remember what it was. He didn't realize I was watching him, and I saw him push Mother's wheelchair down the hallway as if it were a bowling ball. She was in it, and he shot it down the hallway—just hurled it—with her in it. I was so shocked. The chair ricocheted off one wall and then whanged against the far end of the hall to a stop. I didn't do anything. I didn't let him know I had seen what he did. I realize that on some level, he hates taking care of her, and that makes me feel even more guilty for being so far away and for really not wanting to go visit her."

I paused, but Dr. Masserman didn't say anything, so I kept talking.

I told him about the nice autumn picnics Mother and I used to pack for the family and take up into the mountains when I was a girl. "We carried baskets filled with hot fried chicken, baked beans, biscuits, and cobbler," I recalled, letting the delicious smells drift back into my memory. "We climbed up through red and gold leaves until we found just the right spot. . . .

"In summer, the air was filled with the smell of honeysuckle, and when it was so hot we could hardly move, we all went down to the river just outside town, and my brother and I cooled off by wading in up to our knees. Afterward, we ate fried fish and hush puppies, cold watermelon and iced tea. Everything seemed to operate in dreamlike slow motion for me in those days."

"So, little miss, all your memories are happy?" Dr. Masserman asked softly.

"No!" I exclaimed, surprised again by the intensity of my response. "No, not at all."

"Hmm." He cleared his throat but said nothing else.

"Probably the worst event of my childhood happened when I was nine," I said. "I had the mumps on one side and then on the other, and I felt miserable. I'd been in bed for a long time, and one day I looked down and saw blood. I ran screaming to my mother; I thought I was bleeding to death from the mumps. Mother was surprised, but she explained that I was menstruating and was becoming a lovely young woman. It was horrible—much worse than mumps. My breasts also started getting big—which was devastating. By the time I was ten, I was five feet two and had the body of a woman, which made me feel like a freak.

"Neither my father nor my mother ever hugged me or kissed me good morning or good night, so I didn't expect much affection. But after I started my period, Daddy got so cold he rarely spoke to me. That made everything worse. He talked to Mother about me in the third person. He'd say, 'She was late again!' or 'Is she dressed yet?' or 'Why can't she keep her room clean?' "

When I told Dr. Masserman about how bad I sometimes felt, I said, "Through all of it, music was my escape and my comfort. I listened to Ravel's 'Tzigane' and Schumann's chamber pieces, to Bach and Stravinsky."

"I find that with Mozart," Dr. Masserman said in a rare exchange of confidences. "Mozart is often my source of serenity."

I told Dr. Masserman I'd never informed my mother about the affair I'd had with Richard before I divorced my first husband. Nor had I told her I'd gotten pregnant with Richard's child and had an abortion. I'd been so happy when I got pregnant; I loved how slowed down and dreamy I felt. But there was no way to have the baby; it would not have been a happy beginning for a child. Nevertheless, the abortion was heartbreaking.

"When I was growing up, Mother told me if I was smart I would never have kids," I said. "When I married Robin, she told me, 'If you ever want children, wait until you can afford a nurse or a nanny— otherwise it's just *too* hard.' Since the abortion, I've been afraid I'll never have a child. I'm afraid I'll never be a mother. I feel as if I've done a really dreadful thing," I said, starting to cry. "At the time, it seemed like the only way, but now it just makes me so sad."

"This discussion is a waste of time," Dr. Masserman said with a harsh impatience that startled me. "Any fool knows it's all right to get an abortion if that is what's indicated. Your husband had two other children to support, and you weren't even divorced from your first husband! Why in the world wouldn't you do what you did?"

"I don't know. I just can't think about it without crying."

"Don't you think you're being a bit self-indulgent about all this?"

Before I left that session, Dr. Masserman asked me if I had a headache, which I did. He said that was a shame, but some aspirin should help me. Then he carefully folded a tiny paper envelope for me out of a piece of notebook paper, took four aspirin tablets out of a bottle, and put the tablets inside the envelope. He closed it up and handed it to me before I left the room. Over the years, whenever I rummaged in one of my purses, I always found old little flattened paper envelopes that Dr. Masserman had folded to hold the medicines he gave me.

· · ·

Before long, it was too late to tell Mother anything at all about what I'd done, what I'd felt. In October, my father called to tell me Mother had been hospitalized and was in critical condition. Richard and I flew straight to Sarasota and spent several hours at the hospital with my mother before Warren arrived. Then the three of us took my dad out for fresh air and dinner. When we came back, Mother was dead. Dad sobbed and sobbed in Warren's arms. Even though he'd hated caring for her, he went to pieces over her dying. For some reason, I didn't cry. Richard came over to me, and I kissed him. Then I turned around and went in to be with Mother. Sitting there, I still didn't cry. I just sat with her, looking at her pale, motionless face. She was beautiful even after all her pain. I'd been there I don't know how long, when a nurse came in and said, "You shouldn't be here; you should wait until your mother's all fixed up. You shouldn't see her like this; let me get her pretty first."

In December, more than a month and a half after my mother's death, I wasn't talking as easily to Dr. Masserman as I had been before. I wasn't as good at remembering things I thought I'd forgotten. One day I told him, "Sometimes, thinking about my mother, I get this ugly feeling and I can't say anything. I don't know why. I stare at the red and gold feathers in the birds' wings on your screen, and I get this bitter feeling in my throat. I feel as if someone is sitting on my chest and holding me down, but I can't cry and I can't speak."

Dr. Masserman was silent. I had nothing else to say, so I stopped talking. I could feel my heart beating in my chest; it seemed like a drumbeat, a fast drumbeat.

After a long time, I heard Dr. Masserman clearing his throat. From behind his desk, he said, "By your silence, I can see something is bothering you."

What was bothering me most was what I had just reported—the feeling that someone was sitting on my chest. I tried to think of something else that disturbed me. I said, "All those unhappy people."

"What unhappy people?"

"Those people in all those miles and miles of houses on the highway. When we came back from O'Hare Airport, I saw those thousands of little houses filled with all those unhappy people."

"Are they as unhappy as you are?"

"Oh, they are even more unhappy."

"I see."

I heard him writing. It was astounding, but he seemed to take down every word I said. Sometimes I was amazed at how much writing he did. I thought he must be filling in the blanks for me, figuring out what I should be saying, because even when I wasn't talking, his pen was busy.

Dr. Masserman didn't say anything else for a while, and neither did I. I listened to his pen scratching against the paper. Then he told me that anything I said could be useful.

I said, "I still feel like someone is sitting on my chest. I feel like crying. I'm glad I told my mother that I was in therapy with you before she died. . . . I always felt like an outsider in the South; I always knew I was a Yankee, even though I knew how to talk and look like I fit in. . . . You know, I feel silly sometimes, lying here, saying stupid, disconnected things when you don't say anything and I don't know how you are responding to what I'm saying. It makes me feel like you're not there."

Finally, he cleared his throat and told me our hour was almost up, but he would like Richard to come to our next session so we could have a three-way conference. "Frankly, I'm worried, Miz Nole," he said, still mispronouncing my name. "Things were going favorably, and you were free-associating quite well, but now you're closing up. You seem to be blocking. This doesn't give me a chance to help you as much as I might. I know you're having a hard time facing your mother's death, and I think it's worth talking these things over with Mr. Nole."

When Richard and I came in together, we sat down in the leather armchairs and Dr. Masserman sat behind his desk. I looked at my tall, tanned husband, perfectly turned out in his cream-colored silk shirt, cashmere sweater, wool slacks, and custom-made Italian loafers, and I felt a rush of pride and affection. The first time I'd seen him in person was when I auditioned for his singing group in San Francisco; I thought him even more attractive than he'd been on television. Besides being a magnificent singer, he had so much positive energy and talent that I was drawn to him like a magnet to iron. Now Richard flashed his warmest smile at me, and I felt strong and united, part of something larger than myself. Richard reached over and patted my knee, and I put my hand in his. He had been in this office before to see Dr. Masserman, but this was our first time together, and we both were nervous.

After he sat down, Dr. Masserman asked Richard if he had been flying recently. He knew that besides being a successful singer, Richard was a licensed pilot who had his own small plane, a Cessna 172. He asked about the Cessna and confided that he himself loved flying and was working toward qualifying for his pilot's license. The two of them chatted about airplanes, flying instruction, and the dangers of solo flights, as though they were old friends talking over drinks. Dr. Masserman asked a number of questions about the handling and problems of owning and maintaining the airplane, and then they compared a few notes about sailing.

After they talked about airplanes and boats, Dr. Masserman asked Richard about Aspen, Colorado, where we had a condo. Richard and I loved to ski there with our friend and attorney, Dick Shelton. Remembering the fun we had skiing, I squeezed Richard's hand. It made me proud that Dr. Masserman was so interested in him. I thought: If I weren't already married to Richard, I would *want* to marry him.

At that moment, I didn't remember how furious I had been at Richard recently and how, all too often, I didn't enjoy making love with him. This was an incredible contrast with the days when we drove along and laughed hilariously at "Purple People Eater" or sang along with Jack Jones' "Wives and Lovers" or walked in a Sierra snowfall and made love by a fire in his cozy cabin at Squaw Valley, or in an open meadow, or even in the back seat of a convertible. During that time we were intensely focused on each other, and I felt happy and free and womanly. Lovemaking was electrifying.

But things had been different for quite a while. Both of us were hurting, unable to deal with the changes in our feelings. Richard was bitter when I simply went through the motions of lovemaking without really being there. I couldn't seem to overcome my anger at his change of view on my career. It made me feel trapped, and I couldn't let go of my resentment. But at that moment in Dr. Masserman's office, I thought: We can conquer this thing. We have what it takes. I was determined—and excited to think of our enormous potential, of the marriage we would have if we could just work out our problems. I left my reverie when I heard Dr. Masserman's voice pronouncing my name properly. He was saying, "I asked you and Mrs. Noël to come in today because I feel that she and I are at an impasse. Things were going quite well, but since her mother's critical illness and death, she has been closing up, blocking.

"I think a different tactic, a different kind of therapy, is indicated," he said quietly, looking at Richard with intense concentration. "Let me tell you about the success I've had for a number of years with a drug therapy I call the Sodium Amytal Interview." He folded his hands together and looked at me for a moment and then at Richard. He got up slowly and walked over to his bookcase. He leaned down and pulled out a thick green book, opened it to a particular page, and placed his hand there.

"I wrote about this therapy in my book *The Practice of Dynamic Psychiatry,* which was published ten or eleven years ago," he said in his quiet voice. "You may read this if you'd like." He set the open book down on the desk in front of us, and I pulled it over and turned it to look at the cover and the copyright date.

"But let me tell you something about the Sodium Amytal Interview first," he said. "Sodium Amytal is a barbiturate that was first discovered in 1923. It was used extensively and became invaluable during the Second World War, when psychiatric casualties were able to acquire enough symptomatic relief to be quickly returned to the front line. It was also used a great deal as a type of truth serum with former prisoners of war during the Korean War to help them recover from their traumas.

"For a number of years now, I've used the Sodium Amytal Interview with patients having many forms of stress, and it's been quite successful, particularly for those people who are experiencing various levels of immobility." He turned to me. "That seeming inability to open up has become your problem, Mrs. Noël, and this is why I'm suggesting it for you now. I believe it will help you overcome your resistances and open up so that you can get to what is troubling you. I believe it will give you relief from your anxiety and depression over your mother's death and open up new areas of memory for exploration."

"You may wonder how it's administered," he said, speaking so softly that we had to sit forward in our seats and strain to hear him. Dr. Masserman lifted his left forearm and pointed to a vein in the crook of his elbow. "The Amytal is given by slow infusion through this vein in your arm, here in the bend of your elbow. The treatment itself takes about an hour." He looked from Richard to me and back to Richard. "However, after the treatment, Mrs. Noël would be sleepy for quite some time—probably the entire day—so I would ask you, Mr. Noël, to come pick her up and take her home, feed her, and put her to bed for the evening. By the following morning, she should feel perfectly strong again.

"An advantage is that we wouldn't need to go elsewhere to do this. I have a private examination room right here," he said, indicating a door at the end of the room, "and it's equipped with all the things you would find in any doctor's examining room. We can make Mrs. Noël quite comfortable on the examination cot, or she can use the chair and ottoman in there, if she'd prefer it."

Richard interrupted. "I'm not sure I like this idea," he said, clearly agitated, his voice rising. "You say this drug is a barbiturate: that doesn't sound very safe. Aren't barbiturates habit-forming? I'm sure I've heard about people becoming addicted to barbiturates."

"Oh, no, Mr. Noël; both the drug and the procedure are actually quite safe," Dr. Masserman said kindly. "I understand your concern, but this drug has been in use now for more than forty years and is completely harmless when properly used. Since I am the one to control the amount and frequency of the dosage, we wouldn't have to worry about any mistakes being made."

As the two of them talked, I picked up the book and started reading. I saw the word Amytal and all this medical jargon—cc's and mg's and ml/min—meaningless to me. I couldn't understand what I read, but it looked as if it must be important and true. I was frightened and kind of glazed over, so nothing really registered as I looked at the words. I remember thinking: A shot! Oh, God, I'd have to have a shot! I hate shots! As usual, however, I tried to give the impression of being competent and thorough about it all, and so I held on to the book and looked down at the words from time to time.

"I can assure you, I've been using Sodium Amytal with patients for many, many years, and it's a very pleasant and restful experience—one that Mrs. Noël needn't fear in the least," Dr. Masserman was saying. "The entire interview would be conducted in strictest confidence. Miss Laird, my receptionist and nurse, will be ready at all times to assist Mrs. Noël if she should require anything during the hours she is recovering here."

Dr. Masserman leaned toward us.

"I hope you will seriously consider this suggestion, because I believe it might be quite worthwhile as an intervention and alternative," he said. "You two are married people who clearly love each other. We just want to do everything we can to ensure that we can get things worked out for you." He paused and cleared his throat. "It's obvious you're devoted to each other. I see this as a way of speeding up the process, getting to the unconscious more quickly, so we can really work through what's bothering her."

Dr. Masserman was quiet for a moment; when he spoke again, he did so even more softly: "But of course, I don't want you to rush into this decision. You must feel sure about it."

A wave of fear rushed through me as I wondered if this was the kind of thing they used on really crazy people. I put the book, still open, down on the desk, and it stayed there, kind of staring at me, through the rest of the meeting.

Richard looked at me and touched my arm. "I don't like the idea, Barb," he said. "But you're the one who would be doing it. What do you think?"

"I'm not sure," I said. My hands were trembling. "I like the idea of trying something new . . . something that might give me the answers I want," I said. "But I don't know."

I tried to get my thoughts together. "Is this like a truth serum? Is it to get me to say things I wouldn't say otherwise?" While I was speaking excitedly, I was also flooded with mortification that I needed something so drastic. My mind seemed to be going a hundred miles an hour, and my mouth couldn't keep up. "Would I have just one treatment or more than one?"

"Usually, at least several sessions are called for, Mrs. Noël," Dr. Masserman said. "But I have no idea how many Sodium Amytal Interviews will be necessary in your case, because every patient is different. Every patient is unique, so there's no way to predict frequency with any accuracy. There's simply no way to tell what you'll need."

I looked from Dr. Masserman to Richard and then back to Dr. Masserman. "I was just wondering," I said in a small voice, about to ask the unspeakable, thinking of the mental zombies I had seen in movies—inmates crowded together, their mouths slightly open, drooling. "Can you tell me, is this something just for crazy people or something you only give to really *sick* patients? I mean, are many of your patients in need of this treatment?"

Dr. Masserman smiled at me as if he knew just what was on my mind. "Now, my dear, I don't want you to get the idea that you have insurmountable problems. Many people benefit from this type of therapy, and it's only because they're blocked or could use a boost. I suggest it simply because it's a relatively quick and effective way to get you back on your way to healthy thinking and a healthy, happy marriage.

I think it will particularly help you in overcoming your resistance to dealing with your mother's death."

It sounded amazing—innovative but absolutely terrifying. A feeling of hope flashed through my mind: maybe this would let me get through to an understanding of what troubled me about my relationship with my mother. I knew it was something unspoken, something deep and foggy, that was always just beyond me. Maybe if the Amytal helped me work all that out, I would be at a new level of awareness that would help me get on with my life. Maybe it would also help resolve my performance anxiety and my headaches.

"Do you think you might want to take this material home and study it further?" Dr. Masserman asked, indicating his book. "If you'd like to do that, please feel free to do so."

"No," I said with a greater conviction than I felt. I reached out for Richard's hand in reassurance. "I trust your judgment. I'm for it."

When we left Dr. Masserman's office, the book still lay open on his desk. If Richard and I had taken that book home and read it carefully and understood what Jules Masserman had written in it about Sodium Amytal, we would never have agreed to my first Amytal interview— or to any Amytal whatsoever.

In *The Practice of Dynamic Psychiatry* (Philadelphia: W. B. Saunders, 1955), Jules Masserman made it clear that Amytal was *not recommended* for a person like me. He wrote that patients who have deep longings for passivity and protective domination "may form a greater attachment to the procedure (or directly to the physician) than to the intent of the therapy and thus remain fixed in an altered but hardly preferable neurotic pattern." He had to have recognized that behind the strong and capable performer I appeared to be, I was a dependent person who longed to be protected and cared for. It was clear from all the literature that I was a prime candidate for becoming addicted to Amytal and to the physician who gave it to me.

Dr. Masserman also wrote, in the same textbook: "Conversely, patients with latent paranoid tendencies may become suspicious, hostile, and recriminative—a possibility that necessitates the presence of a witness *to refute retrospective falsifications on the part of the patient as to what occurred during the interview.*" (My emphasis.) Dr. Masserman never once had a witness when he gave me Amytal. He gave Richard and me the impression that Billie would be present during my Amytal sessions, but he had me arrive for them at seven or seven-thirty in the morning, long before she came to work. She only came into the room later, during the recovery period.

In his book, Dr. Masserman also said that any insights or gains achieved during the Amytal drug interview *"offer no lasting advantage"* unless they are *"reviewed, accepted, and applied by the patient in actual life."* As it turned out, Dr. Masserman *never* told me anything I said under the Amytal. He never reviewed anything I'd said. The Amytal interviews were blanks in my mind. The doctor acted as if I should know what I'd said—and he always suggested that I was holding out on him—"You *know,* Miz Nole, you *do know,*" he would say—but I had no idea what, if anything, had happened when I was unconscious. I had not one memory, not one clue. (I have been told that Dr. Masserman might have given me hypnotic suggestions not to remember anything that happened under the Amytal. Psychopharmacologists have also suggested that the Amytal might have produced retrograde amnesia.)

It would later become clear to me that I was *never* even remotely a legitimate candidate for Amytal. For a medical audience, Dr. Masserman had written that Amytal was a preferred treatment *only in extreme cases* (e.g., a hospitalized catatonic schizophrenic suddenly unable to speak or a battle-fatigued soldier who had blown up a fellow soldier by accident). He wrote: "Except in the acute stages of catastrophic or traumatic neuroses, little can be accomplished by drug narcosis that could not also be achieved by anamnestic and therapeutic interviews conducted without its use. As noted, Amytal or other drugs may aid in history-taking and in the modification or removal of symptoms, but in most cases, the employment of pharmacologic adjuvants for these purposes is definitely contraindicated."

Had I called any well-informed physician or psychopharmacologist, I would have learned that something highly unusual was going on for Dr. Masserman to even suggest that I might "need" the Amytal more than once. Amytal* simply is not used on a regular basis. When psychiatrists do employ it, it's often given as a diagnostic, one-shot measure: to help a catatonic patient remember things he or she may have

---

*Amytal, a barbiturate used as a hypnotic and sedative, is referred to in pharmacologic literature in a variety of ways, including: Sodium Amytal, Sodium Amobarbital, Amylobarbitone Sodium, Amylobarbitone, Amylbarb, Brevital, Soluble Amylobarbitone. It is Sodium 5-ethyl-5-isopentylbarbiturate, $C_{11}H_{17}N_2NaO_3 = 248.3$.

lost because of a traumatic episode; or to help physicians differentiate between clinical depression and dementia. (People who have memory loss due to depression can often remember under Amytal, whereas truly demented patients get worse when administered this drug.)

Dr. Masserman himself wrote that because Sodium Amytal has "the effect of removing inhibitions in speech and activity," it can facilitate rapport and communication "with morose, evasive, withdrawn patients in early schizophrenic or mild depressive reactions." He notes, however, that "in all such cases" further data and helpful therapy "must be secured without the aid of drugs."

Had I asked a knowledgeable person about it, I also would have learned that although Amytal is rarely used at all, when it is used for legitimate purposes, it's given in a hospital or in an outpatient setting where emergency equipment is available, since Amytal depresses the central nervous system and can stop a person's breathing or create blood pressure problems. *Martindale's The Extra Pharmacopoeia,* a standard drug reference, notes that Amytal is available in tablets or can be given through a deep intramuscular injection, and that it is normally *not* given intravenously, that intravenous injections *may* be given only *"under close supervision, in emergency."* (Italics mine.)

As for the possibility of addiction, which Dr. Masserman dismissed out of hand, any physician would be negligent if he were not completely aware of this danger. The *Physicians' Desk Reference* says in big, bold letters under Sodium Amytal: WARNING: MAY BE HABIT FORMING. In fact, Jules Masserman indicates in his own words, in his own book, that addiction to barbiturates is a real threat. He writes that these drugs are contraindicated because patients "may seek out the drugs (Sodium Amytal and other types) for themselves and *eventually become addicted to them.*" (My emphasis.) Of course, he had assured both Richard and me that I couldn't possibly become addicted, because *he* was experienced, and *he* would be the one controlling the amount and the frequency of the drug.

I didn't know what that experience meant. I didn't know Dr. Masserman had done extensive experiments in the early '40s with alley cats—studying in depth the effects of alcohol, Amytal, and other drugs on the hypothalamus, a part of the brain that regulates emotions and inhibitions. I didn't have any hint that he had spent years getting cats addicted to alcohol and then studying their disorientation and disabilities when he withdrew it from them. I didn't know that he'd studied cats' responses under Amytal or that he had been giving Amytal to his female patients for years—that others, like me, most likely had and would become addicted to Amytal *and* alcohol under his care. It would be a very, very long time before I learned any of those things—and by then a great deal of damage would have been done.

But I didn't make further inquiries about the advisability of using Amytal at that time. Richard and I didn't call a pharmacist, hospital, or medical school to ask about contraindications or standard usage. With hindsight, it's clear Dr. Masserman didn't intend that we take home the book containing a chapter on drug therapy and Amytal which he showed us. I'm sure he was quite confident it would remain on his desk when we walked out the door. We did just what he wanted us to do. But even in retrospect, I understand why we trusted him. Why in the world would a former president of the Illinois Psychiatric Society, a former president of the Chicago Psychoanalytic Society, and a founder of the American Academy of Psychoanalysis steer us wrong?

I made my first appointment for an Amytal interview for two days later. Since the appointment was scheduled for 7:30 A.M. and I was too ashamed to tell anyone I needed something as drastic as Amytal, I furtively wrote "A—7:30" on a small piece of paper and attached it to my calendar with a paper clip. At that moment, I never would have believed how many hundreds of times I would attach "A—7:30" to my calendar in the years to come.

4 The Amytal Interview

JANUARY 1967 On the day of my first Amytal interview, I got to the office at 7:10 A.M., because I wanted time to compose myself and relax before it began. The reception room was empty, and taking deep breaths, I sat and tried to calm the terror I felt. I didn't have words for what it meant to me to give up my consciousness.

I hadn't taken drugs at all in my life, not even marijuana. Many singers and performers I knew got stoned from time to time on pot or hash; many took uppers or downers, they tripped on LSD, mescaline, cocaine, and other drugs. Throughout the country, it was a time of experimentation with illegal drugs, but I'd always been scared of losing control and too chicken to try anything. I drank alcohol occasionally—a glass of wine or a cocktail at a party—but drugs had never tempted me.

I knew the Amytal would put me under—it was supposed to do that. But even though I had decided to take this drug, even though I thought it would help me get rid of the hidden terrors in my life, actually going through with it was something else.

The doctor had told us he would have an hour-long session with me under the Amytal, and then I would spend the day in his examination room sleeping, slowly regaining consciousness, and recovering from the effects of the drug. The only person who knew I was doing this was Richard.

Dr. Masserman opened the door from his office with a bright, kind smile on his face. I said, "Good morning," but couldn't seem to force enough air through my windpipe, and the words came out small, tight, and barely audible.

Dr. Masserman invited me to sit in the chair next to his desk for a preliminary chat. I sat stiff and silent, trying to remind myself that I was choosing to do this to get rid of whatever was inhibiting my life. Dr. Masserman explained the process again. "It's going to be very simple," he said. "Now, it's very important that everything is sterile, so I'll use alcohol on your arm when I give you the shot." He repeated that we would be using his private examining room for the Amytal interview. He said the room had another door that opened into the hallway, and after our interview, when he was back in his own office, Billie Laird would use a key to that second door to check on me and make sure I had everything I needed. "If you ever need a woman's presence, you can call on Billie," he said. "She'll be able to help you stay comfortable while you're recovering."

I smiled at the reassuring thought of Billie checking on me.

"Now, unless you have some questions, I think we're ready to begin."

"Is any part of it going to hurt?"

"Only the injection, and I don't think that will hurt much at all. I think you'll be pleasantly surprised." He looked at me. "Do you have any other questions?"

"I probably do, but I can't think of them."

"Just ask when you do," he said, clearing his throat. "All right, first I'd like you to go in and get yourself ready. It's extremely important that you be comfortable during the interview, so that you don't have any distractions. I believe you'll be more comfortable on the examination cot, since it's made up with pillows and blankets. But if you prefer using the chair and the ottoman . . ."

"No, that's okay," I said, trying to cover up my increasing nervousness. "The cot sounds fine."

"Now, if the pillows aren't just right, you let me know, and we'll get them right for you. And I can get another blanket if you need it, because we've got to keep you nice and warm and comfortable.

"After you go in, now, Miz Nole, it's very important for you to get rid of anything you're wearing that might be constricting, binding, or uncomfortable, because your body must be very relaxed."

"Any clothing?"

"Yes, you should remove any or all clothing that might in any way bind you."

"Like my dress and my slip and bra?"

"Yes, certainly. But don't worry, you'll be properly covered at all times. Just put your clothing on the chair, and then get under the covers. After you're on the examination cot and you've covered yourself, open the door to my office slightly so I'll know you're ready."

I went into Dr. Masserman's small examination room and looked around. There were no windows, but I was happy to see the "cot"— which I'd imagined to be old army issue, was actually a daybed made up with fresh white sheets and a Navaho-style Indian blanket. The room also had a white cabinet filled with medical supplies, a refrigerator, a sink, and an electric hot plate, which sat beside several utensils in shiny metal containers. Steam was rising from an old aluminum pot on the hot plate.

On the wall was a framed article from *Time* magazine with a picture of Dr. Masserman with black hair and a ship captain's hat, standing in front of his sailboat, which he had named *Naiad, Nymph of the Lakes*. The article, which I quickly skimmed, said the doctor had been a violin prodigy as a child, that he wrote poetry and loved sailing.

I slid my black pumps under the easy chair and, after some hesitation, removed my dress, slip, panty girdle, and nylon stockings (these were the days before panty hose), and laid them in a small, neat pile on the arm of the chair. All these things would be binding. I took off my bra and folded it inside my dress, so as to hide it from the doctor's view. My underpants weren't at all binding, so I left them on and went over to the examining cot and crawled under the sheet and the blanket. Holding the covers up around my shoulders, I turned around and opened the door behind me a couple of inches. Then I scrunched down further under the covers and looked around. A large, colorful wool rug hung on the wall next to me. I was studying a painting that hung on the opposite wall, liking the way the ship in it seemed to move through the water, when the doctor knocked lightly on the door and came in.

"How are you feeling?" he asked kindly.

"Okay."

He walked over to the hot plate. "Now, it's your job not to worry about anything at all," he said ceremoniously. "Please watch, and you'll see how carefully I'm going to prepare this injection." He picked up a large, empty hypodermic syringe from a small pot next to the stove and showed it to me. "As you must know, it's important that every piece of equipment is absolutely sterile so that you won't get an infection of any kind. Before you came in, I boiled this syringe for ten minutes to make sure it was completely sterile. Now it has cooled to the right temperature, so it's ready for use."

Dr. Masserman held a small vial of medicine up in the air, inserted the syringe, and slowly filled it with a clear liquid. When he had finished, he tossed the empty vial onto the counter. Then he set the syringe on top of a clean white cloth on a steel tray, beside cotton swabs, alcohol, and a blood pressure kit.

He pulled the ottoman over to the side of the cot, sat down, and asked me to give him my left hand. I clutched the blanket up around my shoulders and carefully pulled out my arm. He held my hand, stretched my arm out on the cover, and lightly swabbed the area around the large vein at the crook with a cotton swab saturated in alcohol. Gently, he wrapped the blood pressure tourniquet around my upper arm and said, "Now make a fist for me." I squeezed my fingernails into the palm of my hand, glad to have some physical pain to distract me from my anxiety.

"Ah, that's good," he said, touching my vein with the saturated cotton to make sure it was ready. "You have good veins!" He smiled at me and carefully picked up the syringe. "Now, you tell me if anything hurts you," he said, placing the tip of the needle on the bulging blue line in my arm. With a sharp, quick stab, he inserted the needle into my vein. It hurt a lot, but I bit my lip and didn't move.

"I hope that didn't hurt you too much, young lady," he said soothingly. "I didn't hurt you too much, did I?"

I smiled and shook my head to indicate that no, it hadn't hurt too much. My blood entered the syringe and mixed with the Amytal solution. Slowly, almost imperceptibly, Dr. Masserman removed the tourniquet and began to depress the plunger and inject the solution, all the while talking softly and reassuringly. I started to relax.

"Sometimes the world can seem like a bad, scary place, can't it?" he said. "But now you'll rest and be happy, and we'll talk." A warm, spreading sensation of peace and joy flooded my body, touching every cell.

"Soon you'll discover that this world can be very warm and very safe," Dr. Masserman said, reaching out and stroking my hair back from my forehead. His hand felt warm and gentle.

"Yes," I said. "Yes." All the tension had drained from my neck and shoulders and lower back, and I felt almost giddy with euphoria. I suddenly had an incredible sense that I was a spirit walking in the universe.

Through some gap in time, I heard Dr. Masserman say, "Now you are warm and safe, and you can talk to someone you trust, someone who is your friend. And while we talk, you can relax completely and realize that the world isn't such a bad place after all."

I didn't know whether I was talking or not. My feeling of joy and tranquillity tasted pink. I was utterly calm and totally open. I said, "It tastes pink and safe." For a few seconds, perhaps a minute, I heard myself talking about the way it felt, but then I felt myself slipping into a space where I didn't know I had a mouth or a body and I remembered nothing. I was transported up and away into a heavenly sphere where I'd never traveled before. It was so deep and far a place, so remote, so soothing, that it was vaporous, a billowing cloud permeated by rosy shades of color, away from this world, away from all consciousness. It was heaven; I was in heaven.

Billie Laird stood over me, her bright eyes concerned, thoughtful. "How ya doing, Barb?" she said, touching my arm. "Can you talk to me yet?"

Billie had a warm, luminous glow around her. I felt myself grinning.

"It's close to noon, and I bet you're hungry," she said, returning my grin. "I'm going to help you get dressed, and then I'll take you down to the bathroom before we have some lunch."

"Oh, no," I said, hearing the words slur and slip as they came out of my mouth and echoed into the distance. "I can go by myself al-lllllrighttttt. . . ."

Billie laughed. "No, you can't go by yourself. I'll bet you can't even get out of bed by yourself."

I focused all my attention on standing up. But my head didn't move off the pillow. It was heavy, a large boulder that wouldn't budge. I couldn't lift it even a fraction, no matter how hard I tried. Nor could I raise my back off the bed. My mind could get up there, but my body didn't follow. Billie put her arm behind my shoulders and helped pull me up to a sitting position. The room tilted left, then it tipped to the right. We were on a boat, steering through the China Sea, and I was laughing. Billie brought my clothes and helped me dress, which wasn't easy, since my arms were not connected to my brain. I flopped them, but I couldn't aim them. I kept saying, "Let me help you," but then I could only giggle helplessly as I watched my rag-doll arms waving around. I'd never seen anything so funny.

Once I was dressed, Billie sat with me until my head cleared enough for the boat to stop rocking and the lights to stop blinking. I heard myself saying, "Blink, blink, signals for the lighthouse!"

Somehow she got me into my shoes and onto my feet and supported me while we took the elevator down three floors to the ladies' lounge— the only woman's bathroom in that old building. By the time we got there, a light show had started again, and I had a bad case of the giggles. I was happily babbling about what fun I was having, but I'd forgotten what to do in the bathroom, and Billie had to sit me down on the toilet seat. When some other women came into the rest room, she quietly tried to shush me. I put my hand over my mouth, but my laughter spurted out and I practically collapsed off the toilet.

Back upstairs, Billie said she wanted me to nap a bit while she went and got us some lunch. She slipped off my shoes, tucked me back into bed, and asked what I'd like to eat. I knew at once I wanted what had always been my favorite treat when my mother and I went out together: chocolate milk and a ham salad sandwich on whole-wheat bread. I fell into a blissful, bottomless sleep. When Billie woke me again, my ham salad sandwich and chocolate milk were on the ottoman beside the bed. It wasn't easy to find ham salad in Chicago, but she had found it. It was like Christmas! My birthday! The best day of my life! I wolfed down my treats and fell asleep again.

Sometime later, I looked up and saw Dr. Masserman sitting on the ottoman beside me, smiling. "That was wonderful," I said happily. "You were right."

"Right about what?"

"That this'd be pleasant. It's more than pleasant; it's heaven."

Dr. Masserman beamed. "So you are feeling happy," he said.

"I feel better than I ever felt in my life."

"Do you remember anything that happened?" he asked me gently.

"It tasted pink. The Amyt . . . tasted pink. . . ."

"No, I mean, do you remember anything you said or did?"

"Let's see. I think I was saying something for a minute, but I'm not sure. Did I say anything?"

"Yes, we talked quite a bit."

"What'd I say?"

For a minute, I thought Dr. Masserman was trying to decide whether to tell me, but he only said, "On some level, you do know everything, every word you said, but it's not important for you to remember it right now. You'll remember when you want to."

He sat and looked at me for a long time. "You did show me something very important, young lady," he said. "What you showed me is that underneath that conscious mind of yours is a very sunny little girl. Did you know you have a very sunny little girl in there?"

"Why, yes," I said, surprised and pleased. I imagined my own little-girl face, smiling and cheerful. I saw myself radiant and shining, glowing the way Billie Laird glowed.

"Why do you think you won't let her out?" he asked.

I didn't know why I wouldn't let her out, and at that moment, I didn't really care. "Don't know," I said, letting my mind follow the picture of light, drifting away from the doctor's face and his questions, back into my own happy feelings.

"Well," Dr. Masserman said. "We'll have these sessions from time to time, and you'll see how it goes. Soon you'll begin to remember more and more. But you've done a fine job today, just fine." He patted my arm, and I felt as though I'd just won a blue ribbon.

"Now, do you think you can walk?" he asked. "Your husband is outside, waiting to take you home."

Dr. Masserman helped me up and supported me until the room stopped tilting. I held his arm, and he walked me out of the examination room, through his office, and into the reception room, where Richard jumped up from his chair and rushed to me with a tender, concerned look on his face. He put his arm around me and kissed my forehead. I was still wobbly-legged and slightly giddy as Richard and Dr. Masserman greeted each other.

"Did she do okay?" Richard asked Dr. Masserman.

"This young lady was fine, but I think she might want to take another nap when she gets home," Dr. Masserman said.

"I'll take good care of her," Richard said, tightening his grip on my waist.

"I think it might be best if she doesn't work tomorrow," Dr. Masserman said.

Richard laughed. "You mean I have to serve her breakfast in bed as well as dinner?"

• • •

In the car on the way home, Richard kissed my forehead again and
said, "Sweetheart, are you going to stay awake long enough for me to
get you into bed?" I felt so loved and happy that I could only giggle
before I fell asleep.

Richard walked me into our wonderful old apartment building on
Lake Shore Drive, ushered me into the elevator and then into our
apartment and straight into our bedroom, where he laid me gently on
our king-size bed. He tried to help me get into my pajamas, but once
again, my arms seemed to have a life of their own. I couldn't cooperate;
I just laughed and laughed, drawing Richard into my hilarity as I tried
to take off his shirt instead of getting into my pajamas. It was hard to
unbutton the buttons, but I got two or three undone and put my hands
inside his shirt, running my fingers across his chest and then trying to
tickle him. Every now and then, waves of sleep overtook me. I lay in
the swell of each wave and rode it, coming back to consciousness and
then being carried out again. One time when I woke up, Richard
brought me a dinner of spaghetti and salad on a tray. I ate ravenously,
put in an order for three bowls of chocolate ice cream, and fell asleep
again. When I came to, I took three bites of ice cream and then fell
asleep as I watched the spoon approaching my mouth, a lump of the
cold chocolate falling toward the covers.

I woke up to sunshine skittering across the carpet. The sounds of
morning traffic blended with the chirp of birds, and I felt marvelous.
Dr. Masserman had told Richard not to let me work or be around
people the next day. I couldn't understand why, but I didn't mind. I
felt strong, whole, and serene, and under doctor's orders, I had an
extra twenty-four hours to enjoy those feelings before I had to see
anyone.

Feeling I was beginning a new life, a perfect life, I ate a breakfast of
eggs, toast, juice, and coffee, and looked at the "Tempo" section in the
Chicago Tribune. As I read the newspaper, however, a dull headache
began to creep over the top of my scalp and settle down into my brain,
my eyes, and the rest of my head. My skin began to itch. I scratched
my neck and chin, my arms, legs, and back, but no amount of scraping
or pressure reduced the itchiness. Even the backs of my legs itched.
No matter how much I rubbed, I couldn't get relief. The tingling, painful
itch came from underneath the skin. I became jumpy and uncomfort-

able. All my senses were turned up to full volume. When I heard car horns blasting or trucks revving their engines or sirens wailing on the streets below, I wanted to scream. Even small noises—running water or doors closing in the hallway or bells ringing for the elevator or barely audible voices from the kitchen radio—irritated and angered me.

Richard had stayed home with me, but if I heard him or saw him, rage flooded through me, made me want to hit him. I snapped at him whenever I had a chance: "Can't you turn down that radio?" "Could I *please* have a cup of tea now?" "Why don't you wear your blue shirt instead of that ugly one?" "What's the matter with *you?* Why are you looking at me that way? Get away from me!" As it was happening, I noticed from afar that I was doing something new, something strange, but I couldn't seem to control the hostility. When Richard asked if I wanted to eat, I crossed my arms in defiance and told him I'd roast in hell first. Later, I became hysterical, crying uncontrollably. My legs ached and jumped and wouldn't stay still, and I felt overwhelmed with a strange dread that my life was finished.

It would be years before I learned that my symptoms on the day following the Amytal were not just a "release of my feelings," but were adverse side effects to the drug. My itchy skin, headache, irritability, and crying fits were classic drug reactions and indicated quite clearly that Amytal didn't agree with me. I was allergic to the Amytal, or I had been overdosed. These days, doctors and patients alike are told to stop immediately any medication that causes such a reaction. Even when an adverse reaction is a known side effect of a drug, substitute medication or a dramatic reduction in dosage is required when such an excessive response occurs. Anything less is medical negligence or incompetence.

Yet two days later, when I met with Dr. Masserman and told him about my extreme mood swings, how my head still hurt and my skin itched and how irritable and scared I was feeling, he wasn't perturbed in the least. He said I should expect such reactions initially; it would probably take me some time to get used to the Amytal, and I shouldn't worry about it. When I told him I was either ecstatically happy or extremely negative and hostile, he said, "Yes, of course. This is all part of the process. You must look at your true feelings, good and bad." He told me he was pleased with my progress. "The negative feelings, in particular, are a good sign," he said. "You need to release your negativity and explore it. You have been artificially positive, and you won't get yourself back into balance unless you are willing to accept all your feelings, no matter what they are. Following those feelings will allow you to work through necessary issues you must face in the process of growing up into a happy, mature, and womanly woman who can enjoy her marriage to the fullest."

After a few more "talking" sessions, where I free-associated but didn't remember a thing from our Amytal interview, I underwent another 7:30 A.M. Amytal session. It was very much like the first one, but this time I wasn't afraid. I was thrilled at the prospect of reexperiencing the pink-filled rush that had carried me into that heavenly place of utter calm. I went into Dr. Masserman's small, windowless examination room as if it were my sanctuary, my launching pad, my fount of inspiration.

Once again, Dr. Masserman was meticulous about the way he handled the tourniquet and the syringe and explained everything to me. He swabbed my vein with cotton doused in alcohol and once again told me what great veins I had. After he had inserted the needle and expressed his concern about any pain I might have experienced, he began slowly to inject the Amytal, and I could feel it beginning to take hold. For a minute or two, I knew I was talking, and I heard Dr. Masserman's quiet questions, heard myself come out with easy answers, saying whatever I wanted to say without anxiety. Then I sank into a blissful ecstasy, floating off on a metaphysical journey that took me into unexplored realms and lasted until I saw, through a haze, Billie Laird's attentive face three or four hours later.

After that second session, I had an Amytal interview at least every two or three weeks, except for vacations and sick times—his and mine—over the next seventeen years. During some periods, I had Amytal every week. On several occasions, I had it three times in one week, and sometimes two days in a row. The ritual was always the same. I would undress and get under the covers, then open the door a crack to signal I was ready. Dr. Masserman would sit on the ottoman by the examination cot, stroke my arm or push my hair back from my forehead, and say the same thing: "Now, you tell me if anything hurts you." It hurt when he injected the needle, but he would always say soothingly, "I hope that didn't hurt you too much, young lady. I didn't hurt you too much, did I?"

I'd smile and shake my head no, he hadn't hurt me. Then Dr. Masserman would remove the tourniquet slowly and begin to inject the Amytal solution, all the while talking softly and reassuringly; I would relax and listen to him telling me to rest and be happy, and I'd know I was well taken care of and safe. As he talked and I interjected a few comments and insights, a sensation of peace and joy would flood my body, and then I would travel to a place that I never found without the Amytal. My adverse reactions to the drug subsided—perhaps he changed the dosage or perhaps my body came to accommodate it better. But I was almost always groggy for the rest of the evening following Amytal, and at least slightly hung over the following day.*

After my first full year of Amytal, I began to feel like a very special soul. I felt more attuned to the world around me. My interest in the arts became stronger, and I was sure I was more creative than I had been before I'd started the Amytal. I discovered Edward Hopper's paintings, began writing vocal arrangements of songs modeled after Simon and Garfunkel's close tonality in "Scarborough Fair," and made weekly forays past Daley Plaza to see the two-hundred-ton "Lady" that U.S. Steel had based on a small-scale version Picasso presented Chicago in 1967.

In the meantime, when I had Amytal, Billie took good care of me, mothered me, put up with my silliness, and always managed to find me a delicious ham salad sandwich for lunch. Sometimes after Dr. Masserman flicked the lights on and told me to get dressed whenever I felt like it, I would put on my clothes and then, instead of passing through Dr. Masserman's office as usual, I would play games, going out the hallway door and sneaking back into the reception room. I'd plop myself into a chair, and when Billie looked up, I'd be sitting there acting as if I were the next patient. Then the two of us would laugh and laugh. I was often giddy and woozy, and at times like that, I thought everything I did was hilarious.

That little examination room became my cozy, special place, where I experienced such joy, such childlike feelings, that I never wanted it to end. With the Amytal, the doctor, Billie, and Richard all paid special, extraordinary attention to me—and for someone who longed to be cared for and babied, what could have been better?

Away from 8 Michigan Avenue, I acted like a grown woman, a

*For further discussion about what actually may have been happening with the Amytal injections, see Notes, page 291.

competent performer. Although I was still plagued by facial pain, I was singing backup for albums with Al Hirt and Ramsey Lewis, and doing commercials. I sang in a sixteen-member chorus backing up Henry Mancini at a live concert at the Auditorium Theatre, where we premiered the song "Two for the Road" just before the film by the same name was due to come out.

More and more, however, my attention was focused on my next Amytal session. I thought of Amytal as ultimate bliss. When I was having a "talking" session and noticed the door to the examination room was closed—indicating that someone else was recovering from Amytal—I would feel a stab of jealousy. I discovered that if I'd had a choice I would rather have Amytal than go to parties, movies, or dinners out.

Sometimes I noticed a strange, unpleasant odor around my shoulders after I had the drug, but I assumed the Amytal had made me sweat and had given my skin a rancid stench. After I got home and felt solid enough again, I would always jump into the shower to wash off the smell.

Also, I realize now, I often had bruises after my Amytal sessions. One time early in 1967, I noticed marks on my arms afterward, and I asked the doctor about them when I went to my next "talking" session. He said, "Sometimes you begin to get excited under the Amytal, and I just hold you down so you won't hurt yourself. I'm so sorry if I bruise you. You bruise awfully easily, don't you?"

From the beginning, there were obvious questions to be asked about what was going on under the Amytal—Why would I be "thrashing around"? Why would I get "excited"?—but those questions never entered my mind. I believed what Dr. Masserman said—that I caused the bruises myself by thrashing around or caused him to have to hold me down.

One time, however, I was bruised on my pelvic area, right on the pubic bone. About two days later, I had another Amytal session, and afterward, in the doctor's office just before I went home, I thought about my pelvis—it was sore. I suppose because of the Amytal, I was more relaxed and spontaneous than usual, and I said out loud, in a kind of shocked voice—speaking as much to myself as to him—"My God, how did I get this bruise? Where did I get this bruise?"

He got angry, and he said, "*Obviously,* you were flailing around on the springs of the daybed and you got a bruise! Now, will you calm down and lower your voice. And if you *ever* raise your voice to me again, young lady, I will never give you another drop of Amytal again, do you hear me? Never!"

How could I get bruised on the springs if I was lying on my back? But I didn't think of the logic. I was mortified by his anger. When I got home, I called him to apologize for having raised my voice!

The next time I came in, the bed was turned around. I said, "What happened?"

"I don't know," he said. "What do you mean?"

"I'm facing different. The bed is turned around differently."

He said, "It is?"

I said, "Yes, look. Before, I was looking the other way."

"Oh, Miss Laird must have made up the bed that way. I wonder why she did that? Oh, it doesn't make any difference, does it?"

I don't know what the difference was, but it must have given him some other kind of leverage, because I never had another pelvic bruise after that.

5 Blind Trust

I skidded around in no-man's-land for many years, it seems, bumping into myself in the dark and finding very little emotional relief outside of my visits to Dr. Masserman's office.

At home, Richard and I quarreled constantly. At one point I took down a jar from the kitchen cupboard and decided to fill it with pennies—one for each day I got through without making Richard angry. If we fought, I took out the pennies and started again from zero. I never got more than five pennies into that damned jar, usually no more than two.

Richard had become quite big in the singing-commercial business, and he often booked other people for jobs when I thought he should have booked me. I decided it would help avoid conflict if I concentrated on filmed commercials instead of singing jingles. Earlier in my career, I'd filmed commercials for Campbell's soup, Busch beer, Chevrolet, and Qantas airlines. I liked doing films and didn't mind switching back to them. But when I landed a network commercial for Bell Telephone that was going to shoot in St. Louis for two days and pay great residuals, Richard said he would not have any wife of his going out of town to work! He was so angry—even though I would have been gone only two days—that I finally turned down the job.

But I couldn't win. Even my work at local studios annoyed Richard, because I had to get up at 6:00 A.M. Filming a commercial always means an early start: they have to find the right costume for you, make it fit, then do your hair and makeup. You do test shots and sit for lighting, listen to arguments about how the spoon is supposed to be picked up and where you're supposed to look and how much to smile, where to put your other hand, whether the salt and pepper shakers are casting shadows. . . . You spend hours doing all that before you start to shoot— and by then you need to go back and get powdered again and put on fresh lipstick, because you've started to sweat. Then the steward for the Screen Actors Guild says it's time to break for lunch, which is an hour, and then you don't feel much like working any more, but you do. Even though it was grueling, the film crews in Chicago are a lot of fun, and I liked working with them.

But Richard complained that I got up too early, or got home too late. If my work didn't rile Richard, then he got angry because I'd forgotten to pick up his pants at the cleaners, or because I'd said something he didn't like at dinner the night before, or because I'd done something else wrong.

After I turned down the Bell Telephone job, Dr. Masserman encouraged me to turn down other jobs as well, so Richard wouldn't feel so threatened. But occasionally, when he met with both of us, the doctor explained to Richard how important it was for me to be working. He reminded Richard that I was a professional musician and I *needed* to cultivate my talents, which of course confirmed and reassured me. After the doctor, Richard, and I all agreed I needed to express myself, I would sail effortlessly through a flurry of music sessions.

Then, for no apparent reason, I'd be hit with an excruciating headache, a pain in my jaw, and unreasonable anxiety, and I'd go back to Dr. Masserman and Billie and my little room. Sometimes when I wanted the Amytal, I would find myself crying during a regular session, acting more unhappy than I felt, which would lead to my asking Dr. Masserman, "Do you think I would benefit from some Amytal?" Even when Amytal wasn't on my mind, he almost always encouraged me to ask for it. He would tell me that if only I could "free myself" with the Amytal, I would be able to express my talents and creativity more fully and become a happier person. Then he would schedule me for another Amytal interview.

Of course, during all those hundreds and hundreds of talk sessions and Amytal sessions, I thought I was involved in a normal therapeutic relationship. I had the impression that it wasn't unusual for legitimate psychoanalysis to go on for a number of years, so even though it wasn't what I'd expected, I accepted it as valid and necessary—particularly since the doctor continued to tell me how much I needed his help.

I realize now how dependent I was, how much power I gave him, but in fact, Dr. Masserman did offer me relief and understanding. Sometimes when I felt painted into a corner at home, he was my only refuge. The support he gave me about my career, and his affirmations of my perceptions, built and sustained my trust in him. I realize now that part of the horror of abuse is being violated by a person who sometimes does genuinely good things for you—which I think he sometimes did for me.

Nothing he did, however, seemed to help Richard and me become closer. I was so desperate for help that I broke one of Dr. Masserman's rules. He'd told me that I had to trust him, and that I should not look into other forms of therapy because they would only confuse me. Nevertheless, I read Eric Berne's popular books, *Games People Play* and *Transactional Analysis*. When I told Dr. Masserman what I'd done, and said I thought Richard and I played some of the games Berne described, he just laughed and said, "Eric Berne is a friend of mine. At best, his ideas are amusing, but for the most part, Berne is just a publicity seeker." With a wave of his hand, he dismissed my idea that Richard and I might benefit from analyzing our "games" and designing new game plans.

At about the same time that I began my sessions with Dr. Masserman, Richard had started seeing Dr. Charles Schlageter, a psychiatrist who shared Dr. Masserman's suite of offices. With both of us in therapy, we thought we'd make real progress. But we didn't. It baffled us that despite the counseling of two excellent psychiatrists, we still squabbled constantly. Several times we went for a couples appointment with either Dr. Schlageter or Dr. Masserman, but our question "How do we stop ourselves from fighting?" went unanswered. The meetings were unrewarding. Richard and I knew we loved and really cared about each other, but we were consistently furious after those sessions.

An unspoken disappointment between us was the fact that we would never be able to have children. In 1968, I had started to hemorrhage and Richard had rushed me to the hospital emergency room, where we learned that because of the IUD I'd used since my abortion, my uterus was all torn up. My gynecologist, who was very kind, recommended a partial hysterectomy and said, "There aren't going to be any babies." Richard was even more devastated than I. Our physician, Dr.

Ivan Keever, came by to see me twice at the hospital and was clearly worried about Richard. The knowledge that we couldn't have a family of our own hung like a shadow over our lives, but I never once discussed my feelings about the hysterectomy with Dr. Masserman. He knew about it because I'd had to cancel appointments when I was hospitalized, but he didn't mention it, and after his negative reactions previously to my "self-indulgent" feelings about the abortion, I wasn't about to raise it.

On the home front, though, Dr. Masserman was helping me learn how to improve my relationships with Richard's children, Sally and Danny.* They lived with their mother but spent large chunks of their holidays with us. We began to have real fun together the summer of 1968, when Danny, nine, preceded twelve-year-old Sally to Chicago for a visit. Danny was an absentminded towhead with a difficult stutter and some pretty severe problems at school, but his cherubic face, bright brown eyes, and infectious giggle made me love him.

That summer, Richard, Danny, and I biked along Lake Michigan and sailed our twenty-four-foot sloop, *Jingles,* out of Burnham Harbor, with Danny and me singing "Yellow Submarine" and "Mellow Yellow" and "Galveston" at the top of our lungs. On the Fourth of July, we took the boat out and had a fabulous view of the fireworks from Soldier Field.

Danny started relaxing with me, but when he and I walked over to Oak Street beach, where other kids were swimming or playing ball, Danny wouldn't go near them. He hung back and tugged on my arm, urging that we go home. One afternoon, after playinng his version of gin rummy, I got out crayons and paper and asked him to draw me a picture. At first he refused, but I begged, and finally he relented. He worked on his picture so long that I expected something quite elaborate. When he handed it to me, however, the entire drawing consisted of small, weak squiggles and circles in the middle of the page that never connected—as if he couldn't join one line to the next. He had used two crayons so lightly that they produced almost no color.

Danny was the only little boy I'd ever really known, so I didn't know if I was overreacting or whether my alarm was justified. Richard and I decided to have Dr. Masserman evaluate Danny. At my next appointment, Danny—looking small and vulnerable in his red shorts and blue

*The names and details of the children have been changed.

Chicago Cubs T-shirt—walked into Dr. Masserman's office while I waited in the reception room. After about ten minutes, Danny strutted out, grinning, and said, "Your turn!" I patted him on the back, handed him his comic book, and walked into the office.

"You're that boy's best friend," Dr. Masserman said after I sat down. "I agree he has some real problems, and I believe he would benefit greatly from seeing an educational counselor." The counselor he recommended tested Danny, and she confirmed that he had severe dyslexia, as well as other learning and perceptual problems—all of which explained why he was so far behind in school. She told us that Danny's brain interpreted letters and numbers in a unique way—not only upside down and backward but even nonsequentially. In order to function successfully, Danny needed to learn how to translate what he saw into more traditional and workable patterns. It was no wonder that he stayed away from other children, who might tease him if they discovered he couldn't read.

The counselor, explaining that Danny's learning problems triggered his behavioral problems, recommended a good private school for students with learning difficulties. We sold our vacation condo in Aspen to pay for it, but the investment in Danny's education was worth every penny. After a tough adjustment, Danny became one of the most popular boys at the school. He lost his stutter, learned to read, and gained confidence.

Dr. Masserman also encouraged me about Sally. I'd said, "This kid is never going to like one thing I do." But he told me to just be myself and accept that she expressed her loyalty to her mother by being critical of and distant from me. Eventually, he said, Sally would relax her guard. He was right, and when she did, the two of us had fun and were very pleased with ourselves too. We decided we looked fabulous—Sally and Barb, the brown-eyed girls. It didn't go unnoticed by me that Dr. M's prediction was right on target.

Dr. Masserman also gave me good advice about how to deal with my father's drinking. After Mother's death, Dad had begun to sell real estate and was earning more money than he'd ever had as a college professor, but he also was consuming enormous quantities of booze. In April 1968, when I was visiting him in Florida, we went to my uncle and aunt's house for dinner, and my dad sat there and gulped down one martini after another, not saying a word. When it was time to go home, he refused to relinquish his car keys. I suggested I drive, and my aunt said, "Brother mine, I think you've had one too many."

"This is *my* new car," he said, his eyes bleary and his words slurred, "and *I'm* driving my new car."

I held on in terror as Dad, talking nonstop about how I was the picture of my mother, how I walked like her, tossed my head and laughed the way she had, careened home. It was a nightmare.

Then in July 1969, Richard and I flew with Danny down to Florida. The four of us watched television as Neil Armstrong walked on the moon. The following morning, Dad decided to surprise Danny with a brunch, and we were all in the kitchen while he started the pancakes. He had been drinking martinis for a couple of hours and seemed happy enough, but he suddenly got angry about something—and the next thing we knew, he was insulting Richard and gesturing at Danny with a spoon. The whole thing ended with his cursing and throwing pancake batter all over the kitchen. Richard and I packed up Danny and headed for home, furious and disgusted, but also afraid for him.

Shortly after we got back to Chicago, I went to see Dr. Masserman. When I told him about what had happened, he advised me to write my father immediately and tell him to quit drinking or I wouldn't see him again.

I went straight home and wrote Dad. I said I was infuriated by his behavior. He'd been drunk for almost our entire visit, and did he realize he'd been drunk in front of a *child* all that time? Did he have *any* idea how harmful that was? I'd been proud to have him as a father, but now I was ashamed; he should find a sanitarium and dry out. It was his choice: keep on drinking and forget his relationship with me, or stop drinking and enjoy our being together again.

Richard read the letter and said it was cruel and heartless. He thought no child—no matter how old—had a right to speak to a parent like that. I should write a more kind and caring letter. I took the letter down and slammed it in the mailbox, determined to get it into my father's hands as soon as possible.

For weeks, I didn't hear from him. I had visions of Dad crashing his car into a bridge, driving at night on the wrong side of the road and running head-on into a truck. I imagined him covered with blood on a highway, police and ambulance lights revolving as a crowd gathered to stare at him. Just when I had given up hope of ever hearing from him again, a letter arrived. He said he was sorry, and it would never happen again. I was overjoyed when I read: "I appreciate your being so honest with me." After that, we visited Dad often, and he never had more than two drinks a day. Mostly he didn't drink at all— and it was Dr. Masserman I credited with saving his life.

I had been seeing Dr. Masserman for five years when, in the summer of 1971, Richard and I separated. I stayed in our home—which by then was a beautiful three-bedroom house on an acre of land in Glenview, a northern suburb of Chicago. I couldn't visualize life without Richard, and I spent a lot of time crying. The only thing that made me laugh was a new TV show called *All in the Family*. But even my hilarity over Archie Bunker's outrageous comments would quickly turn to tears.

When I told Dr. Masserman that Richard had moved out, he shook his head in apparent dismay and said solemnly, "I'm disappointed in both of you, but especially in you, Miz Nole. It's clear that your husband is unsure of your love." He studied his hands for a while; then he said that if I wanted to show Richard how much I cared, I should stop working.

"When are you going to learn how to get along?" Dr. Masserman said, shaking his head sadly. "Your husband needs to know he has a wife. You need to act like a real wife. If Richard can understand he is the most important person in your life, he'll relax. And then later, if you go back to work—within limits, of course—it won't seem like such an imposition."

I accepted the judgment without challenge. And Richard's joy when I announced my intention to stop working and stay at home confirmed the wisdom of Dr. Masserman's advice. Richard moved back, took time off from work, and insisted we take a long vacation in Antigua and sail the Caribbean. It was a wonderful reunion. We swam and sailed and snorkeled, ate long, romantic dinners, lingered in bed, and felt like lovebirds again.

But six months later, when I went back to work, our bond became shaky again. Richard's icy silent treatments resumed and began extending to weeks at a time. When we passed each other in the house, he often looked right through me, refusing to answer my questions or engage in any dialogue. At dinnertime, he'd often leave the house without telling me where he was going. Because he refused to touch any food I'd made when he was angry at me, I stopped cooking. I felt isolated and panicky.

During one long freeze-out in the spring of 1974, I got a severe respiratory infection and laryngitis—I couldn't sing, couldn't work, couldn't talk. Though I was extremely sick, Dr. Masserman demanded that I come to see him. I was too sick to go, but I went, and as a result I got even more run down. My throat was so sore I had to write instead of speak. My physician said to remain in bed, and to get up only for steam treatments in the bathroom. Richard responded with affection. He apologized for his behavior, brought me flowers, rubbed my back and neck, and pampered me thoroughly. I was helpless, and he was the white knight, my rescuer. This clearly made him happy—until I was well and singing again.

What I now understand, but didn't have an inkling of in those days, was that as the child of an alcoholic, Richard had played the hero's role in his family. It's no wonder his role in a marriage confused him. He was hypervigilant about any kind of criticism or possible fault, and he judged himself without mercy. In his child's mind, he felt that if he didn't take care of things and make everything right for everyone, then the family—and, by extension, the marriage—would fall apart. He felt it was *his* responsibility to make everything perfect for us. If I had a career of my own, interests of my own, it meant he'd failed, and he couldn't live with that. His desperation, of course, only suffocated and terrified me, so we went round and round in circles.

Richard was also questioning my need for so many Amytal sessions. "I honestly don't see that it's doing you much good," he'd say. I'd bristle at such remarks. I *knew* I needed the solace the Amytal brought me. Also, I was proud I had begun to tolerate the effects of the drug to such an extent that Richard could take me out to dinner sometimes after a session instead of taking me home to bed. I got into the habit of prolonging the childlike Amytal feeling by joining Richard for a martini before dinner. Richard wondered if martinis were a good idea for me, but I couldn't see how they could hurt me. In self-defense, I would quote my physician: "Dr. Masserman told me gin was the purest and cleanest alcohol." Richard would say he was sick and tired of hearing Dr. Masserman's opinions, which, of course, would lead to another fight.

There were times when Richard and I were so angry that we'd write each other letters, because if we talked, we'd get too enraged to make sense. We would go off to different places and write and write—page after page. Then we would exchange letters, which would set off another round of writing.

In September 1972, we separated again. During this separation, we got counseling from both our psychiatrists. Once, Dr. Masserman looked at us and shook his head. "You're obviously devoted to each other," he said sadly. "Can't you see that? Now what are you going to do about it? Once you start that downward spiral of hurt and spite, it becomes increasingly difficult to rebuild trust. Please don't let yourselves go too far down, or it will be too late."

We had no idea how not to let ourselves "go too far down." But bless us, we tried one more time to get back together—faithfully going to our doctors, but lacking the courage or insight to explore other alternatives or to rely on our own judgments. We never argued about the money we spent on therapy. I was still taking Amytal regularly, believing that ultimately it would help me with my career, my life, and my marriage. And though Richard questioned the necessity of the Amytal and said he was frightened of what it was doing to me, he showed no resentment at paying for it—even though we had to lay out fifty dollars an hour for every session, without any insurance reimbursements.

In the meantime, in spite of our personal problems, my singing was developing. I still had tension in my jaw, headaches, numbness in my hands, and dizziness from time to time, but I was experimenting with more variety and range. By 1974, I was writing music and lyrics that seemed to spring forth after an immersion in James Taylor's music, particularly his album *Sweet Baby James,* which inspired me and changed my outlook on music. James Taylor told whole stories—"Fire & Rain," for instance, explores a friend's death and his response to that loss. His words touched me deeply and freed me to use lyrics to express my own feelings.

I started writing lyrics that were emotional, combined with intricate chord structures that just seemed to be there for me when I sat down at the piano. When I did several arrangements for four-part groups just for the fun of it, the response from my fellow musicians was so encouraging that I began to experiment with various musical styles within the pop-music frame. I wrote some songs for Richard to sing, as well as a simple, sarcastic piece for myself about bad relationships, set to a German-cabaret oompah beat:

> I'd take the indiscretion, self-obsession,
> Each confession, deep depression
> Just to be near you again—at least I think I would—
> But meanwhile, where did you go? Where did you go?

Richard arranged for me to record ten of my songs and asked me to write special material for him, which I did. But then, in early fall of 1974, something strange and frightening happened that interrupted my songwriting for over a year and was the beginning of the end for us. One evening when Richard came home from a recording session, I was sitting at our grand piano, working on a new song. As usual, my dog, Boomer, was sitting up beside me on the piano bench, watching me play. When he saw Richard walk in, Boomer jumped off the bench and hid under the piano, as if he knew what was coming. I didn't. I looked up and smiled at Richard as he walked toward me with a peculiar transfixed look on his face. He stopped near the piano and said softly, with a kind of singsong lilt, "If I ever come home and find you at the piano again, I'll break both your hands." Then he turned and walked out of the room.

Richard had never said such a threatening thing to me before—and I didn't understand how or why he'd said it now—but I felt overwhelmed with fear and sympathy. I was afraid for both of us, and I was sure that Richard's saying something so horrible meant he must be experiencing terrible turmoil. But we didn't talk about it. In addition to the silent treatment, Richard started what I called the sightless treatment, where he wandered around the house half-smiling, looking right through me as if I weren't there at all, as if I were invisible.

At my next session, Dr. Masserman expressed concern for my safety. "I don't think I'd sail with him if I were you," he said. "And I'd think twice about getting into a small plane with him."

Despite my trust in Dr. Masserman, I couldn't agree. I knew Richard had threatened me, but I was sure he wouldn't hurt me. I *knew* he cared for me deeply, and to this day I believe I was right about that. I reminded Dr. Masserman of some of Richard's family problems as a child.

Dr. Masserman said Richard's childhood was irrelevant to the current situation and insisted I was in danger. "You're coming here for my advice, young lady," he said, "and so I tell you, this man will harm you. Watch out. And please, *please,* do *not* go up in his plane with him."

By the end of that session, I was thoroughly frightened, but I went home committed to understanding Richard and working things out. On my own, I was beginning to realize that men can be victims as much as women. The book *Portnoy's Complaint* and movies like *Easy Rider* and *Midnight Cowboy* had deepened my sense of men as vulnerable, uncertain beings, struggling to understand themselves, and I had a growing sense that Richard sometimes felt as hunted and haunted as I did. I knew he was struggling with his past, just as I was, and I thought that if somehow we could break through the barriers between us, we would be able to have a viable marriage. At home, though, Dr. Masserman's cautionary counsel kept replaying in my head, arguing with my own beliefs but making me extra cautious and distant around my husband.

Then one night, all of Dr. Masserman's admonitions seemed to be justified. Having dragged myself home from a recording session with a terrible headache, I was eager to go to the bedroom to do some exercises to relieve the pain. But first I walked into the den to say hello to Richard. He looked sad and distressed, and he reached out his hand, touched my face, and suggested we make love. I said, "Give me a half hour to get rid of this headache first." Then I went to the bedroom and did some stretches and neck rolls and other exercises I'd learned to help me overcome my headaches. After that, even though I wasn't overly eager, I came back, willing to make love. Richard's eyes were glazed over, and he started giving me his usual freeze-out.

I said, "My headache is gone. Here I am."

He said, "Yeah? Well, it's too late. I don't care about it anymore."

We started our typical repetitive routine, and he said, "You forced me to marry you!"

I got furious and gave my usual response: "I'm sick of hearing that! Do you think you're so weak that I could have told you what to do? You were the one who got *me* to marry *you!*"

I was usually more adroit verbally than he was and could best him in an argument. He hated my one-upping his lines, but my only joy when we were fighting was to attack him verbally, so I went blithely along. He became furious, though, and suddenly screamed, "I could kill you!" He grabbed a log from the hearth and threw it at the wall, but it hit the television set instead and shattered the glass screen.

I screamed and went tearing out of the den, saying, "That's it! That's it!" The ruined television set and the word "kill" were last straws for me; I thought they totally verified Dr. Masserman's prediction.

I ran to the bedroom and started jamming sweaters and underwear and jeans into a suitcase. I could hear Dr. Masserman's voice saying, "This man will harm you. This man will harm you." Richard came into the bedroom to watch me pack. I was shaking with fury and felt scared to death. When I bolted past Richard with my suitcase, he said, "Where the fuck do you think you're going?"

"I have no idea," I said. "Just away from here!"

I got into my Mercedes and started driving. It must have been nine o'clock, and I drove and drove. About four hours later, I'd reached Rockford, Illinois, and didn't have a clue how I'd gotten there. I drove past a motel, turned around, and got a room there for the night. The next day, I drove to Galena, a hill town close to Dubuque, Iowa, and checked into another motel. On the third day, I drove across the river and spent the night in Dubuque. For the next four days, I went from motel to motel, charging my bills to credit cards. I watched TV, cried, drank, cried some more, drank, walked around the towns, and wondered what to do about my life. Boomer had died from a malignant tumor two months before, so I cried and cried over him, and I cried and cried over Richard and me. I had no idea about how to correct the course of events that seemed to be determining my life, nor did I have any idea how I could start over. I felt I didn't have a chance on my own. I thought: I've had this gorgeous house and this wonderful Mercedes—where can I go now? What kind of house can I find? How poor will I be? I'll probably starve to death. I thought: All I know is how to sing! I can't even type! Both Dr. Masserman and Richard had discouraged my singing, and I felt totally second-rate. I had no confidence in my ability to survive either personally or professionally.

Finally, from Evanston, Illinois, I called Dr. Masserman and told him what had happened. He asked me if I thought I could persuade "Mr. Nole" to come in with me for a session.

"Oh, Dr. Masserman. Does that mean you think Richard and I can work things out?"

"My dear, why would you possibly want to?" he said. I started to cry, and he said, "But of course, if that's what you want, then we can work toward a reconciliation."

I drove back home, but Richard wouldn't speak to me for several days. Finally, though, he acceded to my request for a joint session with Dr. Masserman.

The day of the appointment, Richard was late, but Dr. Masserman invited me to come in at the appointed hour. I walked in and sat on the leather couch, acutely aware of the smell of the cloth on top of it: Dr. Masserman rarely changed the cloth and it reeked of accumulated sweat and hair creams and hair sprays. I was experiencing the room as Richard would—he couldn't stand the offensive smell—and so the strength of the odor from the couch that day made me additionally nervous. I looked around the room at the dusty plaques and knick-knacks sitting on yellowed doilies and tried to calm my shaking hands.

Fifteen minutes after I sat down, Richard stormed into the office without looking at either of us and took the chair next to the doctor's desk.

"Well, Mr. Noël," Dr. Masserman said, "I can see that you're quite angry."

"Yeah?" Richard glared at him. "So?"

"I wonder if you'd like to tell us—"

"Get this straight, Doctor," Richard said angrily, looking steadily at Dr. Masserman. "*No.* I wouldn't like to tell you. I'm sick of telling you. What good does it do to tell you?"

The doctor's voice rose in anger I'd never heard before. "Sir, that is hardly—"

"Don't push me, Doctor!" Richard's voice was so low that it was nearly a growl.

"Why did you come here, sir?" Dr. Masserman shouted.

When Richard didn't reply, Dr. Masserman's face turned red and he jumped to his feet—almost as if he were challenging Richard to a duel. "Would you answer me, sir?" he hollered.

Richard stood up slowly. He towered over Dr. Masserman and stared down at him with a look of contempt so extreme that it distorted his features. Then, suddenly, he turned to leave. Dr. Masserman followed him, shouting, "Would you answer me, sir? Would you answer me?"

Richard turned and looked at Dr. Masserman in disgust. "You son of a bitch," he said in a low voice. "Why should I answer you?"

"If you have any interest, sir—" Dr. Masserman began.

"You're controlling her life, you know," Richard said, his voice growing louder. "You say jump, she jumps. You say take Amytal, and she takes Amytal. You and your fucking drug therapy! You and your pronouncements!"

Dr. Masserman's red face was contorted with fury.

"I'm not living this way anymore," Richard shouted. "I've had it!" He slammed the door behind him, and the noise shattered me. I began to sob. I felt so sorry for Richard, and so sorry for myself.

Dr. Masserman, his face nearly purple with rage, wheeled around and pointed his finger at me. "That settles it," he shouted. "You're getting a divorce!"

6 No Way Out

In retrospect, our divorce was literally just what the doctor ordered. Most likely, if we had been left to our own devices, Richard and I would have divorced anyway, but there isn't any question that Dr. Masserman urged us on. At one point, when Richard and I began to date again for a brief period of time, the doctor turned pale at the news and told me in no uncertain terms that Richard had *not* changed and *would not* change. Making a biblical reference, he called my desire to reconcile "giving up your birthright for a mess of pottage," as he said Esau did in the book of Genesis. Another time, referring to my "bad judgment" about Richard, he said, "You act like a spoiled little girl! Sometimes I think I should turn you over my knee and spank you!"

When I stopped seeing Richard and told Dr. Masserman I had directed my divorce lawyer to proceed with the final papers, the doctor smiled broadly, predicted Richard would remarry within six months of our divorce, and congratulated me for "facing the facts." He cited the Bible again, then said he was quite pleased with my "progress." Richard and I were both miserable, but Dr. Masserman was happily congratulating me for finally coming to my senses.

He told me how pleasing it was that I was opening up to him and willing, at last, to take responsibility for the way I chose to behave. I was thrilled. Bolstered by his approval, I started to believe that perhaps I was in the process of growing into the stronger, healthier woman I wanted to be.

Another salve for my low self-esteem came when I discovered I wouldn't starve just because I was separated from Richard. I got a job singing with Dick Judson and the Sunshine Brass five nights a week in a large, elegant ballroom at the Drake Hotel, where people came to watch the shows. JoAnne Judson and I sang Beatles songs and other contemporary music, as well as old standards; we wore costumes and did dance routines orchestrated by a choreographer.

As for my Amytal sessions, however, I faced a dilemma. Obviously, I could no longer ask Richard to take me home after the Amytal, and after Amytal I was in no shape to drive by myself. My logistics were further complicated by the fact that Richard, who preferred the suburbs, had taken an apartment in the city, and I, the city-lover, had stayed in our suburban Glenview house—too many miles to go when I was still woozy from the drug. I thought I might have to stop the Amytal, but Dr. Masserman insisted that I must have someone who could help me out.

Dick and Mary Shelton, our good friends and former skiing buddies, filled the bill. Dick, whom I considered my mentor, was an entertainment lawyer who handled contracts for me. He loved my Mercedes, and at one point after my separation from Richard, he offered to buy it. I hadn't wanted to let go of the Mercedes, so we decided to share it, which felt quite natural, since he and Mary were like family to me. They were the only friends I had told about the Amytal. I thought it would color people's opinion of me, and I was still quite ashamed of needing such drastic drug treatment. For several months, one or both of the Sheltons picked me up after the Amytal sessions and dropped me off at the Drake, where I either paid for a room or used the dressing room that was available to the Sunshine Brass. A couple of times, Dick and Mary tucked me into bed in their guest room. They couldn't have been more gracious or supportive, and I was grateful.

Following my divorce, Dr. Masserman's concern for my well-being seemed to intensify. "I'm worried about you," he said often. "I can see how unhappy you are by the way you hold your body." I'd assure him I was all right, but he'd shake his head.

"I see that you're very sad today."

"Yes."

"You're lonely and you're frightened too."

I'd nod in agreement.

"Poor sad, lonely, frightened little girl. What do you think would help you?"

"I don't know."

"The last time you were feeling this way, the Amytal seemed to help you."

"Maybe some Amytal would help me. Do you think it would?"

"Yes. Yes, I think it might."

By the end of the hour, it would be obvious to both of us that the only way I could get to the bottom of what was troubling me was with another Amytal session. From the moment he wrapped the tourniquet around my arm and plunged the needle into my vein, I floated off into that pink space I loved—which, certainly, *must* be doing me some good. Under the Amytal, I never worried or was anxious, my head never hurt, my jaw never hurt; I never felt a thing.

Sometimes in the late afternoon when I got up, dressed, and went into his office after having been knocked out from the Amytal for the day, Dr. Masserman would say, "I believe that we're getting somewhere with the Amytal interview." Then he would schedule me for a second session, later in the week, or even the very next day. I didn't have a clue about the danger I was facing. What would Dr. Masserman have done if I had stopped breathing, gone into shock, or suffered any of the other dangerous and sometimes fatal effects of intravenous injections of Amytal?* He had no emergency equipment; he didn't even have a receptionist or a nurse in the office early in the mornings, let alone an anesthesiologist, when he gave me Amytal intravenously. If I had overdosed or stopped breathing, that would have been it. I would have died right there in his "examination room."

Once that year, after Patty Hearst had been caught and was on trial for robbing a bank, I asked Dr. Masserman about brainwashing. I said I didn't think it was fair for Patty Hearst to be found guilty or to be punished. After all, she had been kidnapped and tortured by the group she later joined for the bank robbery—and wasn't brainwashing just like temporary insanity? Dr. Masserman frowned. "A person is always completely responsible for what he does, Miz Nole," he said. "I like to think of mental disease as just that: dis-ease, not some version of the Svengali and Trilby story. If you rob a bank, you go to jail!"

Although Dr. Masserman's pronouncements didn't always make sense to me, his predictions about my ex-husband proved to be right

---

*Martindale's *The Extra Pharmacopoeia* states that Amytal should be given *only* under close supervision and indicates that intravenous injections of barbiturates are extremely hazardous.

on target. Six weeks after our divorce decree was final, in 1975, Richard did remarry. When Dick and Mary Shelton broke the news to me, I felt as if I had been jolted by lightning. The fact that Richard married again in only six weeks, not six months, made Dr. Masserman's forecast look charitable. I was miserable. Every time I turned on the radio—in the car, at home, at a friend's—I'd hear the song "Love Will Keep Us Together," by the Captain & Tennille. I was always bursting into tears and switching off the radio, but for a while, it seemed I couldn't shake that song or my sadness.

Then, to my own credit, I believe, I accepted the finality of Richard's remarriage and propelled myself into action. I moved out of the house in Glenview and found an airy one-bedroom apartment to rent on Dearborn Parkway in the city, near Mary and Dick Shelton's building. My time began to fill up with rehearsals, fresh material, new and old friends.

When our divorce settlement was final, I got some stocks and bonds as well as some money from the sale of our house. I wanted to handle my own investments, but my first major financial decision was a disaster. After losing the entire sum I'd invested, I decided I wasn't such a hot businesswoman after all. I was still driving my Mercedes, but for a while I lived on peanut butter sandwiches and TV dinners. Somehow, though, feeling poor didn't feel all that bad. I was making a living—which I hadn't been sure I could do—and I was having some fun. I loved being back in the city, able to go to concerts, hear jazz groups, and run in the park again.

All in all, most areas of my life seemed to be running smoothly. The one bugaboo I couldn't seem to work out after I moved back into Chicago was how to continue the Amytal sessions. I didn't want to keep imposing on Dick and Mary, and I had work commitments five nights a week. I told Dr. Masserman I might have to stop the Amytal, but he said he thought I still needed it and that he would reduce the dosage to make sure I could continue it. Under the new system, I canceled any appointments for the day and arrived at the Michigan Avenue office at either 7:30 or 8:15 A.M. Then, by 3:00 P.M.—instead of the former 4:30 or 5:00 P.M.—I was steady enough to get myself home in a taxicab.

Over time, however, the whole Amytal process had shifted into a slightly less than perfect experience. Billie was no longer available to care for me in the examining room, because besides being Dr. Masserman's secretary-nurse-receptionist-bookkeeper, she was now his book assistant, getting his new manuscript ready for publication. That cut out Billie's company as well as her ham salad sandwiches. Billie and I always talked before my regular appointments in the reception room—we even went to a few concerts together so we'd have more time to talk. But I missed her being part of the wakening process following Amytal.

My new routine was to stock the refrigerator with my own ham salad sandwiches and chocolate milk before I left home for an Amytal session. I'd also arrange my bed so I could crawl right into it and doze for a while when I got home. Because the dose was lighter, I also set out a bottle of gin for making myself a martini. Gin, "the purest and cleanest alcohol," gave me the boost I needed to keep that state of bliss going until early evening, when I'd take a shower and start to snap out of it. Then I'd put on makeup, one of my long sequined gowns, high heels, dangling earrings, and long gloves, and go to work on the band-stand at the Drake Hotel.

Not long after I got established in my new apartment, I gave up singing at the Drake and took a full-time job as a singer and rep with Jerry Liliedahl, a brilliant, charismatic producer who had formed a new jingle company—Lilidahl [sic] Productions. Jerry was extremely talented; he wrote grab-you-in-the-gut jingles that played behind the filmed commercials on television. His music and lyrics for United Airlines won all sorts of awards, as did many of his spots. Jerry and I hit it off well and together went after the best national accounts. Business got good fast. We picked up accounts with Pizza Hut, Hamm's beer, Cheerios, Schlitz, Red Lobster, Frigidaire, and Sears. The work was demanding, and we operated at an almost frenzied pace. In addition to selling, I was singing on spots, including ones for Schlitz, Red Lobster restaurants, Cheerios, and Hamm's ("From the Land of Sky Blue Waters").

Except for the times when I had to be "out of town" for Amytal, I worked sixteen-hour days. We got so busy we had to bring in another writer, as well as an office manager, Nancy Waller, who became an extremely good friend—one I'm still close with today.

Nancy and the man she lived with, "John Harriman," and I began going out to shows and movies together, and it wasn't long before they introduced me to John's brother. "Tony Harriman" and I were both surprised to discover we shared an eclectic musical taste—everything from the early French classical composers to jazz to Jennifer Warnes, Jethro Tull, The Band, Leon Russell, Smokey Robinson, and Cream. We found it easy to overcome our mutual shyness, and within a few months we had become lovers—not living together, but together; not in love, but good friends. Neither of us was looking for marriage, but we had fun, laughed a lot, and enjoyed each other immensely. Tony wasn't at all like Richard. For one thing, he was ten years younger than I was, but it didn't bother him, and strangely enough, it didn't bother me. We *felt* the same age. Tony was cerebral, affable, funny, and boyish, with rumpled blond hair and the broad shoulders and narrow hips of a swimmer. He was from a wealthy family, but he had no interest in material things. For three years, he'd lived in one small room in Paris and survived as a housepainter. He had a master's degree in French, and at the time we met, he was studying for a doctorate in economics, living off a teaching fellowship and a generous stipend from his parents. When we were together, day or night, we felt free and easy. We'd get out one of our favorite records and bop all over the apartment.

When Lyric Opera was doing Wagner, we'd be there. Tony and I sometimes spoke to each other in French, which I loved. We talked for hours about world events and current issues—something neither my husband nor Dr. Masserman had ever been willing to talk to me about. The two of us rode the Chicago el all over the city and made up stories about the people we saw. We often felt touched by the variety of people and the real-life vignettes we witnessed on those train rides.

When I told Dr. Masserman what great fun I was having with Tony, he reacted wrathfully. He said it was *obvious* Tony was not looking for marriage, and since he was also ten years younger than I was, the relationship was a waste of time. It was an absolute rule of thumb, he said, that if you must date a younger man, he should never be more than six years younger. Besides that, I should be seeing someone *much* more responsible than Tony.

I didn't have any argument for Dr. Masserman's mandate on age, but when I rebelliously objected that our relationship wasn't a waste of time, that fun was *important,* and that I wasn't looking for marriage either, Dr. Masserman said, "Well, you'd better be careful, young lady, or you're going to end up old, tired, and all alone. I would hate to see that happen to you."

• • •

Not long after he gave me that warning, Dr. Masserman suggested I might enjoy coming to his home for a session, to see where and how he lived. I was surprised, but I agreed since his invitation seemed rather quaint and intrigued me. I'd read that Freud and Jung actually had some patients visit in their homes, and I thought that, perhaps like them, Dr. Masserman was planning to use his home and his family as part of my therapy. I also was curious about Mrs. Masserman. I'd seen her briefly in the office once and I thought it would be interesting to meet her. I agreed.

Dr. and Mrs. Masserman lived in an elegant but run-down Tudor apartment house on East Sixty-seventh Street, about three miles from the University of Chicago. A brown awning covered the double entrance doors. On my arrival, a doorman ushered me into a huge lobby with greenish stone walls, and I took an elevator up to the Massermans' apartment. Dr. Masserman opened the door to my knock and showed me into his living room; Mrs. Masserman was away, he said, and he was sorry she would be unable to meet me. He introduced me to his housekeeper and cook, a regal, light-skinned black woman who appeared to be in her early seventies. When she left the room, he said she had "always doted" on him.

The doctor led me across the living room to a large window that offered a perfect view of Jackson Park Harbor and Yacht Club. Then he took me into what he called his music room and showed me his two prized musical instruments: a 1709 Albani violin and an Albani viola, made in 1712. He said they were the only two perfectly matched Albanis in the world. They were extraordinarily beautiful.

We went back into the living room to talk, sitting on furniture that I remember as soft, loose, and honey-colored. He had many books, and there was an old-world, cluttered, slightly shabby quality to the surroundings. I wondered if perhaps the doctor hadn't invited me to his home to show me the kind of life he thought I should live—one unconcerned with status and elegance. Maybe this was his way of saying I shouldn't be so conscious of fine furniture, classic refinements, station and grandeur, but should instead focus on the intellectual aspects of life, which were ultimately most valuable.

By the end of the hour, when Dr. Masserman steered me back across the long living room to the window overlooking the harbor and the yacht club, I was feeling rather good about myself, thinking perhaps this session was a prelude to the eventual ending of my therapy—a graduation of sorts and a tribute to my well-being. Afternoon light danced on the water below us, and Dr. Masserman pointed out a sailboat—his own form of therapy, he said, *Naiad, Nymph of the Lakes,* a thirty-two-foot yawl anchored some distance from the harbor's main dock.

"You know, don't you, young lady," Dr. Masserman said softly near my ear, "that you have been badly victimized by your husband?"

"Yes," I said, suddenly feeling my spirits sink. "I suppose you're right."

"And it will take a long time for you to get over it."

"A long time?" I asked, feeling chilled. "How long?"

"One cannot undo the harm overnight. You must be patient, and of course, I will help you all I can. I'm here for you. But I want you to realize that you're the type of woman who should be married. You simply must not enter into dead-end relationships like the one you have with this Tony."

"But you don't understand. . . ."

"Now, none of that, little miss. You'll see. One day you'll meet the man you're going to marry." He put his hand on my shoulder, and we looked out the window at the harbor. "When you do, you'll bring him out to the *Naiad,* and then we three will sail together."

I didn't say anything, but I was thinking: I will *never* marry again. *Never.* I enjoy Tony, and it's great to be with someone who doesn't care that I spend hours writing music and doing my job. He is exactly what I want. Exactly what I *don't* want is marriage.

As much as I respected Dr. Masserman, his harping on Tony's unsuitability made me increasingly annoyed and uncomfortable. I wasn't deterred from seeing Tony, but it was beginning to look as if the doctor was demanding that I choose between worlds. In the one he recommended, I could stay sheltered under his redeeming care, where the fragile part of me could be safe while the rest of me blossomed and found meaning. In that world, I needed to accept his advice and direction without question. He depicted my other option as a vast, subterranean land of cruel reality, where, without his sure-handed guidance, my hidden terrors and mysterious fears would surely consume and destroy me.

When it came down to it, though, I was tired of therapy. I was tired of having to report on all my activities and thoughts two or three times a week, not to mention the time I had to set aside for my therapy appointments and Amytal sessions. My friend Nancy Waller insisted I didn't need a psychiatrist, which was what Dick and Mary Shelton had been saying for years. My work was going well; I was happy and having fun, so I wanted to try to go it alone. I talked myself into believing Dr. Masserman might even be pleased I was trying to stand on my own two feet.

When I told him I wanted to stop therapy, however, his eyes widened, and he said with a note of alarm in his voice, "It's the money, isn't it? You're in a brand-new job, and you're worried about money." He sounded positively dismayed. "Oh, my dear, did you think I wouldn't understand?" he said softly. "For a while, certainly until you feel more prosperous, I'll cut my fee in half."

I was so shocked and confused by this generous response that for the time being, I kept on with both the Amytal and the regular sessions, paying twenty-five dollars per hour rather than the previous fifty dollars.

By late May of 1976, however, I'd been in therapy for over ten years, and I was determined to stop. I was well established in a good job, I'd had a raise, and I was feeling pretty powerful and ready to be on my own, without Dr. Masserman. Also, I didn't feel I was making any discoveries about myself or growing because of anything I was learning in therapy. It no longer seemed a creative exploration into my psyche; it was more like a chore—sometimes like running the gauntlet, defending myself and my choice of friends—and I honestly thought it neither constructive nor useful at this point. Dr. Masserman had also started putting down my singing on a rather regular basis. He told me at one point that I should remarry so that my husband could support me; then I wouldn't have to try to support myself by singing. That assessment was more appalling than I was willing to admit or deal with at the time.

I knew I wanted out.

I practiced what I would say, and when I finally got up my nerve, I said firmly, "The time has come, Doctor, for me to try it alone, at least for a while."

Dr. Masserman stared at me with a look of total bewilderment. "You simply don't understand," he said after a long silence. "You still have *many* unresolved problems."

"I do understand. It's just that I feel the need to—"

"The matter is closed. Until you realize you have problems, that you're wasting your life with that young man, there's no need for further discussion." He got up from his desk and stood with his back to me, gazing out the window.

I felt swamped with remorse and panic, but I was still determined. "I'm so sorry, Doctor—"

"The matter is closed."

"Does this mean you don't want me ever to come back?"

Sternly, he turned to look at me again. "When you're ready to face some modicum of reality, when you're ready to listen to me and accept my help, then of course I'll welcome you back."

That parting upset me, but I didn't miss talking to Dr. Masserman. I did miss the Amytal and thought about it a lot. Tony kept a stash of pot in the antique wooden box on my coffee table, and we smoked it occasionally; it gave me a little bit of a jolt. More often I had martinis or joined Tony in drinking Jack Daniel's. It wasn't the real thing, but it worked quite well as a substitute for my Amytal.

With the help of the alcohol and pot, I managed to stay away from the Amytal and Dr. Masserman for more than a year. During that time, I'd made frequent trips to New York to meet with ad agencies on behalf of Lilidahl Productions. I loved being in the city, and I usually had dinner and caught a Broadway show with good friends who lived there. In December, I had flown to New York to do some singing commercials, including one for AC/Delco Batteries that was turned into seventeen spots of varying lengths; it paid for a trip to Paris and eventually allowed me to buy my apartment when the building became a condominium. In another stroke of good fortune, Dinah Shore heard some of my songs and decided to perform them on her network television show. Then, as a result of the Dinah Shore show, Chappell Music in New York offered me a year's contract as a songwriter.

My work was going exceptionally well, but I was hit with some major stresses. My brother and I had moved our father, who had been very ill, into a nursing home. Richard, my ex-husband, had left his new marriage, become depressed, and called me to talk. Then my favorite colleague and wild man, Jerry Liliedahl, underwent a personal crisis and closed down Lilidahl Productions. By then I was vice-president of the company, and I had been making a lot of extra money from bonuses and residuals. Jerry was extremely apologetic, but when he terminated the business, I was secretly relieved. We had done good work together, but I was exhausted, tired of the frenzied, sixteen-hour workdays.

Fortunately, I found several good studio jobs right way. But the unstructured schedule that goes hand in hand with free-lance work was calamitous for me. With free-lancing, I was sometimes extremely busy for several days in a row, and then I wouldn't have any work at all for three or four days. On days when I had no bookings, I started feeling there wasn't any reason to get up in the morning.

By September 1977, I knew I was in trouble. I fell off in my song-writing, and Chappell's rep didn't renew my contract. Tony and I had started doing a lot more pot, and the Jack Daniel's was disappearing faster than before. We partied hard, singing and dancing late into the nights; we went to movies and restaurants. But when I was by myself, I spent a lot of time playing Stevie Wonder's "Ordinary Pain" and staring at the moon.

Finally, feeling shaky and confused, I returned to Dr. Masserman in late September. I'd hoped he would be glad to see me, but he was indifferent and detached, almost callous. When I told him Richard had been ill, alone, and in need of friendship, he said in a bitter, antagonistic voice, "So Mr. Nole is your swain once more?"

"Well, no," I answered, "but we're friends."

"And this man Tony is part of your life still?"

"Yes, to a certain degree."

"Well, you've made your own decisions. Why come to me?"

"I need help."

"Yes, that's what I told you a year ago."

"Please, Dr. Masserman, don't be angry with me," I said, holding back tears. "I think I'm in trouble." Then I told him about Tony and the pot and the Jack Daniel's. He nodded knowingly.

"This is what I was afraid of," he said in a voice full of disgust. "When you left, this is what I feared. Not only have you insisted upon maintaining relationships with two men who are unfortunate choices, but you choose to make yourself unavailable to life itself. Now it's up to you and you alone. What are you going to do?"

"Well, I don't know," I said. "Do you think some Amytal would help?"

"Do you think it would?"

"I think it might."

Over the next couple of months, the Amytal, strangely enough, did not help. For some reason, it gave me no ecstasy. It simply knocked me out and left me feeling hung over and shaky. I'd go home afterward and crawl into bed, overwhelmed with depression. I had no idea then that depression is a predictable side effect of Amytal: I was in such bondage to my situation that it never occurred to me to go to the library and look up information about the drug I was taking.

My regular psychotherapy sessions with Dr. Masserman didn't depress me as much as the "Amytal interviews" did, but they left me unhappy because he was clearly angry with me. If I talked about feeling depressed, he would act disgusted with what I said; he'd shake his head in resignation and say, "When are you going to learn how to get along with people?"

When I complained that one of the married band members I worked with was always coming on to me and wanting to sit and talk for hours when he drove me home, Dr. Masserman said, "What's wrong with that? The poor man needs to have someone to listen to him. You can't always have things your way!" When I said I'd told the musician he should go into therapy, Dr. Masserman said, "What kind of friend are you to say a thing like that!"

On another occasion, I complained about the jingle business, saying I wasn't singing the songs I wanted to sing, writing the songs I wanted to write, or selling the songs I wanted to sell. Dr. Masserman responded, "You're like the millionaire who's disappointed at having only three million dollars because he thinks he should have ten million dollars. Now, I could walk around disappointed because I didn't win the Nobel Prize, but do I? No. I have patients to treat and books to write."

Because Dr. Masserman was always so angry at me and it was always so depressing to see him, I left him again in mid-November 1977. It was a relief, and I returned to my work with renewed enthusiasm. I read the *Chicago Tribune* and *Le Monde,* along with *Women's Wear Daily, Elle,* and other fashion magazines, and one day I read a fascinating article about the Japanese fashion designer Kenzo, one of the hottest designers in Paris. I loved his style and imagination, and I started buying and wearing the charming Kenzo homespun tops, skirts, and pants fashioned after the peasant clothes of the Japanese, and the starched, immaculate white shirts and pleated skirts reminiscent of Japanese schoolchildren. Kenzo's clothes gave me a clean, calm feeling and led me to begin reading about Japanese culture and eating at Japanese restaurants, where I was introduced to sake.

In the meantime, Nancy and John had moved to New York, and I visited them there. We ate out, saw *A Chorus Line* and *Dracula* on Broadway, haunted jazz clubs, and went to movies. After seeing Diane Keaton's clothes in *Annie Hall,* I shopped for hats and fancy neckties with Nancy. She had an eye for Parisian styles, and while I stuck to Kenzo and my new hats and ties, Nancy bought clothes designed by Karl Lagerfeld and Yves Saint Laurent.

In March 1978, I took a three-week vacation trip to Paris and, among other things, visited Kenzo's shop, Jungle Jap. I had a wonderful time in Paris, but I was lonely, and I realized when I came home that I still had a feeling of emptiness and futility. I often woke up wondering what my life was all about and wishing for a close, nurturing relationship. I also longed for Amytal. I remembered how Amytal made me forget everything and somehow altered my view of the world, at least for as long as it was in effect. Now it seemed I didn't have any real respites. Since I'd started free-lancing, I was spending more and more time alone, often listening to music and drinking sake for hours until I fell asleep.

In the larger world, Jane Byrne was about to be elected Chicago's first female mayor, and Margaret Thatcher was about to become Britain's first woman prime minister. I was on the board of AFTRA (American Federation of Television and Radio Artists), and we were making big plans to push the Equal Rights Amendment for women. Although I had some measure of success with my career, I couldn't help but notice that while other women were getting stronger and hitting their stride, I was feeling ineffective and fragile. I still got terrible headaches and pains, and when I was performing, I often got dizzy or felt faint.

Dr. Masserman had always told me, "You're doing this for attention." He said I manufactured my physical symptoms "in a futile attempt of the unconscious to control the situation." So I *understood* that these things were psychosomatic. But that didn't make them easier to deal with—particularly when I couldn't shake them. I called the American Psychological Association and asked for the name of a therapist, whom I saw eight times. I liked him, but I also realized how long it would take to fill him in on all the details of my life. Besides that, he wasn't an M.D., and he couldn't give me Sodium Amytal, which I desperately wanted.

• • •

In September 1979, I returned to Dr. Masserman once again. Initially, he was haughty and sarcastic about my return, but when I told him I'd been drinking large quantities of sake, he softened, and scolded me for being "a bad little girl." He seemed quite pleased to hear that Tony and I had drifted apart, and he said he wasn't surprised by the dissolution of that relationship, nor was he surprised about my drinking. He told me that if I weren't such a spoiled little girl and if I had just listened to him in the first place, I wouldn't be in all this trouble now.

"Yes," he said, "when little Barbara doesn't like the way the game goes, she takes her little football and goes home."

Dr. Masserman told me that during the time I'd been on my own, "out making trouble for yourself," he had been hard at work as president of the American Psychiatric Association—something that required tremendous commitment and a great deal of traveling. Later I would learn that in Tel Aviv and Jerusalem, Dr. Masserman had collected signatures from leading Israeli psychiatrists on a statement designed to foster cordial professional and personal relationships with their Egyptian colleagues; he had presented that letter to the Egyptian Psychiatric Association. He had helped draft a document condemning the misuse of psychiatry for political, racial, or religious purposes. I also learned that Jules Masserman had been the first president of the APA to conclude his presidential address at the APA's annual meeting by playing the violin to illustrate the therapeutic effects of music. He had chosen the theme "The Future of Psychiatry as a Scientific and Humanitarian Discipline in a Rapidly Changing World" as the focus for that meeting, which had been held in Chicago in May 1979.

Despite his elevated status among his colleagues, however, Dr. Masserman's office looked and smelled virtually the same. Billie Laird always said that the doctor was too cheap to hire a cleaning lady, and it was probably true. The office was as dusty as ever and even more cluttered; the walls were adorned with several new accolades and pictures of him with celebrities, among them Rosalynn Carter at the White House. He had added a number of framed letters acknowledging his many contributions to mankind and the field of mental health. Wood and ivory figurines and knickknacks from around the world had also multiplied on the dusty tops of his desk and bookshelves. He would often identify who had given him which item—"That was a gift from the president of Portugal" or "That was given to me by So-and-so of the World Health Organization in China."

Dr. Masserman delighted in talking about his responsibilities as APA president, and now, more than ever, his phone rang during our regular therapy sessions. If the call was local, he would say he was in session and would phone back, but if the call came from overseas, he would cover the mouthpiece and say, "Could you excuse me for just a bit? I must take this call from Moscow [or Paris or London or Vienna]." Afterward, he might enlighten me on the conversation: "That was So-and-so from the International Society for . . ." He told me about increasingly frequent eight-to-ten-day trips, as well as a two-week "Invitational Tour" to the People's Republic of China on behalf of the APA. He said I shouldn't worry, though—his schedule shouldn't interfere too greatly with our sessions.

Dr. Masserman scolded me for being so dependent on my sake and gave me a simplistic brochure he had written called "Tommy the Tipsy Tabby." It apparently was based on research he had done at the University of Chicago in the forties and basically affirmed that even cats can't function properly if they get addicted to alcohol. He scheduled me for Amytal—"which might help us get to the heart of your problem"—and gave me a prescription for Antabuse, explaining that it would make me ill if I consumed any alcohol. "Your habit of drinking sake and of boosting the Amytal with gin might eventually get out of hand," he said, explaining that "Antabuse is the most efficient way of *preventing* a real problem."

"I thought Antabuse was a serious thing that was only given to people who were confirmed alcoholics," I said.

"No, no, that's not the case at all," he said with a chuckle. "Don't worry; in your case it's just a preventative."

Dr. Masserman also gave me a flu shot, which he did every fall.

I wonder what I would have done if I had had any idea what Dr. Masserman was doing to my body in giving me Amytal *and* Antabuse. In the drug manufacturers' product information published in the *Physicians' Desk Reference,* doctors are explicitly warned that Amytal "may result in psychic and physical dependence" and that it "should not be administered to persons with known previous addiction to the sedative/ hypnotic group, since ordinary doses may be ineffectual and *may contribute to further addiction.*"

It doesn't take a doctor to know that "dependency" and "addiction" are interchangeable words. The fact that Dr. Masserman was prescribing Antabuse for me made it extraordinarily clear that he *knew* I was a person with a "known addiction" to alcohol. It also had to be clear to him that I was already addicted to the Amytal; or if for some reason that wasn't clear, he had to have known at the very least that I was a prime candidate for Amytal addiction.

In fact, it seems it would have been difficult for him *not* to know how addictive Amytal was and not to know that my addiction to Amytal would dramatically increase the probability of my becoming alcoholic. A contemporary of Masserman's, a well-known authority on the subject, had written that Amytal is "as addictive as heroin or morphine" and that addiction to Amytal certainly might provoke and lead to other addictions.*

But of course, I didn't know these things, and I was too addicted and too bound to Dr. Masserman to question his judgment. Like an obedient child, I went along with him. He told me that taking Antabuse for six months would break my drinking problem, and then I could resume the occasional use of wine and spirits.

Martindale's The Extra Pharmacopoeia says: "Dependence is characterised by a strong need to continue taking the drug, a tendency to increase the dose, a psychic dependence on the effects of the drug, and a physical dependence on [its] effects."

After six months, as planned, I stopped taking the Antabuse and began drinking an occasional glass of wine in the evenings. Initially, this didn't appear to pose a problem for me. I felt good about not drinking so much and directed my energy into positive channels. Besides my singing, I'd become interested in improvisation. Second City, a well-known comedy company, had an excellent workshop only six blocks from my apartment, so I took intensive classes there and loved it. It was like child's play, and it opened my mind and my feelings tremendously.

At the time, I was doing a lot of acting in commercials, as well as in industrial films, which are usually thirty to ninety minutes long and are made for training employees or orienting business clients. I identified strongly with other actors, and when Peter Sellers died in 1980, I was very sad. I told Dr. Masserman I couldn't understand why, when

*Louis Robert Wolberg, *The Technique of Psychotherapy*, 3rd ed., 2 vol., New York: Grune & Stratton, 1977, pp. 892–94.

Peter Sellers was so gifted, he shouldn't have enough happiness to live to be ninety-six, like Pablo Casals, the cellist. Dr. Masserman said, "Actors are not very happy people, for the most part. I'm surprised you haven't noticed that by now." Was that true? I *hadn't* noticed. I guess I thought everybody was happier than I was.

During my spare time, I volunteered to work as a nursing assistant with babies at Children's Memorial Hospital. Since my hysterectomy in 1968, I had accepted that I would never have a child of my own, but I had a strong desire to learn about babies. The yearning had crept up on me by surprise. I had found myself looking at babies and little children on the street or in the supermarket with fascination and longing. I realized that I'd never changed a diaper in my life, and since I'd been a grown woman, I'd never even held a baby in my arms. I wanted to carry and rock a baby. I wanted to put my cheek next to a baby's cheek and come in contact with those bright little eyes and tiny fingers. I wanted to learn how to nurture a child and, perhaps, be nurtured in the process.

As a volunteer nursing assistant, I started in the surgical ward, where I took care of little heart-surgery patients on my free mornings. I'd hold them when the doctor put in an IV, and then I'd cuddle and rock them until they calmed down. I played with kids whose mothers weren't there, and I spent a lot of time with kids who had no parents. One sixteen-month-old Hispanic boy named Butch particularly won my heart. I was so taken with him and his family that I started to study Spanish. Butch and the other Spanish-speaking kids loved my baby Spanish phrases and always helped me add to my vocabulary.

Later, I began to work in the neonatal ward with tiny babies who were out of their incubators. Often they were hooked up to tubes and monitors. Sometimes their mothers couldn't visit or feed them because they lived too far away; sometimes their parents had virtually abandoned them because they couldn't cope with a sick or premature baby. The nurses were glad to have help whenever I came. Usually I stayed for four hours at a time to feed and hold these tiny human beings. Sometimes an infant hadn't learned how to suck yet, so I'd put the bottle in her mouth and manipulate the nipple to give her the idea, coaxing her to suck. There were a lot of preemies, and sometimes I would be asked to put my hand into the incubators to touch and rub them, so that they'd have some physical contact even though they couldn't be held. One baby I saw was so small she could fit in a nurse's hand. I changed tiny diapers, and sometimes I just carried and rocked babies who needed affection and warmth. I fell in love with them all.

Each time I went to the hospital and worked with those children or infants, it made me happy. I was gratified and thrilled that I was so good at taking care of them. When I told Dr. Masserman that I thought the experience was very good for me, he acted irritated, shushed me, and changed the subject. The next time I brought up my feelings about working with the babies, he said, "What a waste of time—taking care of other women's babies!" He sounded jealous. He said if I wanted to do something worthwhile, I should go teach music on the adolescent psychiatric unit at Northwestern. So I volunteered there as well, but they needed routine, predictable hours, and because of my own inconsistent work schedule, it didn't work out.

I still think that taking care of those babies in the hospital was one of the most significant experiences in my life. I felt nurtured and nurturing, softened by the interaction I had with those small, beautiful people. It should have struck me as strange when my therapist told me it was a useless way to spend my time. But I'm grateful I had the gumption to stay on the job despite his condemnation.

When I began dating again and had purely platonic, standoffish dates with a man I had no interest in, Dr. Masserman said it was a good sign. But whenever I met or went out with someone who I thought was terrific, Dr. Masserman invariably tried to show me where I was wrong. If I reported on a particular man as impossible or unattractive, Dr. Masserman would try to persuade me that this one was an excellent prospect. "You're so willful!" he often said. "Don't you know how to get along with people?"

He gave me some rules to follow when it came to my relationships with men:

Dating should last about two months before sexual relations start, although a woman certainly should let a man know right away that she's no cold cookie.

Never allow a drunken friend of the opposite sex to come to your apartment late at night and stay over. The doormen might talk! It doesn't matter if the male friend shouldn't drive; a woman's first consideration must be protecting her own reputation.

Never do *anything* that will hurt your reputation.

Never tell a man you've been married twice before. A woman appears unstable in that light.

At one point, I told Dr. Masserman that I looked much too bosomy in an industrial film I had done recently for a realty company. I thought the reason I hadn't gotten a couple of jobs I'd auditioned for was that I was too bosomy on camera. I liked making films, and because I wanted to do more filming, I'd consulted a plastic surgeon about having a breast reduction. I thought I'd like to do it, I said, but I thought I probably should examine my feelings about it first.

Dr. Masserman looked horrified and repulsed, as if he might faint. "Do you realize the awful scarring you would have?" he said vehemently. "Your breasts look just fine! In fact, some people would call you beautiful. So why would you do a thing like that? Men like their women attractive, not scarred!"

It didn't occur to me to wonder how Dr. Masserman could say my breasts looked "just fine." How would he know? Why was he so clearly repulsed at the idea of a breast reduction or scars?

I scrapped the idea of plastic surgery because I didn't want to be repulsive to men, but my reason for considering the breast reduction had been professional, not personal. I had hoped that, ultimately, filming would replace my studio work altogether. My main problem with the studio work was hearing the sound track properly. For jingles, the background music is prerecorded and then played back electronically as the performer adds in the singing. I wore headphones to hear the music, but the sounds got distorted for me and I could hardly tell what key the music was in. Sometimes when I was listening intently to the music, I'd get dizzy; I'd have to hold on to the wall or a table to keep from losing my balance. It was frightening. I'd consulted two hearing specialists. The first one said my hearing was excellent, and the second wondered if the problem could be emotional.

When I explained these difficulties to Dr. Masserman, he smiled knowingly and said, "What am I going to do with you? You still cling to the childlike idea that Daddy's little princess doesn't have to do anything she doesn't want to. If a situation becomes a little difficult, she just gets sick or feels faint. How many times are we going to have to go through this before you begin to understand?"

I had no idea how to apply this judgment to my situation or rectify my behavior, but I figured I must be to blame somehow, and eventually, perhaps, I would understand how to work it all out.

Not long after this, I woke up after an Amytal session to find my bra lying loose on my breasts under the blankets. I couldn't imagine what I could have been doing. Had I stood up or run around? Before receiving the Amytal, I had removed my bra, folded it inside my shirt, as usual, and put everything in a neat pile on the chair. Why in the world would I wake up with my bra spread across my breasts? I felt frantic with worry. Remembering the bruises I'd had, I started wondering just what I did when under the Amytal. How crazy did I act?

When I agonized out loud over what I had been doing with my bra, Dr. Masserman angrily told me to stop these uncalled-for outbursts. He called me a "spoiled brat" and said I would have to quit behaving like this or he would have to stop giving me Amytal.

I felt horrible! I apologized at once and, as was usual these days, left our session upset and depressed.

When I got home, I called him to apologize again for my "uncalled-for" behavior.

7 Out of Bounds

During the years following my divorce, and again after my return to him in 1979, Dr. Masserman frequently implied that I should learn to "open up" new perspectives. More and more, it seemed, he was treating me like an equal.

In 1979, after he had gotten over the worst of his anger about my departures, he suggested that rather than always lying on the couch and free-associating during our regular therapy sessions, I could sit in the chair next to his desk from time to time and speak with him directly. He told me that the Amytal treatments, which I had at varying intervals, would be "greatly enhanced" by face-to-face chats during our other sessions. I was proud and flattered when he told me he thought I was "perceiving the daily realities" of my life, and I was relieved to think how, under his care, I had grown so much that he was treating me like an adult.

Dr. Masserman also began to give me frequent invitations that he said would help me open up the new vistas he spoke about. Often, he invited me to go out flyng with him. He knew I had flown a great deal with Richard, and he speculated that I must miss the expansive view of the world flying offered. I didn't miss flying at all, and each time he invited me to go up in his plane, I easily found an excuse not to go.

It wasn't so easy to turn down his requests to go sailing. He made it sound important that I go out with him on his boat, and he interpreted my refusals as indicators of my lack of interest in really becoming a psychologically stronger, healthier woman. Sometimes he urged me to change my plans so that I could go. "It's therapeutic," he would say, reminding me that being on the water "gives one a different perspective on life."

He confided that sailing, like music, let him escape the pressures of his profession and was "self-administered therapy." During one therapy session in 1980, he gave me a blue folder that contained an autographed copy of an article, "Poetry and Music in Flight from Futility," that had been reprinted in a journal called *The Arts in Psychotherapy*.

I took it home, and the following evening I settled down to read it. In his paper, Dr. Masserman said his lifelong loves were music, sailing, and science—"all partially exclusive, yet aesthetically inseparable." He noted that he had written a song, "Lullaby at Sea," for "the temporary recipient" of an early romantic attachment. In what seemed to be a rather grandiose comparison, he likened the breakup of that romance and his subsequent songwriting to the legend of Mozart's composing the second movement of his G-Minor Symphony Concertante "during his courtship of Aloysia Weber, and finishing the symphony with a lilting devil-may-care dance tune when Aloysia spurned him." Dr. Masserman, "in accord with the Mozartian legend," then wrote two other poem-songs, "Life Is Strange" and "Sailing Song," which he called a "lilting sea chantey."

I thought Dr. Masserman's lyrics and music were extremely simplistic—particularly lines like "Life is strange, full of mystery/In all this world I must walk alone/Yet I yearn and seek endlessly/To know that I'm more than a rolling stone." At the same time, I appreciated having the reprint and enjoyed the praise of *my* therapist by the editor in chief of the journal, Dr. Paul Jay Fink. He introduced Dr. Masserman's article as "a beautifully written bit of personal reminiscence and self-perception" that reflected a "rare contribution of simplicity and complexity." Dr. Masserman, he said, had been "rightfully honored for his massive contributions to the fields of mental health, science and the humanities."

Reading the article made me further appreciate Dr. Masserman's love of the sea. I, too, loved to sail, and even though I didn't feel comfortable about the idea of sailing with Dr. Masserman, it embarrassed me always to turn down his invitations.

At the time, I was often able to decline gracefully his invitations for a weekend sail because I had a steady job as a vocalist every Friday and Saturday night at the Metropolitan Club, a fancy private club in the Sears Tower Building. But my excuses seemed to wear thin. Finally, in the summer of 1980, flattered by his persistence and thinking I was wrong to feel so much discomfort, I agreed to meet him on a weekday afternoon for a sail.

The day was sunny and beautiful. Feeling slightly nervous, I drove to the Jackson Park Harbor and Yacht Club.

Dr. Masserman was waiting on the dock, wearing rubber-soled shoes, shorts, a long-sleeved shirt, and a captain's hat. He was smaller and slightly more bent than he had been when I first met him. Now he had hearing aids in both ears, but he still looked the preeminent psychiatrist, even in his sailing clothes. He took my hand to help me down into a dinghy. I commented that the generous breeze blowing across the water promised good sailing, and we chatted as if we were friends. I couldn't help but notice that the guys at the yacht club were watching us as Dr. Masserman rowed us slowly toward his boat, which was anchored in the harbor. I felt as if we were on parade—and that on some level, Dr. Masserman was parading me past those men. But I didn't resent it.

When we got to the *Naiad,* I helped Dr. Masserman unload a picnic basket he'd brought onto the deck. He was proud of his boat, and with reason. I'd been on many sailboats, and this one was a beauty. She was a two-masted fore-and-aft-rigged sailing vessel with the smaller mizzen mast in front of the rudder. The teak had been oiled and polished to a brilliant luster, and all the brass fittings gleamed.

Before we set sail, Dr. Masserman suggested that we eat the light supper his housekeeper-cook had sent along, and we sat down on the deck to a delicious meal of baked chicken, rice, and salad. Dr. Masserman talked about his recent travels, the need for world disarmament, and lessons we should learn from the Greeks. He was erudite and sophisticated, and as usual, I was mesmerized. Even though I had traveled a great deal myself and had been surrounded by material comforts, I wasn't exposed often to such scholarly dissertations and literary references, so I was impressed. Also, on the water, I appreciated how much more easily I could hear what the doctor was saying than I could in his office. There, he usually spoke so softly that when the air conditioner was buzzing on summer days, I often couldn't hear him at all, and since he was going deaf, I sometimes laughingly wondered to myself if we were doing mime routines, with neither of us hearing much of anything the other one was saying. On the water, however, I heard him clearly and I assumed he heard me as well.

After our supper, the wind was still up, and we sailed smoothly out of the harbor. Dr. Masserman gave me the tiller for a while, but soon I was sitting at the bow, letting the spray hit my dangling bare feet. I was comfortable and would have liked to stay there the entire trip, but when I looked back at the helm, where Dr. Masserman was steering, I felt rude, so I worked my way back and sat beside him as we returned to the harbor. It had been a pleasant trip, but somewhat awkward, so even though he suggested several more outings on the *Naiad,* that was the only sailing or flying invitation I accepted from him. When I had free time, I preferred spending it with friends.

About a year later, on September 16, 1981, my father, in the hospital for minor surgery, died of a heart attack. I should have been prepared for his death, but I wasn't. I floated through his funeral, where dozens of southern women came up to me and said things like, "Oh, I had your daddy for music appreciation, and he was the best-looking thang!" I came back from his funeral feeling like an abandoned child—sad, bruised, full of conflicting feelings. My brother and I were no longer close, and, coming home, I felt like an orphan.

Dr. Masserman suggested that I free-associate from the couch again, and I did. At one such session after my father's death, I was talking away, and then suddenly I had nothing to say. I lay silently for a long time, and then, unexpectedly, I said, *"My father raped me."* I was totally unprepared for that. Hearing myself say those words shocked me so much that I sat up, turned around, and looked at Dr. Masserman. What would he think? Why in the world had I said that?

Dr. Masserman's elbows were on his desk, and his fingers formed a steeple under his nose. He looked at me without comment or response.

I felt myself slipping into a sense of total unreality. "My father never raped me," I said, realizing as I spoke that I wanted to talk about this thing that had just happened, these words I had just spoken.

Dr. Masserman smiled sweetly at me. "Well, in a sense, he did," he said, nodding his head in quick dismissal. "But never mind. Go on with what you were talking about."

That one spontaneous piece of information may have been the only thing I talked about under Amytal that made its way to the surface. But I'll never know. Dr. Masserman never mentioned it again, nor did I. For a few days, I thought about it every now and then, and I wondered why Dr. Masserman was so quick to shrug it off. But I figured that he must have considered it trivial, which was all right with me. I wasn't ready to probe that subject by myself. Just thinking about it filled me with uneasiness and a strange sense of dread.

At our next session, Dr. Masserman asked me to sit in the chair opposite him. Never again did I lie on the couch for free association.

Shortly after that, when I told Dr. Masserman that my blue funk was persisting and I felt as if I couldn't get out of it, he took out a small piece of stationery from his desk and carefully folded it into a little paper envelope, which he then filled with pills. He tucked in the flap and handed it to me. He'd made me these little envelopes before, for aspirin or Dalmane (a tranquilizer) or a few sleeping tablets when he thought I needed them. This time, he said he'd given me enough Elavil, an antidepressant, for a week. He also wrote out a prescription for Elavil, which he said I should have filled. He told me to take one pill three times a day to help lift my depression.

I took the pills, but they didn't agree with me. When I was running, the antidepressants slowed my pulse so much that to get my heartbeat up to training rate, I had to run myself practically to death. I went off the antidepressants and drank martinis instead.

I didn't know that in combination with Amytal, an antidepressant would add enormous depressive effects to my already sedated body. In fact, one of the standard references warns: "Toxic doses and fatalities have occurred following overdoses of Amytal alone and in combination with other central-nervous-system depressants." When I reported to Dr. Masserman that the martinis I was having every day made me feel better, he put me back on Antabuse.

"Am I an alcoholic?" I asked him.

"No, you are *not* an alcoholic," he said with a chuckle, "but the Antabuse will help you make sure you never become one."

"But it can kill you if you drink."

"Then don't do it."

"It seems like it's a safer idea to join AA," I said, laughing at my own joke.

"That's not funny, young lady," he said. "Don't ever get the idea you can drink all you want and then get cured by a bunch of amateurs who don't know what they're doing. And don't think I don't know what I'm talking about. I've helped organize a number of Alcoholics Anonymous chapters. And don't get ideas about treatment centers at hospitals. If it goes on your record that you've had treatment, it can ruin your reputation—and you should know that a woman has to be especially careful about these things."

From time to time, for no apparent reason, Dr. Masserman gave me little gifts. Before my divorce, the only gift he gave me was a book called *Body Dynamics,* on the dynamics of exercise, by Gertrude Enelow. When I began reading it, I discovered that he had written the foreword.

After my return to him in 1979, however, he almost always brought me something special when he came home from traveling abroad. From Russia, he brought me a recording of the Pyanitsky State Russian Folk Choir. In London, he had picked up a recording of Maria Callas and Joan Sutherland singing coloratura arias. I think that on some level, I felt as if he were my daddy, bringing me home a present from a trip—something my own father had never done.

He also gave me professional medical journals written in French, which he'd saved for me from Paris, and he began presenting me with more autographed copies of his own articles. I wasn't impressed by his writing style, which seemed florid and obtuse, but I accepted the articles with appreciation, assuming he was giving them to me because he thought I was smart and interested in his intellectual pursuits.

Usually when he gave me trinkets and other little things, he said he thought they would interest me. At one session, he handed me a large brass coin two times the size of a silver dollar. "You might like this," he said. "I got it at a dinner they gave for me at Northwestern. Why don't you keep it?" The coin had "Northwestern University" engraved on it. I was so naive and hungry for approval that I was thrilled with his thoughtfulness and the special consideration he was giving me. His gifts made me feel as if I were an exceptional patient, a favorite.

In the spring of 1982, Dr. Masserman made it clear that I was one of his favorites when he proposed that I join him and a few other patients on a July trip to Paris, where he would be presiding at the Fourth International Conference of the World Congress for Social Psychiatry—a pioneering organization (originally the American Society for the Study of Social Psychiatry) that he and some of his colleagues had founded in the early 1970s.

Dr. Masserman said that my going to Paris with this group of his patients and friends was a perfect way for me to form new friendships and experience Paris with a group of sociable people. It would be a broadening experience and get me out of my shell. Initially, I refused, but during the next several sessions, he kept telling me how good it would be for me and how important it was for me to join his entourage and to broaden my horizons.

He told me that Mrs. Masserman would be unable to accompany him, and asked, since I would be the only unattached woman in the group, if I would serve as his hostess at a cocktail party he was giving at the Petit Senat of the Palais du Luxembourg. Since I spoke French and he did not, he said he would like me to be his translator as well as his hostess. He said he knew I spoke the language because I had been flown to New York to do three Toyota spots in French, which indicated to him that my accent must be excellent. I was complimented, but the conference was scheduled from July 3 through July 9, and I said I really could not afford that much time away from work. Dr. Masserman reiterated that this was an opportunity I shouldn't miss. All too often, he said, I avoided experiences that would be good for me. He also assured me that the group of his patients on this trip would be free to attend the congress or to go off and do as they pleased, so I would have quite a pleasant time. I told him several times that I didn't have the time or money to do it, although I was flattered he would ask.

But Dr. Masserman would not take no for an answer. He pressured, pleaded, and insisted, until one day, finally, laughing, I said, "Yes, yes, all right, never mind my schedule! I'll go! I'll go!"

Dr. Masserman gave me a World Congress brochure that described the Centre Internationale de Paris, where the July conference would take place.

When it came time to go, I was packed and ready—looking forward to taking time off for a vacation. Dr. Masserman had wanted me to travel with him and his other patients from O'Hare Airport in Chicago to Paris, but I said I would join them en route because I wanted to take advantage of a free stop in New York. I flew to New York City five days early to visit Nancy and John and several other friends, and then, on the second of July, I boarded the plane carrying Dr. Masserman and his group to Paris.

On the airplane, I greeted Dr. Masserman, but it wasn't until we were making our way to the Hotel Meridien that I saw the other patients.

That first morning, Dr. Masserman invited me to have breakfast with him. A patient whom I'll call Gerald Epstein came up to our table, and Dr. Masserman immediately introduced us. I asked Gerald to join us, but his response was strange. He said, "No. I'm married." Later, I met Gerald's wife, Beverly, a lovely woman, tiny, with pale-blue eyes and black hair, who resembled the actress Jennifer O'Neill. She was standoffish at first, but she turned out to be a pleasant and well-informed woman, and we became friends. Shortly after that, I met Diane Greenspan and her teenage daughter, Laura.*

The Epsteins and the Greenspans were crème de la crème in Chicago, and I was delighted to know them. In Chicago, we lived within a few blocks of each other, but we had never crossed paths. In Paris, we quickly slipped into the camaraderie and glamour of the occasion. We all went with Dr. Masserman to a number of events, and we were friendly and confiding with each other. I liked Beverly, Gerald, Diane, and Laura immensely, and we formed a special clique—as if we were Freud's chosen children.

Dr. Masserman seemed quite popular with and well-loved by his colleagues, and as president of the World Congress for Social Psychiatry, he was nearly always at the center of attention. Many people commented that Dr. Masserman was a "renaissance man" and "the main force behind this opening of doors" in the psychoanalytic community. It seemed he was known internationally for his interest in social and political issues, as well as for his irreverence toward psychoanalytic orthodoxy. He felt that psychiatry and psychoanalysis tended to be too compartmentalized, too narrow, and should, instead, open communication and contact throughout the mental health fields. As far back as 1951, he had been a consultant in neuropsychiatry to the secretariat of the U.N. World Health Organization in Geneva. He had traveled widely for the WHO and had given lectures and led seminars for psychiatric and psychoanalytic societies in many South American countries, including Argentina, Chile, Costa Rica, Peru, and Venezuela. He'd also been an official representative of the American Psychiatric Association, the Academy of Psychoanalysis, and the U.S. State Department when he gave lectures in Eastern Europe, Asia, the Middle East, and Africa. While I was his patient, Dr. Masserman had been named honorary president of the 1970 Psychosomatic Congress

*All these patients' names are pseudonyms.

in Buenos Aires and president of the Third Congress of Social Psychiatry in Moscow, Leningrad, Budapest, Zagreb, and Dubrovnik. It was heady stuff.

One evening, ten of us—the five chosen children, plus Dr. Masserman and two other psychiatrists and their wives—went to a concert at Notre Dame and then had a late supper at a chic French restaurant. The food was exquisite and the conversation lively and fascinating. Dr. Masserman clearly was our charismatic center, a magnetic force toward whom we all gravitated. It was a revelation for me. At our psychotherapy and Amytal sessions, Dr. Masserman usually acted subdued and concerned, or annoyed and irritable, but in these social gatherings, he was witty and clever. He joked and laughed and quickly engaged with others, including me. He also called me by my first name, which he had never done before.

As his hostess at the Petit Senat, I stayed by Dr. Masserman's side. He often held my elbow as he steered me where he wanted to go. He beamed when he introduced me, and he seemed to be showing me off to his colleagues. From time to time throughout the evening, I translated for him and spoke on his behalf with several French psychiatrists who knew no English. I was surprised at my skill as a translator, and I must admit that I basked in Dr. Masserman's glow. He was the kingpin of mental health—and he had selected me as his hostess and translator. I was one of the elect—a patient touched by the magic wand, blessed with approval. I was delighted that he had insisted I come on this trip, and I felt he had been right: I was making new friends and seeing Paris from a new perspective.

When Dr. Masserman had some free time, he asked me to go sightseeing with him, and several times, only after I accepted, I learned that just the two of us would be together. One morning, he took me to the top of the Eiffel Tower, and we had lunch on one of those levels above the city. I also went out with Dr. Masserman and Dr. John Carlton, the president-elect of the World Congress, to see the Arc de Triomphe. On another balmy afternoon, Dr. Masserman invited me to the Louvre. When we got there, the doors were locked—we had forgotten it was closed on Tuesdays—so Dr. Masserman suggested we get some *limonade* and relax in the gardens of the Tuileries. We sat across from each other at a little table in the shade and sipped lemonade and I read him historical accounts of Notre Dame and the Louvre from the *Guide Michelin.*

As we were sitting there in the Tuileries, Diane Greenspan walked into the gardens with her daughter, Laura, and looked stunned when she saw us sitting together.

"Oh," she said, "I didn't mean to interrupt."

We both assured her that she hadn't interrupted anything, but she turned red, seemed quite flustered, and left in a hurry. I felt she was jealous. I assumed that she was feeling the same kind of possessive jealousy I felt when I was in his office and noticed that the door to the "Amytal" room was shut.

During this excursion in Paris, I heard bits and pieces about the history of the World Congress for Social Psychiatry. I would later learn that Dr. Masserman was one of many people who had responded to a call made a number of years earlier during an international congress of psychoanalysts in Vienna, where Anna Freud read a brief published correspondence between Sigmund Freud and Albert Einstein called "Why War?" Anna Freud said at the meeting that a real void—perhaps one of the most important omissions in the psychoanalytic field—was the study of political aggression.

Because of Dr. Masserman's pioneering interest in humanistic social psychiatry, his response to Anna Freud's challenge didn't surprise many of his colleagues; while the overwhelming majority of psychiatrists were only person-oriented, Dr. Masserman had always shown interest in social and political problems as well as psychiatric issues. His colleagues responded positively when he proposed the American Society for the Study of Social Psychiatry. The group held its first conference—"Concordance vs. Discordance in Human Behavior"—in 1971. Representatives from all over the world were there to examine economic behavior, cultural change, and intergroup relations. Another pioneering aspect of the gathering was that Dr. Masserman's invitations had gone out not only to psychiatrists, psychoanalysts, and Ph.D.s but also to psychiatric nurses and social workers—people often treated with disdain by the psychiatric community.

One of his colleagues at that conference later said, "This was an extraordinary reaching out. Jules's influence was getting these people together to discuss things afresh and to communicate with each other. He had no systematic theory at that point, he was exploring the subject. He got these people to ask new questions—not just to repeat the same old things—and that's real skill. Most secretaries of state don't have it."

A couple of days before our scheduled departure from Paris, Dr. Masserman told us he had been called away to a quickly formed conference in Warsaw, so we, his Chicago contingent, had to fly home without him. I was high on all the excitement of the trip, and on our flight back to O'Hare on July 9, Beverly and Diane and I made plans to get together in Chicago upon our return.

Back in my own apartment, I made calls to get into the swing of work again, but within a few days of being home, I came down with strep throat and was too sick to leave my bed. One of my friends came over with soup. Because I was scheduled for a therapy session, I called Dr. Masserman to cancel my appointment. He insisted that I come to his office, and even though I told him I was too sick to leave home, he reminded me that he was a physician and could check on me. I bundled up and took a taxi to his office, where he ended up taking my temperature—it was 104 degrees—and putting me to bed in his examining room, where I slept for four hours before going home again. He seemed shocked I was so sick. Perhaps he had thought I was avoiding him—or he genuinely couldn't imagine I was really sick because he himself was so amazingly fit. He flew all over the world and would come back to his office right from the airport for appointments. Nothing seemed to slow him down.

8 At the Heart of the Problem

SEPTEMBER 1, 1982 People sometimes say miracles occur when you least expect them. What happened to me on September 1, 1982, in a dentist's office, still seems like a miracle.

It started as an accident at a big band rehearsal, when I collided with a microphone and cracked a front tooth. It was just a hairline crack—a vertical one and barely visible—but I had to have it repaired. In the mouth of a performer, an "almost invisible" crack can look a mile wide. I also was afraid the tooth was going to break off, so I wanted it fixed immediately.

My dentist was away, but I didn't do my usual thing of picking up the phone to ask Dr. Masserman for advice. Most of my medical recommendations had come from him. I was surrounded by his cronies. My ophthalmologist was in his chamber music group; my internist was his protégé and had an office two floors below his; and my throat specialist was one of his sailing buddies.

Instead of calling him, I headed for my gym, remembering that the last time I'd worked out there, I'd been discussing recent movies with a couple of women in the locker room. After we had laughingly shared our favorite scenes of Dustin Hoffman in *Tootsie,* they had started discussing cosmetic dentistry and a dentist located on North Michigan Avenue who was "just marvelous." When I got to the gym and, fortunately, found my locker room buddies there, they gave me the name of Dr. Robert L. Wheeler, D.D.S., who had been doing cosmetic dentistry since 1955.

At my first appointment—September 1, 1982—Dr. Wheeler came out to the waiting room himself to usher me into his immaculate office. He was a tall, friendly-looking man in his fifties, wearing small spectacles and a freshly washed and starched white jacket. After I sat down in the dental chair, he perched on a stool and asked me to explain how I had cracked the tooth. I explained how I had lost my balance, tipped forward, and grabbed the mike to steady myself.

He listened intently and then examined my teeth. After he had finished a thorough examination and taken an x-ray, he said the front tooth would be no problem, but he'd noticed something else that might be a source of distress. If I didn't mind, he'd like to ask some questions that would let me identify and clarify the problem he had noticed. When I agreed, he asked me to open and close my jaw.

"Do you hear that clicking noise?" he asked.

It was a distinct noise; I couldn't miss it. "It always does that," I said.

"Can you feel it?"

"Yes, I always do."

Dr. Wheeler held up a mirror and let me look into it as he directed me to open and close my jaw. "Do you see how your jaw opens in a snakelike motion instead of opening straight up and down?" he asked. I watched as my jaw opened—snaking over to the side as it did so. I tried but couldn't make it open straight up and down.

"Do you have frequent headaches?" he asked.

I was surprised by his question, but Dr. Wheeler didn't seem at all startled when I told him I had headaches at least six or seven times a week.

"Are they across the front of your forehead?" he asked.

"Yes."

"And are your arms, hands, or fingers ever numb or tingling?"

Again I answered yes.

"Do you ever have upper-back and neck pain?"

"Yes, and it's severe."

"Do you ever experience dizziness when you're singing?"

"Yes! Sometimes I have to hold on to the wall! When I cracked my tooth, it started with feeling dizzy."

"Do you ever feel that you're losing your hearing?"

"Yes; when I'm wearing the headphones, I can't hear the music!"

"How frequently would you say you experience pain in your face, jaw, or ears?"

"I'm almost always in pain!" I practically shouted, mesmerized by these questions.

"Do you feel extremely fatigued after you have had a singing performance?"

"Yes," I said, still stunned.

Dr. Wheeler, who was making check marks and notes on a printed paper fastened to a clipboard, continued to question me about a panoply of my symptoms that over the years had been considered "emotional problems." He asked me about pain in my cheek areas, around my eyes, in the front of my neck and throat. He wondered if I woke up tired and whether my hands were frequently cold or lost their power. He inquired about mood swings and asked if I often felt irritable and whether there were times when I had a total lack of concentration.

What amazed me was that *he* was telling *me* about my problems; I wasn't telling him. I was so astonished that I'm sure my mouth dropped open as I listened and answered—moving along with him as if we were in a detective story, compiling all the clues. I had no idea that any or all of these problems of mine were related.

"Can you tell me anything else about what happens when you open your mouth?" he asked.

I told him about how sometimes, when I was singing, I opened my mouth and my jaw seemed to lock, "stick" or "slip," causing terrible pain to shoot through my face. When I was performing, I said, I didn't know what to expect—I always worried about what kind of pain I would have, what kinds of unreliable sounds would come out of my mouth. Would I get dizzy this time? I didn't think to tell him that I'd gone into therapy about these problems, but I did speak of my anxiety about performing. As I talked, he nodded his head knowingly.

"How do you know so much about these problems?" I asked.

"Because they happen to be a special interest of mine," he said. "All of these problems are symptoms common to a dysfunction of the jaw called TMJ—temporomandibular joint dysfunction—which occurs because the surfaces of the upper and lower teeth don't mesh together properly for some reason."

Dr. Wheeler explained that when the hinges which connect the constantly moving lower jaw to the stable upper jaw are out of place—even if the synchronization is off by a few microns—the result can cause intense headaches and other serious problems. When the surfaces of the teeth don't fit together properly, then the teeth "win" and the jawbone moves out of place to make them fit. The pain results from the jaw opening and closing at the wrong angle, pulling to try to *make* the upper and lower teeth mesh properly. This puts constant strain and enormous pressure on the temporomandibular joint and the muscles surrounding the jaw.

He said research has indicated that a large percentage of the population has TMJ dysfunction, but only about 30 percent of the people who have it experience pain, and about 5 percent of them, like me, have severe pain. The objective signs of TMJ are the clicking of one or both of the TMJ joints, deviation in the way the jaw opens (to the left or the right or both), and a limited ability to open the mouth.

"The fact that your lower jaw is out of alignment affects the way you breathe at times," he said. "It affects the way you open your jaw and how far you can open it. It also alters your airstream and your vocal quality. It even has an impact on your ability to move through space. You see, your body tries to compensate for the dysfunction. What you haven't been aware of is how all the musculature in your head and neck tries to compensate and, as a result, makes you move ineffectively."

Dr. Wheeler explained that the lower jaw moves constantly as we talk, chew, and swallow. In twenty-four hours, we open and close our jaws approximately 2,500 times. We swallow once every sixty seconds—or 1,440 times in twenty-four hours. In the act of swallowing, we put enormous pressure on the jaw and impact the teeth against each other substantially. Stress in a social environment only compounds the problem.

"When you're under stress," he said, "you can't go around slugging people, so you clench your teeth, which just adds to the pressure on the mandibular joint and makes the muscles more tense.

"Singers are often dramatically affected by this dysfunction, because you not only use your jaw for all the normal talking, chewing, and swallowing, but you exacerbate it even further because you have to open your mouth wider for singing and you need to articulate words very rapidly. You're concerned about resonance, vocal quality, airstream. And it takes you more time to open and close the lower jaw when you have a dysfunction.

"As a singer, you have to concentrate on how to make your jaw move faster, and that's a real detriment to performance. It's sort of like the law of physics—one object can occupy only one space at one time.

The brain works the same way. If you're thinking about how to create a note, you cannot simultaneously think: How am I going to get my jaw to work straight?

"It looks to me as if you've been in a no-win situation," he said. "You have an extreme dysfunction—and I suspect that in your case, as in others like it, the brain is unable to get consistent messages to the nerves and muscles that are involved in the singing process, and so you have constant interruption of the proprioceptive feedback that allows the brain to interpret information."

I was stunned. I said I'd been having these problems for years, and they made me feel crazy. I told him my internist had told me it was "a case of nerves" and that everyone else, including my psychiatrist, had also told me these things were "neurotic" or "psychosomatic." I told him that I'd gone into therapy in the first place because I was so nervous about these problems ruining my career.

Dr. Wheeler nodded sympathetically, then said firmly, "Well, you can rest assured that this is a *physical* problem. But it's a physical problem that often *causes* emotional problems. It's a clear case of cause and effect. If you have lots of pain, you have trouble coping with everyday events because it takes a lot of energy simply to cope with the pain. If I have a person with TMJ pain, and coping with the pain absorbs fifty units of energy, that leaves her fifty units short for dealing with the rest of her life. This alone can lead to psychological or social breakdowns, irritability, short temper, and worse. This is exacerbated by people telling you the pain isn't real, it's all in your imagination."

Dr. Wheeler then astounded me further. He said, "You also have to keep in mind that we live in a male chauvinistic society, where people in the marketplace and men who are doctors tend to think women are crazy anyway. When a woman comes in and says, 'I have these terrible headaches, and my neck hurts,' and the doctor can't see any visible anatomical reason, he assumes she's stressed or crazy and says, 'Maybe we should medicate you with some Valium or you should see a therapist.'"

Until that moment, I had *never* heard a man say anything about sexism or chauvinism. When Betty Friedan or other women said this sort of thing, I always thought they sounded so angry that it didn't get through to me. Hearing a man—and a doctor—say it shook me up and jarred me into realizing the truth of what he was saying. I didn't realize at the time that the way I dismissed women and believed men was a dramatic sign of my own unexamined sexism and showed how I had accepted the status quo without question.

Dr. Wheeler said that he had handled more than three hundred cases of TMJ and that the vast majority of those patients were women. For some reason, perhaps because women have less collagen tissue than males, 80 percent of the people treated for TMJ are women. And most of those women—before they learn they have TMJ dysfunction—have been told that their pain is neurotic or psychosomatic.

"Usually, if we take chronic-pain patients, they've adjusted their life-styles to the pain, and they've gone through personality changes," he said. "But I've seen that when, by virtue of treatment, we eliminate the pain in these patients, they self-correct. People can think clearly again, they can perform more efficiently. They're not having to compensate constantly. So there's no need for therapy.

"I have a patient, a nurse. She was working in a hospital and had an unwieldy patient she was moving, and somehow she was hit in the left jaw and it broke. She was put back together, but afterward she had headaches, things that couldn't be explained. She was told they'd have to operate again. So they operated the second time, and she became worse. She kept bouncing from doctor to doctor.

"During the course of passing through all these doctors, she became unemployed, she became insecure, she became psychiatrically unstable and underwent treatment, and she became very depressed—which is not unusual with TMJ patients.

"I was doctor number twenty-four. She wasn't the standard TMJ patient—and I can offer a surgical patient only 50 percent of the improvement I can expect of a nonsurgical patient—but I treated her. It is now about a year and a half later. She is out of her depression, she's feeling better about herself. She's considering reeducating herself because she feels she cannot enter the nursing profession again."

Dr. Wheeler told me he didn't believe in injections, drugs, or surgery to correct the TMJ dysfunction. "I believe we've been created to function *comfortably*," he said, "and the purpose of noninvasive treatment is to get the jaw back on track with its innate neurological program for normal, relaxed function."

Dr. Wheeler told me that after all the cases of TMJ he's handled, it still isn't possible simply to look and figure out the correct position for someone's jaw. He showed me a hard pink plastic device, which he called a splint. It looked like a small retainer in the shape of a turtle shell. He said the mouth splint gives structural support for the teeth and jaws and slowly coaxes the jaw back into its natural, physiologically correct and comfortable position. Each patient requires her own unique splint that gets her back into alignment.

I signed up for a splint on my first day in his office, and within a month I had been x-rayed, had plaster casts taken of my upper and lower teeth, and been fitted with a little pink splint that fit securely up against the roof of my mouth and changed my bite when I shut my jaw. Dr. Wheeler said the x-rays indicated some kind of severe trauma to the jaw. I remembered a story I'd been told, but only vaguely remembered, about how, when I was young, I'd been hit hard in the face with an icicle the size of a baseball bat. My face had been so badly swollen and bruised that I'd stayed out of school for a week.

After I'd worn the splint for only four days, I couldn't believe the difference. I felt more relaxed and confident and had an amazing feeling of well-being. Within three weeks, my voice teacher had asked me to sing Mozart's "Allelujah" at his church. It was as if, all of a sudden, I was a new person in there. When I wore my splint, my mouth opened up easily and my voice had a ring to it that it didn't have before. I had more room in my throat, more tone quality and resonance.

I was so thrilled with the enormity of the differences, with the further possibilities that existed for me if I corrected this condition, that I dutifully wore my splint day in and day out, even though it sometimes made my teeth ache or felt uncomfortable. Dr. Wheeler often remolded the splint, sometimes as often as twice a week, to accommodate the changes taking place as my jaw slowly found its way back into its natural position.

Within six months after I began wearing the splint, the hoarseness I'd complained about for so many years had disappeared. The quality of my voice was different, and Dr. Wheeler explained that as my jaw worked naturally again, my throat muscles could relax and the chambers in my throat could open. Resonance balance is related to the various tubes and chambers in the throat and nasal passages, so enlarging the size of the chambers was changing the acoustics and the quality of the sound that came out.

Even more wonderful was that the improvements in my voice and my ability to perform with ease didn't go away. On a Monday, I could sing certain scales or exercises or hit particular notes easily, and by Friday, I could do them the same way. I'd try a song in the evening and attempt it again the next morning, and my throat was still open and the sound was consistent. I stopped losing my voice, and I began to trust that my capabilities weren't suddenly going to leave me. The voice, the tone, the quality, were not going to disappear.

"As your throat has relaxed, your throat muscles have probably become larger as well," Dr. Wheeler explained, "and so the efficiency of your total machine is much improved. Eventually, it will require even less energy for the same performance."

By the time I'd worn the splint for a year, all the headaches, neck aches, backaches, and facial pain that had plagued me for so long were gone. When I worked in the studios with headphones, I could hear the music with no problem whatsoever, and I never got dizzy unless I happened to be dancing and spinning in circles! Over the next two years, Dr. Wheeler rebuilt nine of my back teeth so that my jaw got the structural support it needed from the teeth, and I wore the splint only if I was tired or particularly stressed.

After I met Dr. Wheeler and was so excited to discover the source of my headaches, dizziness, and all, I told Dr. Masserman what I had learned about the TMJ dysfunction. He said he understood "the problems with the mandible" and commented that "this dentist sounds like a competent person," giving me his permission to proceed with treatment. I didn't bother to tell him I'd already begun the work and wasn't waiting for permission. Since he gave the clear impression that he didn't think TMJ dysfunction or treatment was very relevant, I took his response as some kind of cue and didn't mention Dr. Wheeler again for quite some time.

Many months later, however, when I was sitting across Dr. Masserman's desk from him, talking about the amount of quality work I was getting, how thrilled I was to be performing it and how happy it made me feel to be pain-free, I blurted out, "I thank the good Lord that I found Dr. Wheeler."

Dr. Masserman turned practically maroon, and said furiously, "Just get one thing straight. That is purely a dental matter! You still have plenty of emotional problems, and don't you forget it!"

I didn't understand Dr. Masserman's resentful, almost jealous outburst. It's hard now to believe that I let him talk that way to me, but at the time, I was frightened of his anger and extremely concerned that he might threaten to cut off my supply of Amytal again. I never thought of myself as addicted, but somehow I knew I needed the Amytal too much to risk alienating my source. So I started keeping my mouth shut about Dr. Wheeler when I was talking to Dr. Masserman. But I praised Dr. Wheeler to my voice teacher and to other singers, and it was clear to me that my life was different because of his intervention. After so many years, it was extraordinary to be free of pain.

By the time 1984 rolled around, most of my old anxiety about singing was gone. My jaw was in near-perfect alignment, and my mouth had literally opened up. I sang better than I had ever sung before and began to reap the benefits professionally. During the summer, I did some especially rewarding concerts—and didn't experience that old, deadening fatigue afterward. I sang a lot of jazz and performed two recitals—one a collection of German lieder and the other a Debussy program, including a song cycle called *Le Balcon*—for a master class at Northeastern Illinois University.

I later performed two hours of French pop music during a reception introducing a Degas exhibition at the Art Institute, and in addition, I was invited to join the faculty of the oldest music conservatory in Chicago, the American Conservatory, where I would give private instruction in vocal jazz. This was a tremendous honor, and I knew now that I was up to doing it and doing it well. Two years before, I wouldn't have been so sure of myself.

In the meantime, Dr. Masserman suggested that I stop studying voice with the teacher I'd been working with for several years. He said he himself could advise me on my music. I was surprised. I knew Dr. Masserman disliked pop music and pop singers. Billie Laird told me that every time she had pop music on the radio, he would come out, frown, and change the station to classical music. I didn't imagine that Dr. Masserman could advise me in an area of music that he found so distasteful, so I didn't ever consider leaving my voice teacher. I did, however, bring in some of the music I had written and some recordings I'd made, and he gave me some of his own music, which I thought was so inferior that it embarrassed me even to see it.

Dr. Masserman gave me a critique of my compositions, saying he thought my melodies were "simple but adequate." He reiterated a suggestion he'd made earlier—that I should marry, so my husband could support me. That way, he said, I could satisfy my desire for music by volunteering to do things—such as singing in a church choir, which would be an appropriate use of my talents. He said he thought it was "too hard" on me to have to earn my own living.

If I'd had any consistent self-esteem, I would have walked out of his office then and there and never gone back. But of course, I didn't. Instead of holding onto my recent successes and feeling angered by Dr. Masserman's sexist remarks, I felt cowed and defeated. I even went so far as to think seriously about joining a church choir.

I maintained my regular appointments with Dr. Masserman, both for my therapy sessions and for the Amytal, and I always had my pre-session sessions with Billie Laird, who over the years had become a good friend. Billie, who'd never married, had a soft spot for children and was passionate about people and political causes. From photographs, I'd "watched" the two boys she'd raised grow from toddlers into handsome teenagers.

Billie, who was sixty-three, had always worked extremely hard for Dr. Masserman. But for quite a while, I had been noticing that her attitude toward her boss was changing. These days she was quite tense in the office. She was usually annoyed with Dr. Masserman, and she often complained about being overworked, which she was. She also was furious that Dr. Masserman underpaid her and wouldn't give her medical insurance. When Billie was sick, Masserman would give her shots or medication, but she had no money to go see any other doctor. She needed to have dental work done, but she didn't make enough money to pay for it.

Billie began to suggest to me almost every time we talked that I really didn't need a psychiatrist anymore. "This is so expensive, Barb," she said in June of '84. "I really don't think you need to be coming here. I think you should quit."

Whenever I set up an Amytal session with her, she frowned and shook her head. She told me several times she didn't think I needed the Amytal. Of course, I suspect now that she well may have discovered what was going on during Dr. Masserman's Amytal interviews and was trying to warn me without coming out and saying it. But I'll never know for sure.

Billie Laird died of a heart attack at home in her sleep on July 7, the day before she was scheduled to go on a vacation. Diane Greenspan called me, very upset about Billie's death, and I joined her and Gerald Epstein, who had also been with us in Paris, and went to Billie's wake. We learned from Bette, Billie's twin sister, that Dr. Masserman had paid the expenses for Billie's wake and funeral but refused to attend either one. At the time, we commented that the poor man must have been too broken up to make an appearance.

At my next appointment, a dark-haired, attractive woman named Peggy Karas was sitting at Billie Laird's desk. All traces of Billie's papers and ashtrays and presence were gone from the gleaming surface of the desk. A few papers were stacked neatly in one corner of the desk, and the appointment book was carefully placed in the center. Seeing the tidy order of things gave me a pang of grief and longing for Billie. Just then, Dr. Masserman came out of his office and engaged in some cheerful banter with Peggy before ushering me inside. He told me Miss Karas was learning his office procedure quite quickly, and he hoped I would become good friends with her, as I had with Miss Laird. He said nothing else about Billie, and after our usual exchanges, he asked me if I thought some Amytal would help us get to the heart of things. Of course, that's what I'd been angling for all along, so in perfect agreement, we set up yet another Amytal interview.

I knew I was dependent on Amytal, but I never suspected I was addicted. After Dr. Masserman left for his late-summer sailing vacation on the *Naiad,* I was surprised at how much I thought about Amytal and craved it. I wanted my Amytal with a fierce hunger—not unlike a wild craving for a cigarette or a candy bar or an ice cream cone. I sometimes felt socked with such a strong desire for it that I thought I could practically kill to get it. But I had no idea that was addiction. All I knew was that Amytal wasn't like anything else—not like sex, not like liquor, not like sleep. Somehow it was absolute happiness. Complete escape.

During that summer—in spite of my undetected Amytal addiction— I was always able to pull it together for a show. In fact, I never missed one performance with any band I was booked to work with. I especially loved big-band work and the spontaneity of performing live, sur-rounded onstage by brass and woodwinds and percussion, with that gorgeous sound coming at me from all around. It made me feel more alive and focused than anything else I did.

By myself at home, however, I used up all the pot that Tony had left behind. I went out to lunch by myself and had two martinis. At dinner, I had wine and brandy. I was missing my Amytal. About a week before Dr. Masserman's return, I remembered that a new psychiatrist had taken over the empty office in Dr. Masserman's suite. Dr. Victor M. Uribe had been trained by Dr. Masserman at Northwestern University, and I had seen him once when I was waiting for an injection and Dr. Uribe popped into the office to have a word with Dr. Masserman. I was already under the covers on the daybed, but the door was open and our eyes had met.

I phoned Dr. Uribe, thinking that since he knew about the Amytal, he could give me some to hold me until Dr. Masserman's return. Dr. Uribe said he would be glad to talk to me if I came in, but he would not give me Amytal. He asked me why I wanted it, but otherwise he didn't even want to *discuss* Amytal with me. I had no interest in talking; I only wanted Amytal.

When Dr. Masserman returned, I told him I felt as if I were going to jump out of my skin.

"You're probably somewhat nervous about starting your teaching at the conservatory, aren't you?" he said.

"That's part of it, I guess."

"Yes, and I think perhaps you're ready now to have what we call in psychiatry an 'Aha' experience—when one suddenly begins to realize that his way of thinking is no longer bringing him any rewards."

I sat listening to Dr. Masserman and realizing on some "Aha" level that we were once again playing the game of words he required for me to get my Amytal. With the newfound confidence I had gained from having my TMJ corrected, I felt surer of my own perceptions. I thought: Dr. Masserman knows exactly what I want. He *knows* I want the Amytal. Why doesn't he just give me the Amytal and get it over with?

"I don't know," I said out loud, playing the game. "That could be it. And maybe I'll feel better tomorrow after I've had my first day of teaching."

I paused. Then I said, "But I think maybe I'd get somewhere with some Amytal. What do you think?"

"Yes," he said. "I think this is just the time you would benefit from looking into yourself. Why don't you come in on Friday?"

We made the appointment for 7:30 A.M., Friday, September 21, but Peggy Karas called and asked me to change it to 9:15. I thought: Oh, shoot! I have to make Xeroxes and I wanted to get out of there by three and miss the rush-hour traffic. With a later appointment, I wouldn't get out of there until four-thirty. But of course, I agreed; I'd do anything for Amytal. I hung up feeling despondent about Billie and sad that I couldn't talk to her anymore. I didn't like Peggy Karas, and I didn't like her taking Billie's place.

9 *Medical Treason*

AFTER THE AMYTAL: SEPTEMBER 21, 1984   After Dr. Masserman blinked the light on and off, I'd usually lie there for another half hour, but not this time. Not when I knew what he had done to me. Not when the repulsive stench of his body odor and after-shave lotion wafted up from my own shoulders and made me feel like gagging. Not today, not now, not ever again. As soon as the door was closed, I sat up to see whether I was steady enough to stand. I had to get out of there and get out fast, but to do so, I had to walk through his office. If I went out the door to the hallway, he would wonder what was wrong—and he might suspect I *knew*. I had to act normal and leave through his office. But I couldn't think how to do it. I couldn't think.

I stood up and wobbled from side to side until I could maintain my balance. I was shaking like a limp leaf in a heavy wind, but never mind. I managed to fasten my bra, pull on my black T-shirt and my jeans. I sat heavily on the chair, pulled on my socks, and laced up my sneakers with trembling fingers.

I grabbed my windbreaker from the back of the chair and started to gather up the copies of vocal charts for big-band arrangements and the loose sheet music I'd brought along to photocopy. I kept dropping the music. I thought: I can never pull this off. I can never get out of here looking normal. I tried to count backward from ten and willed myself to calm down. I inhaled and exhaled deeply. I put my purse strap on my shoulder and took several more deep breaths. Then I knocked on the door that led to Dr. Masserman's office.

"Oh, you're up already!" he said in an uncharacteristically loud voice, looking surprised and agitated. "Aren't you a little shaky? Why, you usually sleep longer than this. I did give you a lighter dose than usual, but don't you think you're too groggy? Don't you need more time to wake up?"

From somewhere outside myself, I saw my face smiling what seemed a rather normal smile except for my trembling lip, and I said, "I got up fast because I was so hungry." I noticed his fingers twitching. Was he agitated because he'd just had intercourse with me or because he was wondering whether I knew?

"Oh, well, that's all right," he said, his voice still sounding odd. "I was just about to prepare some lunch. Why don't you stay and have some lunch with me?"

"Oh, no!" I said in a cheerful, little-girl voice I couldn't control. "Thanks, though. I think I really need some fresh air. I have to Xerox this music, and then I think I'll walk a bit before I get a sandwich."

He asked me if I was going to be able to get home all right, and I assured him that I would.

"Well, you be careful, now," I heard him say, as if from a vast distance. "Be sure to take a cab—I don't think you're too steady. And promise to call me as soon as you get home."

Never before had he asked me to call him when I got home.

I watched and heard myself go through the motions of a rational exchange. I said I would call, but it might take a while for me to copy all this music. I told him not to worry, I'd take a cab and be fine.

He said, good, then, he'd see me next week.

I watched myself float toward the door, open it, and close it behind me. I prepared myself to say goodbye to Peggy Karas, but she wasn't there.

On the way out, I automatically picked up the key to the ladies' room, as I always did, and sailed effortlessly down the hallway. When I neared the elevators, though, I stopped and thought: I can't do this. What should I do? I remembered that my internist, Dr. Coleman Seskind, was only two floors down. Maybe he could tell me what to do. I stood in the hallway long enough to have actually made the trip down three floors to the ladies' room and up again. Then I sneaked into Dr. Masserman's empty reception room and put down the key and got out of there fast.

I drifted into the elevator, pushed "12," and then, inexplicably, began to laugh. I thought: What a joke on me this is. What a joke. What a joke. I choked on my laughter, which turned quickly to sobs, and I could feel my face pulling and puffing from the avalanche of feeling that overwhelmed me.

Headed toward Suite 1206, I placed one foot in front of the other and tried to think about Dr. Seskind, Dr. Masserman's protégé, who had been my internist for four years. He seemed to be an excellent doctor, but could I trust him? What if he tells Masserman, and Masserman tries to kill me? I thought: Well, Dr. Seskind is a real professional, and he's taken the Hippocratic oath. I have to chance it. I opened the door. Later he would say he'd noted in his records it was twelve-fifteen. He was sitting behind the receptionist's desk, eating a sandwich.

I walked in and called out, "Hi! Anybody home?" Apparently my chirpy, cheerful facade was carrying the day, even though I could hear my heart thumping wildly. "I just dropped by and thought I could have a quick conference with you if you have some free time."

In the privacy of his office, Dr. Seskind adjusted his white doctor's jacket and asked me, "Well, what's up?" He was a small, plump man with a receding hairline, and he looked concerned. I said, "I was upstairs, and . . . well, Dr. Masserman . . . you see, when I woke up from the Sodium Amytal he had given me, he was screwing me."

Dr. Seskind said, "You mean having intercourse with you?"

"Yes," I said. "Intercourse."

Then I said, "I know this is true, but I don't want it to be true. Could you help me figure out if there is the slightest chance I could have been hallucinating? Because I hope I was hallucinating. I would prefer to be wrong about this."

"Barbara, just tell me quickly—don't think, just answer: Were you hallucinating?"

"No."

"Then I want you to get over to Dr. Abel's as fast as you can. Dr. Abel is your gynecologist, right?" I nodded. "You're going to want evidence, and semen disappears very quickly," he said. "I'll call his nurse right now. Go grab a cab, and I'll tell his nurse you have to see him at once."

Dr. Stuart Abel's office was only twelve blocks away, but the noonday traffic moved like sludge. As the taxi inched its way along the streets, I bit my fist, debating whether it would be faster for me to jump out and run or stay in the cab. I was afraid of making the wrong decision, so I stayed in the cab. When it stopped outside the doctor's building, I shoved a ten-dollar bill at the cabbie and bolted up two flights of stairs rather than wait for an elevator. Dr. Abel met me at his door, a frantic expression on his face.

"Barbara, Dr. Seskind called me," he said. "This is a police matter. You must get over to the emergency room at Olson Pavilion as fast as you can. Run. It's only a block and a half. Don't wait for a cab. You've lost so much time, just run like hell. When you get there, tell the first person you see that you've been raped, and they'll take you before anybody else, even if there's a line around the block. I don't know whether there will still be any evidence, but do it. Barbara, I'm so sorry this has happened. I'm so sorry."

I ran the short distance to Northwestern Memorial Hospital's Olson Emergency and walked around a line of waiting patients. A tall, dark-skinned woman sitting behind the counter looked up, aware that I had jumped the line. As quietly as I could, I whispered, "I've been raped." It was the first time I'd said those words, and they made me feel cold all over.

The receptionist was on her feet before I finished speaking. Then she was leading me down a hall, grabbing a gurney, and motioning to a nurse. I lay down on the gurney and they pushed me into a vacant examining area. The air seemed freezing cold, and I was shaking violently by the time the nurse brought blankets. As she tucked the covers around me, I felt so ashamed that I could hardly look at her. I was thinking: What am I doing here? I'd rather go home and get bloody drunk than go through this!

I had just closed my eyes and tried to calm the pounding of my heart, when a man suddenly standing beside me told me he was Dr. Marshall. He introduced me to two more nurses and asked me how I was feeling. Was I warm enough? Comfortable? I told him I hadn't gone to the bathroom since 9:00 A.M., and I really had to go, but he explained that I couldn't until after I had been examined.

Everyone was calm, hushed, very kind. Dr. Marshall explained that the hospital had contacted the police department, and that by law they could do nothing until the police arrived. He said they had also located a "rape victim advocate," who would be down in just a few minutes. "She'll be with you at all times to make sure you're treated well by the police when they question you," he said kindly.

I felt miles away from Dr. Marshall's face, and I was surprised at the warmth of his hand when he patted my arm. I thought: This is a dream. I'm going to wake up any minute now. What does this dream mean? Then I thought: No, it's not a dream. You woke up in Dr. Masserman's office, remember? You went to Dr. Seskind's and you went to Dr. Abel's and you ran here. Remember? You were looking for shelter. You were looking for someone to tell you what to do, and now you're doing what they told you to do.

Soon the advocate for rape victims came in. She was a plump young woman with a friendly and sympathetic expression on her face. Her voice was warm, reassuring, and compassionate. I thought maybe she was really an angel. She held my hand and told me her name was Jeannie Patrick;* she'd been raped too, so she knew how awful this experience was for me. She told me there was counseling at the hospital. I said I didn't feel like talking about it. "You've got to talk to begin your healing," she said. "If you bottle it up, it will come back and make you sick. You really need to talk and talk and talk and talk some more, because that's the way you'll get better. Get it out."

Jeannie stayed right beside me when a plainclothes detective named Jack Kelly and two uniformed patrolmen arrived about half an hour later. Detective Kelly, who seemed gentle as he asked questions, gave me his card, which showed me he was in Unit Area 1 of the Violent Crimes Detectives Division. He assigned me the case number F 358809. The case number made everything seem real, believable: This *is* happening.

Dr. Marshall took cervical smears and vaginal specimens as well as blood samples, which he turned over to the police for the crime lab. The policemen stayed in the back of the room, and when Dr. Marshall finished, an Officer Fleming, who had been standing in the corner, stepped up next to me in the cubicle and said, "Ma'am?" He was wearing his patrolman's uniform, brass buttons and all, and I hated him immediately, even before he began interrogating me. Just his standing there sent a chill down my backbone. "Ma'am," he said, starting his interrogation, "are you sure you weren't with your boyfriend, and you just got mad at him?"

That made me so angry I couldn't think of a thing to say. It was hard for me even to get my mouth open. But after I had finally explained what had happened—it came out in fits and starts through my em-

*This is not her real name.

barrassment—he asked me if I wanted to press criminal charges, and I said I didn't know. I said I'd have to talk to my lawyer. I couldn't think; I realized later that at the time, I had no *plan;* I was just trying to get through each one of these excruciating minutes.

In a caustic, disbelieving voice, Officer Fleming asked, "You mean to tell me you were knocked unconscious by this drug, ah, Sodium Amytal?"

"Yes."

"And this psychiatrist was raping you when you came to—is that right?"

I was getting even more angry, but I answered, "Yes, sir."

"And you say you've been going to this psychiatrist for about fifteen years for psychiatric treatment?" The contempt and ridicule in his voice made my charges sound ludicrous, impossible, as if I had to be totally crazy.

"Yes, I have."

"Now, wouldn't it be better to assume you might have been dreaming all this?"

"No," I said. "I was *not* dreaming."

"Where were you last night, ma'am?"

"I was at home."

"With a boyfriend, maybe, ma'am?"

"No, I was alone."

"And you're saying that you couldn't have been dreaming this?"

"I was *not* dreaming this," I said, feeling like a little animal, hissing at him.

"But you could have been, couldn't you, ma'am?"

"Yes, I suppose I *could have been,* but I wasn't."

"Thank you, ma'am."

I felt like shouting at him. Did he think a woman would go to the hospital—get herself wheeled in to be poked and prodded and disbelieved and totally humiliated, with people asking insulting and irrelevant questions that had nothing to do with anything, and not even allowed to pee—just to have a little fun with these guys or waste their time?

I turned to Detective Kelly. "I wasn't dreaming," I said.

"No, it's all right," he said, patting my hand. "It's all right."

I turned to Jeannie Patrick, who was still holding my left hand and squeezing it. "I wasn't dreaming," I said.

"I know you weren't," she said.

The doctor gave me ampicillin, along with a stabilizer of some sort, to guard against venereal disease and advised me to come back in six weeks for a booster shot. It was about five o'clock in the afternoon by then. I was sure my bladder was going to burst when Dr. Marshall finally told me I could go to the bathroom.

Just before I left the hospital, Jeannie Patrick gave me a hug and handed me a card with her work and home numbers on it. "Remember, Barbara," she said, "you need to talk about this to other people. Just do it. Talk to anyone who will listen. And please call me if you want to. Anytime."

By the time I found a cab and got into it, I'd started flipping out. I didn't even know where I was. It occurred to me that Dr. Masserman had died. I put my arms around myself and rocked back and forth, saying, "Oh, a great man died today. A great man died. Dr. Jules H. Masserman died. Now I must go on without him. What a pity he's gone! Now I'll have to always remember the things he has taught me, because he's gone, he's gone, he's gone!"

At home, I stayed nuts. I made myself a nightcap of gin and frozen lemonade and crawled into bed with all my clothes and my shoes on and rocked myself back and forth between sips of my drink. When that glass was finished, I got up and went to the kitchen for another bracer, and then went back to bed, got up and paced, went back to bed again. Finally, I got up and took a shower to get the dirty smells off my body. I paced, and then I took another shower. I didn't want to remember what had happened. I turned on the television, and they had a rerun of *Hill Street Blues* on one channel and an old Jackie Gleason and Art Carney *Honeymooners* show on another, but I couldn't concentrate on anything, so I turned it off. I wanted to call a friend, but it was too late, and I felt so crazy that I wasn't even sure I could sound coherent.

As the hands of the clock inched their way toward dawn, the reality of what had happened started sinking in, and it made me so furious that I started kicking the bed. I kicked and kicked until I hurt my toes and fell back onto the bed, crying. I couldn't believe I had wasted all those years with Dr. Masserman. I leapt out of bed and rummaged in my chest of drawers until I found the large brass coin Dr. Masserman had given me with "Northwestern University" on it. I ceremoniously carried it out to the incinerator chute and threw it down. There was silence as it fell, and I heard a ping when it landed at the bottom. I hoped it would get covered with garbage and burn and melt and turn to ash.

By daybreak, my mind was going over and over what had happened and accepting the reality of it. The great man had *not* died; he had raped me. I still couldn't bear to think that it had happened more than once. I wouldn't let myself consider that possibility yet.

Mainly, I wanted to call my friend, mentor, and attorney, Dick Shelton. But it was only 5:00 A.M., and I knew that the day before, Dick had started a home chemotherapy treatment for bone cancer. A nurse-specialist was to have hooked him up to a portable machine that would allow him to be completely mobile. Dick Shelton was a wonderful athlete, and it was hard to imagine him sick. He was the one who had taught me to ski when I was scared to death of it. He would ski backward himself as he coaxed me down the slope: "Come on, Barb, you can do it, you can ski!"

I waited until seven-thirty, and then I called. When I heard Mary's friendly, familiar voice, I tried to stay calm. I asked how Dick was feeling and whether he could handle some serious business.

"What is it? You don't sound so good."

"I woke up from Amytal yesterday and Dr. Masserman was having sex with me," I said, starting to cry.

"Barb, say that again?"

I did, and Mary said, "Get over here right now. I'll put on the coffee."

When I got there, Dick, who towered above me, wrapped his thin arms around me and smiled down with his lopsided grin. The sight of his smile, his freckles, and his wonderful fringe of red hair was so welcome that I instantly felt more sane. I was worried about his health, but he said he was feeling terrific, even though a tiny machine in the pocket of his jacket was feeding chemicals into his body through a needle strapped to his arm as we spoke.

When he and Mary and I sat down to talk, over Mary's lovely china teacups, I felt the comfort and familiarity of our relationship. Dick asked me to tell him everything.

When I finished talking, Dick said angrily, "This is unbelievable. The guy is famous. He's practically a celebrity. How could he be so stupid? Jesus, how old is he anyway?"

"Seventy-nine."

"He's nuts," Dick said. "He's got to be nuts!"

"Why did he do this to me?"

"No, Barbara, that's not the question," he said. "The question is, what are *you* going to do about it? Are you going to go after him?"

"I think I want my money back."

"Damn right you do—and you're going to get it! I'm going to find you an attorney right now. I'll find you a good personal-injury attorney, and you're going to get that son of a bitch.

"Now, as soon as you think you can do it, I want you to sit down and write out everything you can remember—every single detail. Don't wait too long, or you'll start to forget."

I protested; I couldn't possibly write it all down.

"Yes you can. Wait a couple of days, until you've calmed down, but do it. I want you to be prepared to answer everything. You're going to get him, Barbara. I know you can do it."

A wave of grief and outrage hit me. I felt so betrayed. So stupid. How could he do this? I started to cry again, but Dick diverted my attention by focusing on a more immediate issue. "Are you singing tonight?"

I told him I was supposed to sing, but I didn't see how I could. He told me that I could do it, I just needed to go home and get some sleep. "Sing tonight," he said, "sleep tomorrow, and come over tomorrow night for supper."

It was 10:00 A.M. when I walked home and crawled into bed. I tried to sleep but couldn't. I tossed and turned until it seemed ridiculous to stay prone, so I went into the kitchen and finished off the last of the gin and lemonade I'd been drinking all night. Then I dressed and went to the store, trying to figure out what would make me sleep. I decided margaritas and some heavy Mexican food should put me under. I was right; after half a quart of margarita mix and an enchilada dinner, I slept for about five hours.

I woke up just in time for a soak in the tub before dressing for work. I could hardly stand the idea of putting on any of my sexy performance outfits. I wished I owned a tent or something else that would totally hide my body. I put on the loosest outfit I could find—a pale-gray satin skirt and a matching jacket lightly beaded with pearls and copper-colored sequins. I had never been so exhausted or looked so terrible for a performance. My face was puffy from crying and drinking and lack of sleep; my head throbbed, and I hurt all over. I was going to show up for work looking like a monstrosity; the band would take one look at me and go into hiding.

As I tried to cover my splotchy face with makeup, I kept replaying what Dr. Masserman had said the previous morning as he was filling the vial of his syringe with Amytal. "This makes me think about the peaceful feeling it gives me to sail," he'd said in his soothing, hypnotic voice. "You know, there's nothing like sailing. It's so tranquil and healing, it gives you a whole new perspective on life. Now you're going to be able to take a little sailing trip of your own. The only difference is that you'll do it all right here."

I had watched as my blood entered the tube of the syringe and mixed with the Amytal solution. My body had relaxed with pleasure as the doctor lingeringly, almost imperceptibly, began to push the plunger back in and slowly inject the solution, all the while talking softly and reassuringly. "You've been troubled lately," he'd said, "but now you are nice and safe, and you can talk to someone you trust, someone who is your friend. And while we talk about what's troubling you, you can relax completely and realize that the world isn't such a bad place after all."

"Tell me about trusting someone who is my friend and the world not being such a bad place!" I screamed now. "You hypocrite!"

I slammed my makeup case shut, fastened my jacket, and ran out, trying to contain the tears that seemed to gush out so easily. I got to the banquet room at the Palmer House on time and looked nervously at the guys warming up. I felt like hell, but I was lucky. I had forgotten it wasn't a big-band night. I wouldn't have to see or deal with all sixteen guys. Avoiding sixteen musicians just isn't possible. We'd all known each other a long time, and joking around was the way we worked together. Tonight it would be just me and four pieces—piano, bass, drums, and guitar, a pretty quiet group—and we would be playing for an Illinois Bar Association convention, which shouldn't be too demanding. Additional good luck was that we would be performing in an elegant and rather dark banquet room, where I wouldn't have to face the glare of a spotlight.

I must not have looked quite as bad as I thought, because when I got up to start singing, none of my band buddies said, "What's wrong with you?" That helped me relax a little, even though everything seemed totally unreal and I knew I wasn't normal. I was so turned off and tuned out that I could barely hear myself singing the lyrics of an exquisite Brazilian piece, Jobim's "If You Never Come to Me." When the piano man went into Jimmy Van Heusen's most porcelain love ballad, "But Beautiful," I heard my voice lifting through, as if it were disconnected from the rest of me.

Fortunately, I found a long, soft sofa in the corner of an enormous ladies' room, where I could curl up during my breaks and try to calm myself. None of the guys seemed bothered by my quick disappearances, since I always returned on time. After I got back from our biggest intermission, one of the lawyers requested a Chuck Berry or Little Richard rocker, and we broke into a twangy, raucous version of the old favorite "Johnny B. Goode." The lawyers loved it. It looked as if the entire bar association was on its feet, dancing, clapping, whooping it up. Quite clearly, these lawyers were ready to party. We turned up the sound system for "Rock Around the Clock," and for the rest of the night, I let myself loose.

I turned up my own volume and belted out those songs so loudly I was practically screaming. The crowd yelled and clapped with us as we jammed on songs by Elvis, Bob Seger, and more Chuck Berry. The singing and boogying to "Old Time Rock 'n Roll," "Blue Suede Shoes," and "Twist and Shout" brought me alive again, and in a piercing moment of clarity, I laughed out loud at a feeling of strength that came to me like a gift: My music will see me through this damn thing—no matter how long it takes.

As Dick Shelton and I started searching for a lawyer to represent me, I got up my courage to call Peggy Karas and cancel my scheduled appointments with Dr. Masserman. It was the most difficult call I had ever made, because I was still imagining that Dr. Masserman would try to murder me for telling anyone what he had done. I told Peggy I would be leaving town for a while, so she should cancel my appointments until further notice. No, I did not need to talk to Dr. Masserman, thank you. No, I did not want to make another appointment yet. I would call when I got back, I said, hyperventilating as I lied.

After a week went by, Detective Kelly called to tell me that the police lab showed no evidence of semen in any of their tests.

"Does that mean I can't fight him?" I asked. The thought of backing away from a lawsuit had become unthinkable to me.

"No, no, don't look at it that way," the detective said. "You may not have much success in a criminal court, but you can still file a civil suit. Get a lawyer, and good luck."

I was a wreck. As each day and night went by, I couldn't shake the pictures in my mind. I barely slept. Just when I'd find a comfortable place in my pillow, I'd sit up again, seeing Dr. Masserman's bare buttocks gleaming in the light of the examining room. I'd hear the jingle of the coins as he pulled up his pants, and I'd break out in a sweat, gasping for breath. This was the man I had thought of as my father, my guide.

Sometimes I'd lie in bed and be plagued by why this had happened to me. Was it my fault? Was this what I deserved? Was I some worthless piece of ass? Was this the only purpose I could serve for men, including Dr. Masserman? For years, people looked at me only because they thought I was pretty or had a sexy body. In grade school and high school, boys talked about my large breasts, and as I got older, men, even both my husbands, looked at me as some kind of trophy. They might give me gifts or take me out to dinner and pay attention to me, but they never really tried to get to know *me*. I had an A average in college and was ranked third in my graduating class, but I got attention for my looks, not for my ideas or energy or knowledge.

With Dr. Masserman, I'd believed it was different. What an idiot I'd been to think he liked my mind and was intrigued by my thoughts. What a fool I was to believe he understood and respected my passion for singing and writing music. What a moron I'd been to convince myself that he had real affection and concern for me, the person, not the beauty queen. How crazy I had been to trust his attention. In Paris, I'd had this high-minded image of myself as a translator and a woman of stature, but Dr. Masserman had kept me at his side as the "pretty little miss" who was his private joke. I pictured him standing there, smiling at his admirers and laughing to himself: I screw this woman, but she doesn't know it. She's too empty and stupid to know what's happening to her. And better yet, she's too dependent and passive to do anything about it even if she knew. But then, she'll never know. Ah, yes, what a kick life can be!

If anyone deserved Fool of the Year Award, I did. I screamed and cried about my own stupidity.

But Dr. Masserman was wrong about one thing. I wasn't too dependent and passive to do anything if I found out. He might think I was stupid, but he had chosen the wrong woman to put this over on. I woke up late, but I woke up, and nothing was going to stop me from getting even with him for what he'd done to me.

10 The Singer v. the Psychiatrist

I stepped from the private elevator into the penthouse suite of the old building on East Wacker Drive. From a large picture window, I could see the Chicago River below us, but the immediate surroundings weren't nearly as appealing. The gray marble floor of the reception area contributed to the streamlined, Art Deco design of the room. I was feeling nervous and insecure, and the sight of the severe upholstered furniture didn't cheer me. Dick Shelton had said this law firm would be grand, but he hadn't told me to expect anything quite this dramatic.

Dick had been excited about setting up this appointment so quickly. "The head of the firm told me that Leslie Graves* is terrific," he said. "She's not only a female—and I think it would be great for you to be represented by a woman—but she's a senior partner, which means she's tough and can handle the job. Can you take her that report I asked you to write? Did you finish it?"

"No; I didn't know I'd have a meeting so soon," I said. "I've tried to write it, but so far I haven't been able to get a word down on paper. Every time I try, I either feel crazy or I start sobbing. I'm sorry, Dick. It's ridiculous."

"No, it's not; it's understandable. You'll be able to do it. For now, just go ahead to the meeting and tell Leslie all the facts."

I wasn't in the reception room long before I was ushered into a more

*This is not her real name.

traditional office, where I met a plain-looking but sharply dressed lawyer in a pin-striped suit and white blouse. She stood, extended her hand, and said in deep, self-assured tones, "Leslie Graves." In a timid, frightened voice that shamed me as I heard it, I said, "I'm Barbara Noël."

I felt Leslie Graves's brisk head-to-toe appraisal of me and was glad I had worn a sophisticated navy-blue suit with an elegant blouse. At least I didn't look as dumb as I sounded. I took a chair on my side of a large walnut desk. Ms. Graves opened a manila folder and began to fire off a series of no-nonsense questions in an abrupt, unfriendly tone. I wondered if she and Officer Fleming had gone to the same school of etiquette.

"You were in therapy with him for *how* long?" she asked.

She wrote down a note and then looked at something in her folder and read out, "He was *president* of the American Psychiatric Association? *And* the American Academy of Psychoanalysis? And the World Congress for Social Psychiatry?" She sounded incredulous but not mocking.

I wasn't prepared, and as she began asking me questions, I had a hard time pulling answers out of the air as quickly as she wanted them. At the end of twenty minutes, she stood, cutting me off in midsentence. "I don't think we can help you," she said, closing the folder in front of her. "There's no case here. But thank you for coming in." She nodded a goodbye and sat down before I'd even closed the door.

I walked back through the reception room, got into the private elevator, and felt totally deflated. Talking about rape was degrading and complicated in the first place, but I had thought somehow it would be easier talking to another woman. I walked all the way home, feeling stupid. I was angry at myself for having gone to the appointment unprepared. I probably had sounded just as nervous and befuddled as I felt, and that certainly had not helped me present my case. Was I going to do this thing right or not? By the time I got to my front door, I was ready to put everything that had happened on paper.

I didn't bother to eat. I sat down at my typewriter and worked through the night. By morning, I had seven single-spaced pages enumerating every detail of what had happened in Dr. Masserman's office on Friday, September 21. It was thorough, and writing it had jogged my memory. I had forgotten that Dr. Masserman said he had given me a lighter dose than usual. But it made sense. I remembered his saying,

"You're so tense and upset that it doesn't take much Amytal to knock you right out." Probably the lighter dose combined with my recovery from the TMJ dysfunction gave me the strength to wake up to this unbelievable scam.

Even though I was feeling more rational about what had happened, I needed to talk it all out with someone. I didn't want to burden friends—Dick and Mary had listened and were listening more than enough. Besides, I thought it wasn't fair to burden friends with so much emotional baggage. I hadn't called Jeannie Patrick, the rape advocate, and wouldn't, simply because she wasn't someone I would have sought out otherwise. She had been extremely sweet and compassionate at the hospital, but she was an unsophisticated young woman, and I felt she simply didn't have enough life experience to be a confidante of mine. What I didn't realize at the time was that I probably would have been much better off talking to her than seeking the help of some of the professionals I did end up talking with.

Instead, I reverted to my patterns of secrecy and privacy and focused my attention on finding a new therapist. Even though Dr. Masserman had failed me, I still believed there were good professionals who could help me understand and deal with the experience. Since that time, I've had people ask, "How could you ever have trusted any therapist again?" But I believed in therapy and was steeped in the idea of it being extremely important, healthy, and healing. I still look at psychotherapy as an essential tool for self-understanding and insight, and I feel it was the man who let me down, not the process. The existence of a rotten individual didn't mean the whole batch was tainted. It never even crossed my mind not to try again.

The first therapist who came to mind was my friend Nancy Waller's former psychiatrist, Dr. François E. Alouf. Nancy and I had been walking down Michigan Avenue one time when we ran into him, and she introduced him to me. He was a slender, attractive man with a French accent, and in her opinion, he was quite a wonderful therapist. I also knew she wouldn't mind if I saw him, so I called and told him I was a friend of Nancy's and I'd met him once on the street. He asked what the problem was, and in as few words as possible, I told him. When I said the therapist had been Dr. Jules Masserman, I heard a deep inhalation, and then absolute silence. For a moment, I wondered if the phone had gone dead. I said, "Hello?" He cleared his throat and said he would have been happy to see me, but he was just too busy and couldn't possibly fit me into his schedule. He recommended a psychiatrist whom I'll call Dr. Ted Weitz.

When I walked into Dr. Weitz's office, I was struck by the contrast to what I was used to in terms of psychiatrist and psychiatrist's office. The man was totally put together—tall and attractive in a three-piece brown suit made out of the finest wool. He wore an ivory silk shirt, a coral tie, and perfectly polished shoes. When he crossed his legs, brown silk socks covered every inch of skin. His mustache was perfectly trimmed, and his nails were manicured. No scruffy bedroom slippers, droopy socks, or rolled-up sleeves for this guy.

His office was equally stylish—Danish modern with simple, clean lines, decorated in tones of brown, gold, and soft orange. He had a couple of posters on his walls—nothing like the jillions of plaques, letters, and pictures Masserman displayed. Unlike the jumbled piles of old magazines I was used to, Dr. Weitz had a number of new magazines aligned on a teak coffee table. They seemed to be there more for appearance than for reading. No paper or object in the entire office looked out of place, and every surface was immaculate. No dust, not a speck. No bad odors, no smells of sweat, aftershave lotion, or hair oil.

Dr. Weitz sat in an upholstered chair, and I sat on the edge of a stiff corner sofa. I told Dr. Weitz what had happened to me, and he listened with his head raised at an angle, intent. Apparently I hadn't mentioned a name, and so after a while, he broke in with, "Who did this?"

When I told him, he said in a shocked voice that enunciated every syllable loudly, "*Dr. Jules Masserman?*" He shook his head and then said, "My God, is he still practicing? How old is he?"

After I told him, he said, "Are you aware that this man was the head of psychiatry and neurology at Northwestern University?"

I said I was, and then Dr. Weitz asked me to tell him more.

I did. I came back for a second session, during which Dr. Weitz said, "I wonder why you're thinking this happened."

"I get the distinct feeling you don't believe me," I said.

"Actually, I do find this rather hard to believe," he said. "But I might be able to help you."

Before the end of the hour, Dr. Weitz cleared his throat and paused for a moment before speaking. "I think I'd be willing to see you a few times to help you understand why you are thinking this way," he said, crossing one manicured hand over the other. "If you can understand why you assume this thing happened to you, then you should be able to find a way to go back into Dr. Masserman's care and work through your real problems with him. I think it's important for you to work through these issues with him. But I can see that you need to find a way to go back, and I think I can help you do that."

I was sitting with my arms crossed tightly in front of me, and I felt my grip tighten. "No, thank you," I said with as much dignity as I could muster. "I will never go back to Jules Masserman after what he did to me. This was not a fantasy."

At home in the middle of the night, I thought: Who is ever going to believe me? After all, I'm only a singer—I'm only a woman—and Dr. Masserman is a famous male psychiatrist. What's worse is that I'm a *patient*. How can I expect any other psychiatrist to believe me? They'll all think I was just having a transference fantasy. Or they'll say it was wishful thinking.

For the time being, I gave up my search for therapeutic help. Dick Shelton, however, wasn't giving up on finding a lawyer.

Within a week, he had unearthed another personal-injury attorney. This one, Flynn, wasn't with a big, hot-shot firm, but, Dick said, he was a partner in a small, respectable LaSalle Street firm; he was thorough, he knew his law, and he was "hungry for challenging and interesting cases."

For this interview, I arrived armed with my seven-page, matter-of-fact report, which made me feel stronger and more confident. I walked down the grand old marble hallway of the eighth floor, listening to my heels clacking. Inside Flynn's extremely small reception room, I nodded at a receptionist sitting behind a glass partition and sat down, prepared to wait.

Within moments, John Michael Flynn* poked his wide, ruddy Irish face into the reception room and smiled at me. "Which one are you?" he asked, his full head of sandy-colored, curly hair framing his smile.

"I'm the one who got raped by her shrink."

I followed the six-foot-three-inch Flynn down a narrow hallway to his dinky, cluttered office, where his voice seemed to fill every corner

*This is not his real name.

of the room. John Michael Flynn, it turned out, loved show biz and blarney, and before we went into my case, he asked me a lot about my work. He had friends who were radio people, and he wondered if I knew them. I immediately liked this man and felt comfortable with him, but I couldn't anticipate how all this would translate when it came to my case.

When Flynn finally got down to business and began to read my report, he read it slowly, occasionally looking up and shaking his head. I wondered whether he, too, would disbelieve me, and as I watched him read, I was almost holding my breath. When he finished reading, he flipped through the pages again and said, "That son of a bitch. That son of a bitch."

He stared out the window and was silent for a while. Then he looked back at me. "I'll be honest with you," he said. "I've never handled anything to do with psychiatry. Personal injury of a physical nature has been my field. You know, somebody gets beat up by a cop, and I go after the cop for wrongful assault. Or somebody gets knocked down by a city bus, or he falls down a defective store escalator—that sort of thing."

He picked up my report again. "You were with this guy for a long time," he said. "You didn't say how old he is."

"He's seventy-nine."

"Seventy-nine?"

His secretary came in with coffee for us and then closed the door quietly behind her.

"Are you familiar with the dead man's law?" John Michael Flynn asked me. I said I'd never heard of it. "Well, the dead man's law means we could file a suit and spend plenty of money getting the case together, and then if this guy dies, there's no case."

He leaned back in his chair and sighed deeply. "Let me do some thinking," he said. "To be frank, I'm concerned about whether I'll be able to handle this by myself, but the whole thing makes me so mad that I want to take it on. It'll take me a day or two to decide, but I'll write you either way."

Three days later, an envelope arrived in my mailbox with John Michael Flynn's name and address in the top left-hand corner. My hands were shaking as I tore it open. Inside, I found a short note saying he'd decided to represent me, along with a contract delineating the terms of our agreement.

A week later, we met again for four hours, and then twice more, until Flynn felt he had a complete picture of me and the situation. Because there was no corroborating evidence, no witnesses, and no sperm, he had decided that a civil suit, not a criminal suit, was the appropriate action to take. In several states, it is a felony for a psychiatrist to have sex with a patient, but Illinois isn't one of them. And although the case would appear to be criminal, Flynn said that the case boiled down to my word against Dr. Masserman's. The length of my treatment and a predisposition of many judges and juries to believe that a professional's credentials would preclude such behavior added to its vulnerability as a criminal case. Medical negligence and personal injury could be proved more easily. Dick Shelton agreed fully with Flynn's assessment, as had the detective. Flynn asked me if I would like to use the anonymous name "Doe" on my suit against Dr. Masserman; since this case was sexual and involved a rape, I was entitled to anonymity. He explained that once he filed the complaint at the city court, it would be a matter of public record. It would be delivered to the defendant, Dr. Masserman, by a representative of the sheriff's office. And after that, anyone could go into the courthouse and ask for it and read all the details. Using "Barbara Doe" would mean I wouldn't have to deal with any personal repercussions from making my name public.

"No," I said. "I want to use my real name. I'm afraid, but I don't want to hide behind a pseudonym. I want Jules Masserman to know that Barbara Noël is mad as hell."

I didn't get mad often, but when I did, look out. One time at a carnival, when I stepped up to a counter to play a game of hitting balls with a baseball bat, the hawker at the counter copped a feel of my breasts as he started to hand me the bat, and it made me so mad that I grabbed the bat out of his hands and whacked him over the head. Later, I would learn that a lot of this explosive anger on my part was from repressed rage, but I didn't mind that I had it when it was aimed at deserving targets.

On October 9, 1984, John Michael Flynn filed civil complaint No. 84L 21302 in the Circuit Court of Cook County, Illinois. The complaint, *Barbara Noël, Plaintiff* v. *Jules H. Masserman, M.D., Defendant* charged Jules Masserman with two counts of intentional assault and battery and medical negligence. It charged that the defendant "committed an unlawful and tortuous battery and assault" by "intentionally and maliciously injecting the plaintiff with a needle and the contents of a syringe, and placing his penis and other parts of his body [sic] in the plaintiff's vagina." It also charged that the defendant was guilty of ten separate acts of negligence and described the damages ("severe and permanent physical and mental injuries," my having "been forced to expend diverse sums of money for hospital and medical care, for drugs and medicine, etc. . . ."). It asked for a judgment against Jules H. Masserman, M.D., "in excess of $15,000" on each count, the jurisdictional minimum for the Circuit Court of Cook County to hear the case.

The following day, Flynn called to tell me he had filed the complaint and it had been sent to the Cook County sheriff's office. The sheriff's office would serve the complaint on Dr. Masserman at his home. This sounded quite efficient, but Flynn cautioned that the complaint would not be served right away. In fact, the sheriff's office had such a backlog that they probably wouldn't actually get to it until sometime in early December.

"Look, Barbara, is there any possibility that this guy might call you because you're not going in to see him?" Flynn asked me.

"I hope not, but I don't know," I said. "It's possible, of course, since I just disappeared."

Flynn said he didn't know much about psychiatrists, but he knew about human nature, and it seemed to him that Masserman might start to get jumpy if he hadn't heard from me. "Look, if he does call, don't say anything to him," Flynn said. "Don't talk to him, no matter what. Just give him my name and number."

I was freaked out at the very idea of Masserman calling, but I wrote down Flynn's instructions and put a copy by each of my telephones, praying I wouldn't have to use them.

Two days later, however, on October 12, when I got home from teaching at the conservatory, I called my answering service for messages and got one asking me to call Dr. Jules Masserman. It had been exactly twenty-one days since I awakened in his office. Twenty-one days since I had discovered what he was doing. No way would I return his call.

I walked into my bedroom and started to change my clothes, when my private telephone line rang. Very few people had this number, and Dr. Masserman wasn't one of them, but I looked at the phone and listened to it ring four or five times before I mustered the courage to pick it up. The voice on the other end made chills go through my body.

"Miz Nole," said the soft, familiar voice, mispronouncing my name as usual. "This is Dr. Masserman calling. I've been quite concerned about you. Miss Karas said you'd canceled your appointments because you were going out of town—but it's been three weeks now." He paused, perhaps waiting for a response, and then asked, "Are you all right?"

"I'm fine."

"Now, I think it's time you came in to see me," he said in his gentlest voice.

I didn't say anything. I was frozen in place. I was thinking: Oh, my God, he must have found this number in Billie's records.

"Miz Nole? Why aren't you answering me?"

I grabbed the piece of paper I'd put by the phone. "If . . . if you have any questions, please call John Michael Flynn at . . ." I stared at the number. "Just a minute. At 998-0999."

I looked at the mouthpiece and said, "I'm going to hang up now." Then I replaced the receiver, shaking from head to toe and feeling exactly as I had after I discovered that Dr. Masserman had raped me.

Within seconds, my private line rang again.

"Now, Miz Nole," Dr. Masserman said, "I don't know why you're upset, but—"

I interrupted him. "Doctor, please call Mr. Flynn at this number: 998-0999. Goodbye."

I hung up, and the phone rang again. I picked it up immediately.

"Miz Nole, you're not making any sense," Dr. Masserman said anxiously. "You're terribly upset. Miz Nole, what's wrong?"

I didn't answer him. I felt so frightened that I was barely breathing.

"You—" I heard Dr. Masserman inhale loudly and begin to breathe hard. "You—you know about the Amytal!" he said.

His words registered like Morse code in my brain. I tried to stay calm. "If you have any questions, please call Mr. Flynn at 998-0999. Goodbye."

I hung up the phone, shaking and sweating. He had said it. He had actually said: *"You know about the Amytal."*

The phone rang again, and for the fourth time, I picked it up.

Dr. Masserman's voice was frantic. "I didn't get the number! What's the number?"

"It's 998-0999."

I hung up and paced my room, drank a glass of water and paced some more. Would John Michael Flynn be there? What would they say? Surely Flynn would call me soon.

Within ten minutes, the phone rang again. My hands were shaking so badly that I could barely pick up the phone. I was so shocked when I heard Dr. Masserman's voice once again that initially I could barely understand him.

"You're suing me!" he was shouting. "You're suing me! Oh, please come in and see me. We'll talk this thing through. Won't you come in?"

"No."

"Is it money you want?" he said in a shaky voice. "I'll give you money. I'll give you anything you want."

I didn't say anything, but I could hear him breathing, and then it sounded as if he had begun to cry.

"Barbara, dear," he said, "how could you do this to me? I've been a respected member of the medical community for over forty years."

"I'm sorry," I said. "I really am sorry."

I hung up the phone, and I *was* sorry. I really was. I certainly did not want to be doing this, but I had to. He had raped me. It was a sorrowful situation, but he was the one who had created it.

Within minutes, my private line rang again. I could hardly bear to pick up the phone. I let it ring and then picked it up without saying anything.

"Are you scared?" I heard John Michael Flynn saying. "Can you put two words together?"

"Barely," I stuttered. "I'm just so glad it's you. I can't believe he called. What happened?"

"Well, we had a nice conversation," he said. "The guy is more scared than you are—he could hardly talk. You're telling the truth, all right. Damn it, I knew you were."

After the initial thrill of filing the lawsuit and having Masserman make that telephone call, I became terrified at the thought of leaving my apartment. I knew it was irrational, but I thought: Now that he knows I know, Dr. Masserman will try to kill me for sure. I had a mental picture of him skulking across the street from my building, waiting to kill me. I imagined if I tried to leave my building, he would take aim with a high-powered rifle. Or maybe he would hire a sharp-shooter to kill me for him.

It seemed crazy to think these things, but I couldn't help myself. I didn't know that this kind of fear is common to many victims of rape, but it is. Apparently, many people find themselves terrified after being raped because the assault has left them feeling vulnerable, powerless, and so near the possibility of death that their sense of reality has a dent in it—almost as if their nervous systems have been rewired for trauma. Another reason for being so afraid is that it's a screen for murderous rage—the flip side of wanting to kill the perpetrator.

I zigzagged through all those fears and feelings, always seeing a rifle barrel glinting from behind bushes or trees, running into stores for cover when I felt too exposed, and, at home, running to take another glass of wine or another martini to fill the void when I was too shaken to sleep. Remembering it from this distance, I can still feel how disoriented and peculiar I felt, but I can also see more clearly just why I was so disturbed. For one thing, I was going through withdrawal from the Amytal. For another, my whole world had been turned upside down. My trusted therapist was not at all who I thought he had been. His behavior was twisted and sick. And that sickness loomed so large in my mind that I didn't know if it had limits. Again I thought, if he would rape me, why wouldn't he also kill me?

Fortunately for me, I had other commitments. I still had to go to work, even when my head wasn't in it. While we were endlessly waiting for the lawsuit to be served, the music of my professional life gave me some windows of sanity and grace, however small. I did my usual work, as well as being female vocalist with Peter Duchin's band whenever he came to town from New York for society benefits or parties. But teaching my voice students at the American Conservatory of Music was the most satisfying. While we worked together, my students gave me views into their lives that helped me forget my own trauma.

A conservatory student who particularly touched me came sweeping into my studio one afternoon in tight jeans and high leather boots. Nataschè had just arrived from Vienna and was bursting with ambition. "I want to be a jazz singer," she said in a smoky voice thick with an Austrian accent, as she shook out her long brown hair—part of which was painted bright pink.

"You'll be dynamite," I said, laughing at the wonderful enthusiasm this nineteen-year-old radiated. "Singing jazz with that gorgeous accent will knock 'em out."

I worked with Nataschè for more than a year and a half, and felt such kinship with her that it seemed I was working with a younger, smaller version of myself. Her initiative and stamina matched my own; I could always trust her to do her homework and do it well. But as Nataschè's vocal exercises got tougher and she began the process of learning new material, I started to see more of the frightened girl emerge from underneath her spirited and charismatic exterior. I also noticed that from time to time she squinted her eyes or shook her hands. Once, after she had been singing for a while, she clutched the back of her neck in a gesture that was all too familiar to me. When I asked her about it, she admitted that she often came in with severe headaches that caused her to feel dizzy and lose her balance. She hadn't mentioned it because she was afraid I would think it was just performance anxiety.

Nataschè's problem brought out the mother in me. I walked her over to Dr. Wheeler's office, and he found that she, too, had a jaw out of alignment. She got the help she needed without ever having to hear about it being an "emotional" problem or something she was doing "to get attention." In the months to come, I found TMJ in two other students and helped them get the correction they needed. These incidents bolstered my determination: Not one person I knew would *ever* go through what I did.

By February 1985, John Michael Flynn was getting nervous. The suit had been filed, and I had answered long lists of questions—preliminary interrogatories—from Masserman's lawyers. The interrogatories elicit information that tell the other guy's attorneys who you are. I had to write down the details of my birth and family history, and my medical, educational, psychological, and financial background. Flynn had given a similar set of questions to Masserman's lawyers, and the doctor had answered them.

This was part of what made Flynn feel nervous. Even though I'd told him Masserman was a big honcho in the psychiatric community, Flynn was astounded by the man's prominence and could hardly believe his eyes when he got Masserman's extraordinary curriculum vitae from the topflight law firm that represented him. The vita was thirty pages long and included every professional office he'd held, every award he'd garnered, and a bibliography of a dozen books and hundreds of articles he'd written.

Masserman's lawyers informed Flynn that the charges were patently absurd, the delusions of a patient who had a personal vendetta. They told him Dr. Masserman was fully trained as a psychoanalyst at the Chicago Psychoanalytic Institute, a fully accredited member of the Chicago, American, and International Psychoanalytic Associations, and a fully accredited training analyst, the highest professional recognition attainable in the field. As a physician, Jules Masserman was "quite concerned" about me: I was *not* a well woman and I should still be under his "care." His lawyers said that the doctor would be happy to consult with any other psychiatrist who was treating me. They also gave Flynn the strong impression that proceeding with this case would be extremely embarrassing to him professionally.

Flynn had been unable to find any psychiatrist who would testify as an expert witness against Jules Masserman. Even though the police lab had come back with no evidence of rape, Flynn had been sure that the frequency of the Amytal injections alone constituted medical malpractice. But if he couldn't get anyone to testify, how could we win? At the outset, Flynn had told me he was "just a personal-injury attorney—good when somebody gets physically injured on someone else's premises," but that he didn't know *anything* about psychiatry. Now that lack of knowledge was really bothering him. Flynn wrote me a letter saying we should discuss dropping the case.

Because Dick Shelton had become sicker and had to make a second trip to the Anderson Cancer Center in Houston, he turned me over to his partner, John Hastings, at Shelton, Kalcheim and Hastings, who agreed, as a favor to Dick, to guide me through the legal labyrinth facing me. They didn't do personal-injury or malpractice cases, or they would have represented me themselves. Dick had asked John to go with me to talk to Flynn, telling me ahead of time, "Don't worry, Barb. John Hastings will help you until I get better. You have a *good* case; believe it. Keep believing it."

"Look," Flynn said as the three of us sat around his cluttered desk after the preliminary greetings. "For all we know, the guy will be dead by April, and then we'll have no case. The other thing is, frankly, this man is too big. He's just too big. No other psychiatrist is willing to speak against him in court. What fellow professional is going to risk his career to do that? There's no criminal evidence of rape, and it's only your word against his."

Flynn said he was sorry, but he wanted out. "If I were you, Barb," he said, "I'd give up. That man is going to cream you. Give up, just give up."

When I said there was no way I was going to give up, Flynn said, "Look, *nobody* will want to handle this. No law firm is going to be willing to put in so much time and money with so little hope of success." When Flynn and I said goodbye to each other, he told me he would

try to give me as much time as possible to find a new lawyer before
he legally withdrew from the case. Even though he was quitting, I was
grateful that he had done as much as he had; he had said, "Let's go
get the son of a bitch" at a time when I needed that support.

Flynn was right about how hard it would be to find someone else
willing to represent me. Maybe if I'd had a lot of money and the lawyers
were sure of getting paid, they would have been willing to take it on.
But I didn't have an independent income, which meant I couldn't pay
in advance. Handling the case on contingency meant that the lawyers
would get money only if they won the case.

When I met with John Hastings a week later, he said he hadn't had
even a glimmer of success in finding someone to represent me. "Every
lawyer I've contacted has as much as laughed at the idea," he said,
shaking his head in discouragement. "They feel it's a sure loser."

I felt bleak, but there was something very strong in me, and I wasn't
going to quit. "I know it's only one woman's word against the word
of a famous psychiatrist," I said. "And it's even worse because I'm a
singer and performer, not someone in an upstanding occupation. Maybe
if I were a nun, or a schoolteacher or lawyer or businesswoman, they'd
think they could make a better case. But I'm not giving up."

As we sat talking, John's secretary came in with a telephone message.
He read it and broke into a smile. "Good timing," he said, handing it
to me.

I read the message: "John: Linda Mensch [an attorney formerly with
Shelton and Hastings' law firm] returned your call. She remembers an
excellent man, a former state's attorney, who is also a clinical psychologist, now teaching at John Marshall Law School, named William
K. Carroll. He's nearly impossible to reach, so keep trying."

I called his number at least fifty times over the next few days.
Sometimes it would ring and ring, and other times an answering machine came on and I left messages. One day a man answered the phone
with, "This is Bill Carroll."

"Mr. Carroll!" I said, so surprised and pleased that I could hardly
contain myself. "Oh, Mr. Carroll, hello. This is Barbara Noël!"

"Oh, hello!" he said, sounding equally elated. "You're of the North
Carolina Noëls, aren't you! How is your mother?"

What? "Mr. Carroll, I'm sad to say I'm not part of that family," I
said, recovering my equilibrium. "My call is of a business nature."

"Oh? Well, then, I'm in conference right now," he said. "Could you call back later? Thank you." He hung up.

I couldn't believe it. I pulled out some stationery and began to write Bill Carroll a letter. I explained the reasons for my call: eighteen years, the suit, and the reluctance of my attorney to continue with it. I concluded the letter: "Four and a half months have passed since it happened. . . . Not only was the sexual act unconscionable, but also the length of treatment was unnecessary and manipulative. The nature of the case, the age of the doctor, and my anger equal someone who hopes you will find time for her as quickly as you can."

Within four days, Bill Carroll called, and we set up an appointment. At the time, I didn't realize I would be seeing someone who, besides being a clinical psychologist and an attorney, had dealt in depth with the subjects of sexual dysfunction, sexual perversity, and criminal sexual behavior. Nor did I know he was the author of a controversial book, *Human Sexuality: New Directions in American Catholic Thought.*

Bill Carroll's office was at John Marshall Law School, a red-brick building on Plymouth Court, in downtown Chicago. I took the elevator to the sixth floor and wandered down a narrow hallway to a tiny office with a sliding glass door, shelves lined with double layers of books both standing and stacked, and a desk piled so deep with papers, books, and newspapers that it was hard to imagine how the man was able to clear enough space on any surface to write even a note. Bill Carroll, a short, slightly plump man with pink cheeks and light-blond, slightly receding hair, sat in the midst of the paper-strewn chaos, with an expression in his pale-blue eyes that reflected relaxed curiosity, thoughtfulness, and a jovial sense of humor. He made me feel so comfortable that I guessed he was probably the favorite professor of every John Marshall law student.

I explained everything, including all the lawyers' doubts, and ended with, "Even if I don't have a case legally, could you just do *something*?" Bill Carroll had listened carefully, and he smiled at the desperation in my plea.

"Well, it doesn't sound out of the question to me," he finally said. "It sounds as if there could be a good case here. There's just too much nudity going on—and for such a long time. Also, it sounds strange that he got you there so early in the morning and kept you on this drug for so long. . . . Let me talk to Flynn and do some calling around before I get back to you."

I didn't hear from Bill for several weeks, but he was doing his homework. He had been dealing with other people's secret aberrations for a long time. He knew that status or reputation had very little to do with a person's inner life, so my story did not seem as improbable to him as it had to others who heard it.

He also knew—perhaps better than I did—what it takes for a woman to file a complaint like this. Later, he would say, "Any woman has to be pretty determined to do something like this, because there's a tendency, even though it's waning, to take a position that there's something wrong with people who have ever seen a psychiatrist or a therapist. A woman faces the perception that she may honestly believe what she's saying—that it *is* what's in her mind—but it *really* is just wishful thinking. . . . So she has to fight an uphill battle, and she faces the real possibility of just being pooh-poohed.

"Also, it's embarrassing," he said. "It's embarrassing for what actually happened and it's embarrassing to have been fool enough to have believed this was part of the therapy package, that her relationship with the therapist was unique, and that the therapist personally felt for her. For a woman to actually file a complaint, all these difficulties have to be surpassed by a feeling of outrage. Her anger has to surpass the anticipation of being embarrassed or rejected by the authorities and even by the disclosure to her own family."

When Bill Carroll finally called me and we met again, he told me he had talked at length with John Michael Flynn and received his files. He confirmed that Flynn had been very much influenced by Dr. Masserman's credentials and history and the respect in which he was held by the profession; consequently he had become persuaded that my claim was highly improbable.

"Because I've dealt in a therapeutic way with a lot of professionals with considerable credentials and histories and so on, who have their own Achilles' heels," Bill Carroll said, "I'm not quite so thrown off by the fact that this is a man of great reputation. Even men of great standing and prestige can have conflicts and obsessions . . . or perhaps even strange scientific theories they believe they are testing out."

Bill said that since he'd last seen me, he'd been learning quite a lot. "This case won't be easy—especially since you perceived his behavior at that stage of just coming out of a semiconscious state, which will make it a very difficult thing to prove.

"But I've consulted with a psychiatrist colleague of mine who specializes in research in drug therapy—a man with qualifications comparable to Dr. Masserman's—and there's something in the history of the therapy Dr. Masserman has been conducting that suggests something was quite awry.

"One of the disturbing things is that there is some indication that you had trouble with alcoholism and had potential for other addictions as well, and yet this drug that Dr. Masserman was using is a potentially addicting drug. So that doesn't seem appropriate. It indicates this whole thing ought to be investigated more fully."

Bill told me that the interrogatories contained a lot of interesting material from Masserman, who admitted quite openly to his use of Amytal. Then he surprised me by asking if I was in debt to a lot of people.

I told him no, I was always current with my bills. My only debt was on my condo, and I always made my mortgage payments on time. Why?

"Well, according to Dr. Masserman, you owe a lot of money all over, and you've been terribly behind in your payments to him."

"That's not so. I always paid him on time."

"Can you prove it?"

I told Bill I kept good records and was sure I must have every canceled check and every bill anyone had sent me over the past ten years. My ex-husband would have some sort of accounting for the years before that.

"You and Mr. Noël are on friendly terms, then?"

"Yes." Richard now lived in San Diego with his fourth wife, Nancy, but we'd had lunch the last time he was in town for a recording session, and I'd told him about what had happened with Dr. Masserman. Richard had always hated the man, but he was appalled nonetheless and terribly saddened that I'd had to go through such an ordeal. He was supportive of my legal action against Masserman, but thought that the charges should be criminal, not civil, and that the man should go to jail.

"Well, then, would you contact him about any earlier payments he made to Masserman?" Bill asked. "That will help. Now, as to the injections of Sodium Amytal. Can you give me an accurate record of how often you received them?"

"No, not really," I said, thinking of the tiny pieces of paper with "A—7:30" that I'd clipped to my datebook and taken off after the appointments. "I rarely marked the specific dates in my book because I didn't want anyone to find out I had to have drug therapy. There were times, though, when I'd cancel other appointments the day of the Amytal—and that would give you some idea. I think maybe Richard could help me on the earlier dates."

Bill said he believed we might have a good malpractice action. I went home and got out my old calendars and checked for dates of appointments. Papers piled up all over my living room floor as I searched through back tax records and canceled checks. I called Richard and then went through his old records too.

Ten days later, I came back to Bill Carroll's office with my arms full of all the information he had asked for, plus a letter from Richard explaining the payments he had made to Masserman and his knowledge of the frequency of my Amytal treatments during the time we were married. Bill looked at my lists of payments to Dr. Masserman spanning eighteen years and my stack of canceled checks and said that these records, along with the statements Masserman had made in the interrogatories, gave us quite substantial ammunition for legal action.

"I'm itching to work on this case *if* I can find the right person to work with," Bill said, reiterating that since he was a law professor, he personally had no staff, office equipment, secretary, or assistants to do legal research. He said he'd previously worked on cases with partners who had more resources than he did, and they had worked well.

"Masserman may be big," Bill said, "but he's not well liked by a lot of people in the psychiatric community. This is going to be fun." Then he leaned back and looked at me. "Are you aware that you're addicted to Sodium Amytal, both physically and emotionally?"

"No, I never got that impression," I said uneasily.

"Did you know that in his interrogatories he claims you're an alcoholic?"

"No. He told me clearly that I'm *not* an alcoholic."

"But he put you on Antabuse in September 1979. Why did he do that?"

"He told me it was to make sure I never became an alcoholic."

"Well, even if you didn't show any signs of being an addictive personality, the Sodium Amytal shouldn't have been given to you more than once. That's the opinion of experts I've talked to. We've got a real case here, Barbara, *if* I can find a partner."

John Michael Flynn filed a motion of withdrawal as my counsel, and on May 18, 1985, the state court notified me that I had three weeks to formally deliver evidence of new legal representation, or the case would be dropped.

While Bill Carroll looked around for another lawyer to join him in pressing a malpractice suit against Masserman, I focused a lot of my anxiety on Dick and Mary Shelton. Dick had taken a turn for the worse, and Mary had returned with him to the Cancer Center in Houston. I called them there and let them know that Bill Carroll had remembered a lawyer named Kenneth Cunniff, who might be willing to work on the case. Ken had been away at the state capital for several months, preparing briefs against crooked judges and lawyers in one of the Greylord corruption cases.

When Cunniff got back to Chicago, we set up a meeting at his law office. Unlike Bill, who has a laid-back manner, Ken Cunniff is a high-wire act, all business. He's a runner and an avid skier, and he's intense, full of energy, and extremely focused. He has an undergraduate degree in philosophy and, like Bill, is a former state's attorney and a professor at John Marshall Law School.

Ken Cunniff said he'd read all my information, but he wanted to get a few things straight. "You say Dr. Masserman never told you that you had become an alcoholic?"

"No, never."

"But did you actually talk to him about it?"

"Yes. When he put me on Antabuse the second time, I asked him if I was an alcoholic. He said no, but this would make sure I didn't become one. I said I thought Antabuse was such a serious drug that only confirmed alcoholics took it, but he kind of laughed and said no, that wasn't the case at all."

"Was he aware that when you'd go off the Antabuse, you'd start to drink again?"

"Yes. He put me on Antabuse for only six months at a time. I always told him what was going on with me, although I made things sound worse than they were when I wanted him to give me Amytal."

"There were times you *knew* you wanted Amytal?"

"Oh, yes! I craved it."

Ken Cunniff nodded his head and tapped his pencil. "I want to assure you that I believe you," he said. "I absolutely believe you, and I think you'll be thoroughly credible in a courtroom. But the question is whether Bill and I can prove your case without corroborating testimony. Bill and I have to go over all this information and decide if we can prove your charges. If we think we can prove it, we'll take the case. If we don't think we can, we won't. I'll call and let you know what we decide."

I reminded him that we had less than a week to notify the court of new representation, or the case would be dropped, and he assured me he was well aware of the timing.

On my way home, I bought fresh flowers and stopped at the Sheltons' to feed their cat and put daisies in the center of the dining room table. Earlier in the week, when I'd talked to them, Dick had said, "Barbara, get the place ready. We're coming home." Mary confirmed that Dick was better, and it looked as if they'd be back soon. Now I looked around and thought what a celebration we would have if Dick was in remission and if Ken and Bill took on my case.

A few days later, on May 29, Mary called to tell me it suddenly didn't look so good. Two days after that, Dick Shelton died. I was devastated. I missed him terribly, and the world seemed a much smaller place without him.

When Ken Cunniff called on June 4 to tell me he and Bill Carroll were going to take over my case and would handle the litigation for a contingency fee of 40 percent, I was grateful that I could continue my case against Masserman, but the main friend I wanted to share the news with was no longer around.

11   *Above Suspicion*

Ken Cunniff told me he'd just received a call from an old friend, who he said was going to try to eat me alive during my discovery deposition. His friend Debra Davy, an attorney with Hinshaw Culbertson, was representing Jules Masserman, and she'd called Ken to say she was personally "shocked" when she learned he was representing Barbara Noël, "who obviously is taking advantage of a fine old man who's clearly innocent." In addition, Davy warned, Ken would find that handling this case would prove personally and professionally embarrassing.

"She really believes he's innocent, Barbara, and she's going to be hard on you," Ken said. "She can be tough, and I want you to be prepared for it."

"Well, I guess he's got her fooled," I said. "But look at how long he fooled me."

"I like your spirit," Ken said with a grin. "You're going to hold up just fine. You also have two big strengths: You're accustomed to performing in public under stress. And you're telling the truth."

Ken and Bill Carroll hadn't had an easy go of it preparing for the discovery depositions, which had been postponed three times by Masserman's attorneys. Now, finally, my deposition was scheduled for Friday, September 13, 1985—nearly one year after I had awakened with Masserman on top of me.

At the first discovery deposition, I learned, I would essentially be on trial. Discovery depositions, part of the pretrial court process, start with the plaintiff (me) being questioned by the defendant's (Masserman's) lawyers, while my own attorneys and an official court reporter are present. Next, my lawyers would question Masserman in the same way. Ken told me that Masserman's lawyers would use the deposition process to ask me deeply personal questions in an attempt to determine (or undermine) my credibility and the strength of my position. He also told me that depositions don't occur in a courtoom; my deposition would take place in the law offices of Masserman's lawyers; Masserman's deposition would be held at Ken's firm. Each deposition would last about three hours.

Ken explained that depositions often help people to avoid a trial, because at any time during the deposition process, the plaintiff can call off the suit or the defendant may confess to the wrongdoing he's been accused of and settle for damages. Also, at any time during this period, the defendant, without admitting guilt, can ask his insurance company to make an offer of settlement for damages. If the plaintiff accepts settlement, litigation stops and the case is closed. If the plaintiff refuses an offer to settle the case, litigation continues. If the lawsuit follows through all the way to the end, the whole process can take two to five years, even more.

I wanted to go the whole nine yards; I wanted a trial. But I was scared, of course, that we couldn't win. Ken said that even though a number of psychiatrists and doctors were willing to say off the record that Masserman's use of Amytal was grossly negligent, he hadn't yet found an expert witness willing to testify. We assumed that Masserman himself had made countless courtroom appearances. Bill had heard that he had testified as an expert witness in divorce cases, custody hearings, and sanity judgments, and over the years I'd seen his picture in the paper when he'd been asked for psychological explanations of front-page events—plane hijackings, bombings, murders. He would most certainly be cool under fire.

But even though things looked bad, they were about to look much worse. On September 3, Ken Cunniff called me to discuss a big snag that he'd just encountered when he read over the police reports from the emergency room on the day of the rape. That snag threatened to blow the whole case.

"Barbara, did you tell them you probably were dreaming the entire incident?" Ken asked.

"No, of course not."

"Exactly what did you say?"

"Well, after the officer—I hated that officer—after he said, 'You might have been dreaming,' I said, 'No, I wasn't dreaming.' Then he said, 'Isn't it possible that you were dreaming?' I said, 'Yes, it's possible that I could have been dreaming, but I wasn't.' "

"Well, according to this report, he said you were 'unable to determine whether the incident was a dream or reality.' He said you thought you could have been dreaming the whole thing."

"Oh, Ken, I can't believe it. He just left out the part about 'but I wasn't' dreaming."

"What's done is done," Ken said. "But Debra is sure to bring this up in the deps, so be ready, and don't let it upset you."

When I hung up the phone, I was more than upset. I'd been putting up a brave front so far, but with this new piece of "dreaming" evidence how could I have a case at all? I would come out of this thing looking like a fool at best, an avaricious liar or a psychotic at worst.

And even though I'd bantered with Ken about Debra Davy's believing Masserman, my spirit was just about gone: who wouldn't believe him? We were talking about a renowned psychiatrist and his patient of *eighteen years*. Most people would think that he'd been nursing along a very disturbed woman, trying to keep her from going over the edge, but finally, despite his efforts, she'd slipped into a true psychosis.

Also, Masserman knew all about me, about my vanities and weak spots. He would know exactly what to say to keep me off balance. Ken had said that the defendant usually doesn't appear at the plaintiff's deposition, but I knew Masserman would be there to watch me and measure my composure. The cards were stacked; all I had was my anger and stubbornness. John Michael Flynn was right: Masserman was going to cream me.

Two days later, Ken called again. When I heard his voice, my first thought was: They've decided to drop the case.

"Are you sitting down?" he asked.

"Yes." He laughed. Why was he laughing?

"I thought I'd like to make your day," he said. "I've just finished a long meeting with two women who were also patients of Dr. Masserman's. They want to file lawsuits against him.

"One is a lawyer and the other's a businesswoman, and they've been going over court records to find out if anyone else ever filed a complaint against Masserman. They're good friends, and when they compared notes and figured out what Dr. Masserman had done to them, they guessed they were not the only ones. They thought he must have done similar things to other women patients and wondered whether anyone else had ever sued him. They found your name, and then my name as attorney of record, and they contacted me this morning to see if I would represent them."

"Oh, my God."

"Yes, isn't this nice?" He began to laugh again. "Their stories match up with yours, right down to how deaf he is. One of the women said the sound on his telephone is set up so high that she heard a woman telling him she was never coming in again because all he wanted to do was have sex. The woman was shouting, and this patient heard every word."

"Do they know who I am?"

"No, and I don't want you to meet each other until after this thing is finished. But get this: both of them accepted invitations to sail on his boat and fly in his airplane. Both of them had Amytal for a number of years. And both of them were told to take off their clothes, and they both have memories that confirm how bizarre this all is."

"I can't believe it."

"I thought you'd be pleased to know you have company, especially since one of these women is an attorney and will be an outstanding witness."

"This is amazing," I said. "Amazing. How does this affect my deposition?"

"It doesn't, really," Ken said. "We'll go on as planned. It's at *his* discovery deposition that this information will come out. But I think you're going to feel a hell of a lot more confident when Debra Davy starts to take you on."

"That's for sure." I thanked Ken and added, "By the way, you did it."

"Did what?"

"You made my day."

Though I didn't yet know the stories of the two women who had come to Ken's office that morning, I felt vindicated. It helped just to know they existed. Up to that point, I had been totally alone in this thing. I imagined they may have felt the same way. But now the defense could no longer claim I was just one crazy female patient suffering from some delusion.

At a much later date, I would learn that the parallels between our stories were stronger than I ever could have imagined. All three of us had consulted Jules Masserman in order to overcome some deep vulnerabilities, and he'd used our low self-esteem—as well as our strong will to heal ourselves—to his advantage.

The lawyer, whom I'll call Daniella Biagi, started seeing Dr. Masserman in 1980, when she was thirty-one years old and finishing law school. She went to him because her friend "Annie Morrison" was already seeing him and recommended him highly. Daniella had Amytal treatments for four years and quit seeing him when she moved away from Chicago in 1984. Like me, Daniella had been sexually abused as a child. But unlike me, she was quite aware of it. Her uncle had molested both her and her sister. But even with that knowledge, she didn't realize that the abuse had affected her so deeply, given her a low opinion of herself, and made her a perfect target for a sex offender.

Daniella consulted Dr. Masserman because she was having problems trusting men. As is usual in such cases, she had always felt she must have been at fault for her uncle's behavior. Plagued by those early memories, she found that whenever she got close to a man, she became anxious and began to feel she couldn't have faith in him or rely on him as a friend or lover.

Retrospectively, Daniella said it was odd that even though she told Dr. Masserman about her uncle, they never talked about how being molested had affected her. Whenever she wanted to talk about it, as she did from time to time, Dr. Masserman would say, "Oh, it's nothing you have to deal with." He didn't let her talk about her family, how crazy her mother was, or any other family problems. If she complained about her parents, he would ask, "Why do you go out of your way to seek negative attention?" He diverted her from family matters by focusing on how "bad" and "irresponsible" she was.

"He always treated me like I was a spoiled child," Daniella would say later. "He talked about what a 'spoiled brat' I was, what a 'bad little girl' I was—which always fed into my feelings of worthlessness. I was there because my self-esteem was so terrible. But he was so manipulative. If I was having trouble on the job, it was because I was 'spoiled' or because I 'flitted from one thing to another'—not because it was legitimately a difficult situation or a job I should quit. In fact, I am a very steady, consistent, and responsible woman. But I realize now that he never gave me positive feedback or focused on my creative side or did anything directed at freeing me up as a person. What he did was directed at making me follow him."

At the time, however, Daniella wasn't aware that she was under Masserman's control or that she was doing whatever he wanted in order to be respected by him. "He was a master of persuasion," she says. "I don't know a lot about hypnosis, but it feels like that's what he did to me. He had me wrapped around his little finger. If he had said, 'Make love to me,' I would have. If he had told me to jump off a bridge, I would have. He probably had a whole harem of people like us."

When Daniella first had Amytal, she says, "it was like being initiated, since my friend Annie had already had Amytal. My first experience was wonderful. I slept for a long time, and after I woke up, I felt woozy, but it was a nice feeling. That was the only time I felt good under Amytal. After that, I hated how I felt afterward, because I always felt like a big, drugged slob.

"I also hated getting it. First of all, it was in this dirty little back room, and nothing seemed sterilized. I got my period on the sheets one time, and he may have washed the sheets, but the blood didn't come out. The sheet was always stained after that. He told me the Amytal made my flow much heavier. Also, he would jab at you, trying to find a vein. If he couldn't get it in one place, he would jab me somewhere else. He would jab me in the arms and hands, and sometimes I'd end up with swollen places in my hands. I still have a lump in my hand from where he messed it up.

"After he plunged in the needle and it took, it'd be like two seconds for the Amytal to go in you, and you would just conk out. Sometimes he'd tell me what I said under the Amytal, sometimes he wouldn't. I had no idea if I said anything at all.

"Dr. Masserman used to say, 'It will make you feel better. It will relieve tension. It will relieve stress.' He often told me that being an intelligent, intellectual being, living in my mind, made it hard for me to get to my emotions. Which is odd, because he never dealt with any emotions [during normal therapy sessions]. But that's what he said."

Daniella says it had taken her a long time to begin to trust Dr. Masserman. "When I first started having the Amytal, he told me to undress, but I would always wear a shirt and my panty hose and a slip. He'd say, 'Take off your bra, because it's constricting. Take off your panty hose. You don't want anything confining.' But I'd wear at least my slip, because I didn't trust him. When I finally took off my clothes, I did it as a symbol of trust. I thought: Of course I can trust him. I can let him see me naked. It was really a very difficult thing, but I felt that if I would just trust him, I would unfold. I thought: He's here to help me, and if I can just put myself in his hands, I will grow and do a lot better in my life."

Dr. Masserman used to invite Daniella to "Sunday therapy" at his apartment. "His office was very turn-of-the-century, but his home was more thirties and forties," she remembers. "It was kind of artistic, like out of another era. He had a music room and all these old instruments." Sometimes he played the violin for her. Daniella met Mrs. Masserman one Sunday, "but usually his wife was not around."

Dr. Masserman also used to take Daniella flying on Sundays. "I wasn't supposed to tell anyone that he took me flying, because he said they would think that was very bizarre for a psychiatrist and accuse him of all these things," she says, "so I didn't tell. But I hated flying. He said it would give me 'a new perspective on the world,' but it never did. I used to think: What am I doing up here with this seventy-eight-year-old man flying a little plane that could just blow away? I hated it."

The same was true of her outings on Dr. Masserman's boat. "He had a beautiful sailboat, but again, it was out of a weird era," she says. "It had two sails, and it was all cobalt blue and gold, but it was so removed from the way things are. He used to take me on the boat a lot. I hated it. He said I was too 'iss-o-lated'—that's how he pronounced it; I was too iss-o-lated and I needed to be more calm and friendly. But I never felt good on the boat, I never felt calm. Again, though, these were issues of trust, and those issues were so central for me. He said I would finally develop into a mature, happy woman if I could just trust him."

On a few rare occasions, Daniella went to a therapy session at the Massermans' home on a Saturday; but more often, Saturdays were reserved for Amytal at his office. For more than a year, Daniella had Amytal once a week. During a period of time when she wasn't working, in the spring and summer of 1982, she often had Amytal twice a week. In that same interval, she began to drink heavily. "I didn't do well with unstructured time," she says, "and without a job, I had a lot of free time. I started out drinking with friends, but increasingly, I found myself drinking alone. I would drink in my apartment, and I would drink until I passed out. I would have a huge bottle of wine—wine was all I ever drank. When I look back on it, I think: My God! It's a wonder I survived. I smoked, and once I even set myself on fire. I would just drink myself into oblivion.

"Then he put me on Antabuse, which was a problem. I'd take it, but I never really stopped drinking. I would drink right through the Antabuse, even if I got sick. I told him about it, and he'd say sarcastic things like, 'I can't help it. I set fire to the house, but I can't help it!' Sometimes he would be angry and say, 'Of course you can help it. It's your decision. Why do you want to do that?'

"Every time I had to deal with a man, I drank a lot. Being with a man seemed to precipitate the drinking. The drinking started out as a way to escape my problems, but then I would feel so miserable the next day that I think I was punishing myself with it. It's funny, because five or six years before that, I had been a binge eater. I never had any kind of healthy relationship with food.

"Dr. Masserman knew about all of it. I never kept anything from him. I told him about the binge eating and my drinking and everything. But the more I'd tell him, the more disgusted he would act, and the worse I felt about myself. That's the only way I can describe it."

Daniella's memories about things that happened under the Amytal suggest something entirely at odds with any normal standards of psychotherapy. "One time after the Amytal—maybe I didn't sleep enough—I remember being taken on his boat," she says. "I was woozy, out of it. You have to get in a little rowboat and row out to the sailboat, and I remember just sort of sleeping it off in the boat as Dr. Masserman rowed. Then it was like he was dragging a dead weight to get me on the sailboat.

"I don't remember ever having sex with him under the Amytal. But I remember having some loving times, where I just loved him and had the feeling I was encapsulated in warmth.

"I also remember how I'd take the Amytal and then, boom! I'd be out about six hours, but when I'd wake up, I'd want to go to the bathroom. If I was undressed, I'd have to get dressed again, and I'd have to go through his office, where he'd have a patient. It was really bizarre. I seem to remember there was one time when I walked into his office naked. I remember another time when I walked into his office naked and told him how much I loved him. I worshiped him. It never was sexual for me. It was like a little child, and he was God. He was God.

"Annie Morrison was suspicious; she picked up on him a lot earlier than I did. But we were so vulnerable, we thought we must be wrong. When she got upset, I talked her out of it. I said, 'Oh, no, this couldn't be!' We were with the king. He wrote books and was a violinist—and he had all these successful and attractive women going to him. It was part of the allure: we were with the elite, and there was just no way he could really do wrong!"

Masserman did something obviously wrong, however, when Daniella got pregnant and said she planned to have the baby. Much earlier during her therapy with Dr. Masserman, Daniella had undergone an abortion, and it had bothered her a great deal. She worried that she'd never be able to have another child. So when she got pregnant, she was extremely happy. "I had been going with [the man who became] my husband, and I wanted to have this child," she says. "I hadn't really planned on marrying him, but I had an epiphany that made me decide to do it. In an instant, I saw that Dr. Masserman was just like my mother—very judgmental, and he put people in boxes. . . . I also saw that my husband wasn't like that. He was not judgmental; he had an open mind about things, which is more the way I am, or want to be.

"Dr. Masserman wanted me to have an abortion, and he was very against my marrying this man. He said, 'I'm going to give you some Sodium Amytal so we can really get to the heart of this matter, and this time, I'm going to tape-record what you say, and I'll play it back to you. Then you'll *know* your true feelings—you'll hear yourself say that you don't really want to marry this man or have this baby.' He knew I had a lot of trouble ever getting to the heart of anything. But he had never tape-recorded anything I'd said before.

"Anyway, I was really crazed. I called the Northwestern Department of Obstetrics and said, 'If somebody is pregnant and you give them Sodium Amytal, what would happen?' They said, 'Absolutely don't take it. You absolutely cannot take that.'

"And that's when I started wondering about him.

"But I still gave him credit for the fact that I had a good job and that I was marrying this man I loved and having this miraculous child. I had Dr. Masserman come to our wedding, and I even stood up and toasted him and made an announcement about what a wonderful man he was. He was my mentor. Sometimes, in my own mind, I wondered about it all, but I couldn't stand to think that my king had done anything wrong.

"Right after my husband and I got married [in the spring of 1984], we moved to Denver, and I stopped seeing Dr. Masserman. I still owed him money, though, because when I was first seeing him, he never charged me. He'd say things like, 'Your bill is getting larger, you know.' But he knew I was a poor law school student, and he said I could pay him when I had the money. He'd say, 'Now don't tell anyone, because the IRS could come after me.' He never gave me a bill and I never paid him. Then he finally billed me, and while we were in Denver, I think my husband sent him payments every month that added up to about four thousand dollars."

It wasn't until Daniella and her husband moved back to Chicago, a year later, that she and Annie Morrison compared notes and came to a conclusion they could no longer ignore: their doctor had done some terrible things to them. Annie, by then, was very angry. Despite her many suspicions over the four-and-a-half-year period she'd gone to Masserman, Annie had continued seeing him and had been convinced by him that she, not he, was at fault.

The signs had built slowly. Annie had first consulted Masserman early in 1980, when her second marriage had failed and her teenage sons were having real problems. One son was using street drugs, and the other had found religion. Anne had married very soon after her first divorce, thinking it would be best for her sons, but it hadn't been, and she found herself immersed in guilt. "I felt like a total failure," she says. "It was bad enough to have had one divorce, but two! I didn't seem able to help my sons, and I was clinically depressed. At the time, I was managing a jewelry store, and someone in the store had a son who was a doctor and recommended Masserman. I was feeling so fragile, and they said this man has been around for a million years, and it sounded okay. And to a certain extent, he helped me. I'd been on antidepressants, and he got me off those and I felt better.

"I had seen him for about eight months when he suggested Amytal. It was a very, very vague thing. I remember discussing it with Daniella, trying to figure out what the benefits really were. And he would change his reasons. The first time, he said, 'I want you to have an opportunity to see what it feels like to be very, very relaxed, Mrs. Morrison.' I was desperate and feeling crummy, and I thought whatever he said, I'm going to try.

"The whole thing with Dr. Masserman's persona was he was very mysterious and he was God. It was all very creepy. His office was set up in Freudian style, leather couches from several decades ago. Everything tended to make you feel more like the little girl and him like the master.

"The Amytal would kill my day. I'd lie there sleeping for a few hours and then go home and sleep some more. I'd go in very early—I'd have to cancel a day at work. There was this feeling of 'I don't really want to do this,' but he would make me feel like there was some neurotic reason I didn't want it when it was really so helpful. Then he'd change his story about why I was doing it. I owed him money, and if I didn't want the Amytal, he would say, 'Well, you owe me a lot of money.' I took it to mean: You'd better do it my way, or I'm not going to see you anymore.

"I remember one of the first times after Amytal, he said, 'Most people, Mrs. Morrison, most people after the Amytal become friendly and sociable, but not you. You turned away from me.' "

Annie recalls times when she wanted to quit, thinking it was getting her nowhere. She'd tell him she didn't think she should come in anymore. "He would say, 'You know, I'm not dunning you,'" she recalls. "He would act very concerned and gentle with me when I tried to quit. I was quitting all the time because it was too much at fifty or forty dollars an hour. He kept dropping his price to keep me coming. He charged me very little. By the end, it was twenty dollars an hour.

"He also did bartering with me because I worked in a jewelry store. We spent a lot of time talking about my getting him a necklace for his wife. He had said, 'We can make some kind of arrangement'—suggesting he would trade therapy time to pay for the necklace. So he bought this three-hundred-dollar necklace—it was garnets—and he made a big deal over it: it was quite beautiful. But then he changed his mind about the arrangement; he didn't want to trade time or pay for it." Annie was stuck with the bill.

One of the first times Annie recalled something from an Amytal session, the memory came to her suddenly, a couple of hours after awakening. "I recalled being up on my knees, sort of sitting up, and the sheet was down so I was naked, and I remember him coming in the opposite door, and he came over and started kissing me," she says. "Ugh. I remembered it seemed very real, and then I thought: Oh, no, this can't be. I was just dreaming.

"At our next session, I brought it up, and I was very upset because it had seemed so real. I said, 'I know this can't be true, but I think I remember something happening under Amytal. I know it can't be, but I remember I was on my knees, and I remember you kissing me, and it was really upsetting.' I was crying while I told him this.

"He was very composed and very Freudian about it. He said, 'And why would something like this be so upsetting, Mrs. Morrison?'

"I said, 'Because it would be so inappropriate!'

"He was so cool. He didn't deny it. If he had disavowed it, it would have seemed more true. But this way, it was all on me. It was all my fantasy, my problem."

Annie says that in retrospect, she can't even remember why she thought she was taking Sodium Amytal, "except I thought it would make me better somehow. Also, I knew Daniella was doing it a lot, and I thought: Well, I'll do it too. She's my best friend; I don't want her getting a lot better than me."

Annie, like Daniella, went out flying with Dr. Masserman. Although he invited her a number of times, however, Annie went only once. "It was very uncomfortable for me," Annie remembers. "Once was enough. It was a terrifying experience. I thought: Here I am sitting in this tiny little airplane with this seventy-year-old man who is so deaf he can't even hear what they're saying over the radio. I thought: I'm in the middle of a very serious bad dream.

"My guess is that he liked being seen with attractive women. When I went flying with him, he was walking along with me, all fixed up in his little flier's cap with the earflaps hanging down, and he was strutting along in front of these other men, and I had the distinct feeling: This man is showing me off.

"As time went on, I remember thinking: What the hell is this? I remember him saying, 'Cancel the appointment if you have your period, because the Amytal will make you bleed harder.' I thought: This is absolutely bizarre. But that's how unconfident and confused I was, to listen to such nonsense when my intelligence was saying, 'This is ridiculous, Annie!'

"He would say things like, 'Go in there and loosen up your clothing. Just wear loose things.' Then, more and more, he would be insistent about it. 'I noticed you had some very tight garments on, Mrs. Morrison. Could you loosen up your clothing, or don't wear this or that.' He never just said, 'Take all your clothes off,' but you could tell that was the intention. There was a part of me that was saying, 'This man is trying to get me undressed,' and there was another part of me saying, 'Oh, no, this is Dr. Masserman, and you're a bizarre woman who wants her daddy or something.' I was so willing to think that everything was my fault."

Dr. Masserman told Annie, like Daniella, that she had "bad veins." "He had a really hard time getting that needle in, and it made him very angry. He told me once, 'Ah, Mrs. Morrison, don't get yourself into a car accident, because your veins are so bad.' I was terrified for the longest time that my veins were impossible. And I think now he was just inept. Because since then I've had my blood taken many times, and there isn't any problem. But he tore me up. I'd be bleeding up and down both arms. And he would be as annoyed as hell.

"He used to get extremely angry. I remember one day when he was so angry with me because he couldn't get that needle in. He kept sticking it into me, and I would say, 'You're hurting me,' and he would say, 'This doesn't hurt.' This day he put it in my ankles and my hand, and he had got it in enough so I had some of the Amytal in my system. I was bleeding up and down my arms, but I wasn't all the way under. I was still conscious.

"Dr. Masserman was pacing and real annoyed, and I remember he went to his desk and then he came back in. I was half drugged, and I remember he was pacing up and down the room and rubbing his crotch—masturbating himself with his clothes on. I thought: I must be dreaming. He gave us this sheet to cover ourselves with, but I didn't wear a bra. I was sitting there and feeling very exposed, and bleeding all over the place.

"Then I must have passed out. The next thing I remember was he took some cotton swabs and he was wiping the blood off my arm and he was wiping it on my breasts. And I remember he was really getting off on the stroking of the blood.

"I said, 'What are you doing?'

"He got very angry with me. And I was so confused because I had some of the stuff in my bloodstream, and I was thinking: Am I crazy, or is this man sitting here stroking my breasts?"

At the time, Annie was dating a psychiatrist. He had, in fact, taken classes at Northwestern with Dr. Masserman. After this last incident, Annie phoned him and described the bizarre episode with Masserman masturbating and stroking her breasts with blood. "It wasn't that he thought I was lying," she says, "but he just said, 'It just couldn't be.'

He said, 'Annie, I know you wouldn't make this up, but *Dr. Masserman?* I just can't believe it. Not Dr. Masserman.'

"It was maddening, but it *didn't* seem possible. Daniella and I talked about it, and we both said, 'It just couldn't be!' I convinced myself that I must have dreamed it."

Eventually, it became so difficult for Dr. Masserman to get the needle in Annie's arm that he didn't give her Amytal very often. Instead, he started insisting that she go out on his boat with him—to give her some idea, he said, of what it was like to be outgoing and friendly. She thinks now that he got her on the boat and openly propositioned her there because he had become overwhelmed by the frustration of not being able to get that needle in her arm or the Amytal into her system.

"He would say, 'Many people have been on my boat; Daniella has been on my boat.' He told me that many, many times. He'd say, 'It's just a way of being sociable, Mrs. Morrison. I just want you to see what it's like to be sociable.' 'Why do you want to be so contrary, Mrs. Morrison?' I just never understood the whole thing. I never really understood the exact purpose, but finally, I thought: Well, okay, it's creepy, but I'm doing this to move through my stuff, and this will help. Jules Masserman is telling me to do this, and Daniella has done it; I'm going to go do it.

"The first time, it was bizarre. I was not cooperative. We had some sandwiches up on the deck, and then he said, 'I'm going down below, and you can follow me if you wish.' I didn't want to. It was so horrible. But I just felt like I was failing miserably because I didn't follow him. Then he was real annoyed with me, and he rowed me back to shore. I felt I'd done something to avoid getting better.

"He did the same routine the next time. He offered me sandwiches, and then he started downstairs and said, 'You can come down if you wish.' I thought: Okay, well, I better go down. It was this feeling of 'Don't go down there!' Feeling, 'I can't go down there with that dirty old man.' But the other part of me was saying, 'Come on, this is Jules Masserman; go find out what the next step is.'

"So I went down, and he offered me wine. We had a little wine, and then we were sitting close, and he put his hand inside my shirt and fondled my breasts, and then he kissed me. It was so horrible, this old, disgusting creature. Then—this is unbelievable—he took his teeth out and put them on this little shelf above us, and he kissed me some more. I was thinking: This *isn't* really happening. I can't tell you how gross it was. And then he asked me, he said, 'Would you like to get more comfortable so we can go further, Mrs. Morrison?'

"I said, 'No!' 'Get more comfortable' was his euphemism for taking off your clothes. He always said in his office, 'Wouldn't you like to get more comfortable now?' 'No!' I said again.

"He looked surprised and extremely annoyed. He was always annoyed with me. I didn't do what I was supposed to do. All I knew is that I wanted to get to shore.

"He rowed me back. While he was rowing, I was thinking: I'm crazy. This could never have happened. I was feeling truly on the edge. I thought: This could not be happening, I must be way, way out there.

"And then, when we got out of the rowboat, to make things even more bizarre, he said, 'You know, you're going to be finding out that Miss Laird has died.'

"I said, 'How'd she die?'

"And he said, 'Well, she died suddenly.'

"And I just thought I was in some twilight zone. It scared me. And I thought he was a very, very scary man.

"I was really afraid of him. I was afraid when we would go into that little Amytal room. I used to feel: What am I doing in this room?

"He was taking terrible chances. He must have thought I was a complete imbecile, because there he was necking with me on his boat and I was just disgusted while I was doing it, and that is the most excruciatingly horrible part of the whole thing. It's sickening to me that he's such a megalomaniac. He has no scruples. And he would do anything. There's nothing he wouldn't do. It's okay for him to do whatever he wants. I think he really believes he didn't do anything wrong because he's Jules Masserman.

"But it's interesting how we convinced ourselves that he was doing things for our benefit."

Annie never went back to Masserman after that boat ride. She couldn't deceive herself into believing that what had happened was indeed a dream. As she started putting together the pieces, they added up to terrible betrayal, and she was livid. "It had never seemed absolutely clear that it was all true, but it was," she says. "I knew it was. People tend to think other people jump on the bandwagon in a case like this, but there's no reason to jump on this bandwagon. It was really a coincidence. If Daniella hadn't been a lawyer, we would never have known this had happened to anyone else. I was planning on filing a case against him; that's why we went and looked."

When Daniella moved back to Chicago, Annie told her that she wanted to sue Dr. Masserman. "She wanted to punish him," Daniella says. "I didn't. I was still in denial, and I was even more afraid of my alcoholism being exposed. I was also blaming myself for the whole thing. It took me a long time to get angry, but by the time we went to Daley Center to look up the records, I was starting to get very upset. Comparing notes with Annie was sort of like it had been comparing notes with my sister when we were twenty some years old and discovered that our uncle had molested both of us."

Using the anonymity of the pseudonym "Doe," Annie Morrison and Daniella Biagi filed lawsuits against Dr. Masserman. Their complaints included charges that Jules H. Masserman did not use due or reasonable care in diagnosing their problems, choosing their treatment, or choosing the medication or chemicals to be placed in their bodies. In Daniella's case, he was charged with negligently "administering drugs to Plaintiff knowing Plaintiff was addicted to alcohol." Among his offenses, he was charged with carelessly and negligently:

- failing to respond to the Plaintiff's request for proper treatment . . .
- failing to call for a specialist's help when [he knew or should have known] that a specialist was necessary for proper treatment . . .
- inject[ing] certain drugs, chemicals and other solutions . . . in an attempt to drug or numb the Plaintiff, when the Defendant knew . . . or should have known, that such injections, drugging or numbing was of no medical, psychiatric or diagnostic value . . .
- caus[ing] the Plaintiff to remain disrobed throughout the therapeutic sessions while unconscious, when the Defendant knew . . . such action was of [no] medical or diagnostic value.
- fail[ing] to inform the Plaintiff of the risk inherent in the procedures used . . .
- inject[ing] drugs . . . merely for the purpose of temporarily changing the Plaintiff's condition of health so that the Defendant could take advantage of the Plaintiff sexually.

Their civil complaints, like mine, asked for an amount in excess of fifteen thousand dollars on each count and were filed with the Circuit Court of Cook County. Like me, Daniella and Annie didn't have good criminal cases because they lacked evidence. Again, it was only their word against his, and this made it too difficult to prove criminal misconduct, whereas a civil case proving medical negligence seemed more achievable. Ken Cunniff told me that after our lawsuits were resolved, I could talk to both of these women, but until then, he didn't want us to be subject to any accusations of collusion.

When I later learned about Annie's and Daniella's experiences, I wondered how many other women Dr. Jules Masserman had treated in the same way over the more than forty years he had been a practicing psychiatrist.

12 Facing the Perpetrator

FRIDAY, SEPTEMBER 13, 1985 I sat across a large walnut conference table from Jules Masserman and found myself looking at him with pure contempt. My bitterness shocked me, as did everything else during the first discovery deposition in *Barbara Noël* v. *Jules H. Masserman, M.D.*

Dr. Masserman, the quintessential professional in a crisp pink shirt and an elegant gray suit, was suntanned, fit, and healthy-looking despite his age. He sat quietly, his hands folded together on the table. He had a cane at his side, but it looked new, and I wondered if it wasn't more for show than need.

Debra Davy, his solicitous lawyer, sat beside Dr. Masserman, behaving like a devoted daughter or granddaughter concerned with his every breath under trying circumstances. Even before the proceedings began, she repeatedly patted his arm and whispered little encouragements to him—as if he were the innocent victim of a malicious demon twice his size.

When Ken and I met the court reporter and Debra Davy in the reception room at the Hinshaw Culbertson law offices, Davy grinned and cried, "Kenny!" She had the tan of a tennis player and was smartly dressed and breezy—not the tough-appearing "dame" I had expected. I was admiring the bounce of her shiny brown hair when Ken introduced us. She immediately lost her smile, looked me up and down for a moment or two, and then nodded without a word. Her antagonistic head-to-toe appraisal seemed to gauge not only my looks and my clothes but my intentions.

Initially, in the lawyers' reception room, it had looked as if only Ken, Debra Davy, the court reporter, and I would be attending this deposition. But when we walked down a corridor into the designated conference room, Ken and I were startled to see Dr. Masserman seated at the table. I had to walk past him, and as I did so, I couldn't overcome my knee-jerk southern manners; I said an icy "Good morning, Dr. Masserman."

He nodded but said nothing. I thought: You're not going to shake me up with your rude efforts at intimidation. Debra Davy assigned me a seat directly opposite Dr. Masserman, and he stared as I sat down. I realized he would be staring at me throughout my testimony. I looked at him, thinking: If you stare at me, I'll stare at you.

The court reporter bent over her machine, getting ready to begin. Everything would be recorded according to the Illinois Code of Civil Procedure and the rules of the Illinois Supreme Court. She swore me to tell the truth and the whole truth, and then Debra Davy began to question me. She didn't get far. She said, "Now, Ms. Nole—"

The determination in my own voice surprised me as I slapped the table and interrupted her: "The name is No-elle."

Davy cleared her throat, pronounced my name properly, and launched into a series of quick, matter-of-fact questions about my birth, other family members, dates and places of my education and professional background—everything from where my father got his master's degree to a description of how I went about getting work for commercials.

She reviewed all the years I had seen Dr. Masserman and asked how many times a week I saw him from 1966 through 1984. I had been amazed to discover that my records showed at least 1,256 therapy sessions with Dr. Masserman, and those records were incomplete. She asked why I'd gone into therapy, what I had believed was the purpose of the Amytal, and how often I'd had the drug. I testified that for eighteen years, except for two stretches of time during which I'd quit therapy, I'd had Amytal a minimum of once every six weeks but sometimes as often as three days in a row. I estimated very conservatively that I had been given Amytal a minimum of 180 times.

I testified that although I had believed the Amytal was allowing me to "get in touch with certain memories and beliefs," I never remembered anything from the times I was knocked out, "other than a few fleeting statements at the onset of the drug entering my body."

I noticed that every time the word "Amytal" was mentioned—by me or by Debra Davy—Dr. Masserman's eyes widened or he looked up with a startled expression on his face, as if caught in the middle of a private daydream.

Davy asked me if it would be fair to say that between 1966 and 1984, I had trusted Dr. Masserman. I said it would be fair to say so. She asked if I had loved Dr. Masserman, and I said no. She asked if I had loved him, not as a sexual love, but as a friend and counselor, and again I said no. She asked if I had liked him, and I said yes.

It didn't take long for Davy to get to the dates of my marriages and questions about whether I met Richard Noël while he was still living with his wife and children, whether I began dating him then (Yes), and whether I slept with him and had sexual intercourse with him then (Yes). Her line of questioning appeared to be part of an effort to establish a profile of me as a "loose" woman. I wasn't proud that Richard and I had committed adultery; in fact, I'd been troubled about it and had told Dr. Masserman about it in therapy—which was why Debra Davy now had that information to use against me. Even as I realized that Davy's line of questioning had been influenced by Dr. Masserman, I still felt guilty about the adultery and shamed by having it raised publicly—even in this room.

Then Debra Davy began hammering away at my work, apparently under a false impression from Dr. Masserman that I was a flighty, unsuccessful singer, frustrated with my career and looking for some escape from my bitterness through the fabrication of an incredible story against him. She established that I didn't have an office—not a major lack for a free-lance singer, of course, but it sounded bad. Then she asked me to estimate the income I made as a singer in a normal year.

"Approximately fifty thousand dollars annually," I said. She looked shocked, and I felt victorious. I mentioned that I had turned over tax returns as part of the interrogatories, and the lowest income I had reported for the preceding seven years was $45,000, in 1979.

Ken added insult to injury: "Didn't you get copies of her tax returns?"

Davy next tried to establish that I was in debt to Dr. Masserman—implying another possible reason for my suing him. She asked if it wasn't correct that when I left Dr. Masserman's "care," I still owed him "a sum of money." I said that was correct. She asked if I still owed it to him today.

"Three hundred fifty dollars," I answered, thinking I don't *owe* him a dime, particularly not after having paid him more than $100,000 over all those years.

"You still owe it to him now?"

"He bills me every month," I answered.

When Davy questioned me at length about my drinking, she seemed to want to establish that I was an alcoholic, perhaps to further undermine my credibility. This seemed odd in light of what I now knew was "common knowledge": that alcoholics should never be given Amytal or any other barbiturate. I still didn't believe I was alcoholic, but I told the truth about how, starting in about 1978, I was able to get a nice feeling from drinking small amounts of liquor. "It would take me two martinis, and I'd be passed out," I said. "It didn't take much. I'd drink half a bottle of wine."

She asked me if I drank every day—which I did—from about 1978 to 1984. Dr. Masserman had started giving me Antabuse in 1979 and then gave it to me off and on for six months at a time through 1984. Debra Davy asked me what precipitated my drinking in 1978. I told her it was because I was not seeing the doctor at that time and wasn't getting any Amytal.

"Are you suggesting, then, that you began drinking because you weren't getting Sodium Amytal?" she asked.

"I'm telling you that I began drinking when I wasn't getting Amytal," I said, "and I do remember that the doctor told me that if I ever was to drink, that 'gin was the purest thing,' and I do think that particular liquor mimics the flush of pleasure that Amytal gives."

As I was speaking, Dr. Masserman lowered his head, shook it slowly from side to side, and exhaled loudly. At one point, he took off his jacket, rolled up his sleeves, and loosened his tie. A couple of times I heard him say, "Tsk, tsk," as if I were saying untrue and unjust things. He had a notepad in front of him, and he seemed to be taking copious notes. From time to time after I spoke, he wrote furiously on the pad.

I had been warned that Davy would say derogatory things about me, but I wasn't prepared enough. She continued to try to characterize me as a sexual libertine and asked me if I hadn't talked a great deal about my sexual fantasies to Dr. Masserman. When I answered that I had never talked to him about sexual fantasies, not ever, she raised her eyebrows in surprise. She queried me in a rather harsh voice as to whether I had any venereal disease (No), whether I had fears of men approaching me in bed (No), and whether I "harbor[ed] fears about men sexually" (No). I thought her repeated insinuations about my morals—interwoven with more innocuous questions—were in bad taste. Later, Ken said that those questions were so blatant as attempts to discredit me that they failed.

When we took a short break from the deposition, Debra Davy stayed close to Dr. Masserman's elbow, attentive as he got up, making sure he was the first person to leave the room. I avoided going into the ladies' room at the same time as Davy, but later, when I emerged from the rest room, I saw Dr. Masserman and realized I was alone with him in the hallway. I didn't feel physically at risk; I only hated having to encounter the enemy. He was standing still, almost as if waiting for me, and I would have to walk past him to get back to the conference room. I pulled up my shoulders, took a deep breath, and realized that in my high-heeled pumps, I towered over him. That gave me heart. I walked by him silently, my chin high.

Back in the conference room, I permitted myself a moment of self-congratulation. But under Debra Davy's attacks, it didn't take long for me to feel like a shamed little girl again. It was lucky that Davy was so aggressive and inaccurate; it made me mad enough to keep me clearheaded and in control while I testified.

When she started questioning me about what took place on September 21, 1984, she went at it in different ways, sometimes leaving the subject and then returning to it later. Going over the sequence of events in the examining room, I testified to everything that had happened and then said I had seen Dr. Masserman from the back as he was washing his genitals at the sink—or giving an indication of doing so from his elbow movements. I said I closed my eyes and rolled my head back so I would appear to be asleep. I'd heard the sound of change jingling, I said, and assumed he was getting dressed; then he came over, pulled my pants up, and covered me.

"What pants? Underpants?" she asked.

"Underpants."

"You assumed Dr. Masserman did this?"

"Whoever was in the room, nude, with a suntan and white buttocks and with a bald head—yes, ma'am," I answered.

Debra Davy then asked me why I pretended to be asleep.

"Have you ever been raped, ma'am?" I asked.

"No."

"It's scary," I said.

"Did it hurt?"

"No, not physically."

While I was testifying, I noticed Dr. Masserman glaring at me, and I glared back with equal vengeance. Debra Davy asked me if I recalled the individual who had his penis inside me having an orgasm.

"I recall sounds that would indicate that an orgasm might be happening," I replied. "I have no knowledge that it actually did. I had no feeling that it actually did."

"Did you climax?"

I could hardly believe my ears. "No," I answered sharply.

"When you heard the sounds of an orgasm, do you mean vocal sounds?"

"Vocal."

"Grunts, that sort of thing?"

"That's correct."

Altogether, the deposition lasted more than four hours. At the end, Debra Davy stood up, put her hand on Masserman's elbow, and steered him out of the conference room with gentle deference. Ken asked me to wait for him downstairs in the lobby, so I went to the elevators alone. As I was standing there, the court reporter, carrying her speed-typing equipment, joined me. We got into the elevator together, positioned ourselves several spaces apart, and smiled awkwardly. "I'll bet you're going to get some lunch as fast as humanly possible," I said, trying to be light. "You must be starving."

"Yes, just as soon as I drop off this equipment," she said. "Say, tell me something."

"What?" I said, suddenly afraid she was going to ask me something about the lawsuit, which wasn't allowed and could be cause for throwing out the case.

"What commercials would I be able to hear you on?"

In the lobby, Ken greeted me with a smile and the reassurance that I had "sailed through it beautifully." I was worried I'd gotten dates confused, but Ken told me I was credible and solid, and he wouldn't hesitate to have me testify in front of a jury.

"I think Debra Davy was malicious," I said. "But it's obvious she doesn't believe me."

"A strange thing is that women tend not to believe other women,"

Ken said. "It's men who tend to believe women. If we get to trial, we're going to try for an all-male jury."

"It's as if the truth has nothing to do with anything," I said.

"Don't worry about that," Ken said. "Wonder instead how Dr. Masserman will handle it when we spring his two other patients on him during his discovery deposition."

On the way home, I stopped and bought fried chicken and a pint of chocolate ice cream. After a feast to celebrate my deposition being over, I slept soundly for more than fourteen hours.

Ken told me that since my discovery deposition was now a matter of public record, it was legally safe for me to contact the other patients whom I knew and had been concerned about. The first friend I spoke to about Dr. Masserman was "Linda Jass," an actress. Linda and I, who knew each other from auditions, had run into each other in Dr. Masserman's reception room a few years earlier. Initially, we had both been a little surprised and embarrassed, but we'd bonded over our mutual "secret" of being in therapy, and after that, we'd gotten together several times. I called her a few days after I'd made my deposition, and we met one afternoon at a downtown deli. I was nervous about how to explain what had happened, but over cups of decaf espresso and Danish pastries, I told Linda the whole story.

"That's criminal," she said. "I wouldn't put it past him, not one bit. He's such a disgusting, egotistical bastard. I stopped seeing him because he was such a creep." Linda said he had talked her into taking Amytal, "as an aid to get to the heart of my problem," and she'd agreed on six different occasions.

"He told me to take off my clothes, but I kept on every stitch," she said. "He couldn't even get me to take off my shoes. I guess I just didn't trust him very much! Oh, Jesus, I hope you get him, Barb. If there's anything I can do to help, let me know. And keep me posted on what's going down."

After Linda's response, I felt prepared to talk to Diane Greenspan. Since we'd returned from our trip to Paris with Dr. Masserman three years earlier, I'd spent a lot of time with Diane and her husband. "I have something upsetting I want to talk to you about," I said when I phoned her.

Diane was a sunny woman, always lively and animated. As we sat in her large, comfortable kitchen, drinking tea from porcelain cups, she listened to me intently, but her face began to lose all its usual animation. When I finished, she said in a totally deadpan voice, "Tell me again." I told her again, and there was no response whatsoever in her face. I asked her if she'd ever had Amytal, and she said Dr. Masserman had offered it to her but she had never taken any.

"I want you to know," Diane said stoutly, "that man is the father I never had. My father might have been the best provider in Hyde Park, but he was never the father to me that Dr. Masserman has been."

I had assumed Diane would believe me. But she proceeded to tell me that she didn't ever want to hear me say another word against Dr. Masserman. "The only reason I became friends with you in the first place was because he insisted on it," she said hotly.

"What do you mean?"

"I was very upset and jealous when I found the two of you in the park in Paris," she said. "But he told me afterward that I should give you a chance. He said I should become friends with you so that I'd realize you were a nice lady and there was nothing to be jealous of."

I was astounded. As I listened to her, I realized that she adored the man; she worshiped him. She loved him in the way Debra Davy had tried to intimate I did; but I had never felt like that. I have since learned that most people, myself included, feel "Nobody can talk about my father but me." I had accused her "father" of doing something to me that she didn't want to believe.

Little more than a week after I talked to Diane Greenspan, the results of my visit to her were manifest. Ken called to tell me he was sending me a copy of a letter that he and Bill had just received from Debra Davy, in which she said Dr. Masserman had learned and informed her that "Ms. Noël has been calling his patients [and] telling them, in lurid detail, about her alleged rape by Dr. Masserman." She said I must immediately stop calling Dr. Masserman's patients, or they would be forced to seek an immediate injunction and sue me for slander.

Ken said that although a suit against me would not stick, I should probably just keep quiet for the time being. Masserman's discovery deposition was less than two weeks away, and it would be better not to incur any more of Davy's wrath or complicate the issues.

Diane's betrayal—I was sure it must have been hers—upset me deeply. Despite Ken's admonition, I felt I must speak to her again. I finally called and said, "Do you know what's happened? I've gotten a letter from Dr. Masserman's lawyers threatening me with an injunction and a slander suit.

"Who could have told the doctor?" I probed. "Could it have been you?"

Diane excused herself. In a moment, she returned and said, "Well, Barbara, in answer to your question, well, at least now maybe you'll leave that poor, dear man alone."

When the day came for Jules Masserman to be deposed, we waited for him and Debra Davy and the court reporter to arrive at Ken's old Barrister Hall law office on LaSalle Street. Ken and Bill were lively and cheerful. Today it was their turn to ask the questions, and today they would spring the two other patients on Dr. Masserman. The stories of those two women not only introduced new evidence but corroborated my reports. I looked forward to seeing Masserman squirm; yet at the same time, I dreaded it.

Across a conference table from me once again, Jules Masserman seemed to have shrunk. It was November 7, 1985, not quite two months since my deposition, but he seemed more wizened and puny than I'd ever seen him. With his glasses on, he looked like someone in a plastic Groucho Marx nose, with glasses and mustache attached.

Because of Bill Carroll's background as a psychologist, he was the one who would depose Dr. Masserman. After Masserman was sworn in, Bill began his questioning with such deliberate courtesy that for a while I almost wondered whose side he was on. But then I began to see how the courtesy paid off. Masserman was flattered. He was smart and articulate, a man used to having center stage, and he explained things as if he were teaching a class of medical students, often warming to his topic and saying more than was necessary.

A big surprise at the beginning of this deposition came when Debra Davy put three small sheets of paper into evidence as the sum total of Dr. Masserman's notes on me for eighteen years of treatment. One extra three-by-five-inch paper had the date 1967 on it and was separate from the three other sheets, which appeared to have been torn from a spiral notebook. Those sheets contained abbreviated, sketchy notes dated 1979, 1980, and 1981. All three pages of notes appeared to have been written in the same ink, in the same small handwriting, as if they had been prepared hastily in one sitting. He had written "Hates All Men" and "says boyfriend raped her." "Hates father, raped her when 15." I found it incredible that he didn't even try to make the notes look official or well organized or even thoughtful.

Bill asked, "Doctor, are these three pages that you presented to us this morning . . . the totality of your notes on Barbara's treatment?"

"To my knowledge, yes, sir," Masserman said. "Other than the daily schedule, which I keep in [an] appointment book."

". . . I believe, Doctor, that you said you have seen her over the last eighteen years."

"Yes, sir."

"One page you presented us with does not have any year noted on it. . . . The second page that you present us with indicates the year 1979, the year 1980, the year 1981, and I believe the year [1984] . . . and there is a third page which does not indicate any year as well. But that does not add up to eighteen years. So, Doctor, apparently you have seen Ms. Noël in some years in which you have presented us with no records of your notes for those years, is that correct?"

"That's correct."

Dr. Masserman explained that the small card dated 1967 was an "admission note" from when he first saw me; admission notes, he said, are kept separately from the treatment records, which he keeps in a "confidential drawer for patients' records."

Bill asked him if he was sure of that 1967 date, and Dr. Masserman later corrected it, saying, "That first appointment was March 7, 1966."

"Now, when you obtained these notes, Doctor, that you gave us, these sheets of paper, were they separate sheets of paper like I see before me now?"

"Yes, sir." Dr. Masserman paused and looked heavenward, hands clasped, as if in deep thought. Then he explained that the notes had been in a spiral notepad and that he kept each patient's record "on a different pad of paper."

"Now, were there any other sheets in that spiral except these two?"

"No, there were not."

When I looked at those three pages of notes, I was stunned. I thought: What were you doing all that time you were writing as I talked? You wrote so much that I thought you were taking down every word I said! I looked at him and realized in a flash of wonder that during all those psychoanalytic hours I paid for, Dr. Masserman probably had been writing any number of his four hundred–plus professional articles, his thirteen books or chapters of books, letters to colleagues, or perhaps his poetry and music; he probably listened only rarely to a word I said. Even during my deposition, he'd written down many more notes than he had scrawled across those three little pages.

Dr. Masserman testified that he couldn't recall how many times he had seen me and that his records wouldn't reflect it, "because I clear out [my] records every five years or so. Otherwise they would accumulate to an impossible extent."

This admission was remarkable. One psychiatrist reviewing the case later said, "It's unheard of for a psychiatrist to get rid of his records; we keep records for years, because we often end up being lifetime consultants to people. The IRS lets you destroy your records every five years, but we don't do that in psychiatry."

Dr. Masserman testified I had initially sought his assistance because: "She was having difficulty with her second husband. She was having periods of depression and anxiety, spells of anger. She was having thoughts of suicide." He said, speaking in a reluctant but gracious voice, that if he were forced to label my symptoms in terms of categories recognized by the American Psychiatric Association, he would say, "Personality maladaptable with episodes of anxiety and depression and suicidal preoccupation."

That was the second time he'd said I was suicidal, but I had never discussed suicide or even considered it. I angrily scribbled a note to Ken. "Suicide? No way!" Then, still unsure of myself, I wondered: Could I have been suicidal all those years and not known it? Could he have known that and kept it from me?

Bill asked him whether at any time during the eighteen successive years he had had any occasion to change his diagnosis. Dr. Masserman answered, "Yes; I had occasion to add to it."

"When was that, Doctor?"

"When she described episodes of alcoholism."

"I see."

"With details such as she could hardly open a bottle of liquor without finishing it."

I had never been the kind of drinker who could hardly open a bottle without finishing it, and Dr. Masserman knew that. I was glad he'd said it, though, because it jolted me into realizing that this and the suicide business were just his way of trying to discredit me.

Bill's demeanor remained gentle as he worked his way through to the subject of Dr. Masserman's method of psychotherapy. "I'm a trained psychoanalyst," Dr. Masserman said, sighing deeply as if it were a test of his patience to be forced once again to explain the obvious. "I applied analytic principles, which consisted of trying to trace through the origins of her discomforts as expressed currently with regard to behavior modification. [I] counseled her as to how she could readjust her career to more modest objectives which she could attain."

When Bill asked Dr. Masserman whether he had at some point "enlisted the help of Sodium Amytal into this treatment," Masserman said he had but could not recall when he first administered it to me. "I do not keep continuous records of patients for a number of reasons: confidentiality is one," Dr. Masserman said. "Once I get to know an individual, it is not necessary to keep detailed accounts."

He said he did not keep a record of each time he administered Amytal to me or any other patient; he occasionally would make a note "when there was something very significant."

When Bill homed in on the subject of Sodium Amytal,* Debra Davy grew more and more wary and was quick to object and show anger at the slightest hint of disrespect in the questioning. She was right to be wary, because by now Bill was quite knowledgeable about the standard use of Amytal. He had done his homework, and he had talked to a number of people well versed in psychopharmacology. Medical experts agreed:

Amytal is a dangerous and potentially lethal drug that induces a sleep-like state and lowers the inhibitions of the person taking it. While it was often used after its introduction, in the 1920s and during World War II, it never proved effective as an aid to normal therapy.

Amytal is rarely if ever used in a private practitioner's office. It is a central nervous system depressant and should be administered under the most careful of circumstances in a hospital or in an outpatient setting where a trained anesthesiologist is present, and oxygen and equipment for resuscitation are readily available.

When used for diagnostic purposes, Amytal normally is given in tablet or capsule form; intravenous injections of Amytal are extremely rare

---

*"Sodium Amytal" and "Amytal" are names that can be used interchangeably; they refer to the same substance, amobarbital sodium, a short-acting barbiturate.

and should be given only in emergency situations, under close supervision.

There is *no* medical reason to use Amytal on a regular basis, nor one
that justifies its continued or prolonged use.

Giving Amytal on a repeated basis not only is not standard care; it is
bad practice.

The factors of having patients come in to a private office so early in
the morning, asking them to undress, and keeping them asleep or groggy
all day indicates that something clearly unusual and extremely odd is
going on.

It would be medically negligent to use this drug on any person who
is a known substance abuser.

Amytal is addictive and produces a strong need to continue taking the
drug and increase the dosage. Dependence on the effects of Amytal is
both physical and psychic.

Pharmacologically, it makes sense that a patient receiving Amytal regularly will become addicted to alcohol as well. Alcohol and Amytal create
similar effects and are "cross-tolerant," which means they hit some of the
same receptors in the brain. Thus, a hit of Amytal is somewhat like a hit
of alcohol or a drunk on alcohol. Which is why so many people in the
1950s—Marilyn Monroe being one of them—used alcohol together with
barbiturates when the latter were prescribed more regularly. They are
both fundamentally central nervous system depressants and create the
same kind of high.

With his patient probing of Jules Masserman's practice of administering Sodium Amytal, Bill Carroll was about to score several vital
points. In his wildest vision, Bill hadn't dared to imagine that Dr.
Masserman would respond as he did to questions about his use of
Amytal. He thought Jules Masserman was a very intelligent man and
probably a creative and original thinker—which no doubt would make
it fascinating to hear a genuine explanation of his alleged behavior,
perhaps a therapeutic theory about sex with patients under Amytal.
But Bill's fear, of course, was that Masserman wouldn't even admit to
using Amytal. If he denied using Amytal, or denied using it more than
once, we wouldn't have had any way to prove that he did.

But Dr. Masserman surprised us. He never denied using Amytal. In
fact, his answers indicated that administering Amytal was, for him, a
routine, common practice. And although he had been chairman and
a faculty member of Northwestern University's department of psychiatry and neurology, he gave no indication that he knew his use of

Amytal was very far afield from standard medical practice. Did he think that the fact he himself used it made it acceptable?

When Bill Carroll asked, "Now, Doctor, within the theoretical framework of your therapy plan, what was to be the role of Sodium Amytal?" Dr. Masserman answered, "It was used only on occasions when she was seriously depressed, was agitated, exceedingly anxious, and required some relief from excessive tension and discouragement. [It also provided] communication and relief, and some indication as to what was troubling her particularly at the time."

To Bill Carroll's inquiry regarding the percentage of his patients he had prescribed Amytal for, Dr. Masserman replied, "I do not recollect, sir. I have had hundreds of patients." When Bill pressed him further, for numbers in the last five years, he said he had prescribed it for "five or six" male patients. As for female patients: "It is very difficult to say. I believe there have been only a dozen in the last five years that had Amytal."

"Now, how do you determine, Doctor, which patient is to receive Sodium Amytal and which is not?"

"By the same criteria. A period of intense anxiety, depression, suicidal preoccupation, which if relieved would encourage the patient to continue under better circumstances in dynamic and corrective therapy without Amytal."

"At the time, it's given basically for relief?"

"Yes. . . . [It] is also to establish communication, rapport, and to elicit fantasies and preoccupations that can be used afterwards in a therapeutic way."

"So the information that you obtained can be used later in a dynamic way?"

"Yes, sir."

"But at the time elicited, it is not available for the dynamics of psychotherapy?"

"No, sir, that isn't so," Dr. Masserman said with a sigh. "Because it is my function and my procedure that after the patient does come back to full consciousness to recall what we talked about and to expand on it, for the purpose of better insight."

". . . is the situation that the patient must be told what was elicited during the state in which the patient was under the Sodium Amytal treatment . . . ?

"It's often not necessary to tell the patient what he or she talked about, because there is a certain modicum of recall. The patient is not completely unconscious. Memory is not totally abolished."

"Is the level of unconsciousness related to the level of dosage of Amytal as administered?"

"It varies a great deal from patient to patient, as you know. And only enough Amytal is administered so that communication is preserved."

"So there are times when the patient is not able to recall what you believe was the communication from the patient at the time the patient was under the Amytal treatment?"

"Well, that again is only a partial statement because very often in later intervals full conscious memories confirm what has been brought out under Amytal."

"But on those occasions does the patient recall that the patient made these statements under the Amytal?"

"Quite frequently."

"But not always?"

"Not always."

Shortly after that line of questions, Debra Davy interrupted to ask Dr. Masserman if he wouldn't like something to drink. Although he said no, she called for a break anyway.

When we resumed, Bill Carroll asked Dr. Masserman if his views on the role of Sodium Amytal within psychiatric treatment had changed since 1955. Within the field, of course, perceptions of the drug had changed dramatically. Even Dr. Masserman himself had written that Amytal usually didn't provide more information than a psychiatrist could elicit in a normal psychotherapeutic exchange.

But Dr. Masserman answered that his views on the drug hadn't changed. "Only with added experience as I use it . . . [which is] that for acutely disturbed episodes it is preferable to prescribing drugs that the patient can abuse, because it is under the control of the physician."

"So . . . [in your] medical judgment," Bill asked, "is [it] preferable from a medical point of view to prescribe Sodium Amytal for the kind of relief that a person might otherwise be inclined to seek from heroin, cocaine, alcohol, or some other drugs?"

"Of course," Dr. Masserman answered. "And since you mentioned alcohol, very often it prevents the individual going off on an alcoholic binge, providing the relief necessary to make the alcoholic binge un-necessary."

I didn't know it at the time, but Bill was dazzled. "Have you published this view that you have just expressed anywhere, Doctor?" he asked.

"I need not do that. . . . It is so much a matter of good practice that it was described in my 1955 book, thirty years ago."

"So the view that you just expressed that it is better to make use of Sodium Amytal in the place of other forms of relief that might be sought by a patient, that view was already expressed in 1955?"

"It was anticipated. It has been refined since by further experience. . . ."

"Did you indicate there that you believed it to be better to supply this form of drug rather than some other form of drug?"

"By implication, yes, sir. I would prefer to give Amytal than have the patient commit suicide, for example."

"Or to go on a drunken binge?"

"Yes, sir." Dr. Masserman said, sighing and giving the impression that this line of questioning was far beneath him but he would persevere. Debra Davy patted his arm.

"Are you aware of anyone with credentials in the psychiatric or psychological field who has taken a different view from you as to the beneficial effect of using Sodium Amytal in dynamic psychology?" Bill Carroll asked.

"I have run across no such articles."

"Well, then, can Sodium Amytal become addictive under any circumstances?"

"It cannot, because it is a Category Two drug and can be obtained only by prescription."

"If someone has access to it, can it become addictive?" Bill Carroll probed, with utmost cordiality in his voice.

"Sodium Amytal is not furnished in tablets and so on," Dr. Masserman answered irritably.*

"Doctor, my question is, and I am sorry to interrupt there, my question is, is Sodium Amytal the kind of drug which one can develop an addiction to if he or she has access to it?"

"It is a barbiturate, and one can develop addiction to barbiturates. But it [Amytal] is used intravenously."

I had been holding my breath until Bill built up to that question.

---

*Sodium Amytal, or Amylobarbitone, is available in tablets and in capsules, as well as in an elixir and powder for reconstitution as Sodium Amylobarbitone in injections, according to *Martindale's* and *Physicians' Desk Reference*.

Now I heaved a sigh and looked at Ken, who was grinning. Dr. Masserman's answer was nonsensical—using Amytal intravenously made no difference whatsoever to its addictive propensities. But even though what he said wasn't a strong admission, Masserman had finally conceded that a barbiturate could be addictive. Underneath his reserve, Bill seemed to smile as well.

Bill continued, and in answering his questions, Dr. Masserman admitted that it was "very rare" for anyone else to be present when he administered the Amytal to a patient. Then he contradicted himself by saying, "On the other hand, there is always my nurse present in the next office. The doors are kept open in between." He said he did "not recall" whether there was ever a time he administered Sodium Amytal to Ms. Noël or any other patient when his "nurse" was not present.

Bill asked him if he made any representation to any patients that someone would always be present while they were under the Amytal influence.

"It is my custom to explain Sodium Amytal before I ever give it to anyone," Dr. Masserman said, clasping his hands together. "Its advantages, its possible disadvantages, the fact that everything would be considered confidential, what was going on, and that if at any time they wished anyone else present, my secretary would be available."

"So they would have to ask for someone to be present before that person would be present?" Bill queried.

"Yes. But I would point out that since everything was confidential, they would have to take that into consideration."

Bill then asked, "Where did you administer this Sodium Amytal to your patients?"

Dr. Masserman replied, "In the cubital fossa, where the veins are prominent."

"No, I'm sorry," Bill said with a laugh. "Touché. In what room within your office suite did you administer the Sodium Amytal?"

"I am a neurologist and physician. I have an examining room with the blood pressure apparatus and stethoscope and cot for examination, where I do physical and neurological examinations. That same cot is used for the usual reclining position when Amytal is administered."

"For the effective use of Amytal, is it necessary to have a patient undress?"

"No, sir."

"Is it your statement that you did not require any of your patients to undress for the purpose of receiving the Amytal?"

"No, sir," Dr. Masserman responded. "All I ask for is to bare one arm or the other arm."

"You do not know if they were dressed or undressed?"

"When I come in, they are generally covered with a sheet and a blanket furnished on the cot."

"You have no recollection of any occasion when Ms. Noël received Sodium Amytal from you in the room you have just described while she was unclothed, except for her panties?"

"I have no such knowledge."

"Now, when the patient has been administered Sodium Amytal by you for purposes of relieving their agitated condition, do you remain in the room with the patient until the Sodium Amytal effects are deleted and the person returns to consciousness?"

"No, sir," Dr. Masserman said, looking disconcerted. "That would be three or four hours."

"What do you do while the person is in that room you just described?"

"I see other patients in my office immediately next door, with a soundproof door in between."

Dr. Masserman said that he or his nurse would, from time to time, go into the examining room "to make sure that the patient is relaxed, communicative, in good physical condition." He said that no one else could go into that room, because "the door to the outside [hallway] is locked. The only other door is to the office where I am seeing other patients."

When Bill asked him what the "usual dosage was," Dr. Masserman said that from his own recollection, "Dosage was *generally* 0.2 to 0.3 grams [of Amytal] in 5 percent solution of distilled water." He said he recalled that on September 21, 1984, he administered 0.2 ½ grams of Amytal to me.

Bill turned rather abruptly to the subject of whether Dr. Masserman had a boat, where he kept it, and what it looked like. Ken, the sailor, then took over the questions, saying, "Doctor, I'm fascinated by your boat. Can you describe the interior of your boat?"

Debra Davy looked alarmed. "You know something," she said. "What is the relevance of his boat?"

"It will become apparent," Bill said.

Dr. Masserman, led through the questions by Ken, described the boat as a thirty-two-foot steel yawl, blue with a brown deck, with three tiers, and including a galley, a salon, a head, an engine compartment, and sleeping quarters with a couple of bunks.

Later, Bill asked Masserman to describe the sleeping quarters, where two bunks converged. "What is the decorating scheme in that forward sleeping quarter?"

"The same; yellow."

"It is yellow," Bill repeated. "Was it yellow in 1984?"

"Yes."

"The summer?"

"Yes."

Debra Davy interrupted. "Are you thinking of adding a count, Counsel?"

"You'll see," Ken answered.

Bill then returned to questions pertaining to September 21, 1984, the day I woke up with Dr. Masserman raping me. Masserman seemed quite effusive as he seized the opportunity to discredit me.

"[That day] she repeated a great many of her concerns," he said. "She had requested Amytal on two previous occasions, I believe on September 4 and 17, and I thought it inappropriate to give it to her then. But this time she had a litany of special concerns. She had lost her job with a band. She was not securing any other engagements. She was in financial difficulty. She was having unfortunate relations with a number of men at the time, none of which had turned out satisfactorily. She was depressed, anxious. She had been drinking. And therefore again requested Amytal. I told her that I had not planned to give it to her because I was due to leave the office at some time before noon and this was about 9:30 or so. But since I thought it would be appropriate—at that time she had not had it very frequently that year—I asked her to go into the next room and as usual make herself ready for it."

"Now, when you said 'make yourself ready for it,' what did you mean by that?"

"As is usual, to lie down on the cot, cover herself over, only have her arm available for the Amytal. And then I proceeded with routine [sic] in preparing the Amytal. Would you like the routine? It's very simple."

Bill nodded.

"It's a small vial of 0.5 grams of Amytal, prepared by [Eli] Lilly [& Co.]. I have 10-cc vials of distilled water. I very carefully boil a syringe, use a new needle because I am very careful not to get any of Ms. Noël's blood in contact with myself because of her promiscuity and the prevalence of AIDS.

"After boiling the syringe and using a new needle, I extract 10 cc's from the bottle of distilled water, inject that into the vial without shaking to avoid any aeration, just rotation. Remove the solution then in the syringe, use alcohol on the extended arm, the cubital, and inject it not faster than one cc per minute, so it takes ten minutes, fifteen minutes for the initial injection. Inject only enough so that Ms. Noël, in this case, would feel relaxed, quieter, express gratitude for the relief of tension, and begin talking about her difficulties.

"At the time I do recall that, because it was only a relatively short time ago, not eighteen years, she did talk about her continued affairs with—I will use only first names because I don't like to involve other people by identification—with Tony, Frank, John, Robin, with whom she had intercourse some time back, Carleton, with whom she had relations more recently. And her general disappointment and discouragement . . . of not having attained the success in her life that she had hoped for, and that I had hoped for too."

Bill asked him if he'd ever found me delusional, and Dr. Masserman said that I had delusions about my talent, implying that besides my "failed relationships with men," the source of my bitterness was my "failed career"—in other words, I was pursuing this case against him because I was so disillusioned and frustrated from my inflated expectations about my own singing.

"She did have delusions . . . excessive ambition that she could be a prima donna and so on. She occasionally sang a little bit in my office. I could judge from her voice that this was not likely. . . . She did have the convictions that she could use men to promote her career, which I thought was a mistake in her pattern of thought."

Dr. Masserman was exceedingly articulate, and he made himself sound extremely helpful in trying to correct my delusions of grandeur. He's scum, I thought. He's a worm. His denigrating my singing ability wasn't too surprising, though; after all, he had told me more than once over the years, "Don't worry, Miz Nole, you're not a genius."

Dr. Masserman described in detail the stages of waking up from the Amytal—a description that matched my memories. He also testified that he'd administered the Sodium Amytal continuously over twenty-five minutes. Then he changed that and said, "After fifteen to twenty minutes, I withdrew the needle." He said his secretary, Peggy Karas, had, by her own account, checked on me twice on the day in question and had signed an affidavit swearing that she had checked me right after Dr. Masserman left the office at eleven-thirty that same morning. This time frame clearly contradicted my account.

He said he had not seen me since September 21, 1984, so he could not guess "whether she really believes it [the rape] or not, really thinks it occurred or [whether it's] just a wishful fantasy."

Ken suggested a recess, and I followed him and Bill into a stockroom, where we could have privacy. Bill asked me if Peggy Karas's account of Dr. Masserman's departure at eleven-thirty was possible. I said it wasn't. I had said goodbye to Dr. Masserman, and after a few minutes of disorientation in the hallway and a return of the bathroom key, I had gone down two flights to Dr. Seskind's office. Dr. Seskind was a very precise man, and his records showed I had arrived in his office at 12:15 P.M.

Ken and I complimented Bill on the job he was doing. "Boy, is this guy slippery or what?" Bill said. "Try to get a straight answer out of him! I'm exhausted."

We went back to the conference room, and Bill resumed his questions about what the doctor had done when he left his office. Dr. Masserman said that he had gone to Northwestern University's medical library.

"Now, did you withdraw any books at that time?" Bill asked.

"No, sir. I had donated my library to Northwestern University. I was checking up to see what they did with it."

"Did you have a conversation with someone at this time?"

"Just looked through the files."

"Could you give us the name of anyone who saw you there at that time?"

"No, sir. I just consulted the files to see where they had placed my books."

When asked if he later returned to his office, Dr. Masserman answered, without irony, "I don't recall, sir. That day didn't mean anything special to me at the time, because there was an Amytal session just like any others for the past many years."

Dr. Masserman denied absolutely that he was on top of me or inserted anything into my vagina on September 21, 1984. He testified that he had been married to his present wife for forty-three years and in response to a question whether in the last five years he had had sexual intimacy with any other woman besides his wife, he answered no.

"Any sexual contact?" Bill asked. "Have you fondled any other women's breasts?"

"No, sir," Dr. Masserman answered, looking up in exasperation.

"Have you touched any other women's genitals?"

"No, sir."

"Do you believe, Doctor, that physical, sexual stimulation by a therapist does have a proper role within a sex therapy program?"

"No, sir, I do not," Dr. Masserman said vehemently, shaking his head.

"Have you ever engaged in any sexual contact with your patients?"

"No, sir."

Bill then asked Masserman if he had ever taken any of his patients on his boat. Dr. Masserman said, "Yes. Ms. Noël, on one occasion."

When Bill asked if he had taken any of his other patients on his boat, Dr. Masserman shifted slightly in his chair and said yes he had.

"Would you tell us who they might be?" Bill asked.

"A male patient. I cannot use names."

"Any female patients?" Bill asked.

"I do not recollect any."

Then Bill paused and commented that Dr. Masserman must have many acquaintances, and the doctor agreed that he did. Then Bill asked Dr. Masserman if he was acquainted with a patient named Annie Morrison. Masserman's eyes, which had been slightly hooded, jerked fully alert and he answered, "Yes." Bill then asked whether the doctor had ever taken Mrs. Morrison on his boat.

Dr. Masserman looked up at Bill. "I believe on one occasion," he said without hesitation. Then his body began to sag, as though he realized that he had spoken too quickly.

"Did you undress her?"

"No, sir."

"Did you fondle her breasts?"

"No, sir."

"Did you have any sexual contact with her at all on that boat?"

"No, sir."

"Did you tell her that this was a form of therapy?"

"No, sir."

Bill Carroll asked Masserman if he had given Annie Morrison Sodium Amytal, and Dr. Masserman answered that he had. Then Bill pursued a similar set of questions about his patient Daniella Biagi. Dr. Masserman seemed suddenly deflated. He said he didn't recall whether he had ever taken Daniella Biagi on his boat, and, again, he denied ever approaching her sexually. Yes, he had given her Sodium Amytal. No, he had not told her to undress.

Then, just as abruptly as he had begun that line of questioning, Bill began to wrap up the deposition by asking Dr. Masserman whether, over the eighteen years he had me in therapy, he had ever administered any tests to me or had any other professional administer psychological tests. Dr. Masserman said he had not, although he said he was "acquainted with all these tests."

Bill asked him whether he was aware of the malocclusion of my jaw, the TMJ (Yes), and whether he saw "any relationship between the psychological state that you observed in Ms. Noël and that malocclusion of her jaw?"

Dr. Masserman answered, "Only when she said that she was depressed about the impairment of her singing voice because of that condition."

I was only half listening as Ken called for an off-the-record discussion, where he brought up the disturbing fact that Billie Laird's records, which might have shed some light on the frequency of my Amytal sessions, had mysteriously disappeared. Ken requested a search for Billie's records and proposed that the discovery deposition be continued if they were found. Debra Davy agreed.

The next order of business was a decision that the next session, which was to be an evidence deposition on Dr. Masserman, would be videotaped because of Dr. Masserman's advanced age. That way, if he should die before the case went to trial, the video would serve as his testimony in court for the judge and jury. The "dead man's law" that John Michael Flynn had been worried about had recently been changed to allow this kind of evidence.

After Debra Davy had once again gently guided Dr. Masserman from the room, Bill and Ken and I sat down to rehash the events of the day.

"How in the hell did you get him to admit he had those women on the boat?" Ken asked.

"I don't know," Bill said with a sigh. "Maybe he was getting tired, but he just looked up innocently and admitted it, didn't he? After that, I knew we had him."

"But I wonder," I said. "Will he ever admit what he did?"

"Never," Ken said.

"Never," Bill echoed. "Never."

13 Starting Again

MAY 22, 1986   While I waited for the wheels of the legal machinery to crank us into the evidence depositions, I embarked on the kind of therapy I'd been looking for when I walked into Jules Masserman's office twenty years earlier. In fact, it was twenty years, two months, and two days after my first appointment with Jules Masserman when I walked into the comfortable Michigan Avenue office of a relaxed, attractive psychologist named Ann Jernberg. All I knew about her was that she had a Ph.D. in psychology, was highly recommended, and had been practicing since the 1960s.

Ann was smaller than I, with brown hair and one of the most empathic, playful, and responsive faces I'd ever seen. I explained I was having troubles because I was in the throes of a lawsuit. "I don't want to offend your profession," I said, "but . . ." I told her the story and ended with, "If you don't believe me, I'd be willing to take a test or something."

She looked at me and said earnestly, "I believe you."

As it turned out, she had heard about the lawsuit and knew Dr. Masserman. She was right with me when I talked, and she responded with remarks such as, "That must have been terribly hurtful" or "That must have made you incredibly angry." No one had ever said anything like that to me before. If I said I felt a certain way, she'd confirm, "Of course you feel that way."

The difference in this therapy—real therapy aimed at helping me grow—was astonishing. With Masserman, the spotlight was almost always on him, on pleasing him, on keeping him from getting angry. It was amazing to express my feelings and discover how angry I was. Suddenly I had feelings pouring out that I'd never been able to express. From the first moment, it seemed, I was beginning to look at fragments of a puzzle that would someday make sense as a whole picture of my life. With Ann's help, I eventually would have a chance at understanding what was going on inside me and discover the hidden childhood issues that were central to my entire involvement with Jules Masserman.

Even in our initial session, Ann began to encourage my independence and feelings of self-worth by helping me put words to my confused feelings. "Think about it," she said. "You're in the process of breaking free of Jules Masserman entirely. You're going to be feeling pretty angry and lost as you go along. But the more we talk, the more you're going to be able to see for yourself just how much strength you really have. What's important now is for you to know what made you start fighting Masserman right away, as soon as you discovered what he was doing to you. So first, tell me what you were like as a child."

That day, I walked out of Ann's office into the fresh spring air with a new sense of myself, remembering the tenacious four-year-old I'd been—full of energy and very stubborn. Learning how to be a good, sweet little girl and behave had never been easy for me, though I'd thoroughly mastered the form. Ann and I had both laughed when I said, "I'm beginning to get the idea that Jules Masserman didn't know he was messing with such a feisty little kid!"

One of the first big questions I got to after a number of sessions was: On some subconscious level, did I know what he was doing to me all those years? Did I *decide* not to remember?

Ann gave me her radiant smile. "I wondered how long it would take for you to ask those questions," she said. "Of course, I don't know, but several theories have evolved from studies."

"You think I knew, don't you?"

"Yes, I do, but *only* on some very deep subconscious level. Patients who have been hypnotized and asked to describe what happened to them previously in surgery have been able to remember entire conversations in the operating room, including all the remarks that were made about them. And in your case, the anesthetic, the Amytal, was not as strong as surgical anesthesia, so it would be logical to assume that on some level you knew.

"In other studies, we've found that many adult victims of childhood incest block out their experiences entirely. I think that's what you did. I suspect your situation with Masserman was just like incest. He was the child-molester, and you were the child. And just as a child has some secret contract between her and her tormentor and fears grave punishment if she tells what's going on, you also lived in some sort of frightened secrecy."

"I was tired all the time."

"I think the weight of all the secrets you were carrying around was exhausting. You've described being afraid and confused for no apparent reason. Well, this might be the reason."

Something else occurred to me. "If that's true, then I must have *decided* to wake up."

"Yes, you probably did. And I suspect it was because you felt strong enough to face reality."

I recalled that Dr. Masserman had talked about the "Aha" experience—his term for psychological insight. "And it wasn't long after that when I woke up and said, 'Aha! This is what's been going on,' " I said. "I wonder if he was telling me to wake up. But why would he want to? Did he want to be found out and punished? Or did he think I'd wake up and be happy that he was 'romancing' me or something?"

"Now you're getting into areas that are fascinating, but I don't suppose we'll ever get any concrete answers unless Masserman himself comes forward," said Ann, reaching over and patting my hand. "And that's very unlikely."

By the time the evidence depositions were about to begin, in July, I was realizing that in many ways, I was the same uninformed, immature girl I had been twenty years before. I still hadn't gotten to some of the bigger truths; they were waiting for me and beginning to make me uneasy. In the meantime, I'd gained a new understanding of the irrational fears and nightmares I still was having about Masserman. Ann Jernberg explained it to me when I asked her why I still worried about Masserman shooting me down like a sniper from the bushes. I could understand why I felt that way right after it had happened, but almost two years had passed since then, and I was tired of being hit by sudden terrors.

"That feeling is called post-traumatic stress disorder," Ann said. "A good deal has been written about it, but almost all of it has been centered on Vietnam veterans. Have you read about flashbacks?"

"That's not possible," I said. "It sounds as if you're saying that a sexually abused woman has gone through something like Vietnam."

"Think about it. Change one word—war—and the story is your own. What you've been going through is not only unthinkable, it is also shame-based, like Vietnam. It has the same horror for you, the same sense of unreality, just like war. You keep thinking about it, talking about it, dreaming it over and over, hoping to change the ending so that you can say to yourself, 'Oh, it was just a dream, so now I can forget about it and go on with my life.'

"But I can't forget about it."

"Of course not, but you're facing it and talking about it, and those dreams will subside. I promise you."

I dreaded the evidence depositions so much that summer that I often found I could hardly get out of bed on the mornings I didn't have studio work or singing engagements scheduled. But my stubbornness drove me on and carried me deeper into the battle. For one thing, I decided I ought to learn more about Jules Masserman and the trail that led him from Chudnov, a small village on the border of Poland and Russia, where he was born in 1905, to Chicago and his standing as one of the most eminent psychoanalysts and educators in the world. I remembered that a note at the bottom of one of the autographed articles he had given me referred to an autobiography. I wanted to read that autobiography, but I couldn't find it in any bookstores or libraries. Ann Jernberg suggested that Northwestern University's medical library might have one, since he was on the faculty there. I called, but they said no one was allowed into Northwestern's medical library unless they were faculty, staff, or students.

Then one day when I was at Dr. Wheeler's getting my jaw tested (it was in very good alignment now), he mentioned that he was on the faculty at Northwestern. He agreed to see if they had the book, and only a few days later, he handed me a hard-cover tome, *Psychiatric Odyssey: Memoirs of a Maverick Psychiatrist,* by Jules H. Masserman, published in 1971. I held it in my hands and looked at it with fascination and repulsion, wondering what I might learn from it about the inner workings of the man who had had such an impact on my life.

People say that writing an autobiography is a rare move for psychiatrists or psychoanalysts, and after I read his book, I knew why most of them are too smart to do it. His book was six hundred pages of self-indulgence, describing what he called "forty years of the vagaries,

vices, vicissitudes and vicarious victories of a vagrant psychiatrist."
Amazingly, in all those pages, Dr. Masserman devotes little more than
a total of one and a half pages to his birth, his younger brother, his
parents, and his early childhood.

Masserman's father, Abram,* immigrated to America from rural Chu-
dov, and when Masserman was five,† he, his mother, his infant brother
and an aunt followed by steerage and landed at Ellis Island. Jules recalls
long lines of fellow immigrants, heavy bundles, and efforts to try to
convey in Russian to whoever would listen that they wanted to get to
his father in Michigan, which they assumed was a village just a few
miles from New York.

Masserman, who became a U.S. citizen when he was twelve, writes
that the family settled in a marginal slum section of Detroit, in three
rented rooms over his father's tailor shop. Since his father always
professed to being a scholar and philosopher, his mother bore the
burden of learning American ways and helping in the shop, as well as
washing, cooking, mending, keeping house, and saving money for her
sons' educations. It is to his mother's diligence that he credits the
family's ability eventually to buy their own home, but finances were
difficult until he became a doctor and his brother, Ted, became a
lawyer.

That Masserman spends so little space on his childhood seems almost
reasonable: the unhappiness cries out from the lines he did write. In
a telling reference to his family's dynamics, Masserman writes that his
mother never gave up trying to get him to practice so that he would
become a musical virtuoso, whereas his father, "in one of his not
infrequent rages against an unappreciative and discordant world, once
splintered my viola." Masserman reports that his parents divorced after
twenty-five years of marriage, and that afterward he rarely saw his
father, who moved to another city and remarried.

Masserman's father sounded detached and rather dull, except for
violent outbursts, while his mother was the strong one, revered and
honored. He describes her as "the most gentle, modest, intelligent and
kindest human being" he has ever known.

Initially, I was amazed to read that a man so arrogant and self-
assured claimed to have been terribly shy and insecure as a boy. In

*Some references call his father Abraham.
†In some accounts, Masserman's family immigrated in 1908, in others, 1910.

his autobiography, he says he rarely had time to enjoy himself with friends, and what little social life he did have was "impaired" by persistent adolescent acne. While he was in high school, he worked three evenings a week and summer vacations as a drugstore clerk. In 1922, when he was seventeen, he took a six-week summer course at Sandusky College of Pharmacy, passed the Michigan state boards, and got his license as a registered pharmacist. This increased his summer income in the drugstore, as did teaching children "how to hold a violin and draw a bow so as to delight their uncritical parents."

In summing up his development, Masserman says: "social confidence and sexual experiences came late, and subsequent overcompensations, along with a retained avidity for long hours of intensive work, study and recreation, have made for a full but strenuous life." (Reading that, I thought: Wow, I'll say he overcompensated. Maybe he had to knock women out for sex because he felt he had to get even with them for having rejected him when he was young.)

The rest of the book documents Masserman's quick climb to the heights of power and influence within his chosen profession. After high school and junior college, he attended the Detroit College of Medicine in 1926. His first two and a half years of medical school were stressful; he came down with tuberculosis, had a kidney removed, and felt "tested and martyred rather than adequately instructed" as he studied mummified cells under a microscope and examined dry bones and nerve filaments in the skins of cadavers. But during his junior year, in 1929, he had two major breakthroughs: he dealt with real patients, and he had his first lecture in psychiatry, given by Dr. Harry August, a clinical instructor who much later would be trained as a psychoanalyst. Dr. August lectured about how intense anxiety from forgotten childhood experiences was sometimes reevoked by stress in adults and could produce deviations in the way the body behaved. Then he gave examples of patients he had cured by psychotherapy alone.

Masserman says he was intrigued when Dr. August demonstrated group hypnosis on the entire class and when he discussed genetic constitution versus behaviorism and the popular analytic theories and techniques of Freud, Adler, Jung, and Sullivan. Psychoanalysis was new, adventurous, and exciting then. Freud was still living at Berggasse 19 in Vienna, and the International Psychoanalytic Association had been in existence for only twenty-one years. *The Ego and the Id,* in which Freud laid out his complex understanding of mental functioning, had been published in 1923, and *Inhibitions, Symptoms and Anxiety* had come out in 1926.

By 1929, when Masserman was first learning about the power of the unconscious, even the American Board of Psychiatry hadn't been founded. (It was started in 1934.) In all of America there were only about thirteen hundred psychiatrists and far fewer psychoanalysts— many of whom had been trained by Freud himself or by Karl Abraham, Otto Rank, Sandor Ferenczi, or Hanns Sachs, all close adherents of Freud, or by the exiled Carl Jung.*

As I read about Dr. Masserman's resolve to acquire the knowledge and skills of psychiatry and his entry into the field, key words—like his desire to see patients "with or without supervision"—would set me off, and I'd have to go back and reread in order to really get the meaning. He wrote a lot about sexual practices all over the world; he was so hateful toward women and talked so cavalierly about sex and incest that it really made me very angry.

In one quote that jumped out at me, he seemed to be basically saying that when it came to sexual interactions between men and women, there was no right and wrong, there was no such thing as sexual depravity:

> "In storied Cathay, Wong Shih'cheng, in *The Golden Lotus,* put it thus: 'The world is based upon continuous interaction between male and female principles, therefore one cannot say that anything so done is out of depravity, or that any sexual passion is evil.' The term 'anything' in the above quotation is comprehensive enough to include . . . nearly every conceivable variation of sexual technique, partner and orifice, including cross-species intercourse among pastoral and agrarian peoples openly practiced throughout Africa, India, Asia and Polynesia; indeed, in only a few Western cultures can terms such as 'polymorphous perverse sexuality,' 'carnal sin,' etc. have any deprecatory meaning." (p. 286).

When I was his patient, Dr. Masserman had often commented on my having been married twice, and he had referred in his discovery deposition to my "failures" in marriage. His references made me feel guilty and inadequate—which he may or may not have realized. So I was surprised to learn from his autobiography that he had been married

---

*Even today, only about 19 percent of the 43,000 psychiatrists in America have received some psychoanalytic training, according to estimates from the American Psychiatric Association.

not only two but three times. Before his senior year of medical school, he had married a "gentle, unassuming young woman" named Jeanette, the sister of one of his fellow students. It sounds as if he later felt he had ignored and mistreated her. When he graduated from medical school in 1930 and wanted to get as far from Detroit as possible, he applied for and received an internship in San Diego. He left Jeanette behind, claiming that he could not support her on his stipend and that even if he could, they would have very little time together. He says she accepted the arrangement without protest and returned to live with her family, but she died nine months later from an undiagnosed cancer, leaving "a dark cloud of pity and remorse I shall never eradicate from my conscience."

Masserman might not have suffered too much over her death, however, since he writes of basking in San Diego's clean, fresh air, enjoying the nearby mountain vistas, the clean beaches, and sailing trips in a catboat he bought for thirty dollars. And after his internship in San Diego, he began his quick climb through the ranks. He did a residency in psychiatry and neurology at Stanford University in Palo Alto and then accepted a chief residency in psychiatry with the Baltimore City Hospitals, where he had an opportunity to train under the famous Adolf Meyer at the Phipps Psychiatric Clinic of the Johns Hopkins University Hospital. Dr. Meyer both fascinated and inspired Masserman. Even though Meyer attracted and trained many disciples, including Stanley Cobb, Edward Strecker, Spurgeon English, Maurice Levine, and other leaders in the field, Masserman notes that Dr. Meyer didn't appear charismatic either in personal style or in manner. He also observed that Adolf Meyer spoke in long, pompous sentences sprinkled with obscure words and esoteric comparisons—something Jules Masserman would later confess with pride that he himself was accused of doing.

As I read his memoirs, I noticed that when Masserman talked about his patients, he often described them with a subtle contempt, conveying the feeling that patients came to him because they were spoiled or lazy or couldn't solve their problems on their own. In one passage, for instance, he says neurotic behavior may be "face-saving and escapist to those who practice it" (p. 274). In another, he writes that patients often parade their difficulties for the sake of titillating the therapist.

By the time the July 1986, evidence deposition loomed, I knew more than I had about Jules Masserman's life, but that knowledge didn't do anything to reduce my sense of foreboding. Bill Carroll's research into the addictive qualities of Sodium Amytal had led him to believe I was drug-addicted—a view I simply could not accept. I was willing to allow Bill to proceed in that direction only because I so badly wanted to win my suit against Masserman. Since we couldn't prove he'd raped me, perhaps we could prove that he had made me an addict and an alcoholic. It didn't seem to correctly address the issues, but since my avenues for bringing criminal charges against him were blocked, I agreed to the approach.

I still did not believe I was addicted to anything. Somehow I had managed to accept what the Amytal had done to me while at the same time I denied having a dependency on it. I figured, "If I smoke grass from time to time or drink my martinis, it's only because I need to get through the latest ordeal with at least some comfort." Also, I never bought marijuana. I was given it. And no one ever suggested I buy it. The way I looked at it was: You can buy gin, but a lady does not buy marijuana, because it is illegal. It's given as a gift. I figured any real addict would purchase her own pot and get into heavier stuff as well— so of course that made me exempt.

I walked into the Hinshaw Culbertson law offices on July 25, 1986, with an underlying fear that I was about to be massacred. I wasn't going to tell anybody or jinx my case, but I figured "proof" of my nonaddiction was the fact that the year before, I had stopped drinking and smoking for five months. A *real* addict couldn't do that. I would hold on to that belief as a way of keeping myself strong, no matter what Bill said or did.

Because evidence depositions can be used in the actual trial, Debra Davy, the defense attorney, would begin questioning Dr. Masserman and then Bill Carroll would cross-examine him, just as if we were in a court of law. This time, too, a video camera was there to record Masserman's testimony. The camera was focused on Dr. Masserman throughout his statements, as he shifted in his seat and loosened his tie and as Debra Davy patted his arm, encouraged him, or told him not to speak.

Debra Davy began her direct with a long-drawn-out inquiry into the doctor's credentials. It was easy for him to go on at length about them, since he'd trained for so long and done so much work in the field.

With his suit jacket off and his elbows on the table, Masserman spoke confidently and articulately. When asked about his years of formal training after medical school, he smiled and said quite modestly, in a voice filled with charm, "The difficulty is, I'm still in training." He spoke less modestly of his publications: "There are 450 of those," he said. "It would take a book by itself [to list them]."

When questioned by Davy about psychiatry and psychoanalysis, he launched into a lengthy intellectual discourse, quite erudite, on unconscious motivations, sexually aggressive motivations that are usually not consciously recognized, free association, and the interpretation and analysis of dreams—a process that ultimately permits insight into the self. He spoke of the differences between psychologists and psychiatrists (the psychiatrist is a physician) and smiled from time to time as he spoke, nodding at Debra Davy and the invisible audience as if he were a scholar giving a guest lecture. He explained in some detail that although there are some 213 different forms of therapy practiced in the United States,* he personally practiced "comprehensive therapy," which included an awareness of psychological factors affecting the individual as well as the individual's social relationships and his or her beliefs and fantasies. The goal of treatment, he said, was always to diminish "unnecessary anxieties, reduce dangerous promiscuity, unrealistic ambitions, and to modify so people can attain within the limits of their capacity and open up creativity, as well as to broaden their social relationships and perspectives."

When Debra Davy turned to the use of drugs in the course of therapy and asked Dr. Masserman to specifically describe Sodium Amytal "for the judge and jury," Dr. Masserman took the opportunity to use examples from the three pages of notes he had written about me as a way to explain the use of Amytal.

"It's a barbiturate, Sodium Amytal Barbital," he explained in a voice filled with patience, "which was used in the First and Second World Wars to help individuals get over great stress, and that's where its properties were discovered. . . . It is described in practically every standard textbook of psychiatry. Its principal use is during periods of special stress and agitation to furnish a period of relaxation, relief. Those are the physical effects. The psychological effect is that there is a certain

*As president of the American Psychiatric Association, Dr. Masserman advocated and appointed a Commission on Psychiatric Therapies to review as many as possible of the currently practiced therapies, to examine their rationale and practice, and to elicit the common dynamics that are effective from those that are extraneous or counterproductive.

release of what has been troubling the individual, so that he or she speaks more frankly. For example, you get expressions like 'I hate all men.' That sort of thing comes out. Or 'I hate my father. He raped me when I was fifteen.' That sort of thing comes out. Or 'I never did like to work' or 'I remember that my father wanted me to be a great prima donna, and, uh, I have to be a prima donna or else I'll never be satisfied myself.' That sort of thing comes out."

Under Debra Davy's gentle questioning to justify why he had such meager notes on all my years of therapy, Dr. Masserman explained that he only kept notes of "significant events in therapy, but not a daily record. I don't keep records on patients I've seen for so long and know so thoroughly because it's stereotyped and repetitive."

When she asked him how many patients he had treated over the years, he shook his head in mock horror and said, "I have no idea! There's no way to count!" When she asked him if it is permissible for a doctor to have a physical or sexual relationship with a patient, he said, "As a physician, I can do a physical exam," he said. "Outside of that, it is not permissible to have sex with a patient; it is unethical."

When Debra Davy asked about me, Dr. Masserman's eyes clouded over, and he looked tired and angry. He held his pen between his hands as he said, "I treated Barbara Noël for seventeen or eighteen years. I last saw her in 1984. . . ." Debra Davy patted his shoulder and said, "You're doing fine."

Once again Dr. Masserman characterized me as "subject to episodes of alcoholism, of self-isolation." He said I'd had "an unsuccessful marriage and was having a second one." He noted, "She kept encountering disappointments in her career, in her engagements, in her sexual relations with a number of men . . . and she would become despondent, hopeless, and consider suicide."

He said he gave me a sleeping pill, Dalmane, and an antidepressant to relieve "states of tension, anxiety, and hopelessness." He also said he had prescribed one or two capsules of Serax sometimes, or Temazepam, to help me sleep "in circumstances of real agitation." He said he also prescribed, "at times when it was indicated, Amytal." He did this so that he would have an opportunity to talk to me about "things that had been troubling"—such as "when she was frustrated about having a sex affair with a homosexual physician" or "when she was losing her job with a band" or "having an unsatisfactory sex affair with Tony, her junior." Under these circumstances, he said, "it was helpful to her. . . . And she was always grateful for it."

Debra Davy asked Dr. Masserman if he could state what some of my problems were.

"A number of problems," Dr. Masserman said, tsk tsking. "She had difficulties securing job assignments such as commercials, singing commercials, because many of them went out of style, and, uh, Dick Noël, her second husband—whom she married, by the way, in the hope that he would promote her career—divorced her instead and no longer recorded her. And so these opportunities aggravated her when they became infrequent."

Debra Davy asked him to describe my troubles with men.

"Well, they varied a great deal," Dr. Masserman said, shaking his head as if this was a real shame he was describing. "She had a fairly continuous relationship with a younger man named Tony. She had various relationships with a number—I will not use their last names. Frank. She had some relations with her former husband [and] a younger man named Tony, and she was particularly enamored about a John. . . .

"As a matter of fact, I was hoping she would marry one of them, because it would have settled her down and helped her in two ways. One, it would give her a base of operation so she wouldn't have to depend so much on the income from her career, and secondly, then she could continue singing, but in ways that would not necessarily make it the basis of her livelihood. She could continue doing something like singing in choirs.

"In fact," he said, putting his fingers together in a steeple and raising his chin, "I sent her to a Dr. Diamond for an appointment as a music instructor [for] Northwestern University's [adolescent care unit] and so on. These things she could do and do very well."

Debra Davy asked Dr. Masserman if I'd ever had affairs "with more than one man at a time."

Dr. Masserman said, "I believe so."

Then she asked him if I had affairs with married men.

He said, "I can't be sure of that. . . . [But] she began her relationship with Dick Noël when she was still married to her first husband."

When she asked him to recall his last visit with me, to describe "what stands out" about that visit, he said, "She was increasingly concerned about her lack of work and her need for funds. . . . [She] was having big disappointments about her singing career" and had been disappointed because "some songs she'd written, that I helped her write on some occasions, had not done that well."

Ken looked at me and raised his eyebrows. I couldn't help smiling.

The idea was absurd: Dr. Masserman was trying to take credit for helping me compose music. And since he said my music was so mediocre, why would he want that credit?

Dr. Masserman went on to say that on September 21, 1984, he hadn't slated me for Amytal but agreed to give it to me because I was so despondent. He said, "I asked her to go in the other room as usual and bare an arm, but I never asked her to disrobe. She did so, and—"

Debra Davy objected and asked that the last remark be stricken. Ken Cunniff objected and said, "Let the record stand."

Dr. Masserman continued his testimony, saying that after he gave me Sodium Amytal, we talked about my concerns. "I reassured her that after all she could be a successful singer provided she cut down on her expectations about being a prima donna. She could do very well in light opera if she wished to, she could write songs. She was a good musician. She could write melody and counterpoint and she was a fair lyricist. And I encouraged her about these things. Then I left. . . ."

When Bill Carroll began his cross-examination, the anger in his voice surprised everyone. Dr. Masserman looked especially startled, since Bill had been so solicitous and friendly at the previous deposition. For nearly an hour, Bill spent time comparing records that had been kept by Dr. Masserman with those kept by Billie Laird. Billie's books had at last been found, as if by magic. (Dr. Masserman said he and Ms. Karas had searched and searched and finally found them.) The discrepancies between the doctor's records and Billie's were dramatic. In 1979, for instance, Dr. Masserman's records showed that I had fourteen visits and Billie's records thirty-five. In 1980, it was twenty-six visits according to Dr. Masserman, sixty-three according to Billie.

At one point Ken Cunniff interrupted to complain about Debra Davy's coaching her client in a way that wouldn't appear on the video. "Ms. Davy," he said, "I object to your touching the doctor to keep him from answering. If you wish to object, please object, but please don't keep touching the doctor each time to stop him from answering questions you don't wish to be answered."

"I'll touch him anytime I want," Davy shot back. "I object that your question is unclear as to which records you are referring to."

Bill asked Dr. Masserman to examine a freehand drawing I had made of his office suite and asked if the rendering of the room and its furniture was correct. Dr. Masserman soberly studied the drawing for a few minutes and then looked up. "Not accurate," he said, shaking his head in seeming disgust.

"Would you please point out to us what is inaccurate about it?"

"There's an oblong here marked 'day bed,' " he said. "I have no beds in my examining room. I have an examining cot."

The entire group of us broke into laughter. Even Dr. Masserman chuckled.

But when Bill Carroll began to question Masserman about the addictive qualities of Amytal, the mood of the deposition turned deadly serious. "Barbiturates are addictive, are they not—yes or no, Doctor?"

"Some barbiturates are addictive," he said. "Amytal is not."

"Doctor, you are acquainted with Louis Wolberg, and, Doctor, you have told us, have you not, that Dr. Wolberg's writings on Sodium Amytal would be a good authority for us, have you not?"

"I gave you a copy of his description of Sodium Amytal techniques taken directly from his book *Techniques of Therapy*."

"All right, now: is Dr. Wolberg a reputable authority in this field?"

"Dr. Wolberg is internationally famous," Dr. Masserman said.

"Now, Doctor, Dr. Wolberg writes in his book: 'An addiction problem as serious as that of narcotics is dependence on barbiturates and minor tranquilizers.' Do you agree with that statement, Doctor?"

"Depending on what is meant by barbiturates. There are many kinds. Some are obtainable, some are not."

"Now, Doctor, do you agree with this statement of Dr. Wolberg in the next paragraph: 'Short-acting barbiturates, Pentathol, Seconal, and Amytal are particularly addictive. They are truly as addictive as heroin or morphine and give the individual . . . an even greater problem.' That is a quote from the Department of Health, Education and Welfare. 'Like alcohol, they are intoxicating, producing confusion, uncoordination, and emotional instability.' Do you agree with that statement?"

"No, sir; that is not completely accurate." Dr. Masserman's skin was pale; he looked extremely uncomfortable.

"Now, do you agree with Dr. Wolberg when he says on page 894, 'Single addictions are rare. Accordingly, removal of one substance does not lessen the craving for others. Indeed, it may provoke the addict to try new experiments with other potentially exciting or calming materials.' Do you agree with Dr. Wolberg?"

"Yes, providing you remember he said 'may' and not 'does.' "

• • •

After a short break, Bill Carroll continued his cross-examination of Dr. Masserman, going over the familiar ground of the number of times I'd had Amytal, my difficulties with the malocclusion of my jaw, and its effect on my emotional life. Then he went back to the issue of the boat and got Dr. Masserman to admit that he'd taken female patients besides me out on his boat. Bill asked, "Doctor, you used the boat as part of your therapeutic program with your patients, then, didn't you?"

"Only as a therapeutic help," Dr. Masserman answered. He maintained that he did not have any women undress on his boat. But he admitted that he had also taken various female patients flying in his airplane.

Then Bill said, "Now, on September 21, 1984, when you administered Sodium Amytal to Barbara Noël, there was no one else in that room besides yourself and Ms. Noël, isn't that true?"

"During the interview, yes. No one else then."

"And so there is no one who can tell us besides yourself and Ms. Noël what you did during that Amytal session, isn't that true?"

"There was no one present during that interview," Dr. Masserman said, sighing deeply. "I've already answered that."

"Now, Doctor, isn't it true . . . that when you began treatment [of Barbara Noël] in 1966, you found her to be a maladjusted personality? And then with the passing years, some twelve to fifteen years, you added to that diagnosis that she had become an alcoholic, isn't that true?"

Over Davy's continued objections, Dr. Masserman answered. "You've asked me the same question several times. I've always answered yes."

"And so you began in 1966 treating her with Sodium Amytal, and she became addicted to Sodium Amytal, did she not?"

"No, she did not."

"And then in 1979, you began to give her Antabuse, didn't you?"

"I began to give her Antabuse long before that."

"And so what happened, Doctor, is that under your care over these eighteen years, she went from a person you described as being maladjusted, and she turned into an alcoholic in your care, didn't she?"

"She didn't turn into an alcoholic in my care. She elected to become one."

"So she *elected* to become one while she was under your care for eighteen years?"

"I did everything I could to prevent it."

"But despite all that you did over those eighteen years during which you gave her an addictive barbiturate known as Sodium Amytal, she became addicted to alcohol when Sodium Amytal was not available to her, isn't that true?"

"That is not true."

"You destroyed this woman, did you not, Doctor?"

Debra Davy objected once more, and Jules Masserman turned to her with a searching look.

Bill Carroll then entered into the record that even with Dr. Masserman's initial rate of twenty-five dollars per hour, later raised to fifty dollars per hour, I had paid him nearly $100,000 out of pocket, without benefit of insurance. A furious Debra Davy then took another forty-five minutes in redirect, allowing Dr. Masserman to try to cover his tracks and refute whatever damaging testimony he may have given.

I couldn't focus anymore; the smears about my "promiscuity" and "disappointments" all sounded the same to me.

Then, six hours after it had begun, the deposition was over. The room was charged with emotion. Debra Davy slapped pages of paper together in apparent fury, and Jules Masserman's hooded eyes looked angry, confused, and exhausted. He had loosened his tie and rolled up his shirt sleeves, and he had the appearance of a rumpled, tired old man.

Bill Carroll and Ken Cunniff both seemed calm and professional, but the minute the doors closed behind us, we burst out in jubilant congratulations. We all thought Masserman's performance on videotape would lead to a guilty verdict by any jury. I complimented both men on the remarkable work they'd done and laughed out loud at our apparent victory.

But despite my elation over the prospect of beating Masserman, something was gnawing at me. All the way home, I kept seeing those eighteen years go by. I saw myself at Mother's bedside right after she died; I saw myself driving the Mercedes in the dark the night I left Richard; I saw Richard storming out of Dr. Masserman's office and heard Dr. Masserman's voice again: "That settles it! You're getting a divorce!" I saw myself stirring my martinis, jittery and impatient when I wasn't getting my Amytal.

I thought: It's true, that man did a heinous, unconscionable thing to me, year after year. But as I turned the key to open the front door of my apartment, I faced a new truth about myself: Yes, he did horrible things. But what about my role in it? On some level—even if it was subconscious—I let him do it. I allowed myself to be his victim.

The nasty little secret Ann Jernberg's persistent questions had aroused in my mind and that I could no longer avoid was this: I had followed Jules Masserman's script. I had remained in a perpetual fog that kept me from experiencing reality. Since the time when I'd turned into a ten-year-old child-woman with breasts and a period, I had been passive. I'd kept smiling, and I'd never really grown up. Masserman had dosed me with emotional abuse and allowed me to stay suspended in a state of nongrowth, and when I was very, very good, he had given me an ultimate fog-out, which he called Amytal. I had colluded in my own victimization.

His crime had many names—rape, negligence, physical and mental cruelty, malpractice. But I was guilty too, guilty of being his accessory by allowing myself to be his victim. I made myself say it out loud: "Without my cooperation—even if it was unconscious—there could have been no crime."

14 Pieces Begin to Fall into Place

I stood in my living room and stamped my feet, slammed my book onto the floor, sat down and cried. Nothing dramatic had happened. There was no "event" on which to pin my bad mood. I didn't have the slightest notion why I was upset; it was just another day like many others, when I was constantly irritable and got mad or cried if two words happened to rub together wrong.

And even though I still insisted I wasn't a drug addict or an alcoholic, I had walked around for ten months following Masserman's deposition with at least a small amount of alcohol in my system from lunch to bedtime every day. In truth, this is what I had been doing most of the time for the past several years.

I was overly sensitive and constantly on the brink of blowing up, but I somehow managed to continue working regularly. From time to time, I sang at big sports banquets or at political events attended by Mayor Daley, Governor and Mrs. Jim Thompson, Vice-President Bush. I appeared as backup on the same bill with the Four Freshmen and with Bob Hope in front of two thousand people, but I sang automatically and hardly noticed what I was doing.

More often than not, I was on the edge of boiling over with rage, and I walked around barely contained. Almost every time I performed with my favorite band, with guys who'd been like family to me, I thought I'd had it, I was going to quit. I suddenly couldn't stand anybody.

I had no awareness of the energy it took for me to keep hiding from the secret memories of my childhood.

I also wouldn't allow myself any comprehension of the fact that at least one of the reasons I was always on the brink of boiling over was the alcohol in my system. I'd start at lunch with a martini. Then I'd have a glass of wine in the afternoon and move on to a highball before dinner and some more wine before bed. It wasn't excessive, I rationalized. The alcohol was just enough to take the edge off my distress and rage at Jules Masserman. After a session with Ann, I'd stay dry for a couple of days. And then, boom! I'd find an excuse and start all over again.

At one of my therapy sessions, Ann gave me a folder of information about a place called Onsite. It was a therapeutic program in South Dakota, run by a woman named Sharon Wegscheider, whom Ann knew from workshops and conferences they'd attended together. Ann described Onsite as rather like a retreat, since it had strong spiritual overtones and addressed problems people were experiencing from having had severe emotional traumas, like rape, incest, or the violent death of a loved one, along with problems of addiction and alcoholism. Twenty-four people at a time went to Onsite, for eight days of intensive group psychotherapy—just what it might take, she said, for me to get free of Jules Masserman.

"That sounds interesting," I said with an automatic but cautious smile, turning the papers over in my hands. What I really meant was, "That sounds scary; forget it."

Ann was forbearing. "Well, it's just something for you to think about," she said, letting the subject go.

Once or twice after that, I thought fleetingly about Onsite. But it was much easier to immerse myself in the legal machinations of my fight against Masserman. There wasn't much I could do about what was happening, but I could obsess about the outcome—which I did, endlessly, through the remainder of the summer and the early fall that followed Jules Masserman's evidence deposition. I even spent time worrying about what to wear in court when the day came. I went over and over what I would say—even though there was a question of whether there would actually be a trial.

The next step in the legal process was a pretrial hearing, which had finally been scheduled for October 8, 1986. At that hearing, Ken Cunniff and Bill Carroll, on one side, and Debra Davy, on the other, would present in court all the work that had been done over the previous sixteen months. Neither Masserman nor I would attend that hearing. But when it was completed, the pretrial judge would decide whether we had a credible case with which to proceed. If he thought we had a valid claim, he would give us a court date for the trial. If he decided we didn't have an appropriate action, he would simply throw it out. And that would be that: we'd be finished.

Ken and Bill told me not to be too hopeful about a trial. A great deal depended on which judge was assigned to the case. Some judges were sympathetic in cases like this one, but some weren't.

On October 8, I got up early and brewed a pot of strong black coffee. Then I made myself a big breakfast of scrambled eggs, toast, and orange juice and sat reading the *Chicago Tribune* distractedly as I ate, thinking all the while about Ken and Bill walking around a big conference table, putting thick pages of legal papers together and getting everything ready to go to court.

The next thing I knew, I was walking over to my closet and pulling out my "court" clothes, surprising myself as I grabbed the hangers. I knew I wasn't allowed to go to the hearing, but I got myself all dressed up anyway and laughed as I did so, realizing that I must be trying to pull off some kind of voodoo. I put on my pretty white blouse, gray skirt and the navy-blue blazer Nancy Waller had given me, and added my pearls. I put on a light layer of makeup, stepped into my navy heels, and then, standing erect and behaving in an extremely formal manner, I looked through the newspaper to see what was on at the movies. I circled a foreign film I'd wanted to see and then went out to see it. I was one of the only people in the theater, but I bought myself popcorn and had a pretty good time. Afterward I walked slowly home. I took off my high heels and sat down in my favorite chair, waiting for the phone to ring.

"You should be pleased, Barbara," Ken said when he finally called late that afternoon.

"Tell me, tell me."

"Well, the judge we got wasn't the one we wanted, so we were sweating. But he went over every scrap of paper in front of him, and when he was through, he looked over at us and said, 'Good work. Keep digging.' "

"What does that mean?"

"It means we're going to get a trial date."

"Are you sure?"

"Absolutely."

Of course it was wonderful news, incredible. But after I hung up, I sat by the phone feeling oddly depressed. I began to imagine the trial scenario: Masserman was speaking to the jurors, earnestly pontificating about all my so-called "sex affairs" with men. He was explaining with heartfelt sincerity how hard he had tried to dissuade me from my promiscuity. The jurors were nodding their heads in sympathy for this poor old man. They listened to his endless list of professional credentials and raised their eyebrows in amazement. This was a man of great stature. Maybe they could get his autograph for their children. Then I was on the witness stand, saying I hadn't been interested in anyone sexually since Tony, and they were nudging each other and thinking: Sure, look at her. She sings in nightclubs and says she's dated but hasn't had any interest in sex; tell us another one. On the witness stand, I was wearing sedate business clothes, but then the fantasy took an odd turn: I was sitting there testifying in my sexy black sequined evening gown. How could I have worn the wrong thing? Now they'd never believe me. There wasn't a chance of beating Jules Masserman, not a chance.

I came out of my daydream with a jolt. I couldn't afford to feel so intimidated. I told myself, "Don't worry; you won't wear sequins in court. You'll be credible. It doesn't matter if you're a singer."

A few days later, Ken called me again, but this time the news wasn't so good. "Our trial date's been set," he told me over the phone. "But we're going to have a long wait."

"What's long?" The year we'd been through had been long enough.

"It's set for 1990. That's four years from now, provided there are no delays."

"There has to be some way to get it moved up. That's too far away."

"Believe me, with the courts as loaded as they are, it's the best we're going to get," Ken said.

I sat down, barely able to concentrate.

"Now I want you to listen," Ken was saying. "We're going to have to make some decisions. First we have to realize that by 1990, if he lives that long, Masserman will be eighty-five years old."

"Yes, but we have the evidence deposition on video," I said. "Even if he does die, we have—"

"Barb, it just won't be the same. If the guy's dead, the whole emotional element of the case will change, and we could lose. We would be *likely* to lose."

"Then he's already won, hasn't he?"

"No, he hasn't. Let's think about this," Ken said, trying to cut through my despair and anger. "First of all, Masserman's insurance company has made us an offer to settle the case."

"No," I practically shouted. "You know how I feel about that. A settlement doesn't mean a thing. It doesn't make up for anything."

"Listen to me now. They've offered a hundred and twenty-five thou—"

"No. That's bullshit, Ken."

"I agree, Barbara. But please listen to what I have to say before you fly off the handle."

I took deep breaths and tried to make myself calm enough to listen.

"First of all, I want you to think about agreeing to a settlement," Ken said. "I know you don't want to do it, but I want you to listen to why I think it's a good idea. In the first place, I would get you as much as possible from the insurance people. I've done this many times, and I know how these guys think. I want you to *know* that I'll get you the very best price. Also, if you settle out of court, I *promise* you that Bill and I will do everything possible to help you get Masserman's drug license and his medical license taken away and have him censured before a group of his peers."

"Ken, it's not the same."

"No, it isn't. But think about it. If we can go after him right now, you're going to save a lot of his patients from even one more day of abuse. If you wait four years, that's a lot more abuse for all those other patients. Stopping him would have to make you feel like this was worth it. . . . Barb?"

"I'm thinking."

"That's good. Why don't you think about it for a while? We can make a decision later. Will you call me?"

When I hung up, all I wanted to do was cry. For more than two years, I'd focused my energy on beating Jules Masserman in court. Over and over, I'd pictured myself facing him down in front of a jury and proving my case. To get this far and have to give up was beyond imagining. When I thought of court, I wasn't thinking at all of saving any of his other patients. I was wrapped up in my own ego, my own rage.

I called Ann in tears, but her answering machine picked up; she was in session. Then I called Mary, and she wasn't home. Nancy was out of her office. Other friends who knew about the lawsuit didn't fall into the category of people I really wanted to talk to about this. It was one thing for them to know, but quite another to intimately discuss my emotional ups and downs. I had confided in so few people that I couldn't find anyone to talk to now when I needed desperately to talk. It seemed I'd never been so low; I thought I'd hit bottom.

But I was wrong. Three nights later, on a Saturday night, I hit an even lower point. I was singing with a trio that played for smaller events, and it was one of those nights when the music didn't come easily to anybody. When you're working live, you can't always stop and talk things out, and it's hard to break the tension. That night, all I could think was: I want out. I was edgy and getting increasingly irritated; the piano and the bass seemed to be off track and not about to self-correct. Then I signaled for a slowdown at the end of one of my vocals, and the guys missed it. I got irate and began to slow the tempo by stamping my foot. I was furious as I stomped out the rhythm—not unlike a counting horse or a two-year-old having a public tantrum. As soon as the song was over, I stalked off the bandstand. The bandleader called for a break and followed me out into the hallway.

"What in the hell were you trying to pull up there?" His voice was soft, more concerned than angry.

"It was insulting," I snapped at him. "The musicianship was non-existent. Who needs this?"

"Barb, you know you shouldn't do something like that right up there on the bandstand."

"You don't like it?" I said. "Then get somebody else. I don't have to put up with all this shit. Nobody up there is helping me out. I'm all by myself up there!"

My bandleader looked at me silently for a long time. Then he said, somewhat bewildered, "I thought you loved us like we were family."

I burst into tears and ran off to the ladies' room.

When I finally got myself together enough to go back up on the bandstand, I was embarrassed but still angry, and I just couldn't figure out why I felt so shattered. I sang, they played, and we made it through the rest of the night doing the music almost by rote. I couldn't manage to look at anyone, and a subdued, perplexed mood seemed to surround all of us through our last number.

Afterward, my friend Frank, the piano player, drove me home. We didn't talk. I sat on the front seat with my arms crossed in front of me and my eyes closed. Frank hummed a little and tried unsuccessfully to start some conversations, but finally, just before we got to my home, he looked at me and said, "You better do something about all this, kid. You're falling apart."

Ann fitted me in for a Monday appointment. As soon as I sat down in the comfortable chair across from her, I said, "Ann, I can't take it anymore; I'm even messing up on the band now. I've got to get myself together." I asked her to tell me more about the Onsite program.

"One of the most important things is that you'd be with people whose problems are like yours," she said. "As I mentioned, a lot of the people who go to Onsite have suffered traumas. Others have difficult family problems. Much of the therapy centers on relationships and problems that stem from drug addiction and alcoholism."

Ann told me that the director, Sharon Wegscheider, was a therapist, was cofounder of a group called ACOA, Adult Children of Alcoholics. She had done extensive research into the family patterns created by addictions—alcoholism, drug dependency, compulsive gambling, workaholism, eating disorders. Her husband, Joseph R. Cruse, M.D., had been director of the Betty Ford Clinic in Palm Springs before coming to Onsite. The other staff members were also experienced therapists.

"Okay," I said, gripping the arms of my chair. "I'm going to do it. But I'm scared to death."

"You'll do fine," Ann said. "The fight in you that got you this far will serve you well at Onsite."

Ann asked if she should check right then about openings, and I listened as she called Sharon Wegscheider in South Dakota. Listening to Ann's end of the conversation, I was frightened, but I also felt strangely alive and optimistic. When Ann told me that Onsite had an opening on November 17, I said, "I'll take it." Ann discussed my situation at length with Sharon and said she would write a letter recommending some of the issues they should try to cover with me while I was there.

"I've sensed that you have a feeling of being deserted," Ann said to me. "And I would guess it was at a very early age, just past infancy. I want Sharon and the people at Onsite to start there with you and work through all those childhood experiences. After that, you can work through your ordeal with Masserman from a stronger position."

"I'm feeling pretty enthusiastic about all this," I said.

"So am I."

"But I'm also really nervous about it. What if I hate it? What if it doesn't work for me?"

"You can leave anytime you want," Ann said. "I promise you that. You don't have to stay all eight days unless you want to. You're nobody's prisoner—you're the boss. And you don't have to feel like a failure if you choose to leave. It might work for you, but it might not. All I'm asking is for you to try."

I determined to purge myself in more ways than one. I called Ken and said I'd decided that I would agree to a settlement, so he was free to go back to Debra Davy and Masserman's insurance company and negotiate a better offer. I didn't want to do it, I wasn't happy about it, but Ken's assurance that he and Bill Carroll would do everything possible to get Masserman's drug license taken away and have him censured by his peers made it less noxious than it would otherwise have been.

Eight or ten days later, Ken and Bill called me back. Masserman's insurance company had offered $200,000. Ken said this was a real victory; a tangible result—money in the hand—was a much better outcome than a trial date four years in the future that might or might not materialize. Making this settlement would provide some closure. Bill reminded me of the many lawyers who had turned down the case because they thought it couldn't be won. He said the size of the settlement meant we had prevailed. And even though Masserman wasn't literally admitting his guilt, a $200,000 settlement would indicate to anyone that something was seriously amiss.

I didn't know it at the time, but Daniella Biagi and Annie Morrison were also agreeing to settle their cases and feeling dissatisfied about it. Money didn't make up for their pain. They didn't want to resolve their cases this way either, but like me, each felt forced to by the logic of the situation and the lack of alternatives. Like me, they also hoped that if they settled now, it might somehow save Masserman's other patients from further abuse.

On October 18, 1986—two years after I had started the process— I went to Ken's office to sign the settlement papers. Ken's delight in having won me such a good sum was contagious. Soon he had me joking and laughing. But when I walked home afterward, I didn't have any laughter left. Masserman's insurance company had agreed to pay $200,000 to me and $25,000 each to Daniella and Annie, but the money was irrelevant. It was an enormous letdown. Nobody knew what he had done to me and to those other women. And he was still treating patients every day, still playing God, still giving women Amytal and who knew what else.

As it turned out, the settlement definitely did *not* signal victory. In fact, it didn't seem to have any effect whatsoever on Jules Masserman. One week after I had signed the papers, Ken Cunniff got another reprimanding letter from Debra Davy. This one asked Ken to make sure that "Barbara Noël has the courtesy" to "stay away from Rio de Janeiro" in November and "not interfere with an award ceremony in which the World Congress for Social Psychiatry will honor Dr. Masserman for a lifetime of meritorious service to mankind."

Masserman was about to be celebrated, not censured.

Maybe if I'd had a more aggressive, politically oriented personality, I would have taken this letter as an invitation to do something public to shame the man. But the thought of actually trying to disrupt that event never crossed my mind. I said, "Tell her not to worry, Ken. I won't be going to Rio."

Rather than Rio, I would in fact be going to Rapid City, South Dakota, to receive intensive therapy at Onsite. That therapy would, I hoped, help me recover from something other than the doctor's "meritorious service."

For a number of days, I'd been preparing for my trip to Onsite. I had written pages and pages about my family history and what had happened with Dr. Masserman. (I didn't write anything about my drug or alcohol addiction; I was still telling myself I didn't have any problems with substance abuse.) I also made a mandatory visit to my doctor for a physical exam. Onsite required that my doctor send them a health assessment to confirm that I would be able physically to handle their program.

Perhaps because I felt I couldn't do anything about it, I was particularly angry that Jules Masserman was still a practicing, much acclaimed psychoanalyst and psychiatrist and that not a word about this scandal had been written by the press or by anyone in his community. Instead of being questioned or condemned, Jules Masserman was being lauded throughout the psychiatric community. There must have been whispers, at the least. But although many of his colleagues must have heard about the charges against him, they were apparently able to dismiss or ignore them. Indeed, despite any private concerns some individuals may have had, the psychiatric community seemed to close ranks and go out of their way to pay homage to Jules Masserman.

In September 1986, the American Association of Social Psychiatry, a branch of the World Congress for Social Psychiatry, and the Illinois Psychiatric Society held a grand "Festschrift" dinner to honor Jules H. Masserman—the founding president of AASP and the former president of the IPS—for his outstanding contributions to the field. The dinner was held at the Hyatt Regency in Chicago.

In Rio de Janeiro in November 1986, less than a month after his three out-of-court settlements, Jules H. Masserman was honored by the Eleventh World Congress of Social Psychiatry. In an extraordinary outpouring of praise and affection, members of the World Congress for Social Psychiatry paid tribute to the man they had named Honorary Life President. Dr. John Carlton, president of the World Congress, with whom Dr. Masserman and I had gone sightseeing with in Paris some four years before, called Jules Masserman "the most prominent psychiatrist in the world."

15 Admitting My Addictions

While Jules Masserman was receiving a standing ovation in Rio that November, I flew alone to the Black Hills of South Dakota for my eight days of intensive therapy. For an entire week, I hadn't had a drink or smoked any pot. Martinis were what I missed most, but Onsite required us to cleanse our bodies of any toxins before we arrived—which meant no alcohol, drugs, or cigarettes for anyone. I'd been tempted to drink, but I'd stuck to my resolve.

The small Rapid City airport looked rather barren when I arrived the afternoon of November 16, but I quickly got a cab and headed for Onsite. I'd known it would be cold in South Dakota, but I wasn't prepared for two feet of snow. I warmed up on our drive through the hills, however, and was awed by the expansiveness of the land, the thick green pines and incredible quiet. Sharon Wegscheider told me later that some people think the Black Hills are holy. Indian burial grounds are there, she said, and she selected the place for Onsite because of the deep sense of peace that came from the landscape itself.

When we arrived at the snow-covered meadowlands and stone buildings of St. Martin's, a Catholic complex that housed Onsite, as well as a church, school, and hospital, I met our "housemother," a couple of therapists, and some of the other participants, who had come from as far as New Mexico, Indiana, and Florida, and as near as Colorado and Wyoming. Like me, the other new arrivals were trying to present themselves as open and friendly, but their smiles were forced and their laughter was nervous. We all reached out with awkward, overly enthusiastic handshakes as we were introduced, and I found myself thinking: What am I doing here? Twenty-three of us—seventeen women and six men—would be housed in dormitory-style rooms on separate floors.

After we got settled, we had an early supper and then congregated in a large room on the third floor. As I sat down, I looked up to discover a pair of intense brown eyes examining me. The woman was about five feet two, sturdy and fit, and she somehow reminded me of a drill sergeant as she studied me intently, almost seeming to read my thoughts. When I found out she was one of the therapists, I thought: Oh, no, I don't want that one. Don't let me get her; she'll tear me to pieces.

In the "great room," all twenty-three of us sat in a large circle, along with seven therapists. Sharon Wegscheider and Joe Cruse told us that they and our other therapists had been victims of dysfunctional family behavior themselves and had experienced what we were going through. Some were recovering addicts or alcoholics, and they intimately understood the process we were about to undertake. Although many things we would be required to do might not make sense to us initially, we should try to trust that the methods ultimately would help us work through our problems.

I got angry when I heard the rules, which included mandates against smoking, running, and medication—not even aspirin—unless it was vital to a medical condition. I couldn't stand the idea of not running every day. But then Sharon explained that emotional pain is often "medicated" or numbed by running and smoking, as well as by drugs or alcohol. The reason not to use even aspirin, she said, is that often emotional pain is the cause of headaches, backaches, and stomachaches, so it's important to allow these pains to surface in order to get in touch with them.

Another rule was that at Onsite, we were never to be alone. Since one of our big goals was to build trust with other people, we could walk the grounds in groups of three or more, but never alone and never in pairs. We knew how to be by ourselves, but we didn't know how to be with others. So if we wanted to read, or even if we wanted to take a nap, we had to go to the great room to do it. And if we couldn't sleep at night and wanted someone to talk to, we could go into the great room, which was open all night long and where a therapist was always available.

After the therapists told us about themselves and the program, we had to introduce ourselves and tell why we had come to Onsite. When it was my turn, I said hello to the rest of the group, told them my name, and for the first time, described publicly what Dr. Masserman had done to me. I felt ridiculous as I tried to explain that I knew I must have known what was happening all along but had been too frightened to wake up and accept the truth. I told them that even now I didn't remember sex or anything else that happened under the Amytal. When I finished speaking, I felt like such a fool that I got up abruptly and walked back to the room I shared with three other women. That's that, I thought. This is not for me. I had seen it in the faces of those people in that room: they thought I'd gotten what I deserved. I pulled down my suitcase. I had to get out of there. Ann had promised I could leave anytime I wanted, and that time had come. No way am I going to put myself through any more torture.

I started throwing things into my suitcase. I'd probably have to wait until morning to leave, but I was sure I could catch a plane the next day. Then I heard a knock, and I looked up to see a man from Dallas named Andy opening the door a little bit. "Can I come in?" I looked at him angrily, not trusting him for a minute. Andy walked toward me with a shy smile.

"That took guts," he said, "just comin' out and sayin' what you did. I want to thank you, 'cause it helped me say my piece. Would you come on back downstairs? We sure could use you." Andy put his hand on my shoulder in a friendly, nonthreatening way. I looked at him and felt myself smile. We returned to the great room together and sat down. Some of the people in the room greeted me, others smiled. I thought: Maybe this is going to be okay.

The next morning, I grew even more optimistic. We had breakfast at seven, followed by meditation in the chapel and then daily chores. The St. Martin's sisters cooked and cleaned for us, but we each had a daily housekeeping task. My job was to clean the sinks in the women's bathroom. I scrubbed them until they gleamed, and then I went down to the great room for the first class of the day.

Sharon Wegscheider gave classes on the way families behave as units and how dysfunctional families, in particular, play highly structured roles that are an integral part of the disease. Joe Cruse, who was a doctor, gave classes on "The Biochemistry of Feelings" and taught us that chemically dependent people have substances in their brains that cause them to react to alcohol and drugs differently than people who are not physiologically disposed to addiction.

In the group therapy sessions we had in the late morning, after lunch, and again before dinner, we worked in small "family" groups. The idea was for us to role-play situations that re-created our early life experiences so vividly that we would live through them emotionally once again. Letting out the pain and grief and rage of our traumas— whether early or recent—would then allow us to open the wounds, release the poison, and heal.

I was pretty unnerved when I learned that my small-group leader was Carole Keller, the tough, commando-type therapist I'd seen earlier. During a morning class in the great room, Carole had firmly established that I couldn't bullshit her when one of the therapists asked me a question and I couched my answer in my usual defensive wit. From across the room a harsh, curt voice shouted, "Barbara!" It was Carole Keller, and the whole room cringed.

I looked up meekly and said, "Yes?"

"Cut out that phony stuff!" she said. "Why don't you be yourself for a change?" I don't know which was my stronger response—anger at her for shaming me or the feeling of shame itself—but I realized she was somebody who could help me, even if I hated it. I was rather leery of the six other people in my group—a psychiatric nurse, a psychiatrist, a psychologist, an alcoholism counselor, a nun, and a housewife. I later wondered if Carole hadn't purposely put me in this group so I would have to deal with four mental health professionals who were fallible human beings, something that forced me to cut through my automatic tendency to attribute godlike status to such people. Even if it wasn't intended, it worked. I soon learned that all of us came from families with common compulsions—from alcohol and drug addiction to work-aholism, compulsive gambling, and religious fanaticism. None of us had been cuddled or hugged as children, and we all pulled back in fear when the therapists asked us to put our arms around each another. We had developed patterns that allowed us to numb ourselves and disregard our own feelings. We were out of touch with ourselves and our real emotions. So now we had to learn to let ourselves feel vul-nerable, learn how to relax and how to show affection as well as receive it. Touching each other's faces with our eyes closed, putting our hands on each other's shoulders and whispering words of affection helped us start to get in touch with the child inside—a child each of us had been unable to allow and accept.

One of my favorite people in the group was "Cathy." We hit it off from the first day, even though we were totally different. I walked like my mother, head high, spine straight, and when I was scared, I smiled and laughed a lot. Cathy walked with her head down, looking at the floor, and never managed more than the suggestion of a smile. But it was Cathy I trusted to lead me about with my eyes closed, and it was Cathy I first hugged and was finally able to embrace for nearly a minute.

By the fourth day, I was ready to be the main subject in the role-playing we called "sculpturing"—where each member of the group plays a family member or some other person vital to the story of the "star." My head ached terribly, and my stomach was churning. I began by talking about my early life and picking different group members to play my ex-husband Richard, my mother, my father, and my brother. I chose Sister Josephine to play Dr. Masserman. I started from the time when I was two years old and then worked into my marriage with Richard, and finally I got into my relationship with Masserman. Carole Keller, acting as director, then fashioned a scene where "Richard" literally dragged me to "Masserman," who pushed me back to Richard, who dragged me around the room and handed me over to Masserman again. By the time we got to the rape, I was exhausted, and when Sister Josephine as Masserman lay on top of me, breathing in my ear and making orgasmic sounds, I started screaming, "Get off me! Get off me!" I didn't move, but I kept screaming.

I could hear people in the group crying, and I could hear Carole yelling at me, "Are you going to take this? How long are you going to take this?" Suddenly I felt myself struggling to push "the doctor" off me. I removed one of my sneakers and threw it at something. Then the handle of a "bataka," a stiffly padded pillow shaped like a bat, was shoved into my hands, and I gripped it tightly and started swinging it at a pile of big, soft pillows, screaming at the top of my lungs, "Get away from me! I hate what you did to me! You hurt me, you hurt me! Get away!" I slammed into those pillows with more strength than I would ever have imagined possible. When I stopped, exhausted, Carole and the others started hitting me softly with the big pillows, and I heard Carole yell, "Are you going to let him get away with this? Are

you going to take this? What are you going to do about it?" My rage
at being pushed boiled over, and I grabbed up the bataka again and
wielded it with new force, screaming, "You took my life! You took my
life! How could you? How could you?"

I finally collapsed in sobs, and then I felt Carole Keller's arms around
me, cradling and rocking me. "Sweet, precious Barbara," she said.
"You've been hurting so bad. But now that little child inside of you is
coming out. Now you're going to be able to take care of her and comfort
her and let her laugh and play." The rest of my group came over and
hugged me and held me.

The next day, when we settled down on our pillows for our small-
group session, Cathy was clutching her stomach, her face ashen and
glistening with sweat. I thought she must be sick and should lie down,
but Carole Keller said this was a sign that Cathy was ready to do her
work, and she led her into the center of the circle and asked her to
describe the pain. Cathy rocked back and forth in agony and said that
the pain was green and slimy.

"How old are you now?" Carole asked softly.

"Eight," Cathy said, starting to cry.

"Where are you now? Are you back home on the farm?"

"I'm in the barn. . . . Oh, it hurts so bad!"

"Are you being punished, Cathy?"

"It hurts!" she screamed.

"Let the pain out now," Carole ordered, passing her hand upward
from Cathy's stomach to the top of her head. "Let the pain come up."

"It hurts. Oh, it hurts."

"Let the pain come out of you."

"Oh, my God, there's something in my mouth."

"What is it, Cathy?"

"I don't know."

"You know, Cathy. Tell me what it is."

"Oh, God, oh, God. It's a penis."

In that moment of shock, I blocked out any awareness that something
similar had happened to me when I was a little girl. But I felt like
throwing up as I listened, felt the horror Cathy was feeling and the
comfort of Carole's arms around her as Cathy smiled from the relief
of finally having found the courage to remember the incest she had
suppressed all those years.

• • •

On my sixth day at Onsite, Carole asked me to kneel in the middle of our little group, alone, with my eyes closed. I did it without hesitating, much to the amusement of the group. "Boy, talk about faith and trust," someone commented, as they laughed at my newfound eagerness.

As I knelt there, no one said or did anything for more than a minute. Then I felt a soft pillow hit me gently in the face. "This is what he did to you," Carole Keller said, hitting me again and again. "Are you going to take it? Are you going to keep on taking it?"

I stayed where I was, my eyes closed and my arms limp at my sides, feeling utterly confused as I felt the soft pillow striking my face again and again. Then I heard Cathy and George and the other members of my group yelling at me: "Christ, Barb, do something! Aren't you going to fight back? Fight back, Barb, fight back!"

Now they all had pillows, and they were bumping and pushing me with the pillows, and I began to scream, "No! No more!" Carole handed me a bataka, and I started swinging it. I beat the hell out of a pile of pillows, screaming over and over, "No-o-o-o-o mor-r-r-r-r-re." I finally got too tired to hit or scream anymore, but I continued kneeling, my hands still clutching the handle of the bataka. From somewhere, I heard Carole shouting, "How did all this leave you, Barb? How did the doctor leave you?"

"Alone," I said.

"What else?"

"Angry!"

"What else?"

"Unhappy!"

"No," Carole Keller shouted. "No, Barb. He left you a drug addict!"

I said nothing.

"Say it, Barb! Say, 'I am a drug addict.' "

I couldn't open my mouth.

"Say it, Barb," she said softly. "Say, 'I am a drug addict.' "

The room was totally quiet. I opened my mouth and the words stammered out: "I . . . am . . . a drug . . . addict."

"Say it again. That's good. Say it again."

"I am a drug addict," I said in a stronger voice. "I am a drug addict."

"Shout it out."

I shouted it. I shouted it about twenty times in a row. Then I opened my eyes and looked around. I looked at Carole and at everyone in my group. "I am, you know," I said quietly. "I am. I am a drug addict. I am."

Carole put her arms around me and said, "That was good, Barb. That was very good work." Then she lifted my chin and said, "No more Prince Charmings for this girl. From now on, only frogs."

On our final day at Onsite, the twenty-three of us who had started and finished this program together sat down for one last time in a large circle in the great room. One by one, we walked into the center of the circle to receive from Sharon a bronze medallion imprinted with the outline of a butterfly. Each of our therapists came into the circle with us, wished us one word, and then briefly evaluated the work we had done.

When it was my turn, Carole came up to me and said, "The one word I would wish you is *reality*. In all my years as a therapist, I have never worked with anyone more willing to accept reality. If anybody in this room is going to make it, it's going to be you."

I looked around the room at the smiling faces of the people I had come to love during this earth-shaking week, knowing that I was just beginning and that when I got home, I would continue treatment for my drug and alcohol addictions. "Yes, but the miracle of this," I said, "is that I've been able to start healing only because you've all been willing to start healing."

In the yard afterward, packed and waiting for the vans that would take us to the airport, we hugged, laughed, and cried as we exchanged addresses and phone numbers. Brothers and sisters in the best sense, we had begun to cleanse ourselves of the hurts and fears we'd been carrying around for so many years.

My plane was the last to leave that day, so I had about an hour to myself. I ate a quick lunch and then wandered around the tiny Rapid City airport until I found the gift shop. In the back, four shelves of furry toy animals sat waiting for people to buy as last-minute presents. There were fluffy white sheep and a collection of pink and blue rabbits with little ribbons and bells and trinkets attached. Then I saw a brown teddy bear on the very top shelf, looking down at me with bright black eyes. That little bear had no ribbons, no little knit cap. She was just a plain little bear with an earnest, open expression. She and I looked at each other curiously for a long time, neither of us moving, until I said, "Come here, Bear."

I reached up from the tips of my toes, and with a little jump, I got myself high enough to bring her down to me. "So there you are," I said to her. "I've been hoping to meet you. Well, how do you do?"

Bear flew to Chicago with me in a brown paper bag. I sneaked peeks at her, and we got acquainted slowly. Once we got home, I took her out of the bag, and we slept for two full days. I didn't know how, but over the next five years, that little bear would play a major part in helping me heal.

Three days after I got home, I was accepted by Grant Hospital's four-night-a-week outpatient program for chemical dependency. The intensive therapy would last six weeks, followed by six months of support-group meetings. At Onsite they'd told me I needed a support group, and I planned to stay with it. Any evening I had to miss because of work, I'd make up on alternative nights. Carole Keller's advice served me well: "Stick with it. Don't give up your support systems. Just keep putting one foot in front of the other and do what you're supposed to do."

Through the end of November and the beginning of December 1986, that's exactly what I did: I put one foot in front of the other. I went to auditions, sang with several different bands, and started composing a set of songs with Spanish and English crossover lyrics. When Ken Cunniff called in early December and told me we'd finally received the check from Masserman's insurance company, I felt some relief. Even though I was still unhappy about feeling forced to settle, I was no longer hanging by threads in my case against Masserman. After Ken and Bill got their shares and I paid for the other legal expenses, my check amounted to $117,945.48—about $18,000 more than I'd paid Masserman over the years.

When I picked up my settlement check, I said, "Okay, now I've got to get his license taken away. Tell me what to do next." Bill Carroll said he'd get me a list of the places I should write.

Partly to celebrate the settlement and partly to have a real rest, I decided to visit my friend Isobel Hellender in California. John Houlihan, the director of the Grant Hospital program, told me that on my vacation, I should go to AA or Narcotics Anonymous meetings. Introductions at such meetings always started with, "My name is Barbara, and I am a drug addict and an alcoholic." John said he'd be glad to get me the names of support groups in California. I said thanks but no thanks, I'd do it myself. But I never did. It was more fun just to enjoy the idyllic weather, spectacular scenery, wonderful food, and supportive company. Isobel and I talked and laughed and visited with friends, and I didn't feel any need for meetings or support groups. I meditated in the mornings for the first few days; then I forgot about doing even that.

16   The Case Goes Public

TUESDAY, JANUARY 6, 1987   My first morning back from
my California holiday, I was drinking coffee and reading the *Chicago
Tribune* when my eye caught sight of a column called "On the Law,"
by Warren, Possley & Tybor, in the business section. The headline
"Shocking Detour on Road of Fame" topped the article. I could barely
trust that I wasn't dreaming as I read:

> Honors have been as plentiful as patients for Chicago psychiatrist Jules
> Masserman. Of late, however, some embarrassing, even shocking legal
> problems have been almost as abundant as the honors.
>
> "He is the most prominent psychiatrist in the world," says Dr. John
> Carlton of Santa Barbara, Calif., current president of the World Associ-
> ation of Social Psychiatry.
>
> In September, Masserman was lauded by the Illinois Psychiatric In-
> stitute and the American Association for Social Psychiatry. In November,
> he was named president for life of the World Association of Social Psy-
> chiatry in Rio de Janeiro.
>
> But according to three Chicago-area women, Masserman, who at age
> 81 has been practicing for 60 years, may be both an esteemed and
> menacing octogenarian.
>
> All three sued Masserman, alleging that, as part of their therapy, he
> required them to disrobe and then made sexual advances while they were
> under the influence of sodium amytal, which is used as a relaxant and
> can knock one out for a period of time.
>
> The individual suits, filed in Cook County Circuit Court, have now

been settled. According to sources, two women, one an attorney and the other an employee of a Michigan Avenue department store, have accepted settlements of $25,000 each. A third plaintiff, a singer-actress who lives on the Gold Coast, received $200,000, sources said.

I froze with embarrassment at being identified as a "singer-actress." Being a lawyer or businesswoman sounded respectable, but a singer-actress could be considered a dilettante. What came next—Masserman's denial—wasn't too surprising.

"There was no such sexual abuse at all," Masserman says. "I would greatly regret any publicity." Debra Davy, his attorney, declined to comment except to say that all allegations were denied.

Masserman is a professor emeritus of neurology and psychiatry at Northwestern University, and author of more than a dozen books and more than 400 articles. "Few but the youngest resident would not know the name," says one Chicago psychiatrist.

The lawsuits' chief allegations were that Masserman induced the women to disrobe and lie on an office couch. They were then allegedly injected with the sodium amytal and, while they were unconscious, he made sexual advances. One woman contended that she awoke to find Masserman attempting sexual intercourse with her. That suit contended that the doctor should have known that such action was in no way medically significant or of any diagnostic value.

Masserman flies small planes, plays the violin and viola, composes music and in a hobby germane to one suit, sails on Lake Michigan. According to that suit, he invited one of the women onto his boat after indicating that "effective therapy could be conducted thereon." The woman alleged that he disrobed her and touched her intimately, "doing so in the name of therapy."

The column reported that all three of us claimed that our experiences had caused "severe shock and mental trauma." It noted that we'd been represented by attorneys Ken Cunniff and William Carroll, and mentioned that Bill was both a professor at John Marshall Law School and a psychologist. It ended by saying, "Carroll admitted that it was the word of the plaintiffs versus the word of the doctor, but contended, 'There was evidence available that would have persuaded a jury' [my emphasis]."

I read the story several times to make sure it was real. Ken and Bill had come through! I tried to call them, but they weren't around. I got more and more elated, thinking about the repercussions of this article. I also got more and more scared, for while I'd accomplished something that showed strength and proved me a capable person, I thought: Now Masserman will kill me for sure.

About noon, I decided to go out for groceries. On my way to the store, I passed one of my favorite restaurants, and without a second thought, I walked in, took a table in the back, and ordered a martini. As soon as it was served, I ordered lobster and a second martini. I was having a grand time until the third sip of my first martini, when my head started to spin and I felt so nauseated I thought I was going to vomit. Without touching anything else, I paid my bill and headed straight home, appalled at what I'd done. I'd celebrated, all right; but I'd celebrated in the old way, and by myself.

When I called John Houlihan at Grant Hospital, he wasn't surprised. "It's like clockwork," he said. "You were exactly on schedule for a relapse. A rule of thumb is that if you leave all your support mechanisms—meetings, counseling, meditation, prayer reading, or group—at the end of two weeks, there's an extremely high incidence of relapse."

"This is awful," I said. "It's as if I had no control over myself."

"But you do have control," he said. "And you've learned a lot from this. First, you know now that you must never give up *all* your support systems. Even if you're sick in bed, you can still read and meditate. You can still call someone. Second, never forget how sick you felt from that martini." He began to laugh. "I think we've ruined your celebrating for good!"

While I recovered my equilibrium from my "celebration," I remained ecstatic about that little article in the *Tribune*. I had more reason to cheer than I knew, for unbeknownst to me, that article was creating shock waves all over Chicago. One reaction of seismic proportions was happening across town, where Shari Dam, chief of prosecution in the Illinois Department of Registration and Education,* was reading the same write-up and wondering out loud, "Why hasn't this guy lost his license? Why is he still practicing? Why hasn't anybody reported this to me?" At that point, she picked up the phone and called Ken Cunniff.

Shari Dam was a dynamo. A tall, energetic woman with flying blond hair and tremendous humor, she was the mother of a preteen-age

---

*This department is now called the Illinois Department of Professional Regulation.

daughter and an accomplished prosecutor, who had heart as well as courage. She'd prosecuted cases similar to this one and knew that these situations generally are much more extensive—and involve more victims—than the initial complaints would indicate. "When I read that article, I was suspicious," she later said. "As a litigator, you become suspicious. I had prosecuted a couple of cases against dentists and other physicians that involved the use of drugs, and as you go through the prosecution of these various cases numerous times, you start picking up patterns."

The distinct patterns Shari Dam was talking about helped her form a mental picture of sex offenders as well as their victims. "The doctors tend to be narcissists—raging narcissists," she says. "They're charismatic, and they get their patients to fall in love with them. They have a tremendous grandiosity. Sometimes they have simply gone 'crazy' for a limited period of time; sometimes this is behavior they've manifested for years. But even when they've been charged with wrongdoing, they hang on and hang on to their innocence. They're usually married and have wives who are extremely supportive of their positions. Their grandiosity and self-righteousness make them operate in a way that's extremely dehumanizing to women.

"What's most important to these sex offenders is their own pleasure," says Shari Dam. "Their gratification is of utmost importance to them. They're very sick people—people with a total, complete lack of impulse control." Because of their sexual obsessions and overpowering drive to get what they want, men like this rarely limit the number of their prey. Thus, the count of victims can be staggering.

Prosecutors, however, rarely learn the true number of those victims. That's because it isn't easy for women to admit to such experiences, let alone to make it public by bringing charges. In addition, the victims in these cases are women with low self-esteem who are not going to be aggressive about confronting any behavior that seems to be somewhat out of bounds or unusual.

"It's the shame, it's being frightened to death and being embarrassed, that prevents them from coming forward," says Shari Dam. "I think women's tendencies are to immediately deny what's happened or could have happened. They're reticent because they have self-doubts. Women have been trained to distrust themselves. If something has happened, it's immediately, 'That couldn't have happened! He wouldn't do that to me!'

"It also gets back to the confidence you put in your medical professionals. The assumption is that these people are okay, that they're healthy, that they wouldn't jeopardize their careers by doing something like this. You think they're too smart, or that such successful people can't be sick. We are so prone to think that the more luminary you are, the more eminent you are, the less likely it is that you're going to do this. That's what we tend to assume."

Combined with that myth was the credibility problem Shari Dam knew her potential witnesses would face just because they'd sought treatment with a therapist in the first place. "The initial hurdle is, 'She wouldn't be going to him if she wasn't nuts,'" says Shari. "So you immediately have this obstacle, and part of it in this case also has to do with our perception of what it means to see a psychiatrist. Frankly, it seems to me that it's the healthier people who say, 'I need help, and I want to work this out and address my problems.' But we're not at that point [of understanding] in our society. So when you put these women on the stand who don't have credentials to match the professionals', people say, 'Well, how can you believe them?' This is just a housewife, or a patient, or a this or that—and *look* at this professional person's credentials. It's a credibility issue."

In this particular case, Shari Dam guessed, if the allegations were accurate, other women would come forward when they read the article. She knew from experience that when victims realize they're not alone, they're more likely to confess to the abuse that left them feeling isolated, ashamed, and frightened. She asked Ken Cunniff to relay her name, number, and address to the plaintiffs and to any other women who might call in response to the article. Ken told her that one of the ladies—me—had already asked for her name and was writing her a letter. He told her that he knew I was willing to testify or do anything necessary to help get Masserman's license revoked.

I had also told Ken to give my telephone number to Daniella, Annie, or any other patient who might call him and want to talk to someone who'd gone through a similar experience. (Since Annie and Daniella hadn't used their real names in their lawsuits, I couldn't call them.) Ken said Shari Dam was certain he and Bill would get calls from other women who'd been victimized by Masserman.

She was right. The day after the article appeared, three more women picked up the phone to call Ken. Others called over the next couple of weeks. Many went in to talk with him. We'll never know how many there were who didn't call, didn't share their pain. But at least ten women, after talking to Bill Carroll or Ken Cunniff, called me to talk about what Masserman had done to them.

The first was Annie Morrison, the businesswoman who had also "awakened" to Jules Masserman and sued him. I was surprised at how relieved and affirmed I felt after talking to Annie about her experience. Annie was extremely forthright, and she was angry. "I imagine this was going on for a long time," she said. "It's a shame no one can get the records, because my guess is that there would be hundreds of women he did this to."

Annie also told me that she was the woman who had heard a patient of Masserman's talking about sex over the telephone. "I was sitting in his office," she said, "and he had that amplifier device in his phone because he was so hard of hearing. Anyway, I heard this woman crying and shouting over a bill he had sent her. He said, 'Well, you have to pay.' She shouted, 'Why should I pay? All you ever want is sex anyhow.' And he said, 'Now, now Mrs. So-and-so, why don't you just pay half.' And he hung up.

"It was a longer conversation than that, but afterward, he said to his receptionist, 'Miss Whatever-her-name-was, change the billing of that to half of whatever it's supposed to be.'

"And I was just sitting there and I was really upset. I said, 'What is going on there?'

"He said, 'Oh, you know; just a crazy lady.'

"And that's what happens when someone is considered a god," Annie said. "Anyone who says anything against him is just a crazy lady. There's always that fear that you're going to be thought of as a crazy lady. Especially when you're so vulnerable."

I told Annie I had felt the same way. I related my experience with Diane Greenspan, without mentioning her name, and said I assumed there were still people who would think of us as simply crazy ladies but that we couldn't afford to let it get to us.

"You know, I have a lot of anger toward him," Annie said, "but I also think he's a pathetically sick person. Really. To do that. It's very sick."

Annie told me that Daniella would call me soon, and we agreed we three should get together for coffee.

Next, a woman I'll call Bonnie Markham called and told me her husband—not she—had been a patient of Masserman's for years. "I always hated the man, Barbara," she said, "and even though he has done my husband a world of good and my husband adores the man, I can believe this happened."

I said, "Maybe your husband adores the man, Bonnie, but from what I've been reading recently, a sick shrink does nobody any good. His agenda is only for him."

Bonnie started to cry. She told me her hatred of Masserman stemmed from an incident a number of years earlier, not long after her son, who had been a heavy drug user, committed suicide. At the time, she was terribly worried about her sixteen-year-old daughter, Vanessa, and thought it might be helpful for her to talk to a psychiatrist. So Bonnie made an appointment, and Vanessa went to see Dr. Masserman. Apparently, during that appointment, while Vanessa was talking about how she felt about the suicide of her older brother, Dr. Masserman said, "What would you do if I unzipped my pants and took out my penis right now?" Vanessa looked at him in disbelief, burst into tears, and got up and walked out of his office, slamming the door behind her.

I asked Bonnie if she had ever told her husband about this incident, and she said she hadn't. "My husband considers him the father he never had," she said. "I just couldn't spoil that for him. Of course my husband thinks your lawsuit is an outrage, and I couldn't talk to him about it at all."

Another woman, who gave me only her first name—Lillian—called the next evening. In a hesitant voice, she said she'd gotten my number from Bill Carroll, and she apologized for calling so late. I assured her it was all right, but then, for a long time, she didn't say anything.

"I imagine you're calling about the *Trib* article?" I said finally.

"Well, yes, but I don't really know how to begin."

"Were you a patient of his?"

"Yes—but oh, I'm so sorry, I think I'm going to cry," she said, breaking into sobs. When her crying quieted down a bit, she said between deep inhalations, "It's just that it was such a shock to read that article. I simply had no idea what was going on. I was his patient for ten years, and for six of those years, I thought he was in love with me. He and his wife were very unhappy together. You knew that, didn't you?"

"No. No, I didn't," I said, so startled that I had to catch my breath.

"Actually, the first time I knew *anything* was when I woke up that time."

"Oh, my God, I can't believe that," she said. "He told me he wanted to marry me. He said he was getting a divorce, but then, when I got a job offer in New York, he told me to go ahead and take it. I was sure there was another woman, so I left. Then when I saw the article, I thought maybe it was you."

"No," I said, feeling my heart beat wildly. "It wasn't me."

"Has anyone else called you about this?"

"Yes; in fact, you're the third, and I know of at least one other woman."

Lillian started crying again. "How could he do this? I should have known! I should have suspected."

I told her I was sorry she had to find out like this, but she said, "No, I'm glad to know the truth. I'm glad you sued him."

"I want you to know that I'm going to try to have his license revoked," I said.

"Good! I hope you do!"

"Well, I was wondering if you could help. You wouldn't have to use your name."

"No, I couldn't do that," she said. "I mean, I live in New York. I'm just in town for a visit."

"That wouldn't be a problem," I assured her. "You could still talk to Mr. Carroll or to the prosecutor for the Department of Registration and Education."

"No, I just couldn't," she said. "You're really strong. I'm not." With that, we said goodbye, and I never heard from her again.

Several of the women who subsequently called said they had never before spoken to anyone about what Dr. Masserman had done to them. One woman, who said she'd been his patient for less than a year when she started sleeping with him in 1967, told me he'd promised her he was going to leave his wife and marry her, but after she'd helped him with a writing project, their relationship broke up. She, like some of the other women I talked to, cried a lot when they talked about how foolish they felt, how used. Another patient who'd had a long-term affair with Masserman outside of therapy said she, too, believed he was in love with her and wanted to marry her "when he left his wife." Yet another woman, also a long-term patient, said she'd virtually written one of Masserman's major books and had been deeply in love with

him. Their affair had begun in 1960, she said. It seemed this was not
a situation where a doctor had suddenly gone senile or crazy; the pattern
stretched back thirty years; perhaps it had been going on all his life.

Just when I was beginning to think that everyone except Annie
Morrison and I had known what was going on, Daniella Biagi called
me. She provided some relief from the despair and sadness of the others
because she was so candid. Humor laced her stories of taking Antabuse,
drinking through the Antabuse, and having Amytal once or twice a
week over a four-year period. Daniella sounded like a remarkably strong
woman outside of her relationship with Masserman. But with him—
the "Master Manipulator," as she called him—she'd been malleable,
just like me. At the time we talked, neither of us realized that our
addiction to Amytal was what had physiologically turned both of us
into the alcoholics we'd become under his care—nor did we know
that he easily could have killed us with what he was doing.

For a while, as we talked, Daniella and I laughed—probably half
defensively, because of how awful it was to have been duped and how
stupid we felt we'd been. But when Daniella told me how, when she
was pregnant, Masserman encouraged her to take Amytal to learn the
"truth" that she didn't really want the baby, I was horrified. Thank
God she'd had the sense to call the obstetrics department and refuse
the Amytal; she was now the mother of a healthy, wonderful little five-
year-old. I was thrilled for her, but her story made me think once again
about what deep contempt Masserman must have had for women. I
remembered how cavalier he had been about my grief over my abortion.
"It's nothing," he'd said. "It's a waste of time crying over it now."

Even with Daniella's story and my own, however, I wasn't prepared
for "Jennifer." She called me on a Saturday morning when I'd just come
in from a run. She told me Masserman had given her Amytal for years,
and when she got pregnant with a child she and her husband had
waited for, Dr. Masserman assured her that the Amytal would not hurt
the fetus. He'd said it was especially important for her to continue her
Amytal therapy in order to discover how she really felt about the
pregnancy. She believed Masserman and let him give her the Amytal.
But the day after one Amytal injection when she was about five months
pregnant, she hemorrhaged and lost the child. I could see that she still
didn't blame the drug, or the doctor, for her miscarriage. But it was
obvious that her grief and rage over losing that baby were intertwined

with confusion about Masserman and the Amytal. I didn't know then whether the Amytal had anything to do with her child's death, but I did later learn that taking a barbiturate during pregnancy could be damaging to the fetus.

Like Lillian, Jennifer said she didn't have the courage to give me her full name or to help in getting the doctor's licenses revoked. Her husband didn't know about her suspicions, and she couldn't risk his finding out. She confessed that she was wondering if there was any possibility that the baby had been Masserman's, not her husband's, but that line of inquiry was too distasteful to follow, it made her too sad; and so we ended the conversation with that thought hanging in the air.

None of the new women I had spoken with so far had decided to sue Masserman, and most of them said they were unwilling to go through the distress of any such public complaint. Some even resisted the suggestion that they call Shari Dam to help stop Masserman from victimizing others. I recommended counseling to several women—and for the two or three ex-patients who sounded as if they were considering lawsuits, I suggested they decide soon, before the statute of limitations ran out. The limits differed in length and depended on a variety of factors, but in most civil litigation cases against a therapist in Illinois, charges would have to be brought within two years of the alleged incident involving the defendant.

A particularly sad and disoriented woman called and said she wanted to see my therapist so that she, too, could "get well" and get over what Jules Masserman had done to her. I gave her Ann Jernberg's name and that of another therapist I'd heard was very good, but she never made contact with either of them. She called me a number of times, however, and each time, she seemed farther away from the possibility of ever healing. She told me that Masserman had been "just like a father" to her, and she was very confused about what he had or hadn't done. I wondered if she was on drugs or was drunk some of the times she called, but her disorientation flustered me so that I never knew how to ask her about it.

One day, approaching my apartment door after a jazz concert rehearsal, I heard my phone ringing and ringing. I finally picked up, and "Laura Davis" told me she was another former patient. Laura sounded smart and quick, and when I told her I was going to try to get Masserman's medical license revoked so that he couldn't continue his abuse of other women, she said she'd do anything necessary to help. Laura, an urban designer, was a classic example of a woman who initially doubted her own perceptions and suspicions about Masserman. When she read the *Tribune* article, however, she said she cried uncontrollably, because it confirmed that she wasn't crazy.

Laura Davis had inadvertently discovered yet another victim of Dr. Masserman's. The day she saw the article in the *Trib*, she called up a woman friend who was a lawyer. The lawyer had seen the article, and she spoke of a roommate from law school who had been treated by Dr. Masserman years before and would feel quite vindicated by this whole thing. The roommate had tried to tell her friends what this man Masserman was doing, and they wouldn't take her seriously.

Apparently, this law student had received a number of obsessive and obscene phone calls at home. Though the caller was anonymous, the student figured it was Masserman because she wore heavy wooden clogs to his office, which she took off when she got on the couch for analysis, and Dr. Masserman would make comments during the sessions about her feet being sexy. Her anonymous caller displayed the same kind of foot fetish. No one else she knew ever saw her feet or made such remarks. The calls frightened her, but she never pursued the matter because she didn't think anyone would believe her. She wasn't even sure her friends did—and once again, of course, the reason was Masserman's prominence.

Laura Davis first saw Jules Masserman in 1979, when she was twenty-eight years old. After a forty-minute interview, he had told her she needed analysis, which would "cost less money than a car and won't take as long as it used to."

"I shouldn't have been there in the first place, probably," Laura said. "He really didn't help me in any practical way. I had panic attacks, and he acted like it was certain that they were real symptoms of something important from my past. I later cured myself of them—completely by accident—about a year after I quit therapy. Our office went to decaffeinated coffee, and I stopped having panic attacks altogether. I hadn't thought much about it, but then one day I had an attack, which really surprised me since I hadn't had one in such a long time. My secretary said to me, 'Did you notice anything different about the coffee? I made it with caffeine.' So it turned out that my big psychological problem was caused by caffeine! It would have been nice if Masserman had suggested to me, 'Try cutting back on coffee and see if that helps,' but he never did. Of course, that's one of the reasons one goes to a psychiatrist, because they know about medicine and the body as well as things about the mind. But he didn't help me there."

Laura had Amytal only twice. The first time, after she'd been going to Masserman for about five months, he said she was "blocking" and needed "treatment in order to be able to talk more freely and with less inhibition."

"Up to that point, I had been lying on the couch, free-associating," she said. "I didn't feel I was blocked. But maybe I was being a little stubborn. We had talked about my childhood, and Dr. Masserman just loved exploring any sexual connotations there might be whenever the subject of my father came up. I came from a very uptight WASP family, and to me, it didn't seem relevant to why I was there. That was part of my problem with the analysis: I wanted a short-term solution to a short-term problem.

"Dr. Masserman suggested I was blocking out important information—implying there was sexual stuff I was refusing to look at [related to the panic attacks]. It was so far out of the realm of possibility if you knew my family, it just couldn't be, but it got me a little worried. I thought: He's telling me I'm blocking, and maybe I am shutting out all this memory, but I don't think so. Anyway, I knew I was being a little stubborn, so I decided I should explore that possibility.

"He told me that under the Amytal I would talk more freely, but I would not remember everything I said. He said that when we got back to regular sessions, I would gradually remember or to some extent he would reveal to me what had been said, so I would benefit. That never occurred.

"The first time—it was in the summer—I went in at seven o'clock in the morning, and he had me sign a release form. It said the treatment was for medical purposes; I'm not sure what it said about risks or anything like that. He had me do a certain amount of undressing, and then I got into this narrow twin bed. I know I couldn't have been wearing any clothing, because my arm was completely bare and you had to get enough off so it would be appropriate to get in between clean white sheets. I do remember having to re-dress after it was all over.

"I remember my arm was outside, on top of the sheets, and pretty much everything else was under the sheet, because it was chilly. The sheets were very crisp and clean. And then he injected the drug. I remember the needle being in quite a long time. But then I went out. That needle could have been in a long time, and he could have kept gradually adding more. It was a fairly sizable vial of clear liquid with a reddish tint to it.

"I just remember the first time from probably the first thirty seconds of conversation. He must have asked me what I was thinking about, and I was looking at the wall and I was visualizing all the people in my life as being a wall and I wasn't part of the wall. It was a strong visual image and gave me a sense of separation. And then nothing, absolutely nothing.

"I remember waking up around twelve-thirty, and I sort of stumbled over to Marshall Field's for lunch. I remember dropping my fruit juice. I wasn't in my normal state of control. I was very uninhibited all afternoon. I went to the office, and I said things to people in a very straightforward way, like I would normally never do. I had large backlogs of work on my desk, and I got through that backlog faster than I ever had before—partly because it was very easy for me to make decisions about how to handle things and partly because I was uninhibited enough that I wasn't feeling guilty about returning [overdue] calls.

"Late in the afternoon, I had a friend come over, and we went out bike riding, and I promptly drove straight into a parked car. Nearly twelve hours had passed since I had been given the Amytal, yet as soon as I got out of my apartment on my bike, I drove straight into the bumper of a parked car. When one does something like that, there's something a little wrong with how you're perceiving things in space.

"So that was the first time. I was really pleased with not being my usual uptight self. I might have dropped glasses and ridden my bike into a wall, but I was very effective and very decisive, because it took away the guilt and worry about things that pile up. I was much more relaxed than I ever had been.

"Two or three weeks later, he wanted me to have Amytal for the second time, and that seemed very soon to me. There was absolutely no cause that I could see for him to say I needed the drug again. I wasn't doing anything like being stubborn or 'blocking.' He just said I needed it again. I didn't object. I was confused, and I don't know if I expressed my confusion to him.

"Although I didn't sign a form the second time, I went in again at seven o'clock in the morning. I remember my arm being bare again, and I remember getting the shot. I remember nothing about any conversation. No conversation, zero conversation.

"I have no idea what time it was or how many hours had gone by or how many minutes it had been when I woke up. But I woke up, and he was somehow on top of me. I have no sense of weight or anything or what his position was because, you know, your perceptions are real strange when you're waking up and you're kind of drugged, but he was on top of me and he was fondling my breasts, and he was repeating over and over, 'Oh, you have beautiful breasts. Oh, you have such beautiful breasts.' And then I fell back asleep.

"All I was paying attention to was the upper part of my body. I don't think he was raping me; I hope he didn't. I have this idea that the sheets were still on top of me and that he was on top of them. That's the sense I have because the whole focus was on my chest. A part that's so horrible to me is that in my drugged state, I felt very flattered and proud. I think I mumbled or groaned, because I was pleased he was saying that. I made some noise to indicate my pleasure. I'm ashamed of that. This is not a man I found pleasant. That's the part that's hard to live with. You have to forgive yourself for it.

"Anyway, then I fell back asleep. And it was quite different the second time. The first time I remember waking up, and when I was ready, I just got dressed and left by the side door. The second time, I didn't sleep quite as long, and he came in to try to shoo me out. He kept telling me I'd slept long enough, I'd slept long enough, I should get dressed and get out of there. He was extremely impatient to have me leave. I was kind of irritated at that, because based on the first experience, when I dropped my glass and had these perceptual problems, I didn't want to leave that soon. I didn't feel ready to leave. But he was pushing me out.

"And then, later in the day, I remembered what had happened, and I thought: Was it real or was I dreaming that? I decided it had been real. I did have some question in my mind, because, you know, you're drugged and it's very strange. But what you do when you have an experience like that—which is somewhat dreamlike because of the drug—is you compare it to other dreams. And when you break it down, it just doesn't compare to any other dream. Because there's the give-and-take of the conversation. There's his closeness—his face was right in my face. It was all the tactile feeling. And, you know, the number of times he repeated, 'Oh, you have beautiful breasts.' And knowing my own reactions—how I mumbled or groaned. . . .

"Sure, you have some kind of shadow of a doubt that it could all be in your head, because there is a dreamlike sensation to the thing. But I couldn't imagine myself having a dream like that. It's too improbable. In dreams, one thing leads to another. In my dreams, everything happens very rapidly, and things that happen in them don't make that much sense. But this was just, you know, one brief clear moment. And my sense of time in this one clear moment was a true sense of time. It was not a dreamlike sense of time. You have to wonder whether your mind can play tricks on you like that. But I simply wasn't willing to believe or accept that my mind would play that actual trick.

"So I decided it was real. I thought: I believe that this did happen, and I don't trust the man—what can I do about it? I thought: One thing I could do is ask him about it. So I thought that through: what would happen if I asked him about it. I decided, He's not going to say, 'Yes, I did that.' He's going to characterize it as something that's going on in my mind, something that I wanted. And I'm going to be left with the burden—and so I thought there would be nothing to be gained in having that conversation. I went one or two more times. I was dying to ask, but I felt no trust, and then I just quit. I just canceled my last appointment and didn't go.

"After I quit, I heard nothing. I received invoices from him for another six months or so. I paid them; now I don't know why I did that. I don't know why I didn't go to an attorney.

"When I read that article, I realized how stupid I had been to pay all the bills and not go to a lawyer. That finally removed the shadow of doubt from my mind as to what had happened and why I had quit and that I was right to quit. It also made me realize that I had been very, very fortunate."

After all those calls, I felt sure that the women who had come forward represented only a fraction of the patients Jules Masserman had abused over the fifty years he practiced medicine. How many hadn't come forward? How many had no conscious recollection of his sexual abuse because they never woke up? I wondered how many of his female patients had become drug-addicted or alcoholic for reasons they couldn't explain. Did they still blame themselves? Did they still secretly feel they might belong in a mental institution, as I had felt? The depth of this abuse and its consequences on the individual lives of women staggered me.

I also had to wonder what had been going on with him all those years. Was his violation of so many women a sign of arrogance or of feelings of inferiority? Was he afraid of women? Was he merely excited about controlling these drugged bodies? I wondered if he struggled over issues of morality and tried to stop, or whether he found it so compelling that he never questioned his actions. Whatever it was that drove him, it was extraordinary that he'd been willing to jeopardize all that he'd achieved in exchange for those moments of gratification. It was horrifying to realize how deeply in need of therapeutic help Dr. Masserman himself had been.

It never occurred to me that Dr. Masserman might, in fact, have been justifying what he was doing in the name of science—continuing research on women that he had begun on cats many years earlier. I had studied abnormal psychology and taken Psych 101 in college, but I never realized it was Jules Masserman's research I was reading about when I studied experimental induction of neurosis. Like me, anyone who took a basic psychology course might not recall his name but might remember his experiments that induced anxiety and conflict in cats (and dogs and monkeys), which he said corresponded to human dysfunctions.

Masserman's long-term fascination with experimental neurosis— which was at the heart of the "biodynamic" principles for which he is best known—began in the late 1930s in a University of Chicago laboratory.* His pioneering work, which was in keeping with the scientific mainstream of the times back then, drew on a tradition of empirical psychology that was influenced by the work of such behaviorists as Ivan Pavlov. Jules Masserman's accounts of these animal experiments in induced neurosis won him a great deal of attention and a large number of scientific grants and awards, including the Lasker Award for research in mental hygiene in 1946.

Masserman's interest, even in those days, however, seems to have been unusually intense. Today, Masserman is still referred to by some people in Chicago as the "Cat Doctor." Early in this research, he personally collected alley cats and took them to his lab, where he carried the animals from their regular cages to a training cage and taught them to depress switches that opened a door and allowed them to eat. At first, the cats were trained to respond to a light flash or the sound of a bell, but they soon learned how to operate the switches directly— and be rewarded with food.

---

*For more on Masserman's biodynamic principles, see Notes, page 298.

These alley cats had lived by their wits, so they learned quickly; they rubbed against the "food door" and purred because they were so thoroughly confident of getting food when they wanted it. They were also friendly to the experimenter, entered the training cages eagerly, and then quickly and effectively operated the switch. Sometimes the cats would press the switch for food even when they were no longer hungry.

Once the cats were confident and content, Masserman began to interrupt their habits and expectations. He would disconnect the switch, interpose barriers, lock the food box or fail to drop in food after the signal was given. When this happened, the animals would reexplore the cage, sit on the switch, play with the wires or barriers, or attempt to attract the experimenter's attention. They didn't express fear about these disruptions and were easily trained to resume working the switch when the food reward was available again.

At that point, Masserman upped the ante. At irregularly spaced intervals, when a cat worked the switch or reached for food, it would instead be hit with a harsh blast of air or get an electrical shock. This created such fear and conflict that the animal would become severely nervous and terrified. Masserman theorized that tremendous conflict was aroused because the switch signal represented satisfaction of the cat's hunger but also threatened horrible trauma.

Masserman reported that animals "crouched, trembled, mewed plaintively, and breathed rapidly, shallowly and irregularly"; their blood pressure increased, and they had a fast, pounding pulse and dilated pupils, "obviously parallel[ing] the subjective experience of normal and neurotic anxiety in the human."

After the air blasts and electrical shocks were started, the cats' aversions were quickly generalized. They resisted being put into the experimental cage and tried to escape; they avoided the experimenter and in many cases showed severe startle reactions and phobic aversions to sudden lights or sounds, to constricted spaces, or to restraint. Masserman found these reactions similar to "acute war neuroses."

Most of the cats refused to touch the switches in the experimental cage rather than risk the trauma. Some of them, Masserman found, became "so severely neurotic" that they refused food in their home cage as well as in the experimental cage. He found it "remarkable" that some animals would starve themselves to death rather than risk being shocked or blasted with air. Others got confused, lost their memories, or became semicatatonic. When some of the animals were force-fed to stay alive, they became "psychosomatic," lost weight, or got diarrhea; others regressed to nestling and nursing movements. Some animals developed compulsive or counterphobic responses: A dog used in one of these experiments developed the ritual of circling the food box three times and then bowing on its forepaws before attempting to eat the food in front of it.

Masserman noticed that some of the animals became "viciously antagonistic" to members of the laboratory staff associated with the traumatic experiences. Cats and dogs who were given free run of their quarters and permitted to chase mice and mate at will showed milder neurotic reactions to the trauma than did control animals who were kept isolated and otherwise inactive.

Learning about this research, I started to feel like a cat myself! It was as if Masserman had trained me to want his lavish approval as well as the Amytal. When he withheld it or got angry at me, then he'd observe my reactions. Just like the cats, I'd tremble and show startle reactions, my pulse would increase, I'd get nervous. Like the cats, I got depressed. I wasn't in control of my environment; someone else worked the switch.

This feeling was intensified when I learned that Masserman also studied the effects of alcohol and Amytal on the hypothalamus, which regulates body temperature as well as emotions, sexual behavior, and inhibition. His extensive interest in the hypothalamus and the neural mechanisms involved in the exhibition of emotional and sexual excitement and sexual behavior may be related somehow to what he later did to us women. Did he study what emotional effects alcohol, Metrazol, morphine, and Sodium Amytal would have on us, as he did on cats and monkeys?

An article called "They're Making People Out of Monkeys" in the *Chicago Tribune* in 1953 described how Dr. Masserman and his research assistant drove monkeys insane—"making them full of fears, frustrations, and phobias"—and then tried to cure them. The article focused on one monkey, Lucretia, whose neurosis was cured by an experimental brain operation "which left her oversexed and slightly stupid, so she will probably never know nor care . . . how much she probably contributed . . . Her brain operation proved that a neurosis can be cured—but at the risk of lessening intelligence."

The article went on: " 'Since most women don't use all their brains anyway, why wouldn't it be practical to sacrifice part of them on the operating table to cure their neuroses?' " asks Dr. Curtis Pechtel, research assistant to Dr. Jules H. Masserman, one of the nation's leading research psychiatrists."

It seems curious that Dr. Masserman was so intrigued with the effects of Sodium Amytal on sexual behavior, autoeroticism, "sham" emotion, mobility, and somatic dysfunctions as far back as the late 1930s and early '40s. It is also intriguing that in 1943, Dr. Masserman was looking into the question of whether the hypothalamus plays any role in the origin or conscious perception of erotic emotion, and not just on the capacity to display sexual excitement that can be induced by a drug or by vaginal stimulation. He suggested that among other things, investigation needed to be done to determine whether animals could be conditioned or trained to adapt to direct hypothalamic stimulation.*

At the same time Masserman was studying the effects of Amytal, he was also doing extensive experiments on alcohol addiction. In a number of experiments, he got cats drunk and compared their neurotic behavior to that of cats who were sober. After injecting them with alcohol, he found that even the cats who would rather starve than touch the dreaded signal switch sometimes lowered their inhibitions and touched the food switch. Nearly half the animals eventually learned that alcohol relieved neurotic tensions and inhibitions, and thereafter chose milk spiked with alcohol instead of plain milk.

One woman who knew Jules Masserman and his future wife, Christine McGuire, at the University of Chicago in the 1940s remembered that Masserman had cats living with him in his apartment. "He'd get the cats hooked on alcohol and then withdraw it," Barbara Cheresh said. "I remember the detail that they used to climb the curtains in his apartment, and when he withdrew the alcohol, they lost their ability to climb. I thought it was *cruel*. I was an impressionable young thing, but it seemed sadistic to me."

Hearing about this, I couldn't help but compare it to the way Dr. Masserman sometimes withheld Amytal from me and then watched to see what I would do to get it.

Sometimes he would schedule me for Amytal and, when I showed up, tell me he'd decided not to give it to me after all. He would say, "I don't think we'll have it today. I don't think you need this." I was tremendously angry and let down when I couldn't get it, but I was

*For more on this research, see Notes, pages 298–299.

afraid to say anything for fear he wouldn't give it to me the next time. Once, I almost burst out crying when he withheld the Amytal. I remember saying, "Why? I canceled all my appointments for the day!" He said, "You're just a spoiled little child. Just because you want it doesn't mean you'll get it."

Daniella and Annie reported similar experiences.

Annie, who hated Amytal, said he always made her beg for it. "He would make me feel I was the one who wanted Amytal," Annie said. "He would say, 'Do you want Amytal?' and I would say, 'No.' And he would say, 'You know, the last time I noticed you seemed a little better after you had the Amytal.' So then I would say, 'Well, okay, then maybe I would like to have some Amytal.' And then he would say, 'Well, you know you can't have this anytime you want it.' It was so bizarre. I would find myself begging for something I didn't even want."

And Daniella remembered, "You were scheduled for an Amytal, okay? And first you'd come in and do the talking. And then he would say, 'Do you really want the Amytal?' Very manipulative stuff. 'You really want the Amytal? If you *really* want the Amytal, then you have to *ask* me for the Amytal.' I was never sure I wanted the Amytal anyway, because I felt so goddamned horrible afterward—out of it, gone, in a different realm—and not very happy. But it would be like he was tantalizing me with the Amytal. Not only would he make me beg for it, but one time he withheld it. He said, 'No, I don't think you really want it.'

"Other times after I begged for it, I never knew what time I was supposed to stand up from the couch and say, 'Now I'm ready for the Amytal.' It was a guessing game. Because if I didn't stand up, I'd blow the time. He'd go, 'Well, there won't be enough time left for the Amytal,' as if it were my fault. Of course, there probably was enough time, he probably didn't even have a patient coming in, but he'd always do that."

Was he playing with us? Was he studying us like he had studied animals? Was he comparing the ways animals and women could be conditioned and controlled?

I remember once when I went for Amytal, I got undressed and under the covers on the daybed, waiting for Dr. Masserman to give me my Amytal injection. He lifted the syringe from the pan the way he always did and said, "Now, you must understand, this syringe was boiled for ten minutes so that it is absolutely sterile. I've cooled it to the right temperature so it's ready for use." He did everything the same every time. It was ritualistic, like magic. This time, as usual, he had prepared everything and pulled the ottoman over by the daybed. He brought the cotton over and the cuff, and he swabbed the vein on my arm with alcohol. He picked up the syringe and the glass vial, and he held them up in his hands, as usual. But then he lifted the vial of Amytal even higher in the air, looked at it, looked at me, and very deliberately dropped it on the floor. Glass and Amytal scattered all over, but he barely looked at it. "Oh, what a shame," he said, with a sweet smile. "And I don't have any more."

17 License to Rape

Jules Masserman's unconditional denial of "all allegations" added fuel to my determination to stop him from practicing therapy of any kind and from administering the "Amytal interview" to unsuspecting patients.

Shari Dam at the Department of Registration and Education was launching an investigation that would eventually help her press formal charges against him, but in the meantime, Jules Masserman had a medical license that gave him access to the bodies and minds of his female patients. With that license, he would still have the opportunity to use them sexually while they were knocked out and, while they were awake, undermine their confidence by telling them what "spoiled little girls" they were.

Besides wanting Masserman's license revoked, I wanted him censured by his peers, so on January 12, 1987, the same day I wrote Shari Dam, I also wrote the Illinois Psychiatric Society and the Chicago Psychoanalytic Society to register complaints against him for unethical behavior in the form of sexual abuse. I attached copies of the *Chicago Tribune* article, said I was the patient who had settled for $200,000, and noted that four or five other women had recently come forward with similar complaints.

Within two weeks, I received a letter from the chairman of the psychoanalytic society's Ethics Committee, advising me that they were preparing to investigate my complaint. The following day, a letter arrived from the Ethics Committee of the Illinois Psychiatric Society (IPS), noting that as the district branch of the American Psychiatric Association (APA), the IPS would be investigating my complaint. An enclosed copy of APA regulations stipulated that each state society should "seek to complete the investigation [of a breach of ethics] and reach a decision within nine months after the complaint is received."

It didn't take that long for the IPS to halt its investigation altogether. In mid-April, Dr. David Hawkins, chairman of the society's Ethics Committee, sent me a copy of a letter he'd written to Jules Masserman, advising: "because this matter is under investigation by the Dept. of Registration and Education, we will not pursue any active investigation on our part as long as they continue their activities. I trust this meets with your approval."*

Fortunately, Shari Dam was proceeding full steam ahead with a case aimed at bringing Jules Masserman to trial and getting his license revoked. I met with Shari's assistants in February, and she interviewed me at length later in the spring. She got copies of the civil complaints and the records Daniella, Annie, and I had filed.

In addition, Ken and Bill had referred at least ten other women to Shari to discuss bringing complaints against Jules Masserman. Many of these women had talked for hours with Ken or Bill or both of them about their painful personal discoveries of Masserman's assaults and betrayals. Ken had been amazed by the similarities in the stories he heard. These women had never met each other; they had never spoken. "Yet they all told the same details, the same stories," he said. And the affinity between the women themselves was startling: "They are very intelligent and very attractive women who had listened to somebody as if he were god," Ken said. "They are all very nice, very good people." Ken commented on how interesting it was that a number of Masserman's patients were quite prominent in Chicago, or were married to men in powerful positions. I knew that in two or three cases, the husbands knew nothing about what Masserman had done to their wives. One woman had said she wouldn't dare tell her husband what had happened because "He'd be mortified." Another had said she

---

*The chair of the committee later said that the Ethics Committee always stops their process if there's an on-going investigation because they don't want to have their documents subpoenaed or used legally by the licensing board or the courts.

thought her husband would leave her if he knew she'd had sex with her therapist.

Along with interviewing me and all the other women, Shari Dam also was talking to medical experts and investigating another civil case against Masserman that had been settled out of court for fifty thousand dollars in February 1985. In that case, a former patient had charged Masserman with medical negligence for having given her permanent scars from his injections of Amytal. She filed her suit in 1983—one year before I woke up to Dr. Masserman's betrayal. She hadn't charged sexual assault, but she had charged that besides causing her "serious and permanent personal injuries, including but not confined to extensive surgery, great pain and suffering, [and] loss of income," he "needlessly injected Plaintiff's arm when it was not medically necessary."

When I met Shari Dam, I was glad she was in charge of the prosecution against Jules Masserman. Although Shari was never at liberty to tell anyone details about the women she interviewed, I later learned that she had been quite disgusted over the patterns of Masserman's behavior that she'd seen repeated in the different individual civil suits. The similarities—early morning Amytal, disrobing, lack of memory, flashbacks of bizarre incidents that left them confused and ashamed— had convinced her beyond doubt that the charges against Jules Masserman were true. "I came to believe those women when they finally said, 'I'll testify,' " Shari said later. "I believed at that point—and we had come that far and I knew every inch of the story—I knew it was true."

Except for me, however, the case would proceed with pseudonyms. None of the other women—married or single—wanted to use their real names; it was too frightening. But once again, in these proceedings, I insisted on using my full name because I still wanted Masserman to know I was mad as hell.

Shari Dam felt we had a strong case. The evidence made it clear that normal standards of medical care were not being met by Jules H. Masserman. And the use of Amytal was *archaic*. "Even if we can't get around the issues of the credibility of whether he did it, I'm gonna sink him on his use of controlled substances," she said. "He initiated and perpetuated addictions—and look at his records. He didn't keep adequate records on his patients when he gave them drugs. Failing to keep adequate records on a patient he has seen for eighteen years: this is totally outside the standard care. Also, he often treated his patients

for physical ailments—for colds and other things. He gave them antibiotics *and* anti-depressants. But where is it in his records? It *isn't* in
the records, because he's a schlock doctor. He's incompetent. Good
doctors keep records."

Shari was looking forward to trying the case; she felt that the rep-
etitions and the numbers of patients who planned to take the stand
would play a big part in winning. She said a good thing about pros-
ecuting for a state agency was that she could play with numbers. For
a criminal court case of rape, for instance, she would have been able
to present only one victim per case. But here, she not only had numbers
of victims willing to testify; she also had ample evidence of medical
negligence and incompetence. "Giving it by himself at seven-thirty in
the morning?" she said, outraged. "What happens if the patient goes
into cardiac arrest?"

When I worried aloud to Shari that the judges would think Masserman was too accomplished and distinguished to have done such
things, her response reminded me of Dick Shelton's. "Look, we have
people in high positions who are sick," she said. "And when professionals assault people physically and sexually, it is rape—even if it
doesn't fit the criminal definition."

"But I'm afraid they'll be sympathetic to him and think we're cruel
for going after him when he's so old," I said.

"Why shouldn't somebody at the age of eighty lose his license?" Shari
said hotly. "Is the argument that once you pass a certain age you're
vindicated for your sins? You don't have to pay the penalty for being
bad? Once you pass sixty-five, can you take a pass to kill or rape, and
since you're over sixty-five you're no longer responsible?"

I looked forward to watching Shari Dam in court. She said it was
going to be a very complicated, messy, and expensive trial, but she
was confident we would win it. Perhaps Jules Masserman thought so,
too, because the case never got to a hearing.

Rather than choosing to respond to the allegations or face a trial,
Jules Masserman and his new lawyer, Ronald Stackler, of Stackler &
Augustine, decided to settle out of court—and out of the public eye.
So it was on that October 7, 1987, close to one year after his out-of-
court settlements with me, Daniella, and Annie, Jules H. Masserman,
now eighty-two years old, signed a consent order, agreeing to surrender
his medical license, his controlled-substance license, and his right to
practice medicine and *any form* of patient psychotherapy, psychoa-

nalysis, or counseling. This last limitation—on his right to practice *any form* of therapy—was an important part of the agreement, because in Illinois, as in most states, it's possible to practice counseling (and to call it "psychotherapy, psychoanalysis, or counseling") without credentials and without a license.

Under the agreement, Masserman could not renew his medical license at any time in the future, nor could he ever renew his controlled-substance license. He relinquished his right to practice medicine or any form of therapy or counseling in all other states in which he was licensed and agreed never to apply for licensure in any jurisdiction in which he was not already licensed. He also was required to return all his wall certificates and wallet cards that indicated he was licensed by the Department of Registration and Education to practice medicine in any form. I imagined with some pleasure Dr. Masserman heaving indignant sighs as he removed the plaques from his walls. I liked the idea of the bare spaces they would leave.

This consent order wasn't a total victory, however. Masserman's lawyer drove a hard bargain. The consent agreement asserted that the respondent, who had been licensed to practice medicine since 1937, "denies all allegations in the four lawsuits," which were settled by his insurers "without his consent." It stated that Jules Masserman knew he had the right to a hearing, the right to contest charges, and the right to administrative review, but that he "voluntarily waived [those rights] because of the potentially exorbitant personal and financial costs," which were "prohibitive," given "his age, his own and his wife's health and their financial condition." I knew that this statement was just his way of affirming his position, but it still didn't seem right.

Some of my disappointment about the wording of that consent order was soothed when I opened the *Chicago Tribune* to the business section on November 10, 1987, and once again was startled by an "On the Law" column. Under the headline "Renown No Shield as Career Shatters," Warren, Possley & Tybor wrote:

> The 60-year career of Chicago Psychiatrist Jules Masserman, renowned worldwide in his field, has ended in ignominy. The fall is no less precipitous than the stock market plunge.
>
> Masserman, 82, voluntarily has given up his license to practice. The action follows allegations, first revealed here, that he forced female patients to disrobe as part of their therapy, then made sexual advances while they were under the influence of sodium amytal, a relaxant that can knock one out temporarily.

A consent order prepared by Shari Dam, attorney for the Illinois Dept. of Registration and Education, has been signed by Masserman and his lawyer, Ronald Stackler.

Masserman has agreed, without admitting that he engaged in any improper activities, to retire from the practice of psychiatry and any form of patient psychotherapy, psychoanalysis or counseling.

The article recounted the settlements and some of Masserman's honors and then floored me by revealing:

Masserman's legal woes are far from over. Two more lawsuits have been filed against him by former female patients. The suits, filed in Circuit Court by attorneys Kenneth Cunniff and William Carroll, each seek damages of $1.25 million.

One woman was a patient from 1979 to 1980 and, according to the lawsuit, disrobed during a therapy session and was administered sodium amytal. The woman "awakened during part of the drug treatment to find the defendant [Masserman] fondling her breasts," the suit states.

The other lawsuit was filed on behalf of a woman who was a patient of Masserman's from 1976 to 1986. It, too, alleges that the woman disrobed, was injected with the drug and later fondled. The suit says she was induced to meet Masserman on his boat and airplane for some of these sessions.

There is little doubt that more lawsuits could have been filed if not for a natural reluctance of patients to subject themselves to potentially embarrassing court proceedings.

"Ten other women came forward after they read your article about Masserman," Cunniff says. "But they didn't want to go through with a court proceeding, because it would be too traumatic."

Masserman was a professor emeritus of neurology and psychology at Northwestern University and is the author of more than a dozen books and more than 400 articles.

Despite his having signed that "final consent order," Masserman was still enjoying his stature as professor emeritus at Northwestern. And he seemed to be remaining immune from any censure by his colleagues. Outside of this news item and the earlier "On the Law" column in the *Tribune,* no other media mentioned the subject of Jules Masserman's transgressions. There was no television report, nor was there anything in the *Chicago Sun-Times* or in any other newspaper or magazine. Was any behind-the-scenes power at work to keep it quiet, or did people simply prefer to stay in the dark?

18 Uncovering My Own Mystery

The power at work to keep childhood secrets hidden from my consciousness was a mighty one. Nevertheless, I'd started a process destined to pull ghosts from the shadows of my mind and cast light on unspeakable subjects.

In the months that followed Masserman's signing of the consent order, Ann Jernberg had helped me realize that I might not be on as good terms with my mother as I pretended. My focus on Mother's Southern graciousness, the way she was always concerned for me and made sacrifices for me, didn't impress Ann. She suggested that perhaps the memory I'd built was mostly fantasy, constructed so I could believe I had a deeply loving, generous mother. When I asked Ann why she thought I had built a fraudulent image of my mother, she said, "It's from the way you interact with me. You come in the door with this look in your eyes, this question: 'Am I welcome here?'—as if you weren't welcome with your mother."

Ann asked me to step into my mother's shoes and write a short autobiography in her voice, not mine. I was surprised at how easy it was for me to express my mother's feelings, but as I did it, I realized that not only was she a real person, with understandable problems, but I was very, very angry at her—almost enraged.

Ann wasn't surprised. "That's good," she said. "You were denied your right to be a child who was sometimes angry, sometimes mean, sometimes jealous or demanding, hateful or annoying. You never had the chance to express yourself and grow through those perfectly normal feelings. You had to press down what was natural in you, so that you could be good and polite and do what you were told, to keep things in balance."

I researched my dad through old pictures, letters, newspaper articles, and concert programs, and then I interviewed two aunts and an uncle about him. They were hazy about his childhood, and his adult life had been spent far away from them. I was also hazy about him. And something particularly odd started happening to me when I explored his life. I noticed that when I studied a faded photograph of him, I went into a kind of amnesia. If the picture of him was taken when I was eight, I couldn't remember being eight. Or seven. Or five. I kept "forgetting" to call my aunt in Oregon with questions about him. Eventually, Ann and I pieced together some of the mystery of my childhood daddy who seemed so disappointed in me. It became clear I could never please him, and after I had physically matured so early, he had distanced himself from me. Over time, he started turning in my mind from "Daddy who hates me" into a troubled person who drank too much, shied away from feelings, and had dark secrets I didn't understand.

Then Bear—my little teddy bear from South Dakota—started to help me figure out some more things. I'd gotten into the habit of keeping Bear close by my side when I was home alone. Sometimes, when I was unhappy or confused, I'd hold her and feel great comfort. If it was cold and I took her out in the car with me, I'd wrap her up so she would stay warm. It may sound strange for a grown woman to have this kind of "friendship" with a stuffed animal, but Bear became a real friend to the frightened little girl inside me.

And in December 1988, it was Bear whom I kept close beside me when I found that I was videotaping every movie and television talk show that focused on incest. As I replayed them, I'd clutch that little teddy to my chest and cry uncontrollably. Sometimes during a moment in a movie when a child was being hurt, I would hug Bear and hear myself crying, "Why doesn't somebody do something? Look what he's doing to that little girl! Please, somebody do something!"

I didn't understand why these movies were so riveting and upsetting to me. When I told Ann about it, she suggested I keep a pad and pencil on my night table so I could write down my dreams when I woke up and use them to help me understand what was going on. I put the pad and pencil by my bed, but I couldn't seem to recall anything when I woke up. One night before going to sleep, I asked Bear to let me dream, and sure enough, Bear helped me remember a couple of strange nightmares. But I still didn't remember much, so I began putting my glasses on Bear at night. I asked her to look hard and help me see what I needed to see. I had a few more dreams, but they didn't break through the enormous wall I had erected around this subject. I took my glasses off Bear and, over the next six months, protected myself by gaining weight. It took twenty-six pounds to make me feel safe.

Then one day, I marched into Ann Jernberg's office and told her I wanted to change my name. I didn't want the name Barbara Noël anymore. "Noël is Richard's name, not mine. And Barbara's what they gave me."

"They?" she said. "Your parents, you mean?"

"Yes, I don't want it anymore. Most especially I don't want Barbara. My mother named me Barbara after her mother-in-law, a woman she couldn't stand, and she didn't even like the name. Every time she said my name, she must have hated it. I don't want to be Barbara; I want to be who *I* am."

Ann looked at me with great interest and said, "You've reached a turning point, you know."

"I have?"

"Oh, yes. When someone wants to throw off her birth name, it's often suggestive of abuse within her family—and she wants to throw that off, along with her name."

"Then why don't I just come out with it?" I started to cry. "Why do I keep playing this game?"

Ann could see that I was still too afraid to face what I was hiding. She told me it was a scary process but encouraged me for having started it. She also suggested I try talking more to Bear. So for several evenings I sat on my bed, propped against pillows, with Bear in my lap. Bear looked at me earnestly with her little black eyes, but she wouldn't talk. One night, though, I realized exactly what was happening.

"I know why you won't talk, Bear," I said, clutching her to me. "You're afraid of something. You're afraid that if you tell, I'll hate you. You're scared that I'll never forgive you for letting it happen."

When I reported my insight to Ann, she said, "You know it's not Bear who's scared of being hated."

"What?"

"It's you. You can't forgive yourself for what happened. But it was never your fault. You were so little and helpless; there was no way you could keep it from happening."

"*What?*" I said, starting to cry again. "Keep what from happening? Is this the way I'm going to spend the rest of my life? Batting conversations that I don't even understand back and forth with a stuffed Bear?"

"No, that's not the way it's going to be," Ann assured me. "I know it doesn't feel like it, but we really are getting somewhere."

A few months later, in the fall of 1989, Ann suggested that I think about having a consultation with a clinical social worker named Beverly James, who specialized in the evaluation and treatment of traumatized children. Ann said she felt that I had all the clinical symptoms of someone who had been deeply traumatized as a child and if I were willing, Ms. James might be able to help us get to the issues that were so difficult for me to face. Ms. James, director of the James Institute in Hawaii, was going to be in Chicago to speak at a convention and would probably be willing to work with me if I wanted to do that.

I agreed to meet Beverly James at noon on Sunday, October 15, 1989, but I wanted Ann to be present. Sometimes Ms. James used hypnosis, Ann said, so we decided that it would help me feel safer to have a videotape of the session, and that way I also could see it and listen to it afterward.

The day of my scheduled meeting with Beverly James, I had a heart-to-heart with Bear before we left for Ann's office. "I'm going to do my best to accept everything you tell me," I said to Bear. "And I won't hate you, no matter what you say."

I was so frightened by the time I got to Ann's office that I could barely speak above a whisper, but Beverly James, a warm, outgoing woman, spent the first hour talking to me and letting me get to know her. She told me that she'd worked with other women who'd been sexually assaulted by their psychiatrists. "The hardest part is that it's the ultimate betrayal," she said. "Here's somebody you open up your heart and soul to, and they take advantage of you. You can be an intact, functioning person, and when a trauma happens, you feel as if you are crazy. Particularly if you have a traumatic shadow experience behind it, something that happened earlier in your life."

Later, when she began gently questioning me about daydreams and fantasies I had as a little girl, I surprised myself by remembering how I had spent nearly every waking hour in a daydream—and associated different parts of myself with different daydreams. I had imagined one part of me as "Little Singer," full of joy and the ability to fly. I'd also had a sense of myself as "Little Tough Guy"—me at the age of four, when I was full of energy and quite sure of myself. Then there was "Lost Girl," who was frightened, confused, and all alone.

Beverly said she would like to hypnotize me and take me back to that very early time so we could understand why I had needed to dissociate and create these little alter egos. I agreed, and Beverly explained that hypnosis was nothing like it seemed to be on television. "Hypnosis is not sleep," she said. "It's only a process of relaxation that allows you to get deep inside yourself. It sharpens your awareness to the point that you actually smell the honeysuckle or taste the fried chicken if that's what you're remembering or thinking about."

Beverly started the process of hypnosis by having me sense how heavy my eyes had become and how relaxed my neck and shoulders and back and chest were. My arms would be like lead, she said, but my hands could always signal to her. My right hand, representing my conscious mind, could indicate "Yes" by wiggling my thumb, or "No" by my forefinger. My left thumb and forefinger could signal "Yes" and "No" for my unconscious mind. If at any time I should want to stop, I could press the palm of either hand forward. I also could use my voice if I chose to do so.

Once I was deep in trance, Beverly asked me, "Did someone hurt you?"

Tears trickled from my closed eyes and I nodded yes.

Then Beverly asked me if any of the parts of myself from childhood could tell her what happened to me or how I had been hurt. More tears. My left forefinger signaled, "Yes." Then Little Tough Guy came forward and said, "It was Little Singer got hurt."

"Now, Little Singer," Beverly asked softly, "will you come forth and tell us where you are?"

"In my room at the old place on College Avenue," I said. "I'm in my old wooden bed."

"How old are you?"

"Five."

"Is it dark?" Beverly asked Little Singer.

"Yes."

"Is someone there with you?"

"Yes."

"Who is it?"

"Ask Lost Girl."

Beverly asked Lost Girl who was there, and Lost Girl moved her head back and forth as if searching for the answer. Then she spoke one word: "Mother."

"Where is Mother, Lost Girl?"

"She's leaning over my bed."

"What is she doing?"

Lost Girl moved her head back and forth again, as if she didn't want to see. "She's putting her nipple into my mouth."

"What is she saying?"

"Bahhrr . . . braaah. Bahhrr . . . braaah."

"What is she doing now, Lost Girl?"

"Putting her finger into my private place."

"How does it feel?"

"It feels good. But I'm scared."

"Now, Lost Girl, look around the dark room. Do you see anything else?"

"Yes . . . it's . . . I see the glow of a cigarette. I can smell the smoke."

"Can you smell anything else?"

"Whiskey."

"Who's there?"

"Daddy. He's watching."

"Then what?"

"He's coming over to the bed."

"What's he doing?"

"He's sitting on my chest. He's trying to put his penis in my mouth."

"And then what?"

"I won't open my mouth. He's pushing his penis against my face. Oh, no! There's wet all over me. It's running down my neck and into my hair." Lost Girl is crying.

"What is happening now?"

"Mother has put a towel across my chest. She's cleaning me with a towel. It feels scratchy."

"And then?"

"And then I'm all alone."

The session went on, and Lost Girl told Beverly James about other times and other incidents. After three years of Ann Jernberg's gentle questions and preparations, and after nearly five hours with Beverly James, the truth was tumbling out. I would never be the same.

Afterward, I spent weeks talking all of this out with Ann. I'm still talking to her about it—and I've realized that the incomprehensibility of this happening to me as a child made me feel I would shatter if I ever knew the truth. I'm still inclined to wish I'd made the whole thing up. I'd still rather tell you about the parties and how glamorous my parents were. And discussing it still makes me very uncomfortable— almost as if I'm discussing someone else's life. But I understand now that some part of me felt that if I ever let it out, I'd die, that it would be the end of me. Some part of that feeling came from being so angry that it had happened at all: a little girl needs to be taken care of, not abused by her own parents. Her parents are supposed to respect her boundaries, not violate them. It was too horrible to believe, but the feisty child inside me—my own Little Tough Guy—came out kicking . . . and knowing the truth.

Ann Jernberg has explained to me that although it's unusual to be molested by both parents, and although mother-daughter incest is not as common as father-daughter incest, it does happen. She reassured me, though, that even though my parents didn't give me the care I needed, somewhere along the line I must have had some good nurturing. The evidence of that, she said, comes with the fact that I'm a strong woman, capable of facing the truth and bonding with and loving other people. She's said that most likely, my mother must have done a good job of nurturing me at some time when I was a baby and tiny girl—probably before I started being a real little individual at the age of five.

I also feel strongly that at some point, my mother came to realize the harm she and Dad were doing to me and tried consciously to turn it around, tried to change herself and make amends. When I was sixteen, she quit being a college voice teacher and singer and went back to school, studied child psychology, and got a degree in education. I think she did that in an attempt to make up for what she had done to me when I was young. She taught third, fourth, and fifth graders, and the school where she worked considered her an especially gifted and caring teacher.

Sometimes now I think it's strange that my mother became crippled with arthritis at such an early age and that she died when she was only fifty-nine years old. I wonder: Was it too hard for her to live with the anguish of memories she couldn't escape and yet couldn't endure facing? I realize I'll never know for sure. Nor will I ever know whether my father felt regretful or distraught about what he did. I hope I'll come to understand why he was so cold and disapproving of me. I do think, however, that Dad was good at blocking it all out—behaving like someone with something to hide, with his overpoliteness in public and his smiles that lasted too long and his laughter that verged on hysteria.

I remember a conversation with my mother when I was about eleven and I asked her if there really was a Jesus.

"Yes, there probably was," she said, "but I think he was only an ordinary man. Also a very good man."

Then I asked her if she thought there was a hell.

"If there is," she said with a bitter, scornful expression, "it's right here on earth."

One result of my search is that I'm out of the private hell my parents constructed, which I maintained with my secrecy. I'm stronger and more comfortable inside myself now that the truth is out. But I'll probably be unraveling it for the rest of my life.

As it happened, I didn't need to change my name. I just needed to uncover the wrenching truth of my past that made me such a perfect target for victimization by Jules Masserman.

Later, when I learned that Daniella Biagi's uncle had sexually abused her when she was a little girl—a fact Masserman dismissed with, "That's nothing. That's a waste of time"—I realized: Masserman chose his victims carefully.

Those of us who had low self-esteem or "shadow experiences" that would help keep us quiet were perfect targets. Besides Daniella and me, how many others had been victimized as children before they were victimized by him? Did he elicit such information while we were under Amytal and then use it himself to keep us in bondage?

A research article I later read compared therapists who abused their patients to child molesters who are classified as "fixated pedophiles." Such individuals "may be well-adjusted in other avenues of life, and people who know them are often shocked and react with disbelief when accusations and allegations are made," wrote Dr. Susan Brayfield-Cave, chair of the New Mexico Board of Psychologist Examiners. "The sexual and aggressive aspects of their behavior are quite isolated and encapsulated from the rest of their lives." These people "have an uncanny ability to seek out passive people who have had prior sexual traumas and focus their attentions on them. The prior history only magnifies the negative impact of the inappropriate sexual behavior" upon the patient.

As with the pedophile, the therapist's predatory behavior "may resemble a sexual addiction, a compulsive preoccupying behavior that is done without regard to the consequences."

Describing Jules Masserman as a sexual predator and fixated pedophile seems approriate given the therapeutic relationship. In an ideal therapeutic context, all of us patients would have been exploring the emotions of our infancies and childhoods with a healthy "father figure" to whom we could transfer our early feelings and fears and work through them—eventually arriving at a place where we could be clear emotionally about how we got to be who we are in our present lives.

But none of us had that chance with Masserman. The balance of power was established when we walked through the door; and that inequality of power was never used for our good. We were only prey for him—and he could exploit us by drawing out the little girl inside who was frightened and alone and used to keeping secrets.

19 Above the Law

I'd won some battles, but I hadn't won the big one: Jules Masserman still hadn't been censured by his peers. Even though he'd been forced to give up his license, he could sit around dinner tables with his colleagues, sipping brandy and bandying stories of being victimized by crazy female patients who had untenable transference problems, "erotomania," or some other kind of "fatal attraction." He could swap anecdotes about patients who haunted their doctors, followed them down streets, phoned their wives. They could complain in unison about the rising costs of insurance owing to all these spurious lawsuits.

Masserman was still able to go to meetings of the APA, the Chicago, American, and International psychoanalytic associations, and other professional events, and hold his head high, maintaining, if asked, that these delusional female patients—only a handful, of course—were all jumping on the bandwagon. He could browse through the collection of books he'd donated to the medical library at Northwestern and continue to enjoy the prestige and privileges accorded him as professor emeritus there.

It didn't look as if his peers were about to censure him either. Three and a half years after I'd filed my initial ethics complaint, neither the Ethics Committee of the Chicago Psychoanalytic Society nor the Illinois Psychiatric Society had scheduled hearings on my charges. Two very courteous IPS members had met with me once and asked me many questions. They also asked me to specify which principles of medical ethics Jules Masserman had violated. That was easy:

1. The patient may place his/her trust in his/her psychiatrist knowing
the psychiatrist's ethics and professional responsibilities preclude him/
her gratifying his/her own needs by exploiting the patient.

The two doctors from the IPS Ethics Committeee told me after that
May 1989 meeting that they would make a decision about the hearing
and contact me within six months. A year later, I still hadn't heard
from them. I never had even one visit or call from the Chicago Psychoanalytic Society. After their initial response to my complaint in
January, 1987, they never contacted me again.

I didn't realize it at the time, but Jules Masserman was in even better
standing with his peers than I could have imagined. While I had been
undergoing drug treatment and trying to recover from his sexual abuse
and betrayal, Dr. Masserman had been working on a book about adolescent sexuality with his officemate, Victor M. Uribe, M.D., a man
Masserman has referred to as "my colleague, student, and disciple."
Dr. Masserman had also established the Masserman International Foundation, at his same old address, 8 South Michigan Avenue.

In fact, in 1989, Jules Masserman's name was still on the roster of
the American Psychoanalytic Association. He was listed in the 1989
Biographical Directory of the American Psychiatric Association as an
active fellow and member of the APA. The directory, designed to "facilitate patient referrals" and "serve as a reference source for the professional community," included him even though he surrendered his right
and his license to practice in the early fall of 1987.

In that same 1989 APA directory, Jules H. Masserman's professional
address was listed as 8 S. Michigan, and his business phone was given,
as well as his home address. His "Customary services" were listed as:
"Couples/Family Psychotherapies; Crisis Intervention; Forensic/Legal
Consultation; Individual Psychotherapies." Had he never stopped practicing?

Masserman and Uribe's book, *Adolescent Sexuality,* was published in
1989. In the foreword, Dr. Harold M. Visotsky, M.D., professor and
chairman of the Institute of Psychiatry at Northwestern University,
wrote: "With warmth and a precise knowledge of the primal roots of
human development and an erudite grasp of anthropology, anatomy,
physiology, and sociology, [the authors] have used their psychiatric

training and experience to produce this expert guide to adolescent conduct, and have woven current scientific theories and research developments into an eminently readable book." He mentioned "the literary capacities demonstrated in producing this lucid exposition."

In their extremely short, large-type, idiosyncratic, and superficial book, Drs. Masserman and Uribe inform teenagers and their parents of such matters of importance as these: "Distinctions between popular culture and frank pornography have become tenuous. . . . Mothers take pride in dressing their teenage daughters 'attractively,' i.e., with special accents on hips, legs, and breasts, while fathers find surrogate virility in their sons' sexual adventures."

An endnote reflecting Jules Masserman's distinct style gratuitously explains: "In a Latin-Iberian tradition the father may habitually spend his mid-day siesta with a mistress, and both father and son may receive sexual favors from household maids."

Dr. Masserman's style also marks a pronouncement on incest:

Contrary to many current concepts, transient and somatically non-injurious parent-child or intersibling sexual relations, even when verified, usually leave no serious adverse effects, and require only judicious avoidance of social and legal traumata. . . .

The Old Testament records several instances of incest long after Adam and Eve: both of Lot's daughters plied him with wine until they could seduce him "to bear his seed." Saul acquired a harem with little regard for consanguinity; Ammon, son of David, raped his sister Tamar while cold sober.

This book is supposed to help adolescents? (Translate adolescents to males, since all the remarks in it seem addressed to boys.) The authors write that they hoped to provide "a more rational, secure and humane world for our youth and their offspring," but look at the security Masserman offered specific children at a time when he worked as a consultant to juvenile court and family court judges.

In one custody dispute, where the father was an alcoholic, a wife beater, and violent with the children, Masserman found the father "lacks general information, imagery, abstract and symbolic thought, and speed and flexibility of judgment." The mother, on the other hand "has an alert intelligence, a friendly, interested, cooperative, and somewhat flirtatious manner and a partially defiant frankness about her attitudes and actions."

So who gets the children?

Masserman, the expert, recommends the father.

Why? Because: "Mrs. N. will not soon have the financial means or the environmental setting for raising them with proper example and discipline unless she marries a man capable of being an especially devoted and competent stepfather."

Why? He reports: "She intends to support herself and continue her extramarital adventures although she has no present intention to marry."

Feeling the ethics committees' decisions were long overdue, I wrote on May 19, 1990, to Dr. Donald G. Langsley, the chairman of the IPS Ethics Committee, and enclosed an article from the *Boston Globe* about a prominent psychiatrist who had been suspended from the staff of McLean Hospital and expelled from the Boston Psychoanalytic Society and Institute after an investigation by the society into charges that he had sexually abused two of his female patients. I reminded Dr. Langsley that three lawsuits reporting sexual abuse already had been *settled* against Masserman; two more lawsuits were pending, and ten more women had come forward against him, causing him to relinquish his medical and psychiatric licenses. I noted that it had been three and a half years since I'd filed my initial complaint. I asked what further evidence they could possibly need.

Dr. Langsley, who happened to be another former president of the APA, was quick in his response. On June 8, he wrote to tell me a formal hearing had been scheduled for Monday, July 16, at 7:00 P.M. at the offices of the Illinois Psychiatric Society. He expected that Dr. Masserman would be called to testify, and said I was "entitled to be represented by legal counsel or another individual of your choice." He informed me of the procedure:

> The allegations against Dr. Masserman will be reviewed, witnesses and documents will be identified and the status of these proceedings will be addressed. The hearing will be recorded. Dr. Masserman will then testify and you may cross-examine him and the panel may also ask him questions. You will also have the opportunity to cross-examine other witnesses who are called to testify.
>
> You will then be permitted to make an opening statement if you wish and then to give testimony. You will be asked questions by Dr. Masserman if he wishes (or by his counsel if he chooses to have one) and by the panel members. You may offer testimony by other witnesses with similar

procedures being followed. You will be permitted to make a closing statement at the end of the hearing.

I was going to have my day in court after all! But I had only one week to find a lawyer. I called Ken Cunniff and Bill Carroll, but they were both tied up with other cases. Ken was conducting a trial, and Bill couldn't take time off from his case on such short notice. Then I called Shari Dam and discovered she was now in private practice in her own firm, Kline, Dam & Associates, and concentrating on health care law, administrative actions, and corporate and injury litigation. "I couldn't take any more of the trauma," she explained. "People just don't realize what awful emotional scars exist years after these incidents. I couldn't take any more of the doctors with their slick stories, willing to say anything to save their reputations. The defense lawyers' tactics can make a woman who testifies look immoral to the point that she's the one on trial, not the doctor. And you know, don't you, that we lost more cases than we won?"

Shari thought it might not be appropriate for her to represent me, so I wrote Dr. Langsley and asked if we could postpone the hearing since I hadn't been able to locate a lawyer on such short notice. To his credit, Dr. Langsley called me right away and said, "Please find someone. It's all set up, and it will be extremely difficult to get it all together again if it has to be postponed." He told me I could bring along a friend, as well as a lawyer.

Finally, in the eleventh hour, just when I figured I would have to go alone, Shari Dam agreed to review my testimony and accompany me to the hearing. Since she'd been at the Department of Registration and Education, she said, she was concerned about any conflict and thus wasn't in a position to say much, but she would be there to give me moral support. "It's going to be ugly," she warned. "You're going to be on trial. I know Masserman's lawyer quite well, and he's tough!"

Laura Davis had also agreed to testify, but we were the only two. None of the other women were willing to go over their traumas in public, nor were they willing to be identified or cross-examined. Ann Jernberg's friend and colleague Terrence Koller, Ph.D., president of the Illinois Psychological Association, agreed to come to the hearing as my friend.

Late on the afternoon of July 16, 1990, Shari Dam met me at a coffee shop to go over my statement. I'd worked hard on it, and she helped edit it. Shortly before seven, we walked over to the Illinois Psychiatric Society's offices, at 20 North Michigan Avenue, and tried the front door. Much to our surprise, it was locked. We knew we were supposed to go to Suite 700, but how could we get in? We finally found a bell to press, and as we stood there waiting, an attractive, elegant-looking woman wearing a simple blue-and-white cotton dress and sandals walked up and joined us.

Impulsively, I said, "Would you be Laura?"

"Barbara?" she said, with a smile of relief. Although we'd talked only two or three times on the telephone, Laura Davis and I hugged each other as if we were long-lost sisters. She was lovely, and had mustered the courage to come by herself without a lawyer or a friend. A few minutes later, when a maintenance man finally let us in and we were in the elevator, I realized I was thinking: How could such an attractive, capable, smart woman as Laura be bamboozled by that little twerp?"

By the time we got to the seventh floor, Shari and Laura and I were chatting somewhat seriously. Laura told us she used to have an office in this building, so she knew it quite well. We walked past an atrium reception area, where big bouquets of fresh flowers complemented elegant dark wood-paneled walls and plush carpets. Some kind of social gathering or cocktail party was going on in the atrium. It was crowded with people standing, eating, and drinking. We noticed a number of psychiatrists smiling, shaking hands, and greeting each other as they gathered around Jules Masserman and his wife, Christine McGuire Masserman, a handsome woman in her seventies. Both the Massermans appeared central to the social activity and were engaged in animated conversations. Laura wondered out loud whether they were simply surrounded by these admirers or whether this reception actually was being held following a dinner in Dr. Masserman's honor.

Dr. Langsley intercepted our little trio and ushered us into a small private room, where Terry Koller soon joined us. We four had to wait there for about forty-five minutes until I was asked to come out to give my testimony. The rules required that Laura not hear my testimony so she had to wait alone in the room for her turn.

The IPS conference room was simple and elegant, and I sat down at a large round table between Terry Koller, on my left, and Shari Dam on my right. Dr. Brenda Solomon, chair of the hearing, who sat directly opposite from me, introduced herself and six other psychiatrists, including Dr. Langsley, who were also on the other side of the table.

Shari sat next to Barbara Stackler, an attorney formerly with the State Attorney General's office, who was serving as Masserman's lawyer for the hearing. To Barbara Stackler's right was a court reporter, then Mrs. Masserman and Dr. Masserman. Ronald Stackler, Barbara's husband and Masserman's other attorney, sat away from the table with Bob Graham, the IPS attorney.

I was nervous but cool as I faced Dr. Masserman, in his pale-gray, tweedy suit, and Mrs. Masserman, a woman with strong Gaelic features, wearing a pretty green dress. As I began to speak, the two of them smiled broadly at each other, and as I progressed, they reacted as if what I was saying was so ludicrous as to be laughable. My statement was succinct. I told where I was born and educated; I said I was a Protestant, worked as a singer, and had begun treatment with Jules Masserman in 1966 for two reasons: marital problems and fear of performing. I told about my Amytal treatments, the unexplained bruises, and the waking up, as well as Dr. Masserman's gifts, his taking me out on his boat, inviting me to go flying with him, and sightseeing in Paris. When I mentioned that for eighteen years he'd consistently mispronounced my name, the Massermans shook their heads and looked as if they were going to burst into uproarious laughter.

Their mocking performances bothered me, but I was so determined to maintain my control that I blocked them out. I stayed on track for at least five more minutes, and concluded: "Using the drug vernacular, Dr. Masserman became my pusher, and I stayed in therapy so I could keep getting my drugs."

Barbara Stackler, with spiked red hair and sharp features, fired questions at me for more than half an hour. She started by asking me if I was taking any drugs that might impair my ability to answer questions. I said no; I never used drugs anymore. Then she asked if I was currently using alcohol. Again I said no.

"How long since you last used alcohol?"

"Three and a half years." (The last time I'd had a drink was that martini I'd had to "celebrate" the article about Masserman in the *Chicago Tribune*; it was my last ever.)

"Have you undergone treatment for alcohol abuse?"

"Yes, I have."

After that, Barbara Stackler mainly focused on trying to pick apart my account of September 21, 1984. I found her so threatening that I concentrated my attention almost entirely on her. Later Shari told me that during the rest of the cross-examination, Masserman's eyes were closed and he was tapping his fingers.

Barbara Stackler asked me to describe what I meant by saying that I had been "familiarly high" on the Amytal.

I told her, "Marijuana is not anything like it. I have tried cocaine and have no memory of cocaine having that effect. Amytal gives you a sensation that is kind of like pure heaven."

Getting to the events of my waking up on September 21, 1984, Barbara Stackler asked if I was aware that both the police report and the medical report from the hospital stated that there was no evidence of rape. I said yes, I was aware of that. Then she said, "Without asking you to speculate, I wonder what a normal reaction would be to awakening from a drug-induced sleep and finding somebody on top of you. Would you describe your reaction?"

One of the psychiatrists, Dr. Stephanie Cavanaugh, interrupted with, "I'm sorry; I don't understand your question."

"I'm asking Ms. Noël to describe her reaction when she awoke and found someone on top of her."

I answered, "I was terrified and almost immediately aware of the need to be very quiet . . . and not let the person know I was awake."

"Why was that, Ms. Noël?"

"Because when someone is raping you, you are afraid that someone might hurt you."

"Ms. Noël, did you have any physical reaction to this terror that you've just described?"

"I had an incredible calm. . . . I opened my eyes and found that I was in the examining room."

"Why were you afraid to move, Ms. Noël?"

"I find that a rather unusual quesiton."

"I don't think so, Ms. Noël, considering what I would construe to be a normal response to waking up to a rape."

"I can't tell you what a normal response is. I can tell you what my response is."

Mrs. Masserman scribbled notes on a piece of paper and passed it to Ronald Stackler. Then Barbara Stackler asked me whether I had told the police that my rapist did not ejaculate.

"I said I could feel no ejaculation."

"Are you sure about that?"

"No, no, I'm not. I'm truly not." I was very embarrassed, but after a long pause, I admitted, "I've never felt anyone ejaculate, ma'am."

"Well, there's a difference, Ms. Noël, between stating that you don't feel it and stating that it didn't happen," she said. "Could it be, Ms. Noël, that you *knew* that the Northwestern Emergency personnel and the police were going to find no evidence of rape?"

"No, that is not right."

"Why not?"

"Because I know what I know. I know what happened."

When I said that, I heard a couple of sighs from the psychiatrists on the panel. I felt they were listening to what I was saying—and that they were far better able to understand my answers than any lawyer would be. I wondered whether the legal nature of this inquisition also made them somewhat uncomfortable.

Barbara Stackler said, "Ms. Noël, you stated today that you believe that you were sexually assaulted by Jules Masserman on several prior occasions."

"Yes."

"Yet in your deposition you stated that Dr. Masserman always treated you with the utmost respect."

"That was before I came to receive good therapy."

"And in May of 1989 or thereabouts, you suddenly decided there had been prior sexual contacts with Dr. Masserman."

"I think I testified to that earlier."

"No, I don't think you did, Ms. Noël. . . . Ms. Noël, when did you have this *divine revelation* that there had been prior sexual contact between you and Dr. Masserman other than September 21, 1984?"

"Well, it was when I recalled quite a few bruises and contusions. I [remembered] pelvic bruises. I had also discovered bruises on my arms quite often . . ."

Some of the psychiatrists asked me questions about the trip to Paris, the invitations to go on Dr. Masserman's boat, and my prior sexual abuse, which I told them I'd only recently uncovered. Then one of the doctors asked if there was any doubt in my mind that this experience might have been a dream.

"It was not a dream," I answered.

"You're a hundred percent sure?"

"Yes."

Dr. Brenda Solomon reminded Barbara Stackler that she had five more minutes. Stackler then asked me the burning question "Did you cheat on your first husband?" When Shari's objection was sustained, Stackler asked whether I'd had an adulterous affair when I was married to my first husband. (Yes.) She also asked if I'd disclosed my childhood sexual abuse to Dr. Masserman in eighteen years of treatment. I said, "No. I didn't know about it."

"Do you suppose you could have disclosed this abuse under the influence of Sodium Amytal?"

"If I did, I would certainly have thought we should have worked through it sometime during those eighteen years."

When my testimony was over, it was Laura Davis's turn. Shari Dam and Terry Koller were dismissed, but before they left, Shari whispered, "You did a great job. Your testimony was strong, and you had a lot of gumption handling yourself." I laughed, which felt good, and then I asked Dr. Solomon if I could stay as a friend to Laura Davis, since otherwise she would be all alone. Dr. Solomon agreed.

By this time, Laura came out, quite nervous and irritated from having had such a long wait. We were as different as ice and fire in our manner. When the court reporter asked Laura to raise her hand, she said, "Why?" Then, after she had sworn to tell the truth, she looked at the panel members and said rather abruptly, "Am I supposed to talk, or are you all going to interrupt me with questions?"

When Laura began her statement, she was looking at Masserman and his wife. Later, she said she couldn't tell if Masserman could hear what was going on or not. "He sat there like a stone, and never, never put his eyes on me," she said. "Mrs. Masserman, on the other hand, looked at me when I came in and looked at me during some of the time I was speaking, and her look just said, 'Who are you to be doing this? To be saying these things?' She looked at me with contempt, like I was unfairly accusing her husband, and how dare I be there? She didn't appear to be defensive; she didn't appear to be disturbed at all by what was going on. You'd think that a person in that position would show some emotion that indicated they had questions, but she just looked at me accusingly. She should have known I had nothing to gain by testifying at that hearing. It was upsetting and humiliating. How could she possibly think I'd be in there making up a story?"

Laura proceeded to tell the panel about her therapy with Dr. Masserman, the two times she'd had Amytal, and how she had awakened with Dr. Masserman fondling her breasts and repeating again and again,

"Oh, you have such beautiful breasts." She was so nervous she forgot to tell them he was on top of her while he was doing this. Afteward, the psychiatrists didn't ask her many questions, but Barbara Stackler badgered her with some thirty questions designed to discredit her story and malign her credibility.

At one point, Stackler said, "You filed a lawsuit against Dr. Masserman, didn't you?"

"Yes," Laura answered.

"And you lost that lawsuit, didn't you?"

"Yes."

Laura tried to explain that she lost the lawsuit only because of the statute of limitations.

I felt as if she needed some help, and she got some when, at another point, Masserman's attorney asked, "How sure are you that this happened? Are you one hundred percent sure?"

Laura answered, "I'm ninety-nine percent sure."

Barbara Stackler said sarcastically, "Ninety-nine percent is not one hundred percent, is it?"

The attorney for the Illinois Psychiatric Society spoke up and said, "Mrs. Stackler, we'll all concede that ninety-nine percent is not one hundred percent."

Then Laura said, "I've told you things that sound contradictory, I'm sure, but I'm ninety-nine percent sure because I was drugged. That's all there is to it."

Then Barbara Stackler lifted some pages of paper in the air and said these were notes Dr. Masserman said he had taken during sessions with Laura Davis. "Would it interest you to know, Ms. Davis," she said, "that on one occasion you broke into your ex-husband's apartment without his permission? And would you be surprised to know that you told Dr. Masserman about the loss of your job and how afraid you were you were going to be broke? And what I'd like to know, Ms. Davis, is how a mother could desert her small son with so little remorse? Now, Ms. Davis—"

"Just *one* minute!" Laura shouted, her voice furious and her shoulder-length dark hair flying as she turned to glare at Barbara Stackler. "You asked me some questions, and I assume you want some answers. Will you allow me some time to answer? You asked me three questions, and I will attempt to answer them one at a time! First of all, my ex-husband and I are on excellent terms! I have a key to his apartment, and I am free to go in anytime. Secondly, how could Dr. Masserman think I was worried about money or lost my job? I've been vice-president of this company for over ten years! And last, *I don't have a son!*"

The entire group looked stunned, and before even Barbara Stackler could recover her composure, Laura jumped up and yelled, "That's it! That's it! I've had it with this craziness. I'm sick of all of you!" She burst into tears and shouted, "I hope I never see any of you again!" Then she went tearing out of the room and down a long hallway. I ran out after her and hugged her as she cried and cried. When I went back into the room, people were out of their chairs, shuffling papers, talking, and there was an uneasy feeling in the air.

Dr. Langsley said, "If you don't mind, Ms. Noël, could you gather up your things now, because we've got to move along with Dr. Masserman's testimony."

Although Jules Masserman had been able to hear us and have us cross-examined, we weren't allowed the same privileges. In all the excitement, I totally forgot about the procedures Dr. Langsley had first described: Masserman would testify first, and then we would cross-examine him. Much later, I would wonder what had happened to that? Why hadn't we followed the prescribed procedure? Eventually I learned I had been erroneously informed about my right to cross examine Dr. Masserman—and that we did, in fact, follow the regularly "prescribed procedure." Dr. Langsley explained that complainants are permitted to make a statement, but they never cross-examine the accused APA member. They may, however, sit in the room for the entire hearing and listen while the ethics panel asks the accused member questions. So, I could have stayed and listened to the panel's questions and Dr. Masserman's answers. But either that wasn't made at all clear to me or I misunderstood when I was asked to gather up my things. Staying for Dr. Masserman's statement and questioning would have been quite interesting, I'm sure. At the time, however, it didn't matter all that much to me. I was only swamped with relief.

When I got home, I threw myself onto my couch and laughed and laughed. I'd finally had my day in court. It was a trial. And I emerged from it stronger and cleaner than ever before. I felt good about the way I had answered questions. Things I never could have said before, I'd said out loud, such as, "The lack of evidence must mean he used a condom."

Being able to say those things was freeing. Most amazing to me was that I felt no shame. When I told Shari Dam how thrilled I was and how being assertive and facing down Masserman had been really cathartic for me, she said, "It was pretty cathartic for me too, finally getting to see the seedy old worm!"

I knew that it would be quite a while before I heard from the Ethics Committee. But I liked looking back on the way I had finished my testimony. For her closing, Barbara Stackler had looked at me with a narrowed gaze and said, "Ms. Noël, may I ask this question once more: As to your description of the events of September 21, 1984 . . . Do you consider your actions [not moving or screaming when you awoke] a normal response to being raped?"

"A normal response?" I said. "What would be a normal response to rape? Well, I can't tell you that. I truly don't know if my reactions were *normal,* but I think my reactions were *healthy.* I made a decision to take care of myself and keep myself safe."

Barbara Stackler looked at me scornfully, as if I'd given her a non-answer. I don't think she had any clue as to what I meant. But I felt at that moment that the distinguished psychiatrists sitting around the table knew exactly what I was saying. I was saying I had taken care of other people all my life. That morning of September 21, 1984, when I woke up, I began taking care of myself. That morning, I began my healing.

20 A Final Verdict

On a crisp October day in 1991, I opened a certified letter from Donald G. Langsley, M.D., chairman of the Illinois Psychiatric Society's Ethics Committee, and read:

Dear Ms. Noël:
   This is to inform you that the American Psychiatric Association Appeals Board met recently and voted to suspend Dr. Jules Masserman from the APA and from the Illinois Psychiatric Society for five years for violation of *The Principles of Medical Ethics with Annotations Especially Applicable to Psychiatry*. This action will be reported to the Illinois Department of Professional Regulation.
   This case is closed inasmuch as Dr. Masserman cannot appeal this decision further.

This verdict came into my mailbox seven years and twenty-five days after I'd awakened to the truth of what Jules Masserman had been doing to me. I thought I would be elated at the news, and for a while I was. I whooped around my apartment, feeling delighted and vindicated. I called up Bill Carroll, Ken Cunniff, Shari Dam, Laura Davis, Daniella Biagi, Annie Morrison, and Terrence Koller to share the pleasure. Then I called Ann Jernberg and set up an appointment.

For a while, I didn't even stop to think why they had only suspended him. But as I walked down Michigan Avenue, I remembered the committee's choices under the APA's "Principles of Medical Ethics with

Annotations Especially Applicable to Psychiatry": If they decided a violation had occurred, they could choose: admonishment—an informal warning; reprimand—a formal censure; suspension (for a period not to exceed five years); or expulsion.

Now I wondered: Why didn't they expel him? Was it just too hard for them to oust their old leader, friend, professor, and mentor? Was it a matter of deference? Trust? Did they think only some of the charges were true? Or was truth really the issue? Whatever the answer was, I realized that their suspension was a verdict of guilt for unethical conduct and a bigger slap on the hand than is usual for many such cases. But, I wondered, doesn't the Ethics Committee realize that giving him only a suspension is an injustice—not just for me and other women, but for all the many good therapists who would never do anything like this?

Much later, I would learn that by suspending Dr. Masserman rather than expelling him, the American Psychiatric Association avoided any publicity that might have stemmed from public notification about their decision. Although the APA "Principles of Medical Ethics" as applied to psychiatrists states that the name of any member who is expelled *must* be reported in *Psychiatric News,* the APA's newspaper, to warn the public, the same is not true for someone who has been suspended. Under their regulations, "The name of any member who is suspended from the APA for ethics violation *may* be reported as deemed appropriate by the district branch of the APA."

In late January 1992, the librarian at the APA reference desk in Washington, D.C., told a caller: "Either they cleared him or there has been no decision on Dr. Masserman's case. We're aware of the situation, but there hasn't been any decision against him, or we would have been notified; we would have had to report it in *Psychiatric News.*" Apparently, the Illinois Psychiatric Society (the district branch) and the APA had deemed it was *not* appropriate to report this news to the public. Why?

Whatever their reasoning, within the organization, the decision to suspend a member of such stature had not been made lightly.

Dr. Langsley, the Ethics chair, explained the lengthy process involved in every ethics case. It starts when case managers investigate a complaint and report back to the Ethics Committee. If the committee decides that a hearing is in order, they appoint an impartial Hearing Panel.

After the haring, the panel determines whether or not their accused member has violated medical ethics, and if so, how to sanction him. Their decision then goes to the District Branch Council, and the Executive session either supports it or remands the case. If they support it, the report then goes to the APA's national Ethics Committee, which reviews the case to determine whether proper procedure has been followed and whether the sanction is appropriate. If they support the decision, they notify the accused member, who has thirty days in which to file an appeal. Then an appeals hearing is scheduled—which can take months. When the APA Ethics Appeals Board (consisting of some past presidents, the speaker of the assembly, and high officers) meets in Washington, D.C., the accused member is allowed to make a presentation with or without a lawyer. The district branch (the IPS in our case) is represented and can comment. Then the Ethics Appeals Board makes its decision. If it upholds the original decision, then it notifies the accused member and the complainants.

Our case went through all of those steps before Dr. Masserman was officially suspended. At any point, the case could have been remanded. But for all the hard work and disappointment that must have accompanied the decisions against him all the way to the top, that APA sanction almost appears not to have happened at all. Laura and I knew it happened because we were told, but no one outside the APA knew it. That's because the APA's decision received no publicity. Like the librarian, no one could have any way of knowing that the APA and the IPS had suspended Dr. Masserman for violating medical ethics. Their decision did not receive even one word of publicity. Aside from the two articles in Warren, Possley & Tybor's "On the Law" column, in January and November 1987, not one other word of publicity about Jules Masserman's unethical conduct had appeared in any newspaper or magazine or on any radio or television program.

By the time I got to Ann Jernberg's office and sat down in a comfortable chair, I was feeling sad and quite upset. I told her it seemed I ought to feel victorious, but I felt miserable. I wondered, was I feeling guilty about turning on this person I'd thought of so highly? Or was I mourning all I could have done and could have been if I'd never gone to Jules Homen Masserman for help in the first place? My life had been permanently altered by my so-called therapeutic relationship with him. And I'd spent thousands of dollars in therapy with Ann, trying to understand my relationship with him, before I'd been able to even begin the therapy that should have taken place twenty-four years earlier.

"Let's explore that," Ann said. "Let's imagine you'd gone to a different therapist, an ethical one, instead of Dr. Masserman. How would your life have been different?"

"Well, for one thing, I wouldn't have been a drug addict," I said. "Even if I *had* been inclined that way, I would have been in recovery within eight months—like I was with you."

Ann agreed on this point.

"Also, if I had gone to a good therapist, I could have come to terms years ago with the child abuse, dealt with it, put it in perspective, and gotten on with my life. Who knows what might have happened then?"

"There I think you're mistaken," Ann said. "Twenty-five years ago, you'd probably have found a good, classical Freudian analyst who would have explored why you had that *fantasy*. Therapists then were still grounded in Freud's revised view that such experiences were Oedipal, and you would have been led to believe this was your imagination, not reality. In those days, people weren't dealing with the issues of childhood sexual abuse the way they are now. The kind of work we're doing is much more recent."

Ann's analysis startled me. I realized I'd been imagining how perfect life would have been if only . . . Of course, I can never know what my life would have been without the detours caused by Jules Masserman. But I do believe that, like other victims of tragic experiences, going through this trauma has made me a stronger and more substantial person than I would have been if it had never happened. And now that I finally realize how the emotional and sexual abuse I experienced during my childhood made me susceptible to Dr. Masserman's deceptions, I understand that the early abuse also triggered my anger and courage to stand up for myself. It made me go after him with newfound loyalty and concern for myself and other women, hoping that the road we all travel will be somewhat easier because of this story.

It's now been almost two and a half years since I was finally able to remember my incestuous past. With Ann Jernberg's good help, I believe I've worked through that trauma successfully and can leave it behind me as I continue in therapy to deal with the empty feelings that still surface from time to time. Recently I've come to understand that my mother was deeply depressed when I was a little girl. Most of the time, she didn't even know I was there. I often played and daydreamed alone for hours on end. Every now and then, Mother would stop what she was doing and look over at me with a startled expression, as if thinking: Oh, yes. I have a little girl. Then she'd give me a wan smile and an absentminded bit of conversation before drifting back into her reverie.

Remembering that subtle emotional abuse hurts me more than any secret nights or eighteen years of put-downs by an eminent psychiatrist. The fact that my mother couldn't give me recognition meant that I grew up without any sense of entitlement. Without that sense of self, I had to fabricate the person inside—which is why I put energy into *looking* real and competent, without ever knowing I was entitled to *be myself*: a person with rights, boundaries, ideas and feelings of my own. That lack of empowerment made me run the risk of being exploited every day of my life.

Today, however, the deep healing has begun—and it continues. I still run my own business, give concerts, sing with bands, do voice-overs, write lyrics, and compose music. I go to concerts and films with my friends, meditate, read constantly, run, and work out at my gym. I love what I do, and I'm beginning to like who I really am. There's a calmness inside me now that stays with me for long periods of time. I feel stronger and more centered. I've lost a lot of time, I know, but I have a feeling that the years to come will be the best I've ever had, each one a bit better than the last. I would wish no less for all women and men who are making similar journeys.

NOTES AND SOURCES
by Kathryn Watterson

The following research notes are meant as an informal guide to help readers understand how this book was written. The origins of material in "reconstructed" stories often seem mysterious and I hope to shed light on that process by documenting what has been involved in the writing of this story. The notes also reflect published sources, interviews, and information that supplement and support Barbara Noël's candid recollections of her eighteen-year association with Dr. Jules H. Masserman, together with those of several of Dr. Masserman's other patients. In most cases, as indicated within the chapters themselves, I have reconstructed dialogues from Barbara Noël's recollections of them, as well as from depositions and from extensive interviews with her and with lawyers, doctors, ex-patients, and others directly involved, who have corroborated her story. We tried to reconstruct this story as carefully and as accurately as possible. The scenes in Jules Masserman's office have been recalled by Barbara Noël in her written remembrances and during our many hours of interviews. They were confirmed in large part by Dr. Masserman's own testimony about Barbara Noël and about his use of Amytal in depositions, as well as by Richard Noël, who saw Dr. Masserman in several joint sessions with Barbara Noël, and by several other of Dr. Masserman's former patients. Dr. Masserman's dialogue and perspective in all instances is drawn heavily from Barbara Noël and other ex-patients' recollections of his words and his way of speaking; from his recorded testimony in discovery and evidence depositions that are a matter of record in Cook County Circuit Court, Cook County, Illinois, and from his written works.

In addition to published sources, these notes reflect some of the information and wisdom gleaned from many people who helped me examine the medical and ethical implications of Jules Masserman's practice and develop a deeper understanding of psychoanalytic history in America. Representatives of the American Psychoanalytic Association and the New York Psychoanalytic Institute were particularly helpful in directing me to documentary sources, as were the staff librarians and Tom Dial at the American Psychiatric Association. Linda Chamberlin, Special Collections Assistant at the Psychology Library at Princeton University, was of invaluable assistance over many months. She helped me search out previous scientific publications of Jules Masserman's, particularly his early research on the hypothalamus as the center of emotion and sexual excitement and a number of his other experiments on cats, dogs, and monkeys, in which he used alcohol and Amytal, morphine and Metrazol—experiments that I believe may have had a direct connection with his later abuse of female patients. The librarians at the *Chicago Sun-Times* and the *Chicago Tribune* were also helpful in letting me go through their clippings on Dr. Masserman.

Others exceptionally helpful in discussing and explaining psycho-therapeutic dynamics, issues, and history were Marie Stoner, M.Ed.; Dr. Margaret Mandel; Susan Gross, M.Ed., Dr. Lydia Katzenbach, Dr. Fred Flach; Dr. Parker Seymour, and Dr. Don Nathanson. I learned a great deal about sex offenders in earlier interviews with Dr. Judith Becker, director of the Sexual Behavior Clinic at the New York State Psychiatric Institute; Dr. Gene Abel, director of the Behavioral Medical Institute in Atlanta, Georgia; Dr. A. Nicholas Groth, director of the Forensic Mental Health Association in Orlando, Florida; Lori Scott, who runs the sex offender treatment program for the Maricopa County Probation Department in Phoenix, Arizona; Lucy Berliner at the Harborview Sexual Assault Center in Seattle, Washington; and Fay Honey Knopp, director of prison research and A Safer Society Program for the New York State Council of Churches.

I also appreciate discussions about medical ethics, legalities, and background information with attorneys Shari Dam and Glen Crick in Chicago, and with Mia Oberlink at Mount Sinai Medical Center in New York and Leigh Beinen, a criminal-defense lawyer who has specialized in the treatment and disposition of sex offenders and currently is undergraduate dean at the Woodrow Wilson School at Princeton University; Dr. Manfred Halpern, who served on the board of the American Society for Social Psychiatry with Jules Masserman; Maggie Filipiack, a pharmacist who was most generous with her pharmaceutical evaluations; and Eric Greenfeld, at the Princeton Public Library. I also thank several notable psychopharmacologists and psychiatrists who conferred with me regularly but who preferred to remain anonymous because of possible professional repercussions from public comments about this case.

PROLOGUE, PAGES 13–18
Dr. Nanette Gartrell, Dr. Silvia Olarte, and Dr. Judith Herman, who conducted a 1986 study of psychiatrist-patient sexual contact, reported that 1,057 male psychiatrists and 366 female psychiatrists responded to their questionnaire—and that 7.1 percent of male and 3 percent of female respondents admitted to sexual contact with a patient during or after psychiatric treatment. Dr. Gartrell, previous chair of the American Psychiatric Association's Committee on Women, wrote that although documentation as to the extent of the problem is limited, "the best available data indicate that 6 to 10 percent of psychiatrists have had sexual contact with their patients and that the majority of psychiatrists have knowledge of such cases but do not intervene." (Gartrell et al., "Psychiatrist-Patient Sexual Contact: Results of a National Survey," *American Journal of Psychiatry* 143, no. 9 [1986].)

In a national survey, psychologists Dr. Valerie Vetter and Dr. Kenneth Pope found that of 1,320 clinical psychologists, half had treated patients who claimed to have had sexual relations with a previous therapist. (Pope and Vetter, "Prior Therapist-Patient Sexual Involvement Among Patients Seen by Psychologists," *Psychotherapy* 28, no. 3 [Fall 1991]: 429–38.) In a similar study of sexual exploitation by psychotherapists of all professional backgrounds, including psychiatrists, clincial psychologists, social workers, and marriage counselors, Dr. Kenneth Pope and Jacqueline Bouhoutsos found that 70 percent of therapists reported treating at least one patient who had a sexual relationship with a previous therapist—96 percent of whom were male. (Pope and Bouhoutsos, *Sexual Intimacy Between Therapists and Patients* [New York: Praeger, 1986].)

In April 1987, Dr. Nanette Gartrell and her colleagues reported that although nearly two thirds of the 1,423 psychiatrists who responded to their survey reported treating patients who had been sexually involved with previous therapists—involvements they considered harmful in 87 percent of the cases—they reported the sexual abuse in only 8 percent of those cases. This led Dr. Gartrell to conclude: "Although the numbers of malpractice claims and complaints before ethics committees and licensing boards have increased in recent years, it is generally agreed that only a very small fraction of these cases ever come to public attention." (Gartrell et al., "Reporting Practices of Psychiatrists Who Knew of Sexual Misconduct by Colleagues, *American Journal of Ortho-psychiatry* 57, no. 2 [April 1987].)

For further information on the incidence of patient-therapist sex, see the 1990 edition of *Sexual Intimacies Between Psychotherapists and Patients: An Annotated Bibliography of Mental Health, Legal and Public Media Literature and Relevant Legal Cases,* prepared by Hannah Lerman, Ph.D., for the Committee on Women of Division 29 (Psychotherapy) of the American Psychological Association.

Jules H. Masserman's professional accomplishments are listed in a wide variety of sources, including *Who's Who in America,* 1980–81; *Current Biography,* 1980; *American Journal of Psychiatry* 136, no. 8 (August 1979), and *American Men and Women of Science,* 1978.

Dr. Harold M. Visotsky made his remarks about Jules Masserman being "psychiatry's ambassador to the world" in response to Jules Masserman's presidential address to the American Psychiatric Association's annual meeting in August 1979. His comment about Chicago's reputation being enhanced by Dr. Masserman's presence was quoted in the *Chicago Daily News* on May 10, 1974.

Dr. John Carlton's remark was published in the *Chicago Tribune*'s "On the Law," column ("Shocking Detour on Road of Fame," by Warren, Possley & Tybor) on January 6, 1987.

The high incidence of young girls who have been sexually molested by adult males has been well documented by researchers for many years. Despite his well-known later writings about incestuous fantasies, early in his career Freud considered *actual* sexual molestation, seduction, and incest to be the source of "hysteria" among the young women he was treating. Subsequent studies have tended to confirm Freud's early observation that in fact these young women were molested; and later in his life, Freud himself acknowledged that the "uncles" who had molested two of his patients were in fact their fathers. Because they were respectable family men, however, "discretion" had made him suppress the information.

Over the past five decades, Alfred Kinsey, John Gagnon, Judson T. Landis, David Finkelhor, and others surveying thousands of women nationwide consistently have found that from 20 to 33 percent of all women reported having had sexual encounters with adult males during their childhood. Judith Lewis Herman, in *Father-Daughter Incest* (Cambridge and London: Harvard University Press, 1981), documents these and other studies and reports that the therapists she and her colleagues interviewed estimated that from 1 to 20 percent of their women patients had a history of incest. After reviewing the research, Herman estimates that *millions* of women have personally experienced incestuous abuse.

Leigh B. Beinen, in her ground-breaking analysis of legal and psychiatric trends in "A Question of Credibility: John Wigmore's Use of Scientific Authority in Section 924a of the Treatise on Evidence" (*California Western Law Review* 19, no. 2 [1983]), points to several studies that have established it is extremely rare for a child to falsify a sex report. Nevertheless, Beinen points out, the legal community, psychiatric profession, medical profession, and social service agencies have regularly ignored or denied children's reports of sexual abuse.

Relevant to how sex offenders pick their victims is Joseph J. Peters, M.D., "Children Who Are Victims of Sexual Assault and the Psychology of Offenders," *American Journal of Psychotherapy* XXX, no. 3 (July 1976). Also see Susan Brayfield-Cave, "Sexual Predators in the Profession," *The American Psychological Association Journal,* April 1990; and A. Nicholas Groth and H. Jean Birnbaum, *Men Who Rape: The Psychology of the Offender* (New York: Plenum Press, 1979).

CHAPTER ONE: UNDER THE INFLUENCE, PAGES 19–23
This incident has been recalled in full by Barbara Noël; she wrote down the details soon afterward, as is explained later. The incident also is a matter of public record: Area 1 Violent Crimes, Case No. F 358809, documenting the Criminal Sexual Assault that Barbara Noël reported on September 21, 1984; and *Barbara Noël, Plaintiff* v. *Jules H. Masserman, M.D., Defendant,* No. 84L 21302, Circuit Court of Cook County, Illinois, October 7, 1984. Dr. Masserman denies this incident ever occurred and points out that the police found no physical evidence of rape.

CHAPTER TWO: BACK TO THE BEGINNING, PAGES 24–34
Jules Masserman's speech emphasizing the "magic" in a physician's words and deeds was given at the North Shore Hospital in Winnetka, Illinois, and reported in the *Chicago Daily News,* March 3, 1960.

The professional profile of Jules Masserman was taken from Volume 32 of *Who's Who in America,* 1962–63, which Barbara Noël looked up before her first visit to Dr. Masserman in 1966.

In his presidential address to the American Psychiatric Association, Jules Masserman paid tribute to Horsley Gantt, who trained with Pavlov, as well as to Adolf Meyer (*American Journal of Psychiatry* 1936, no. 8 [August 1979]). He writes at length about his relationship with Franz Alexander in his autobiography, *A Psychiatric Odyssey: Memoirs of a Maverick Psychiatrist* (New York: Science House, 1971).

Information on the history of Franz Alexander (1892–1964) and Hanns Sachs (1881–1947) has come from a variety of sources, most notably from Paul Roazen's *Freud and His Followers* (New York: Knopf, 1975); Ernest Jones, *The Life and Work of Sigmund Freud,* 3 vols. (New York: Basic Books, 1953–57); Reuben Fine, *A History of Psychoanalysis* (New York: Columbia University Press, 1979); Peter Gay, *Freud: A Life for Our Time* (New York: W. W. Norton, 1988); and Franz Alexander, Samuel Eisenstein and Martin Grotjahn, eds., *Psychoanalytic Pioneers* (New York: Basic Books, 1966).

In *Freud: A Life for Our Time,* Peter Gay notes that Freud's troubled son, Oliver Freud, was in analysis with Franz Alexander in Berlin in the early 1920s.

Reuben Fine notes that Hanns Sachs defined an ideal for psychotherapists when he wrote in 1930 in the *"Zehn Jahre Berliner Psychoanalytisches Institute":* "the future analyst must learn to see things which other people easily, willingly and permanently overlook, and must be in a position to maintain this capacity to observe, even when it is in sharpest contradiction to his own wishes and feelings."

John A.P. Millet, in "Psychoanalysis in the United States," in *Psychoanalytic Pioneers,* writes that 1930 was a "red-letter year in the history of psychoanalysis in the United States." That year, the first International Congress on Mental Hygiene was held in Washington, D.C., and the University of Chicago invited Franz Alexander to become the first professor of psychoanalysis appointed in the United States. Two years later, Hanns Sachs received a similar honor when he was invited to lecture at the Harvard Medical School. In 1932, the Chicago Institute was established under the direction of Franz Alexander.

CHAPTER THREE: IN GOOD HANDS, PAGES 35–50

Articles from the *Chicago Tribune,* the *Chicago Daily News,* and the *Chicago Sun-Times* from 1931 to 1984 document Dr. Masserman's numerous pronouncements on world events and on topics from hippies to the prospects for nuclear disarmament.

Dr. Masserman's written information on the use of Amytal, its dangers, and its habit-forming effects comes, as indicated from "Drugs as Aids in the Psychiatric Interview," in Chapter 4, "Current Behavior or Mental Status Examinations," pp. 48–53, and from Chapter 34, "Drug Narcosis in Diagnosis and Psychotherapy," p. 574, in *The Practice of Dynamic Psychiatry* (Philadelphia: W. B. Saunders, 1955). His dialogue about Amytal, its history and purpose, comes in large part from his testimony about the drug in depositions taken in 1985 and 1986. A great deal of information about Amytal can also be found in *Physicians' Desk Reference, Martindale's The Extra Pharmacopoeia,* and *Goodman and Gillman's The Pharmacological Basis of Therapeutics.* Barbara's "afterthoughts" on Amytal in this chapter were drawn from these references and from my interviews and discussions with medical experts—psychopharmacologists and physicians at the National Institute for Mental Health, the University of Pennsylvania School of Medicine, Jefferson Hospital in Philadelphia, and Harvard University Medical School.

For more information on Amytal's use as a diagnostic tool, see Nicholas G. Ward, David B. Rowlett, and Patrick Burke, "Sodium Amylobarbitone in the Differential Diagnosis of Confusion," *American Journal of Psychiatry* 135, no. 1 (January 1978), and "Drug Narcosis in Diagnosis and Psychotherapy," *The Practice of Dynamic Psychiatry,* pp. 574–84.

CHAPTER FOUR: THE AMYTAL INTERVIEW, PAGES 51–63

The details of the Amytal interview are vividly remembered by Barbara Noël; Dr. Masserman's routine has been consistently confirmed by my interviews with a number of his other patients. In later depositions, Dr. Masserman detailed his procedures for administering his mixtures of Amytal and saline and confirmed his rationale for the frequency and purpose of its administration. His language was as Barbara Noël reported it.

It's difficult to pin down precisely how long different individuals would be unconcious from Amytal. It is a short-acting drug, and according to the chairman of anesthesiology at the medical school of one Eastern university, "With Amytal, you could render someone wholly insensible to outside stimulation, whether it's anything from fondling to pulling teeth to removing a liver, if you judge your dose correctly." He said Amytal usually affects mental processing within one circulation time, builds to a crescendo, and tends to wear off rather quickly—usually within twenty-five to thirty minutes. He said, however, that if you didn't try to awaken a patient afterwards, it's possible that she "might stay groggy or unresponsive for anywhere from a half-hour to seven hours."

On the other hand, two experienced psychopharmacologists reviewing the testimony have said Amytal is a short-acting barbiturate and that it would be impossible to give a person enough Amytal in one injection to keep her unconscious for as long as seven hours; such a large dose would be lethal. They hypothesized that an IV of Amytal might have been administered continuously or another medication added to keep Barbara Noël and other patients knocked out for five to eight hours.

Several psychopharmacologists I interviewed independently suggested that perhaps the Amytal was administered first so as to disinhibit the patient as much as possible during sex, and then a drug such as morphine or Valium was given to keep the women out for the longer period of time to deepen the effect of retrograde amnesia, erasing any memory of what happened under the drug. They suggest that hypnotic suggestions also may have been given for the patients not to remember anything about sex.

The reactions Barbara Noël had to Amytal (and to whatever other drug she might have been given) are classic drug side effects, as documented in *The Safe Medicine Book* (New York: Ballantine, 1991) and other books about hazards of prescription drugs. Adverse side effects to Amytal are confirmed in *Physicians' Desk Reference* (pp. 1112–13), *Martindale's*, and other standard drug references.

A description of "Untoward Effects" in *Goodman and Gillman's* says: "The aftereffects of barbiturates may sometimes be manifested as overt excitement. The user may awaken slightly intoxicated and feel euphoric and energetic; later, as the demands of his daytime activities challenge his possibly impaired faculties, he may display irritability and temper." ("Hypnotics and Sedatives:

Barbiturates," *Goodman and Gillman's The Pharmacological Basis of Therapeutics,* 7th ed. [New York: Macmillan, 1985], pp. 357–58.)

CHAPTER FIVE: BLIND TRUST, PAGES 64–76

Dr. Charles Schlageter shared office space with Dr. Masserman only at the beginning of the time Barbara Noël was seeing Dr. Masserman. When he moved out, that office remained empty until the early 1980s, when Dr. Victor Uribe moved in. (We could not consult with Dr. Schlageter because in 1977 he was murdered when one of his psychiatric patients walked into his office and shot him eight times. Dr. Schlageter's widow, Mrs. Betty Schlageter, has testified in favor of banning handguns.)

Richard Noël, who now lives in California, recalled during a telephone interview the dialogue with Dr. Masserman. His memory of the event matched—almost word for word—Barbara Noël's recollections, although he had not compared notes with his ex-wife.

CHAPTER SIX: NO WAY OUT, PAGES 77–96

Dr. Masserman's reference to "giving up your birthright for a mess of pottage" came from Genesis 25: 29–34. In fact, Esau, the elder son of Isaac and Rebekah, was tricked out of his birthright by his younger twin brother, Jacob: "Once when Jacob was boiling pottage, Esau came in from the field, and he was famished. And Esau said to Jacob, 'Let me eat some of that red pottage, for I am famished!' Jacob said, 'First sell me your birthright.' Esau said, 'I am about to die; of what use is a birthright to me?' Jacob said, 'Swear to me first.' So he swore to him and sold his birthright to Jacob. Then Jacob gave Esau bread and pottage of lentils, and he ate and drank, and rose and went on his way." (*The Oxford Annotated Bible* [New York: Oxford University Press, 1962], p. 30.) Dr. Masserman often made biblical references in his sessions, as well as in his writing and his speeches.

The view that depression is a predictable side effect and the warning that Amytal is habit forming and "may result in psychic and physical dependence" and cause addiction for "persons with known previous addiction," are taken from *Physicians' Desk Reference,* "Product Information." Further information on the addictive qualities of Amytal, also appears in *Goodman and Gillman's* and *Martindale's.*

Although we haven't been able to locate a copy of the brochure Dr. Masserman gave Barbara Noël, in his bibliography he lists " 'Tommy the Tipsy Tabby' (illustrated by Eloise Smith). Alcoholism Res. Foundation, 9 Bedford Road, Toronto 6, Canada, 1957."

Jules Masserman made reference to his travels to Israel and Egypt in "Response to the Presidential Address," *American Journal of Psychiatry* 135, no. 8 (August 1978).

Also in 1978, Jules Masserman edited an article about Sodium Amytal in *Current Psychiatric Therapies,* an annual publication of which he was editor for more than twenty years. That article, by Drs. Luis R. Marcos and Manuel Trujillo, reviewed Sodium Amytal's history, stating that it was used extensively after its discovery in 1923, but following World War II, enthusiasm about the drug receded because of "inconsistencies in results" and "a paucity of controlled attempts at validation." The authors stated that in recent years, clinical use of intravenous Sodium Amytal "has become unusual." According to Marcos and Trujillo, current "knowledge of the basic physiological mechanisms of the actions and effects of Sodium Amytal on the central nervous system remains controversial." The doctors said that rare indications for Amytal's use were cases of hospitalized patients manifesting "profound catatonic stupor to various levels of immobility, mutism, and negativism." (Luis R. Marcos, M.D., and Manuel Trujillo, M.D., "The Sodium Amytal Interview as a Therapeutic Modality," *Current Psychiatric Therapies,* vol. 18, ed. Jules H. Masserman [New York, Grune & Stratton, 1978].)

Before Jules Masserman played the violin at the annual APA meeting in Chicago, he closed his presidential address with: "But now that the time has come, how shall I end? In musical idiom: by repeating themes unnecessarily, as would Tchaikovsky? Or with a bit of terminal grandiloquence, in the style of Grieg? Or with a muted Mozartian modulation? I prefer the latter. . . ." ("Presidential Address: The Future of Psychiatry as a Scientific and Humanitarian Discipline in a Changing World," *American Journal of Psychiatry* 136, no. 8 [August 1979].)

CHAPTER SEVEN: OUT OF BOUNDS, PAGES 97–107

Jules Masserman's article "Poetry and Music in Flight from Futility" was reprinted in *The Arts in Psychotherapy,* vol. 7 (Ankho International, 1980). Dr. Paul Jay Fink's introduction was taken from the same issue. Dr. Fink was president of the American Psychiatric Association, 1988–89.

In his memoirs, Dr. Masserman writes that on his sixty-fourth birthday, he qualified for his private pilots' license by flying a light plane solo over the California mountains, thus fulfilling a lifelong ambition.

Descriptions of Jules Masserman's boat, *Naiad, Nymph of the Lakes,* come from interviews with ex-patients and from Dr. Masserman, in the Deposition of Jules H. Masserman, M.D., in the Circuit Court of Cook County, Illinois, County Department, Law Division, *Barbara Noël, Plaintiff v. Jules H. Masserman, M.D., Defendant.* No. 84L 21302.

In that same deposition, Dr. Masserman confirmed under oath that he had taken Ms. Nöel out on his boat on one occasion.

Information on the interactive and potentially fatal effects of antidepressants and Amytal and the potentially fatal combination of Amytal and alcohol can be found in *Goodman and Gillman's* and *Martindale's The Extra Pharmacopoeia.*

Jules Masserman's involvement in international social and political issues comes from his own curriculum vitae as well as from articles in the *Chicago*

Tribune, the *Chicago Sun-Times,* the *Chicago Daily News,* and the APA's *Psychiatric News* during those years.

The names of Dr. Masserman's other patients have been changed to protect their privacy.

Information about the impetus for the World Congress for Social Psychiatry and the role Jules Masserman played in its formation comes from *Man for Humanity* (Springfield, Ill.: Charles C. Thompson, 1972) and discussions with Dr. Manfred Halpern, Ph.D., at Princeton University, who was a founder and member of the board of ASSSP for three years with Masserman. Dr. Halpern described Jules Masserman as "as warm and caring a human being as you'd want to meet."

The quote about "an extraordinary reaching out" comes from an interview with Dr. Halpern about Jules Masserman's role in opening the organization. "He is not a manipulative man, not a power-hungry man," said Dr. Halpern. "He deserved all the praise he ever got." This view of Dr. Masserman is widely held by his colleagues and has been echoed in many remarks made about Jules Masserman's extraordinary professional life over the years.

CHAPTER EIGHT: AT THE HEART OF THE PROBLEM, PAGES 108–120
Dialogue between Barbara Noël and Dr. Robert Wheeler was reconstructed from Barbara's medical history, from my recent interviews with Dr. Wheeler and from his summary, "A Composite Viewpoint of the TMJ Dysfunctional Singer: A Hidden Handicap for the Serious Singer" (Temporomandibular Joint Dysfunction Institute, 30 N. Michigan Ave., Chicago, IL 60602). Other helpful information came from Gini Hartzmark, "Medical News: The TMJ Syndrome," *Complete Woman,* February 1986, and Jane Hart, "The Terror of TMJ Syndrome," *Cosmopolitan,* September 1985.

In a statement written in support of Dr. Masserman, Dr. Uribe described Barbara Nöel's call: "I asked her to explain why she needed the Sodium Amytal and she said it was not necessary to go into details and all she wanted was the Sodium Amytal. I explained to Ms. Barbara Nöel that I did not consider Sodium Amytal necessary at that time. I told her that if she wanted to talk further with me about her present tensions and preoccupations that I would be glad to give her an appointment . . ."

CHAPTER NINE: MEDICAL TREASON, PAGES 121–132
The effects of a barbiturate, when injected, will cause a sleeplike state and vary in its duration depending on the particular molecule, the particular dose used, and the patient's individualized response to the drug—which can vary widely depending on what she has had to drink and eat, her body weight, and the amount of sleep she has had. As a result, the effects of the drug could vary widely each time it is administered. Barbara remembers Dr. Masserman telling her that he had given her a "lighter dose" on September 21, 1984. If

so, a lighter dose, combined with her metabolism, weight, and other factors, might have allowed her to become conscious.

Area 1 Violent Crimes, Case No. F 358809, documents the Criminal Sexual Assault that Barbara Noël reported on September 21, 1984, at 1400 hours on police beat 1233 to reporting officer Tom Fleming, #5497.

Drs. Seskind, Abel, and Marshall were named in police reports on this case. Their medical records were introduced as evidence during depositions in *Barbara Nöel v. Jules H. Masserman, M.D.*

CHAPTER TEN: THE SINGER V. THE PSYCHIATRIST, PAGES 133–152

"John Michael Flynn" was given a pseudonym because of his wish not to have any publicity about this case. Conversations with him have been reconstructed from Barbara Noël's recollections of them and notes about the conversations she took at the time.

Barbara wrote down her exchange with Jules Masserman right after he called on October 12. During his Discovery Deposition, Dr. Masserman denied having offered Barbara Nöel any money during this conversation.

Bill Carroll's perspective on this case and his take on the secret aberrations of professionals are drawn from my interviews with him in spring 1990.

CHAPTER ELEVEN: ABOVE SUSPICION, PAGES 153–169

Debra Davy, of Hinshaw Culbertson, Moelmann, Hoban & Fuller, called Kenneth L. Cunniff before the first depositions on September 13, 1985.

"Daniella Biagi" and "Annie Morrison" are pseudonyms; neither woman wanted to have to deal with publicity from this case. They first told their stories to Ken Cunniff and Bill Carroll and filed complaints against Jules Masserman in the Circuit Court of Cook County, Illinois (*Sandra Doe, Plaintiff v. Jules H. Masserman, M.D., Defendant* and *Marilyn Doe v. Jules H. Masserman, M.D.*). Both women later talked with Shari Dam, prosecutor for the Illinois Department of Registration and Education.

Following the completion of the out-of-court settlement of their civil cases against Jules Masserman, both Daniella and Annie talked with Barbara Noël on the telephone. However, their stories as told here are drawn from my lengthy telephone interviews with each of them during the spring and early summer of 1991.

All the dangers of taking Amytal during pregnancy are unknown, but it's clear that no responsible physician would recommend it to a pregnant woman because of the potential for damaging both infant and mother. *Martindale's The Extra Pharmacopoeia* states: "Folate deficiency has occurred following chronic administration and hypoprothrombinemia has been reported in infants born to mothers who have received a barbiturate during pregnancy. . . . The toxic effects of overdosage result in profound central depression and include respiratory and cardiovascular depression, hypotension and shock leading to renal failure" (p. 706).

Dr. Masserman denies that he recommended or gave Amytal to a pregnant patient; he emphasizes that he never would give a pregnant woman any drugs other than vitamins.

In depositions, Dr. Masserman admitted under oath that he had administered Sodium Amytal to both "Annie" and "Daniella;" he also admitted that he had taken Annie on his boat, and when asked if he had taken Daniella, he said, "I don't recall that." He denied ever asking either woman to undress or having sexual contact with them.

I saw the scar tissue on the top of Daniella's right hand when I met her in Chicago in April 1992. She says Dr. Masserman used to put the needle into the vein in her hand because he couldn't find a vein in her arm.

CHAPTER TWELVE: FACING THE PERPETRATOR, PAGES 170–193

Information on Barbara Noël's testimony comes from her discovery deposition in *Barbara Noël, Plaintiff* v. *Jules H. Masserman, M.D., Defendant*, No. 84L 21302, 13 September 1985.

Bill Carroll's questions and Jules Masserman's answers are extracted from the discovery deposition of Jules H. Masserman M.D., defendant, in *Noël* v. *Masserman*, taken before Jean Korinko Sweeney, November 7, 1985, 10:00 A.M. Ken Cunniff's office is now at the First National Plaza building in Chicago, but at the time it was at 29 LaSalle Street.

The three pages of notes were *Masserman Deposition, Exhibit 1 and Exhibit 2.*

Counsel's objections and other interruptions or discussions between counsel have been omitted from these quotes unless they are relevant to the discussion.

The agreement on the dangers of Amytal and its prolonged use, plus the information on the "cross-tolerant" effects of Amytal and alcohol, are well documented in medical literature. Although Bill Carroll had researched the dangers of Amytal, the information listed here has been drawn primarily from drug information references and recent interviews with psychopharmacologists and other medical doctors and pharmacists.

Jules Masserman's description of the Amytal routine comes from p. 68 of the discovery deposition of Jules H. Masserman, M.D., defendant, in *Noël* v. *Masserman*, November 7, 1985.

Information on Jules Masserman's childhood is drawn from his book *A Psychiatric Odyssey*, as well as from *Current Biography*, 1980, and *American Journal of Psychiatry* 136, no. 8 (August 1979).

The APA Commission on Psychiatric Therapies that Dr. Masserman appointed to review the rationale and practices of currently practiced therapies included Drs. Judd Marmor, John Nemiah, Seymour Halleck, Byram Karasu, and Stanley Lesse.

CHAPTER THIRTEEN: STARTING AGAIN, PAGES 194–210

Ann M. Jernberg, Ph.D., began clinical work in the Department of Psychiatry at the University of Chicago in 1955. She was senior staff psychologist at the

Michael Reese Hospital (1960–67), and since 1967 she has supervised psychological services for Chicago Head Start Day Care and Parent-Child Center programs. She has been clinical director of the Theraplay Institute in Chicago since its inception in 1969 and is author of *Theraplay: A New Treatment Using Structured Play for Problem Children and Their Families* (San Francisco: Jossey-Bass, 1979) and co-author of *The Marital Interaction: Structured Observation and Intervention* (Chicago: The Theraplay Institute, 1992).

Dr. Masserman's testimony, as well as Debra Davy's and Bill Carroll's remarks, come from Jules Masserman's evidence deposition videotaped July 25, 1986, at the law offices of Hinshaw Culbertson, Moelmann, Hoban & Fuller.

Jules Masserman's professional history is well documented in *A Psychiatric Odyssey* and in *Who's Who in America,* 1980–81; *Current Biography,* 1980; *American Journal of Psychiatry* 136, no. 8 (August 1979), and *American Men and Women of Science,* 1978.

CHAPTER FOURTEEN: PIECES BEGIN TO FALL INTO PLACE, PAGES 211–220
Debra Davy wrote to Kenneth L. Cunniff in late October 1985.

Honors given Dr. Masserman by his colleagues during the fall of 1986 by the American Association for Social Psychiatry, the Illinois Psychiatric Society, and the World Congress of Social Psychiatry were reported in the APA's *Psychiatric News* ("Association Puts Emphasis on Psychiatry's Psychosocial Aspects," September 19, 1986) and the *Chicago Tribune*'s "On the Law" column, January 6, 1987.

CHAPTER FIFTEEN: ADMITTING MY ADDICTIONS, PAGES 221–230
More information on Onsite's approach to therapy can be obtained by writing to Onsite Training and Consulting, Inc., 2820 W. Main St., Rapid City, SD 57702.

The names of group members at Onsite—including Andy, Cathy, and Sister Josephine—have been changed to protect their privacy.

The kind of therapy done at Onsite can be supplemented by reading Sharon Wegscheider's book *Another Chance: Hope and Health for the Alcoholic Family* (Palo Alto, Cal.: Science and Behavior, 1981). Alice Miller's valuable books *Prisoners of Childhood: The Drama of the Gifted Child* (New York: Basic Books, 1981) and *Thou Shall Not Be Aware: Society's Betrayal of the Child* (New York: New American Library, 1986) are useful, as is Claudia Black's *It Will Never Happen to Me!* (MAC Printing and Publications Division, 1850 High St., Denver, CO 80218). See the bibliography for additional references.

CHAPTER SIXTEEN: THE CASE GOES PUBLIC, PAGES 231–251
The "On the Law" column titled "Shocking Detour on Road of Fame," by James Warren, Maurice Possley, and Joseph Tybor, was in the *Chicago Tribune,* January 6, 1987.

Shari Dam's discussion about sex offense prosecutions and the dynamics of sex offenders and their victims—the patterns of low self-esteem found in victims and the narcissism, sexual obsessiveness, and grandiosity found in doctors who have sexually violated their patients—is drawn from my interviews with her in Chicago during March 1990.

Barbara Noël wrote down her telephone conversations with "Bonnie Markham," "Jennifer," "Lillian," and other victims of Jules Masserman soon after they occurred. All we know about these women's stories is what they told Barbara Noël.

I interviewed "Laura Davis," Daniella Biagi, and Annie Morrison and reconstructed Barbara Noël's dialogues with them so as to present their individual stories in greater detail. I called another woman, not mentioned in the text, who had a sexual relationship with Jules Masserman in the mid-1960s, when she was his patient, but she said she did not wish to discuss it, since it was a matter of "ancient history."

The "biodynamic" principles for which Masserman is best known stemmed from his research in experimental induction of neurosis, which led him to conclude that five basic principles underlie all animal behavior. These are: (1) behavior is motivated by an organism's physiological needs; (2) learning and adaptation are contingent on both internal and external circumstances; (3) most frustration gives way to substitute gratification; (4) conflict is the result of mutually incompatible responses that may induce neurotic and psychotic patterns; (5) these patterns can be alleviated by resolving the stresses that created the behavior in the first place.

My information on Jules Masserman's cat experiments comes from a number of sources, including a basic text, James C. Coleman, *Abnormal Psychology and Modern Life,* 3rd ed. (Glenview, Ill.: Scott, Foresman, 1964), and Jules Masserman's many articles on the subject, including "Effects of Sodium Amytal and Other Drugs on the Reactivity of the Hypothalamus of the Cat," *Arch. Neurology and Psychiatry* 37 (1937): 617–28; his book describing his early animal behavior studies on "Experimental Neuroses and Therapy," *Behavior and Neurosis* (Chicago: University of Chicago Press, 1943); and "Intensity of Conflict and Modes of Therapy," in *Principles of Dynamic Psychiatry* (Philadelphia: W. B. Saunders, 1946).

The article about Dr. Masserman's research on monkeys was: "They're Making People Out of Monkeys: Northwestern University Psychiatrists Induce Mental Ills by Subjecting Simians to the Sort of Troubles and Frustrations Most Humans Must Cope With—Then Find Ways to Cure Them," *Chicago Tribune,* May 10, 1953.

Masserman's article "Effects of Analeptic Drugs on the Hypothalamus of the Cat," in *The Hypothalamus,* December 1939, suggests that he became involved in some research on the hypothalamus when he was with Dr. Adolf Meyer at the Phipps Clinic. In his *Principles of Dynamic Psychiatry* (1946), he lists alcohol, Metrazol, morphine, and Sodium Amytal as the drugs used in the study of "Effects of Various Drugs on the Emotional Mimetic Reactions of the Hypothalamus and Cerebral Cortex." In "The Role of the Hypothalamus in Emotion," in *Behavior and Emotion* (1943), he discusses Philip Bard's animal research on the hypothalamus as an influence on "the capacity to display sexual excitement," hypothesizing that since the stimulation of the hypothalamus or the vagina induces reflexive sexual response, it might be only a "quasi-emotional state" like "sham-rage," having nothing to do with the origin or conscious perception of erotic emotion. (Though Masserman cites Philip Bard's studies of sexual excitement and erotic behavior in cats in this and other early references, Bard's work is not mentioned in Masserman's later works that refer to the subject.)

In a chapter on "Neurophysiological Investigations of Behavior" in *Behavior and Neurosis,* Dr. Masserman writes: "Does stimulation of the hypothalamus also give rise to the actual *experience* of fear, rage, or any other affect, as such, in the animal?" He notes that the experimental approach to this problem is beset with difficulties, the most fundamental being that the "emotional" reactions of "erotic arousal, relaxed self-content, anger, and fear" are difficult to evaluate in laboratory animals because these interpretations [by the researcher] are impressionistic. . . . "For instance," Masserman writes, "to show, as Bard had done, that the hypothalamus 'may exert an influence on the *capacity to display* sexual excitement' is not to demonstrate that the hypothalamus plays any role in the origin or conscious perception of the erotic emotion per se, especially since reflex sexual behavior can be induced in . . . the cats by vaginal stimulation." [Emphasis is mine.]

He says that "the significance of such behavior would have to be tested not only in waking animals with an intact cerebral cortex but also by a number of criteria ordinarily applicable to true affective states." For specific investigation, he included the following criteria:

"—Does the activity induced by hypothalamic stimulation persist after the stimulus, as is the case with normal affective states?

"—Does the induced activity modify or displace behavior occasioned by spontaneous affects?

"—Can the animal be trained to adapt to direct hypothalamic stimulation, as would be the case if a significant affective experience were thereby induced?"

These particular observations Masserman made about getting cats addicted to alcohol are documented in a number of his publications, including *Principles of Dynamic Psychiatry* and *Behavior and Neurosis,* and in a black-and-white film, *Neurosis and Alcohol* (Film 5), available through the University of Chicago or the Psychological Cinema Register, State College, Pa.

Barbara Cheresh, who now lives in Boston, was a student at the University of Chicago and a college roommate of Christine McGuire's younger sister, Jean, in their freshman year. Mrs. Cheresh, who took a sociology class taught by Christine, said in an interview: "She was very bright and a terrific looker—

a shining light in many ways. If she gave an eight o'clock class, people came just to see her! Jules was a more distant feature to me; he seemed somewhat ugly and reptilian, also very isolated. He kept to himself, and when we went on the boat, it was us and him. . . . I always thought it was kind of a beauty-and-the-beast romance."

When asked during an interview about any correlation between his animal research and his later treatment of women, Jules Masserman said, "There *are no* correlations."

CHAPTER SEVENTEEN: LICENSE TO RAPE, PAGES 252–257

A copy of the Illinois Psychiatric Society's apologetic letter to Jules Masserman was sent to Barbara Noël by David R. Hawkins, M.D., who was chair of the IPS Ethics Committee at that time.

The American Psychiatric Association sent the 1981 edition of "The Principles of Medical Ethics with Annotations Especially Applicable to Psychiatry" to Barbara Noël and that is what we have referred to here.

I have reconstructed Barbara Noël's dialogues with Shari Dam and described Shari Dam's perspective on this case from my recent interviews with Shari Dam in Chicago.

"Laura Davis" is a pseudonym; the reconstructed dialogue and her recollections are based on our recent interviews.

CHAPTER EIGHTEEN: UNCOVERING MY OWN MYSTERY, PAGES 258–266

Barbara Noël's recollection of her childhood incest was recorded on videotape by Ann Jernberg's colleague Phyllis Booth. Barbara Noël transcribed the tape, and this excerpt has been taken from that transcription.

An interesting and relevant article that discusses symptoms of patients who have been victims of childhood incest ("massive denial and/or repression accompanied by major cognitive and affective deficits; massive panic and depersonalization") is by Anne Bernstein, M.D., F.A.P.A., "Analysis of Two Adult Female Patients Who Had been Victims of Incest in Childhood," *Journal of the American Academy of Psychoanalysis* 17, no. 2 (Summer 1989).

The comparison between "fixated pedophiles" and therapists who abuse their patients comes from Susan Brayfield-Cave, Ph.D., "Sexual Predators in the Profession," *American Psychological Association Journal,* April 1990. Dr. Brayfield-Cave is chair of the New Mexico Board of Psychologist Examiners.

Extensive research on and classification and treatment of "fixated pedophiles" has been done by A. Nicholas Groth, one of the pioneers of treatment for sexual offenders and current director of the Forensic Mental Health Association in Orlando, Florida. For further study of this coercive sex, see A.Nicholas Groth and Jean Birnbaum, *Men Who Rape* (New York: Plenum Press,

1979), and J. C. Holroyd and A. M. Brodsky, "Psychologists' Attitudes and Practices Regarding Erotic and Nonerotic Physical Contact with Patients," *American Psychologist* 32: 843–49.

CHAPTER NINETEEN: ABOVE THE LAW, PAGES 267–279

The first principle of the American Psychiatric Association's "The Principles of Medical Ethics with Annotations Especially Applicable to Psychiatrists" comes from the 1985 edition.

Dr. Masserman's endnote on the "Latin-Iberian tradition" can be found in Jules H. Masserman and Victor M. Uribe, *Adolescent Sexuality* (Springfield, Ill.: Charles C. Thomas, 1989), p. 23.

His discussion about the custody dispute also comes from *Adolescent Sexuality,* pp. 83–91.

His quotes on incest are from *Adolescent Sexuality,* pp. 45–9. Masserman's view that parent-child or intersibling sexual relations usually leave no adverse effects is found on p. 38.

Masserman counsels boys: "Contrary to teenage macho myths, a 'no!' does not *always* mean a bashfully hidden 'yes!' (pp. 41–4). In an endnote to his advice about being wary of "ready consent," Masserman comments: "As male teenagers become aging Lotharios, they may find a challenging "yes!" no longer quite welcome."

The exchanges between Barbara Stackler and Barbara Noël at the hearing of the Ethics Committee were taken from a transcript prepared by Barbara Noël, who taped her part of the proceedings with the Committee's permission.

The exchange between Barbara Stackler and "Laura Davis" has been reconstructed from my interviews with Laura Davis and from a description of her testimony by Barbara Noël since we did not have a transcript of her testimony.

CHAPTER TWENTY: A FINAL VERDICT, PAGES 280–284

Despite the settlement of four lawsuits, a state consent order to relinquish his medical license, the American Psychiatric Association's verdict, and another pending lawsuit, Jules Masserman still denies any medical negligence or sexual assault of any patients.

It is well known that it's difficult for colleagues to censure their peers in any profession. For more information on this issue in the therapeutic community, see Judith Herman, Nanette Gartrell et al., "Psychiatrist-Patient Sexual Contact: Results of a National Survey, II: Psychiatrists' Attitudes," *American Journal of Psychiatry* 144 (1987); and Gartrell, Herman et al., "Reporting Practices of Psychiatrists Who Knew of Sexual Misconduct by Colleagues," *American Journal of Orthopsychiatry* 57 (1987).

Also see "Sexual Misconduct in the Practice of Medicine," by the Council on Ethical and Judicial Affairs of the American Medical Association, *JAMA* 266, no. 19 (November 1991); "New Laws About Sexual Misconduct by Therapists: Knowledge and Attitudes Among Wisconsin Psychiatrists," *Wisconsin Medical Journal* 88, no. 5 (1989); and R. P. Kluft, "Treating the Patient Who Has Been Exploited by a Previous Therapist," *Psychiatric Clinics of North America* 12 (1989).

CHRONOLOGY OF JULES HOMEN MASSERMAN

1931: Receives M.D. degree.

1931–32: Does residency in psychiatry and neurology at Stanford University Hospital, Palo Alto, California.

1932–36: Does psych residency at Johns Hopkins under "dean" of American Psychiatry, Adolf Meyer; works as chief resident in psychiatry at Baltimore City Hospitals.

1936: Appointed instructor at University of Chicago under guidance of Roy Grinker, Sr., chairman of psychiatry.

1936–40: Undergoes psychoanalysis with Franz Alexander at the Chicago Institute for Psychoanalysis.

1940: Certified as an analyst by the Chicago Institute.

1940: President of the Illinois Psychiatric Society.

1943: Marries Christine McGuire, his third spouse.

1946: Appointed assistant professor of neurology and psychiatry at Northwestern University Medical School.

1946: Receives the Lasker Award "for outstanding contributions to the advancement of mental health through experimental investigations."

1947: Begins working at the Veterans Administration Hospital at Downing, Illinois, where he will be chairman of training for the next thirty years.

1948: Appointed associate professor at Northwestern.

1951: Named scientific director of the National Foundation for Psychiatric Research.

1951: Appointed Consultant in Psychiatry to the Secretariat of the United Nations.

1951: Lectures to the British Royal Society and university faculties in Scandinavia and Europe, under auspices of World Health Organization.

1951: Knifed in the abdomen and right hand by a patient he identified as Richard Draney, a dress designer who had called the doctor to tell him, "I'm going to cut your guts out." According to newspaper reports at the time, Draney dropped the knife and fled from the apartment when Mrs. Masserman began hitting him with a fireplace shovel.

1952: Appointed professor at Northwestern.

1955: Makes lecture tour of Brazil, Uruguay, Argentina, Chile, Peru, Costa Rica, and Guatemala.

1957: President of the Society of Biological Psychiatry.

1957: President of the American Society for Group Therapy.

1958: Named director of education for Illinois Psychiatric Institute; heads training program for some thirty-three resident physicians.

1959: President of the Society for Biological Psychiatry.

1959: President of the American Academy for Psychoanalysis.

1964–69: Co-chairman of neurology and psychiatry at Northwestern University Medical School.

1969–71: President of the International Association for Social Psychiatry.

1971: Publishes A Psychiatric Odyssey, and announces his retirement from all APA duties "in favor of younger and more able colleagues;" subsequently serves as trustee, secretary, vice-president, and president.

1972: Executive councillor, the International College of Psychosomatic Medicine.

1972: Executive vice-president of the American Academy of Stress Disorders.

1974: Receives the Sigmund Freud Award from the American Society of Psychoanalytic Physicians.

1974: Appointed professor emeritus at Northwestern.

1974: Honored for "pioneer work in community mental health" by American Friends of the Jerusalem Mental Health Center.

1974: Vice-president of the APA.

1978: Leads invitational tour of the Middle East; presents conciliatory document signed by leading psychiatrists in Tel Aviv and Jerusalem, to Secretary General of the Egyptian Psychiatric Association.

1978: Presides at Seventh International Congress of Social Psychiatry in Portugal.

1978: Takes invitational tour of the People's Republic of China under auspices of the World Association for Social Psychiatry.

1978–79: 107th President of the APA.

1981: APA Forum in New Orleans endorses his "Resolution Against Nuclear War."

1981: Named "Honorary Life President" of the World Association for Social Psychiatry

1983: Leads forty American psychiatrists on invited professional visits to the USSR, where they and Soviet colleagues compare American and Soviet concepts of psychiatric theory, ethics, diagnosis, and therapy.

1983: Lawsuit *Cheryl Russell v. Dr. Jules Masserman,* filed in Cook County Circuit Court.

1984: Lawsuit *Barbara Noël v. Jules H. Masserman, M.D.,* filed in Cook County Circuit Court.

1984: Lawsuit *Sandra Doe v. Jules H. Masserman, M.D.,* filed in Cook County Circuit Court.

1984: Lawsuit *Marilyn Doe v. Jules H. Masserman, M.D.,* filed in Cook County Circuit Court.

1985: Lawsuit *Cheryl Russell v. Dr. Jules Masserman,* settled out of court by Dr. Masserman's insurers against Dr. Masserman, without his consent, for $50,000.

1986: Lawsuit *Barbara Noël v. Jules H. Masserman, M.D.,* settled out of court by Dr. Masserman's insurers, against Dr. Masserman and without his consent, for $200,000.

1986: Lawsuit *Sandra Doe v. Jules H. Masserman, M.D.,* settled out of court by Dr. Masserman's insurers, against Dr. Masserman and without his consent, for $25,000.

1986: Lawsuit *Marilyn Doe v. Jules H. Masserman, M.D.,* settled out of court by Dr. Masserman's insurers, against Dr. Masserman and without his consent, for $25,000.

1986: Ethics Committees of the Illinois Psychiatric Association and the Chicago Analytic Society receive complaints filed against Jules Masserman by Barbara Noël.

1986: Honored at a Festschrift dinner as AASP's founding president by the American Association for Social Psychiatry and the Illinois Psychiatric Association.

1986: Honored at the 11th World Congress for Social Psychiatry in Rio de Janeiro.

1986: Informed that the Illinois Department of Registration and Education is launching an investigation into allegations of his misconduct.

1987: Signs consent order with the Illinois Department of Registration and Education to give up his license to prescribe drugs or practice medicine or *any form* of psychotherapy.

1988: Lawsuit *Cheryl A. Doe v. Jules H. Masserman, M.D.*, filed in Cook County Circuit Court.

1989: Publishes *Adolescent Sexuality* with Victor Uribe, M.D.

1989: Lawsuit *Cheryl A. Doe v. Jules H. Masserman, M.D.*, dismissed because statute of limitations for "healing art malpractice" is two years with an outer limit of four years for "discovery rule cases."

1990: Lawsuit *Robin S. Doe, Plaintiff, v. Jules H. Masserman, M.D.*, No. 87 L 23941, pending in Cook County Circuit Court, charges that from 1976 to October 1986, Defendant treated plaintiff by inducing Plaintiff to disrobe and use the bed, couch, or cot in the Defendant's office; that he told her the disrobing and drugs were necessary to treat her emotional and psychiatric problems; he also induced defendant to meet at his boat and airplane, representing that effective therapy could be conducted thereon; Defendant was also accused of uninvited touching and physical contact.

1990: Testifies at Ethics hearing held about his conduct before a panel of the Ethics Committee of the Illinois Psychiatric Society.

1991: Informed that The American Psychiatric Association Appeals Board has voted to suspend him from the APA and from the Illinois Psychiatric Society for five years for violation of *The Principles of Medical Ethics With Annotations Especially Applicable to Psychiatry.*

1992: Psychiatric Editor of the *International Encyclopedia of Neurology, Psychiatry, Psychoanalysis and Psychology,* and has two books in press. During his lifetime he has written 16 books, 410 journal articles, and 22 chapters; has edited 22 annual volumes of *Science and Psychoanalysis* and 20 annual volumes of *Current Psychiatric Therapies.* He continues to serve as a member of the APA Board of Trustees.

AFTERWORD: AN INTERVIEW WITH JULES MASSERMAN

by Kathryn Watterson

When I arrived at the the old-style, gargoyle-studded building where Dr. and Mrs. Jules H. Masserman live, I was feeling a lot of trepidation. Dr. Masserman and I had set up this interview after a letter and a series of telephone discussions in which I told him I had almost completed a book, written with Barbara Noël, that focused largely on her story, but also included the stories of some of his other women patients who had alleged sexual abuse and misconduct on his part. I'd said I wanted to give him a chance to comment, and he agreed because he said he didn't want it to appear that he didn't have a defense, when he did. Prior to the interview, he said they "weren't sure" whether I could tape-record the conversation, so I brought along a friend who lives in Chicago to help me take notes.

When the Massermans opened the door to their apartment, they opened it only a crack and looked from me to my friend with puzzled expressions. I was startled at the familiarity I felt when I saw Dr. Masserman's face. Of course, I had seen it on videotape from his deposition, but everything about his wiry and slender presence seemed familiar to me, as if I had seen him dozens of times and knew him well. About 5'5", he is fit and looks much younger than his eighty-seven years. At the door, he pursed his lips, and his expression ranged from thoughtful to perplexed to annoyed. Mrs. Masserman, who looked quite angry and upset, was robust, blond, and seemed to tower over her husband. I introduced my friend, Glen, and explained why I'd brought him along. Both Massermans insisted that he absolutely could not sit in on the interview. Glen and I had already discussed this possibility, and so I said fine, Glen could wait in the lobby, but Dr. Masserman said, "No, no, that's all right, he would be more comfortable waiting in the music room."

Dr. Masserman, moving with an easy, fluid grace, opened the door widely and spoke in a warm, charming voice that was slightly strained: "Please come in, please do come in." He took our coats and hung them before he led Glen into a small room and shut the door. Then he closed the door from the hall into a room he called his "home office," where we were standing.

Dr. Masserman looked at me intently and smiled. "Please sit down," he said, indicating the couch. I sat there, behind a coffee table that held a small black tape recorder, a stack of textbooks, and a copy of *Who's Who in the World*. Dr. Masserman sat in an easy chair next to the couch, and Mrs. Masserman sat in a swivel chair facing us.

They set up the conditions of this interview: no one else could take notes for me or witness the interview, and I could *not* tape-record it. Mrs. Masserman said, however, that they planned to tape-record, because Dr. Masserman "has suffered so much injustice" and they didn't want his comments "taken out of context." We argued about this; I didn't object to their taping, but I insisted that the only way I could be sure his quotes were totally accurate was to record the interview. They refused. "I'll tell you what," Dr. Masserman said pleasantly, as if he had just lit upon a solution. "If my lawyer approves, after reviewing the tape, of course, then I'll send you a copy." I didn't expect ever to see a copy of the tape, but I wanted the interview, so I agreed to the conditions.*

Mrs. Masserman turned on the tape recorder and also took notes on a white pad as we spoke. From time to time during the following two and a half hours, she would scribble notes on her pad, signal Dr. Masserman, and hold up the pad to show him what she had written.

Dr. Masserman picked up some papers and began with statements he had prepared. He enunciated his words carefully and formally, without contractions, and I started taking notes as fast as I could.

"I will be straight-forward and honest and give you demonstrable facts. This, then, is an interview on April 15 with Ms. Watterson with

---

* At the time this book went to press, I still had not received a copy of the tape.

Dr. Jules Masserman at my home office . . . If you are interested in the facts," he said, "I can tell you the facts. As I said, I am a very ethical practitioner, and so I cannot tell you confidential information about my patients. I took a Hippocratic oath, and even though I have retired, I still abide by that oath . . .

"I will give you a blanket statement that you will find true and supported. I graduated from medical school in 1930 . . . For the past forty years, under the aegis and supervision of four different universities, I have treated literally thousands of patients. Until Miss Noël's complaint, not a single previous one of my patients—simply not one— ever made one complaint against me.[1]

"I never violated a single ethical standard, and my philosophy has been optimum care in the neurological, medical, psychiatric and psychoanalytic therapy for every patient. The result is, if I could name some of my most prominent patients—which I cannot do—I have files full of sincerely grateful letters for therapy."

I started to ask about his use of Amytal, but Dr. Masserman waved his hand toward the stack of reference books[2] on the coffee table, commenting that his own book "is a classic in the field now." He pointed out the dozens of plaques on his walls that paid homage to him, and invited me to look at his entry in *Who's Who in the World,* saying, "It's an unusual honor . . . it's a rare honor to be in that book."

Continuing his prepared talk, Dr. Masserman said: "I can say a few things about Barbara Noël's treatment. She profited so greatly from Amytal interviews when necessary. I can't tell you *why* they were necessary, because that would be revealing. There were many times more that she asked for Amytal than I'd give it to her. She even asked my colleague for it when I was out of town, which I can prove to you by showing you this letter."

Dr. Masserman handed me a photocopy of a letter from Dr. Victor Uribe which confirmed Barbara's statements that she had asked him to give her Sodium Amytal when Dr. Masserman was out of town in

---

[1]In 1983, one year prior to Barbara Noël's complaint, a patient, Cheryl Russell, sued Dr. Masserman for needlessly injecting her with Amytal and injuring her in the process. Her lawsuit, civil case No. 83L-10063, was settled against Dr. Masserman, by his insurers, for $50,000 not long after Barbara initially filed her complaint.

[2]In the stack, he had two different editions of *Comprehensive Textbook of Psychiatry* by Freedman, Kaplan, and Saddock; *The Technique of Psychotherapy* by Louis Wolberg; and his own book, *The Practice of Dynamic Psychiatry.*

August 1984. Dr. Uribe said that Barbara stated she needed the Amytal because "she was considering making some decisions, was feeling tense and wanted to relax." Dr. Masserman pointed out Dr. Uribe's statement that "throughout the phone consultation," Barbara Noël had "expressed her deepest gratitude and trust toward Dr. Masserman."

Dr. Masserman then showed me a letter from another of his patients, who said that at Billie Laird's wake, prior to September 21, 1984, Barbara Noël had praised Dr. Masserman, saying "[He] was an incisive, dedicated and first-rate physician, superbly trained in the practice of psychiatric medicine."

"The only complaint Barbara Noël ever made—and I will give you supportive evidence of this—came on September 24, 1984." He took back the letter and said, "Had there been any unethical conduct that morning of September 24, 1984—when she said she was conscious— there were no locked doors in my office. All she had to do was to go into the next office and complain.

"Here is another fact," Dr. Masserman said. "My office nurse saw her on two occasions that morning, at my request. I had to be at the university that morning and both times my nurse checked on her, she was fine." Dr. Masserman showed me a copy of Peggy Karas's sworn statement that she had found Ms. Noël "resting comfortably and re- sponding reassuringly."

"She had demanded the Amytal because there were certain crises in her life," he said. "There were many times when she requested it that I considered it not indicated and did not give it to her.

"She had been my patient for *eighteen years*," he said, shaking his head. "When I objected to certain forms of her behavior and said I couldn't continue our therapy if she didn't stop, she'd see another psychiatrist, but she always came back, for reasons you read about [in those letters].

"What happened on that day [September 21, 1984] is relevant," Dr. Masserman continued. "These are the facts. She did not call me back and make any complaints. Instead she went to her medical doctor and to her gynecologist. I do not know what she told her medical doctor, but obviously if he thought it was something serious, he would have taken action. She went to her gynecologist and stated to him that she may have dreamed the whole thing." He handed me a typed sheet of Dr. Stuart Able's notes reiterating what Barbara Noël said she had told Dr. Sorkin—that "She was either raped or dreamt she was raped while under the influence of Amytal in her psychiatrist's office."

Dr. Masserman then continued: "She went to the police with various allegations . . . I can assure you, I would have been arrested like that, except for what a Detective Kelly found, had her complaints been true . . ." Dr. Masserman emphasized what we related in the book—that after a thorough examination, neither the police nor the hospital found any physical evidence of rape. "Had there been any, there would have been a mandatory criminal charge and arrest," he said. "But no action was taken."

Dr. Masserman also mentioned that "a prominent Chicago attorney" [whom we call "John Michael Flynn"] "investigated her allegations and then withdrew from the case." Then he sat back in his chair, folded his hands across his chest, and seemed to relax. He had given his facts—presented his case, given me letters and leads to follow.

"But what about the other lawsuits?" I asked. "Why do you think they surfaced?"

Dr. Masserman, his eyes bright and friendly, smiled sweetly and comfortably. "You put me at a disadvantage because the two other lawsuits—" he said, "I don't know who you talked to—"

I said, "There were five other lawsuits, not two, but of the two I think you're referring to, I talked to both of them."

"Well, the major one—the principle one under my therapy—resumed the practice of law, joined a prominent firm, married a rich client, invited me to her wedding and publicly proclaimed her gratitude in the presence of her father! Neither woman had made any complaints whatsoever. Both left owing me money, but I had written statements pledging to pay me . . ."

"Why do you think their accusations surfaced? Do you think they're based on malice, profit, fantasy?" I asked.

"My attorney advised me to say this . . . Please note that there were no criminal charges filed at any time, let alone rape. The only action filed was to obtain money, to secure money."

I thought about the other women who had talked to the lawyers who had told of similar abuses, but who had decided not to sue. I said, "I should ask—I assume you deny all the allegations?"

"Absolutely, I deny all the allegations," he said, raising his voice in irritation. "I *never* did anything unethical to any patient."

"Then why did you agree to give up your medical license?" I asked. "Why didn't you fight it?"

"I'm glad you asked that," he said, meeting my eyes. "At the time the suit was settled, I had already given notice to the building where

I kept my office that I was retiring at the end of that year." Dr. Masserman said he'd planned to retire because he was "taking a great deal
of time dashing home to feed my wife, to take her to the toilet, to get
her out of bed," because she needed a hip operation. He said he also
was having three operations for prostatic cancer during that time.

"So I was retiring anyhow, and my attorney said, 'Why go through
any more hearings? You don't need to practice anyway!' They projected
three or four more years of hearings."

"What's your reaction to these lawsuits? How do you feel about all
these allegations?" I asked.

"Being a very sensitive person—which I have to be to be a psychiatrist—and now this has come up again—it's been seven years of
unjustified tension, which I have withstood. Many another might not
have." He looked at me with a wounded gaze, not unlike a child who
has been refused a treat.

I asked him if he thought that the APA's Ethics Committee's decision
had stemmed from or was based on the same charges.

"I am a full member of the APA," he said. "They took no action
whatsoever. I am a member of their executive board. See." He handed
me a letter addressed to Past Presidents of the APA, from Lea Mesner,
inviting him to the May 1992 meeting of the Board of Trustees.

"There was also a complaint made to the American Academy of
Psychoanalysis—there was a hearing," he said. "They investigated, and
they judged there was no reason for action.

"After this publicity that she occasioned, contrary to assurance that
there would be no publicity and no culpability, two other associations
which I had founded and been president of—the American Association
of Social Psychiatry and the American Society for Biological Psychiatry—saw no reason for action. And the highest organizational honor
that I have, the World Association for Social Psychiatry—Honorary
Life President—I retain that title," he said with a little shrug and a
smile.

I asked him why he continued to use Amytal regularly, when most
psychiatrists say it fell out of use after the early 1950s because it was
never very effective—that you couldn't get anything with it that you
couldn't get without it.

"With the Amytal, I followed precisely what I wrote in my textbook
and what everybody else writes . . ." he said, pointing again to the
textbooks. "As you'll see in these books, I followed standard procedure,

I followed precisely what everyone else writes, as you can see if you refer to those books . . ."

I said everybody else seemed to think Amytal should *not* be used regularly . . . that he himself had written that the Amytal interview "was a preferred treatment only in extreme cases . . . and that little could be achieved by drug narcosis that could not also be achieved by therapeutic interviews conducted without its use."

He said, "There are many instances in which I only used talk therapy and I always talked afterwards."

I asked him if he had any colleagues who use Amytal on a regular basis, and he said, "Of course I do . . . many."

I asked, "Who?"

"Among others, Louis Wolberg used it frequently." He gestured to Dr. Wolberg's book.

Referring to my notes, I said, "Well, in fact, Dr. Wolberg writes that Amytal is used only in extreme cases—that it's '*sometimes* employed intravenously as an *emergency* measure in quelling intense excitement . . .' and you yourself say that it's used for 'morose, evasive withdrawn patients in early schizophrenic or depressive reactions . . .'" I said it seemed it was normally used only in a hospital under emergency situations.

"No, no. It was used regularly during World War II and ever since then . . ."

I asked him how his early research on the hypothalamus related to his use of Amytal and whether there were any correlations in that work with his use of Amytal with patients.

"From my animal research? No! I wouldn't have used my animal research on my patients!" he said, pulling his head back with a horrified look.

I asked him why he used Amytal so regularly.

"I only used it with patients that had serious crises—to prevent suicide when someone was so desperate and needed relief, or to *prevent* a bout of alcoholism . . ."

I asked, "Didn't you worry about it being addictive?"

"It's not addictive," he said.

I said, "In the *Physician's Desk Reference,* in *Goodman & Gillman's,* in *Martindale's* and every other drug reference, it says it's habit-forming and carries warnings to that effect. Even Louis Wolberg writes that 'Short-acting barbiturates, Pentothal, Seconal, and Amytal are particularly addictive. They are truly as addictive as Heroin or Morphine . . .' "

"Amytal is habit-forming only in the sense that they might try to get drugs on the outside," he said, "and naturally I wouldn't give them any . . ."

I was reeling from the illogic of that statement, but I asked, "What did the people you prescribed Amytal to have in common?"

"They would be people inclined to very severe anxieties, depressions, melancholy, and temptations toward suicide . . ."

"In references they say that it's given rarely, and yet you used it repeatedly over the years—four years, eleven years, seventeen years— and in some cases, every week for months or years. One patient recently told me there were many periods she got it every week. Why did you do that? Did they have that many crises?"

"There have been years with no Amytal," he said. "But during the past year, with Ms. Noël, before September, 1984, there were various crises, more frequent than usual. But the average frequency in Ms. Noël's case was less than two times a year . . . but toward the end, her crises were rather more frequent."

"You gave them Amytal to help them through a crisis every time— all that often?" I asked.

"I would have to judge each case. Before I ever gave an Amytal interview, I would call in the family; I would consult the[m]. Sometimes I would give the Amytal instead of hospitalizing the person and some- times I would hospitalize the person instead . . ."

"Did you ever recommend that Barbara be hospitalized?"

"I can only say what's positive," he said with an apologetic smile. "I did send her to a friend of mine at Northwestern University who helped her by having her do some music therapy at Northwestern with stu- dents . . . I did refer her to other physicians, which shows that I did consult other medical doctors when it was called for."

I said, "Saddoff and Freedman's textbook says Amytal is used only in extreme cases, in emergency situations." I referred to my notes. "They write that with 'catatonic schizophrenia it's *occasionally* success- ful.' and with 'the unusual, short-lived Ganser's Syndrome, it can be effective,' and—listed under 'other psychiatric emergencies'—in cases of 'fugue states—confusion and altered consciousness, IV Amytal can *possibly* be useful.' They also say 'narcotherapy is *infrequently* used in clinical practice' and when it's used, it's for *acute* symptoms.' "

Dr. Masserman waved his hand as if to dismiss all this and said, "There are a great many psychiatrists who are so caught up in analytic thinking that they believe *only* in talk therapy, without using every known therapy—using drug therapy, diet, behavior therapy—I use them all, whatever is called for."

I asked: "Did you use combined drug therapy and talk therapy with most of your patients, some of them, half of them, or . . . ?"

"Less than one per cent," he said.

"You gave Amytal to *less than one percent* of your patients?"

"That's right."

"You mean to say that *all six lawsuits* came from that less than one percent of your patients who had Sodium Amytal?"

"Yes, the six law suits were part of that one percent . . ."

I said, "I'm confused about Amytal . . . From what I understand from talking with others, it's a Brevitol—"

"Brevitol is something different."

"But it's a short-acting barbiturate."

"I never gave barbiturates . . ."

"But Amytal is a barbiturate!"

"Yes, but not in addition to that. I didn't give drugs in therapy . . ."

"But I'm confused about something . . . The patients I talked to—and in your own descriptions—said they were asleep from like 7 A.M. to 2 or 3 P.M. in the afternoon or later, sometimes 4:30 or 5, and then afterwards they were often groggy for the entire evening or into the next day—"

"They're not asleep. They're relaxed, at ease. They were conscious, and just in a relaxed state so they could converse . . ."

"But the people I talked to said they never remembered anything afterwards."

"But they *do*," he said, enunciating the words slowly, and meaningfully nodding his head as he looked at me, as if we two knew the truth. "They *do*. Part of the technique is to talk about it afterward."

"Well, I was wondering, since Amytal is a short-acting drug, did you add a sedative to the Amytal or use a continuous IV drip to help them stay out for that long?"

"No, no, absolutely not! I only gave the standard dose of Amytal. Since you are interested in the technical details, I will tell you that I followed the standard procedure exactly. What they got was a ten-percent solution in sterile water. The usual dose was 0.025 grams. Ask any psychopharmacologist . . . At that dose, they would remember what they talked about and what they were crying over and the like."

When I raised the addiction problem again—didn't it concern him that regular use would be addictive?—he smiled and said, "You didn't ask me the question, 'Why not tablets?' "

"I was going to ask you that."

"I didn't give tablets, because it avoids addiction," he said, repeating what he'd said in depositions. "To be addictive, it would have to be prescribed by mouth. To have them become addicted, they would have to get it by mouth. If it was given by mouth, they could take more and become addicted. And of course I wouldn't give them any more . . ."

"But that doesn't make sense," I said. "If Amytal hits the same receptors in the brain as alcohol, which I understand it does, can't it be just as addictive, and simply cause them to drink alcohol when they can't get the Amytal?"

"I couldn't prevent them from taking alcohol!" he exclaimed.

"But didn't it worry you to give it to an alcoholic?"

"I could give them Amytal—if someone comes in and says, 'I can't stand it and I want to kill myself!' As a matter of fact, I don't use Amytal except in very rare instances where there's some sort of crisis. I don't use any drugs in treating alcoholics because they can easily switch from alcohol to drugs. There's only one drug that's efficacious, and that is Antabuse . . .

"I give Amytal to an alcoholic only if the alcoholic is in some crisis that threatens his life . . . I give it only to tide them over, not as a treatment for alcoholism—only as a treatment for panic."

I said, "Dr. Masserman, do you think people make up their problems or create them for self-indulgent reasons? You write about 'the convenience of a nervous breakdown' and state, 'In an important sense, even chronic alcoholism can no more be considered to be a true "physical disease" than can thumb-sucking or excessive eating—though both forms of self-indulgence may eventually produce serious bodily deformities . . .' "

He responded, "There has never been any research that establishes a genetic proclivity for alcoholism. It can run in families, but that can be by example. It has been demonstrated that alcoholism can be moderated sufficiently for normally adaptive social behavior by skillful psychotherapy and with cultural aid, such as Alcoholics Anonymous."

"In your early research you said that all human research has to begin on animals . . ."

"I said it has to be *supplemented* by research on animals."

"Okay . . . But I'm interested—were there any parallels? What correlations did you find between your early research on cats with Amytal and your use of that drug with your patients?"

"There are no correlations, but since you're interested—please don't consider this relative—I have demonstrated that subjecting cats, dogs, and monkeys to the kinds of frustrations that human beings encounter can produce deviations in behavior such as phobias that become generalized—not just the frustrations I subject them to. For instance, if they're used to eating at a certain trough, but then they encounter frustrations and they have to decide—shall I eat and get an electric shock, or should I avoid the trauma—you see them become isolated. You see these animals become fearful. You see these phobic, depressed, melancholic monkeys. Since you asked, I'm telling you—you'd see them sitting in a corner of a cage refusing to eat—not because of electric shock, but because of a rubber snake in the food box that scared them.

"But that's not the end of the experiment! I demonstrate that the same kind of therapy with animals that is used with patients *cures* them. First, you give them a rest. You get them out of the stressful environment. Secondly, you can use various sedative drugs in mild doses, but then peter them out. You use it to relieve their anxieties so they can start eating again and not be so afraid. Third, you become a psychotherapist personally. You stroke the animals and feed them by hand, guide them closer to the food box, put food in it and keep stroking them while they eat it. If you've established their confidence by being a gentle person—which I am—then the animals will be cured."

Dr. Masserman, warming to the subject, talked on with enthusiasm and obvious pleasure about his animal experiments with alcohol and alcoholism, saying he wished he could show me some of the films of his experiments that are still available. Then he handed me a letter inviting him to a fifty-year Club Luncheon of the Illinois State Medical Society on April 11, 1992, and said, "This demonstrates that I'm a full member in good standing of the American Medical Association."

I said, "One woman I talked with told me that you had recommended she take Amytal when she was pregnant, and another told Barbara Noël that she'd had Amytal and subsequently lost her baby. Did you ever give Amytal to a pregnant patient?"

"She never told me she was pregnant," he said. "None of my patients ever told me she was pregnant."

"Then you're saying you never recommended or gave Amytal to a pregnant patient?"

"Of course not. I wouldn't give them any drugs except those like vitamins that would expedite their condition."

"Do you think it's ever justified for a therapist to have sex with a patient?"

"Of course not!" he said vehemently. "I have sat in on ethics committees in the past and expressed that view unequivocally!!"

"You mention in *Psychiatric Odyssey* that "perverse sexuality has deprecatory meaning only in Western culture . . ." Do you think it's only Western culture—that maybe Americans are too repressed and overly concerned about these ethical matters? Do you think in another culture or in Biblical times, these things would be considered normal or harmless?"

Dr. Masserman raised his eyebrows in surprise, but then looked rather pleased and amused. "Well, that is true," he said. "In many cultures homosexuality was preferable, for instance. In Greek classic times, homosexuality was not only acceptable, but was considered preferable. Socrates initiated his apostles and that was considered a normal thing. Even cannibalism was accepted in some cultures. To be specific—since you seem to like the specific details—even the Caribbean Indians accepted cannibalism. But psychiatrists should not make such broad general statements. I deplore this kind of guerre attitude . . ."

"In *Adolescent Sexuality,* you mention incest can be harmless and can be a non-neurotic experience if it's treated properly. You say, 'Contrary to many current concepts . . . non-injurious parent-child or intersibling sexual relations, even when verified, usually leave no serious adverse effects, and require only judicious avoidance of social and legal traumata . . .' Is that still your position?"

"Well, that's true if the child isn't dragged through the humiliation of testifying and all," he said. "As a matter of fact, there have been studies that say it can be exacerbated by legal proceedings. Certainly, making the child testify can do a great deal of unnecessary harm. There was one example in that book about a girl whose stepfather molested her. The girl didn't want him to go to jail and break up the family . . ."

I said, "Several of your patients talked about your taking them on boat rides or airplane rides or to your home for home office visits and on trips . . . Did you do that to broaden their horizons or for what purposes?"

Before I finished my question, Dr. Masserman interrupted and said, "I never did anything unethical with any patient. But I can add to that. If you wish to check, go to the Cessna Rental Agency at Midway Airport, where I have to register everybody I take up flying. You will find that the only woman I ever took up flying by myself was my wife—at a time she used to fly with me, before I gave it up."

Dr. Masserman also said he had never taken any patient out on his boat. "Let me show you something," he said, asking me to stand up. The three of us stood and looked out the window; Dr. Masserman stood close to me. I had a surreal feeling as we looked out at Jackson Park Harbor and Yacht Club. I remembered Barbara, Daniella, and Annie telling me about their trips out on his boat—being rowed from the dock to the boat and back—and I could almost feel the motion of the water slapping against the side of the dinghy. "See that house?" he said, pointing out the clubhouse. "The one with the green roof? And the dock beside it? I keep my boat in the harbor, and I have to row from that dock to my boat . . ." We could clearly see the dock and the small boats from this window. "I've been a member of that club for thirty years. It's a small club—probably no more than a hundred members. If I was *stupid* enough to take anyone else but my wife out to that boat, she'd know it before I got home!"

"Honey, you didn't mention this, also," Mrs. Masserman said, picking up a pair of binoculars.

"That's right," he said with a little chuckle. "I'm under surveillance at all times . . . Not really!" Dr. and Mrs. Masserman both laughed, as if the allegations were totally ludicrous. They made it sound so implausible and absurd that for a moment I thought, Maybe he has forgotten! Maybe he doesn't believe it! In that same moment, I forgot how in depositions, when asked if he had ever taken patients out on his boat, Dr. Masserman had said, under oath, "Yes. Ms. Noël on one occasion."

And when he was asked, "Have you taken anyone else on your boat, any of your other patients?" he had answered, "Yes, I have." He had denied that he used his boat as part of his therapeutic program, but rather "only as a therapeutic help." He had also admitted, under oath, that he had taken female patients flying in his airplane.

"But why would these different people say that they went out on the boat and the airplane with you?" I asked, trying to regain my equilibrium, and remembering the similarities in the words I'd heard spoken by four very different individuals as they described their years with Dr. Masserman and their struggles to come to terms with his betrayal. These women, along with nine or ten others, had talked to Ken Cunniff. "They hadn't met each other," Ken had told me, "and most of them didn't want to sue. Yet they all told the same details, the same stories— and they all thought he was God."

"Are you saying they were making that up, or having the same delusion or something?" I said.

"See that picture?" Dr. Masserman asked me, pointing out a small oil painting of a gray-blue boat with full white sails listing in rough seas.

"Is that your boat?"

"Yes, that's my boat."

"It's nice."

"I have the same picture in my office."

"You do?"

"Yes, and I have a picture of the plane I flew when I was flying, in my office. I have a picture of my playing a violin, in my office. I'm a person who is down-to-earth and friendly.

"Why do I have these pictures in my office? It is one part of one technique called *transference,* which illustrates by personal example that there are many activities in life that can give more satisfactions than drinking or quarreling or competing or seeking revenge. And so people ask me these things [he asks and answers the questions]:

"Do I sail? What sort of boat?

"A cruising boat.

"Do you sleep on it?

"Yes, my wife and I do sleep on it when we take cruises.

"Oh, do you fly?

"Yes, of course I fly.

"Do you take people up?

"Yes, I've taken friends up, my wife also . . .

"They can make all sorts of fantasies from their own ends . . ."

"So you say they're fantasizing this?" I interjected.

"That's exactly what I'm saying."

After that, Mrs. Masserman made a long statement about how, after nearly fifty years of a "very close and happy marriage," she knew her husband's values and knew "he would never knowingly hurt another human being." She cried over how "unjustly maligned" he has been, and Dr. Masserman comforted her. I said, "If you could have anticipated all of this, is there anything you would have done differently?"

Once again, Dr. Masserman looked amused. He had a whimsical expression while he thought for a moment. "I don't think so!" he said. "I suppose if I'd been all-wise and godlike, it could be said, 'Well, why didn't you see so and so going haywire?' But I'm not God. I've had forty years of relatively good judgement . . ."

The interview was over and we all stood up. Dr. Masserman said, "We probably should let your boyfriend out of the music room." I said he wasn't my boyfriend, but he would probably welcome getting out. Dr. Masserman invited me to look around his music room—and showed me his beautiful old Albani violin and viola. I thought he was starting to say he would be glad to play something for me, but his wife cleared her throat and interrupted, so he didn't finish his sentence. Small stringed musical instruments—"from all over the world"—filled one wall; crossed Balinese swords hung on another. A low plywood cabinet was filled with at least a dozen old violin cases, which he said contained violins given to him by previous patients and friends. He told me he still receives many invitations to lecture all around the world, but that he and Mrs. Masserman aren't doing too much traveling these days.

Dr. Masserman said that as a fellow writer, I might be interested in the two books he had in press. He opened a closet filled with files and writing materials, and showed me his galleys for a book on writing for the humanities, with an introduction by the editor-in-chief of the APA Journal. "I try to broaden the thinking of my colleagues," he said with a smile. "They sometimes can get too narrow and constricted in their thinking."

He pointed out more plaques and honors hanging on the walls. "I'm particularly proud of my testimonials from former students who are coming up," he said. "They're becoming presidents of organizations and departments all over the country . . ."

I had the sensation that I was in a time warp, and after I left, I felt an amazing sadness. I gave a lot of thought to Dr. Masserman's defense—and to his magnetism. I thought it was no wonder he charmed Barbara and his other patients into believing him. He was compelling and appeared so genuine that I had actually *liked* him, even when I was so vividly aware of his wrong-doing. I thought about good and evil—and wondered how Dr. Masserman talked to himself, how he justified what he had done. Did he rationalize that he had helped his patients by his "gentle" stroking?

A couple of days after I got home from Chicago, I called Dr. Donald Langsley, chairman of the Ethics Committee in Chicago, and asked, "Why would Dr. Masserman have said the APA 'took no action whatsoever?' Why would he say he was 'still a full member of the APA?' "

"I can't comment on that," Dr. Langsley said. "All I can tell you is that he *was* suspended. Of course he was notified of that." I asked whether suspension included the Board of Trustees, and Dr. Langsley said, "That's a separate matter; he *is* a past president of the APA."

Next I called the American Academy of Psychoanalysis to ask whether it was true that the Academy had had a hearing, "and judged there was no reason for action," as Dr. Masserman said. Vivian Mendohlson, Executive Director of the Academy, said, "No, we never had a hearing. We never have hearings. We're a pretty small association, and our policy is to adhere to whatever the ethics decisions are by the APA and the American Psychoanalytic Association." She said the Academy had not received any complaint and, although they were aware of the problem, they hadn't been aware that the APA had suspended Jules Masserman's membership.

Finally I called Dr. David Spiegel, M.D., professor of psychiatry and behavioral sciences at Stanford University and a leading expert in the field. I wanted to ask Dr. Spiegel whether the dose of Amytal Dr. Masserman claimed to have used could possibly have kept anyone out for seven to eight hours. I told him that the patients I had interviewed said they had been out from about 7:30 A. M. until 3 or 4 o'clock in the afternoon. "Not from one dose of Amytal!" he said without pause. "It's a short-acting barbiturate. That's why it was used in the way it was [during the war]. Somebody would be under its influence from half an hour to an hour."

I told him the patients remember waking up in stages, that they sometimes had breakthrough memories, but were extremely groggy and sometimes giddy for seven to eight hours. "They could have that response under Amytal, but not for that length of time," he said. "They might be groggy for an hour or two afterwards, but they wouldn't be that deeply affected by it." When I asked him whether a continuous IV may have been used or a sedative added to the Amytal, he said that would make sense. Dr. Spiegel said he didn't know of anyone who still uses Amytal in the normal practice of psychiatry, and that he had never heard of it being used on a repeated basis, since, of course, it is highly addictive.

BIBLIOGRAPHY

A number of books and articles have been especially useful in understanding the issues and implications of this story. These include:

On Patient-Therapist Sex and Related Ethical Issues

American Psychiatric Association, "The Principles of Medical Ethics with Annotations Especially Applicable to Psychiatry." APA, Washington, D.C., 1985.

Bates, Carolyn M., and Annette M. Brodsky. *Sex in the Therapy Hour: A Case of Professional Incest.* New York: Guilford Press, 1989.

Borys, Debra S., and Kenneth S. Pope. "Dual Relationships Between Therapist and Client: A National Study of Psychologists, Psychiatrists and Social Workers. *Professional Psychology: Research and Practice* 20 (October 1989).

Brayfield-Cave, Susan. "Sexual Predators in the Profession." *American Psychological Association Journal,* April 1990.

Freeman, Lucy, and Julie Roy. *Betrayal: The True Story of the First Woman to Successfully Sue Her Psychiatrist for Using Sex in the Guise of Therapy.* New York: Stein and Day, 1976.

Gartrell, Nanette, et al. "Psychiatrist-Patient Sexual Contact: Results of a National Survey. *American Journal of Psychiatry* 143, no. 9 (1986).

———. "Reporting Practices of Psychiatrists Who Knew of Sexual Misconduct by Colleagues. *American Journal of Orthopsychiatry* 57, no. 2 (April 1987).

Goleman, Daniel. "New Guidelines Issued on Patient-Therapist Sex." *New York Times,* B1, December 20, 1990.

Greenacre, Phyllis. "The Role of Transference: Practical Considerations in Relation to Psychoanalytic Therapy." *Journal of the American Psychoanalytic Association* 2 (October 1954).

Herman, Judith, Nanette Gartrell, et al. "Psychiatrist-Patient Sexual Contact: Results of a National Survey, II: Psychiatrists' Attitudes." *American Journal of Psychiatry* 144 (1987).

Kardener, S. H., M. Fuller, and I. N. Mensh. "A Survey of Physicians' Attitudes and Practices Regarding Erotic and Nonerotic Contact with Patients." *American Journal of Psychiatry* 130, no. 10: 1077–81.

Kluft, R. P. "Treating the Patient Who Has Been Exploited by a Previous Therapist." *Psychiatric Clinics of North America* 12 (1989).

Plasil, Ellen. *Therapist: The Shocking Autobiography of a Woman Sexually Exploited by Her Analyst*. New York: St. Martin's/Marek, 1985.

Pope, Kenneth S. "How Clients Are Harmed by Sexual Contact with Mental Health Professionals: The Syndrome and Its Prevalence." *Journal of Counseling and Development* 67, no. 4 (December 1988).

————. "Therapist-Patient Sex as Sex Abuse: Six Scientific, Professional and Practical Dilemmas in Addressing Victimization and Rehabilitation." *Professional Psychology: Research and Practice* 21, no. 4 (August 1990).

Pope, Kenneth, and Jacqueline Bouhoutsos. *Sexual Intimacy Between Therapists and Patients*. New York: Praeger, 1986.

Pope, Kenneth S., Barbara G. Tabachnick, and Keith Spiegel. "Ethics of Practice: The Beliefs and Behaviors of Psychologists as Therapists." *American Psychologist* 42, no. 11 (November 1987).

Pope, Kenneth S., and Valerie Vetter. "Prior Therapist-Patient Sexual Involvement Among Patients Seen by Psychologists." *Psychotherapy* 28, no. 3 (Fall 1991): 429–38.

Roiphe, Anne. "Why You Shouldn't Have Sex with Your Therapist." *Mirabella*, November 1991.

Rutter, Peter. *Sex in the Forbidden Zone*. New York: Ballantine, 1991.

Sexual Intimacies Between Psychotherapists and Patients: An Annotated Bibliography of Mental Health, Legal and Public Media Literature and Relevant Legal Cases. Prepared by Hannah Lerman, Ph.D., for the Committee on Women of Division 29 (Psychotherapy) of the American Psychological Association. Ed. 2, 1990.

"Sexual Misconduct in the Practice of Medicine," from the Council on Ethical and Judicial Affairs, American Medical Association. *The Journal of the American Medical Association* 266, no. 19 (November 20, 1991).

Warren, James, Maurice Possley, and Joseph Tybor. "Shocking Detour on Road of Fame," in "On the Law." *Chicago Tribune*, C1, January 6, 1987.

Warren et al. "Renown No Shield as Career Shatters," in "On the Law." *Chicago Tribune*, C3, November 10, 1987.

On Parent-Child and Child-Related Issues

Angelou, Maya. *I Know Why the Caged Bird Sings*. New York: Random House, 1970.

Becker, Judith V., and Emily M. Coleman. "Incest." in *Handbook of Family*

Violence, edited by Vincent B. Van Hasselt et al. New York: Plenum Press, 1988.

Benedek, Elissa P., and Diana H. Schetky. "Problems in Validating Allegations of Sexual Abuse: Factors Affecting Perception and Recall of Events." *Journal of the American Academy of Child and Adolescent Psychiatry* 26 (1987).

Anne E. Bernstein. "Analysis of Two Adult Female Patients Who Had Been Victims of Incest in Childhood." *Journal of the American Academy of Psychoanalysis* 17, no. 2 (Summer 1989).

Black, Claudia. *It Will Never Happen to Me! Children of Alcoholics, As Youngsters—Adolescents—Adults.* MAC Printing and Publications Division, 1850 High St., Denver, CO 80218.

Butler, Sandra. *Conspiracy of Silence: The Trauma of Incest.* San Francisco: New Glide Publications, 1978.

Edmiston, Susan. "Daddy's Girl: A 29-year-old California Woman Charges Her Father with a 20-Year-Old Murder." *Glamour,* November 1990.

Finkelhor, David. *Sexually Victimized Children.* New York: Free Press, 1979.

Fraiberg, Selma H. *The Magic Years: Understanding and Handling the Problems of Early Childhood.* New York: Scribner's, 1959.

Gagnon, John. "Female Child Victims of Sex Offenses." *Social Problems* 13 (1965).

Ginott, Haim G. *Between Parent and Child.* New York: Avon, 1965.

Ginott, Haim G. *Between Parent and Teenager.* New York: Avon, 1969.

Groth, A. Nicholas, and H. Jean Birnbaum. *Men Who Rape: The Psychology of the Offender.* New York: Plenum, 1979.

Herman, Judith Lewis. *Father-Daughter Incest.* Cambridge and London: Harvard University Press, 1981.

James, Beverly. *Treating Traumatized Children: New Insights and Creative Interventions.* Lexington, Mass.: Lexington Books, 1989.

Jernberg, Ann M. *Theraplay: A New Treatment Using Structured Play for Problem Children and Their Families.* San Francisco: Jossey-Bass, 1979.

Kaufman, Gershen. *Shame: The Power of Caring.* Cambridge, Mass.: Shenkman Books, 1980.

Landis, Judson. "Experiences of 500 Children with Adult Sexual Deviance." *Psychiatric Quarterly Supplement* 30 (1956).

Maeder, Thomas. *Children of Psychiatrists and Other Psychotherapists.* New York: Harper & Row, 1989.

Masson, Jeffrey Moussaieff. *Assault on the Truth: Freud's Suppression of the Seduction Theory.* New York: Farrar, Straus & Giroux, 1984.

Miller, Alice. *For Your Own Good: Hidden Cruelty in Childrearing and the Roots of Violence.* New York: Farrar, Straus & Giroux, 1983.

———. *Prisoners of Childhood: The Drama of the Gifted Child and the Search for the True Self.* New York: Basic Books, 1981.

———. *Thou Shall Not Be Aware: Society's Betrayal of the Child.* New York: New American Library, 1986.

Nathanson, Donald L. "Understanding What Is Hidden: Shame in Sexual Abuse." *Psychiatric Clinics of North America* 12, no. 2 (June 1989).

———. *Shame and Pride: Affect, Sex and the Birth of the Self.* New York: W. W. Norton, 1992.

Peters, Joseph J., M.D. "Children Who Are Victims of Sexual Assault and the Psychology of Offenders." *American Journal of Psychotherapy* XXX, no. 3 (July 1976).

Sanford, Linda. *The Silent Children: A Parent's Guide to the Prevention of Child Sexual Abuse.* New York: Doubleday Anchor Press, 1980.

Wegscheider, Sharon. *Another Chance: Hope and Health for the Alcoholic Family.* Palo Alto, Cal.: Science and Behavior, 1981.

On Amytal, Alcohol, the Hypothalamus and Related Research, Including Selected Works by or About Jules Masserman

"Anxiolytic Sedatives Hypnotics and Neuroleptics." *Martindale's The Extra Pharmacopoeia,* 29th ed. Ed. James Reynolds. London: Pharmaceutical Press, 1989.

"Association Puts Emphasis on Psychiatry's Psychosocial Aspects," *Psychiatric News,* September 19, 1986.

Bard, Philip. "Central Nervous Mechanisms for Emotional Behavior Patterns in Animals." *The Inter-relationship of Mind and Body* XIX. Association for Research in Nervous and Mental Disease. Baltimore: Williams & Wilkins, 1939.

———. "A Diencephalic Mechanism for the Expression of Rage with Special Reference to the Sympathetic Nervous System." *American Journal of Physiology,* 84 (1928).

———. "The Hypothalamus and Sexual Behavior." Chapter XIX in *The Hypothalamus and Central Levels of Autonomic Function.* Proceedings of the Association for Research in Nervous and Mental Disease, December 20, 21, 1939. Baltimore: Williams & Wilkins, 1940.

———. "Neural Mechanisms in Emotional and Sexual Behavior." *Psychosomatic Medicine* 4 (1942).

Goodman and Gillman's The Pharmacological Basis of Therapeutics. 7th ed. Ed. Alfred Goodman Gillman, Louis Goodman, et al. New York: Macmillan, 1985.

Herrington, B. S. "Masserman, Psychiatrists Visit China, Get Glimpse." *Psychiatric News,* February 16, 1979.

———. "Psychiatric Therapies—An Evaluation." *Psychiatric News,* October 2, 1981.

Kabanov, M. M. "U.S.S.R. Psychiatrist Discusses Psychiatry in His Homeland." *Psychiatric News,* September 6, 1985.

Marcos, Luis, R., M.D., and Manuel Trujillo, M.D., "The Sodium Amytal Interview as a Therapeutic Modality." In *Current Psychiatric Therapies* 18. Ed. Jules H. Masserman. New York: Grune & Stratton, 1978.

Martindale's The Extra Pharmacopoeia. 29th ed. Ed. James Reynolds. London: Pharmaceutical Press, 1989.

"Masserman Sets Committees in Action." *Psychiatric News,* January 19, 1979.

Masserman, Jules H. *A Psychiatric Odyssey: Memoirs of a Maverick Psychiatrist.* New York: Science House, 1971.

―――. "Anxiety: Protean Source of Communication." In *Communication and Community.* Science and Psychoanalysis, vol. VIII. New York: Grune & Stratton, 1965.

―――. *Behavior and Neurosis: An Experimental Psychoanalytic Approach to Psychobiologic Principles.* Chicago: University of Chicago Press, 1943. Reprint. New York: Hafner & Co., 1964.

―――. *The Biodynamic Roots of Human Behavior.* Springfield, Ill.: Charles C. Thomas, 1968.

―――. "Comparative and Experimental Contributions to the Dynamics of Behavior." In *Development and Research.* Science and Psychoanalysis, vol. VII. New York: Grune & Stratton, 1964.

―――, ed. *Current Psychiatric Therapies,* vol. 23. New York: Grune and Stratton, 1986.

―――. "The Effect of Strychnine Sulphate on the Emotional Mimetic Functions of the Hypothalamus of the Cat" (with the assistance of E. W. Haertig). *The Journal of Pharmacology and Experimental Therapeutics* 64, no. 3 (November 1938).

―――. "Effects of Analeptic Drugs on the Hypothalamus of the Cat." Chapter XXIII in *The Hypothalamus and Central Levels of Autonomic Function.* Proceedings of the Association for Research in Nervous and Mental Disease, December 20, 21, 1939. Baltimore: Williams and Wilkins, 1940.

―――. "Intensity of Conflict and Modes of Therapy." Chapter XII in *Principles of Dynamic Psychiatry.* Philadelphia: W. B. Saunders, 1946.

―――. "Is the Hypothalamus a Center of Emotion?" *Psychosomatic Medicine* 3 (1940).

―――. "Marital Power: Mary Todd's Influence on Abraham Lincoln in Historical Perspective." In *The Dynamics of Power.* Science and Psychoanalysis, vol. XX. New York: Grune & Stratton, 1972.

―――. "Poetry and Music in Flight from Futility." Reprinted in *The Arts in Psychotherapy* 7: 3–9. Ankho International, 1980.

―――. *The Practice of Dynamic Psychiatry.* Philadelphia: W. B. Saunders, 1955.

―――. "Presidential Address: The Future of Psychiatry as a Scientific and Humanitarian Discipline in a Changing World." Presented at the 132nd Annual Meeting of the American Psychiatric Association, Chicago, May 14–18, 1979. *American Journal of Psychiatry* 136, no. 8 (August 1979).

―――. "Presidential Address: Human Values in Social Psychiatry." Presented at the Fifth International Congress of Social Psychiatry, Athens, September 1974. *Current Psychiatric Therapies,* 1975.

———. *Principles of Dynamic Psychiatry: Including an Integrative Approach to Abnormal and Clinical Psychology.* Philadelphia: W. B. Saunders, 1946.

———, ed. *Psychoanalysis and Human Values.* New York: Grune & Stratton, 1960.

———. "Response to the Presidential Address" of APA President Jack Weinberg. Presented at the 131st Annual Meeting of the American Psychiatric Association, Atlanta, Ga., May 8–12, 1978. *American Journal of Psychiatry,* 135, no. 8 (August 1978).

———. "Sex and the Singular Psychiatrist." In *Science and Psychoanalysis,* vol. 9. "Adolescents, Dreams and Training." New York: Grune & Stratton, 1966.

———. "Some Current Concepts of Sex Behavior." *Psychiatry, Journal for the Study of Interpersonal Processes* 14. William Alanson White Psychiatric Foundation, 1951.

———. *Theory and Therapy in Dynamic Psychiatry.* New York: Jason Aronson, 1973.

———, and John J. Schwab, eds. *Man for Humanity.* Springfield, Ill.: Charles C. Thomas, 1972.

———, and Victor M. Uribe. *Adolescent Sexuality.* Springfield, Ill.: Charles C. Thomas, 1989.

Physicians' Desk Reference. 42nd ed. Oradell, N.J. Medical Economics Co., 1988.

"Referendum Narrowed to Recertification Issue." *Psychiatric News,* October 6, 1978.

Trainor, Dorothy. "Doctors and Nuclear War." *Psychiatric News,* November 6, 1981.

Trustees to Draft DSM-III Criticisms." *Psychiatric News,* XIV, no. 10 (May 18, 1979).

Ward, Nicholas G., David B. Rowlett, and Patrick Burke. "Sodium Amylobarbitone in the Differential Diagnosis of Confusion." *American Journal of Psychiatry* 135, no. 1 (January 1978).

Wolberg, Louis Robert. *The Technique of Psychotherapy.* 3rd ed. 2 vol. New York: Grune & Stratton, 1977.

Other References

Becker, Ernest. *The Denial of Death.* New York: The Free Press, 1973.

———. *Escape from Evil.* New York: The Free Press, 1975.

Beinen, Leigh B. "A Question of Credibility: John Wigmore's Use of Scientific Authority in Section 924a of the Treatise on Evidence." *California Western Law Review* 19, no. 2 (1983).

———. "Rape III—National Developments in Rape Reform Legislation." *Women's Rights Law Reporter* 6, no. 3. Rutgers Law School, Spring 1980.

"Benzodiazepine Sex Fantasies: Acquittal of Dentist." Medicine and Law. *The Lancet* 335, no. 8686. London and Baltimore, February 17, 1990.

Bernheimer, Charles, and Claire Kahane, eds. *In Dora's Case: Freud—Hysteria—Feminism.* New York: Columbia University Press, 1985.

Biographical Directory, 1989. Washington, D.C.: American Psychiatric Press.

Brody, Jane E. "Scientists Trace Aberrant Sexuality." *New York Times,* C1, January 23, 1990.

Carroll, William. *Human Sexuality: New Directions in American Catholic Thought.* New York: Doubleday, 1978.

Delin, Bart. *The Sex Offender.* Boston: Beacon Press, 1978.

Feild, Hubert S., and Leigh B. Bienen. *Jurors and Rape.* Lexington, Mass.: Lexington Books, 1980.

Ferraro, Barbara, and Patricia Hussey, with Jane O'Reilly. *No Turning Back.* New York: Poseidon Press, 1990.

Fine, Reuben. *A History of Psychoanalysis.* New York: Columbia University Press, 1979.

Friedan, Betty. *The Feminine Mystique.* New York: W. W. Norton, 1963.

Freud, Sigmund. *The Standard Edition of the Complete Psychological Works of Sigmund Freud,* trans. and ed. James Strachey. London: The Hogarth Press, 1961.

————. "Civilized Sexual Morality and Modern Nervous Illness." Vol. IX (1908).

————. "Female Sexuality." Vol. XXI (1931).

————. "Three Essays on the Theory of Sexuality." Vol. VII (1905).

Gay, Peter. *Freud: A Life for Our Time.* New York: W. W. Norton, 1988.

Gilligan, Carol. *In a Different Voice: Psychological Theory and Women's Development.* Cambridge: Harvard University Press, 1982.

Greenberg, Joanne. *I Never Promised You a Rose Garden.* New York: Signet, 1964.

Hare, Robert D., and Leslie M. McPherson. "Violent and Aggressive Behavior by Criminal Psychopaths." *International Journal of Law and Psychiatry* 7, no. 35050 (1984).

Jones, Ernest. *The Life and Work of Sigmund Freud.* 3 vols. New York: Basic Books, 1953–57.

Kinsey, Alfred C., Wardell B. Pomeroy, Clyde E. Martin, and Paul H. Gebhard. *Sexual Behavior in the Human Female.* Philadelphia: W. B. Saunders, 1953.

————. *Sexual Behavior in the Human Male.* Philadelphia: W. B Saunders, 1948.

Malcolm, Janet. *Psychoanalysis, the Impossible Profession.* New York: Knopf, 1981.

Middlebrook, Diane Wood. *Ann Sexton: A Biography.* Boston: Houghton Mifflin, 1991.

Nathanson, Donald L. "A Timetable for Shame." In *The Many Faces of Shame,* edited by D. L. Nathanson. New York: Guilford Press, 1987.

Noël, Barbara. *Twilight Sleep.* Unpublished manuscript.

Norwood, Robin. *Women Who Love Too Much*. New York: Pocket Books, 1985.

Olsen, Jay. *Doc: The Rape of the Town of Lovell*. New York: Atheneum, 1989.

Peck, M. Scott. *People of the Lie: The Hope for Healing Human Evil*. New York: Touchstone, 1983.

Psychoanalytic Pioneers. Edited by Franz Alexander, Samuel Eisenstein, and Martin Grotjahn. New York: Basic Books, 1966.

Quen, Jacques M., and Eric T. Carlson. *American Psychoanalysis: Origins and Development*. New York: Brunner/Mazel, 1978.

Roazen, Paul. *Freud and His Followers*. New York: Knopf, 1975.

Stoller, Robert J. *Perversion: The Erotic Form of Hatred*. Washington, D.C.: American Psychiatric, 1975.

————. *Sexual Excitement: Dynamics of Erotic Life*. New York: Touchstone, 1979.

Stone, Leo. *The Psychoanalytic Situation*. New York: International Universities Press, 1961.

Visotsky, Harold M., M.D. "Jules H. Masserman, M.D.: One Hundred and Seventh President, 1978–79." *American Journal of Psychiatry* 136, no. 8 (August 1979).

Waldholz, Michael, "Head Doctor: Doubted and Resisted, Freud's Daring Map of the Mind Endures." *Wall Street Journal*, A1, December 2, 1991.

Watterson, Kathryn. *The Safe Medicine Book*. New York: Ballantine, 1992.

Wheeler, Dr. Robert. "A Composite Viewpoint of the TMJ Dysfunctional Singer: A Hidden Handicap for the Serious Singer." Temporomandibular Joint Dysfunction Institute, 30 N. Michigan Ave., Chicago, IL 60602.

Who's Who in America 32 (1962–63). Chicago: Marquis–Who's Who, Inc., 1966.

Who's Who in America 42 (1980–81). Chicago: Marquis-Who's Who, Inc., 1980.

ACKNOWLEDGMENTS

There is no way I can adequately express my gratitude to those whose contributions of time, understanding, skill, and caring turned this complex, often murky and frightening story into a book I hope will play a part in keeping the field of psychotherapy honest.

Since May of 1986, I have been blessed with the counsel of a most compassionate and knowledgeable woman, Ann Marshak Jernberg, Ph.D., psychologist, author, and artist. After a year of her gentle therapy, I began writing my story, which I called *Twilight Sleep,* and in that process gathered around me a truly remarkable support group. Psychologist Manny Silverman, Ph.D., at Loyola University, gave me counsel and made all his avenues of current research available to me. Bruce Bennett, Ph.D., an expert on troubled therapists, provided invaluable information and advice. Terrence Koller, Ph.D., looked over my writing from time to time and lent his image as president of the Illinois Psychological Association when he accompanied me, simply as a friend, to my July 1990 hearing with the Illinois Psychiatric Society. Psychologist Ted Hurst opened his extensive library of textbooks on psychology to me, and therapist-editor-author Phyllis Booth followed my progress with enthusiastic interest and advice.

I am indebted to my friend Susan Solovy, attorney, former magazine editor, and now a psychologist in training, who got me started on the project, to novelist John Fink, who generously shared his creative talents, and to author Thomas Maeder, for his years of encouragement.